MEDICAL NEGLIGENCE AND THE DUTY TO ADVISE

This book argues that patient autonomy and medical negligence make for strange bedfellows. The emphasis on autonomy has distorted orthodox negligence principles, contributing to uncertainty and angst amongst healthcare professionals while eroding trust in the doctor-patient relationship.

This work takes the current discourse beyond autonomy – which focuses on the rights of the patient, to agency and shared decision-making – which focus on the relationship between doctor and patient. The core argument is built on a review of the theoretical foundations of negligence and the philosophical conceptions of autonomy. Provocatively, this work argues against a rights-based approach to negligence – which can be confrontational – in favour of a human obligations approach, which is collaborative and thus well suited to the doctor-patient relationship.

Drawing on the theoretical analysis, the book identifies doctrinal anomalies in the duty of care, standard of care, causation, and damage. It critically analyses landmark UK Supreme Court cases, including Chester v Afshar, Montgomery v Lanarkshire Health Board, and McCulloch v Forth Valley Health Board, arguing that the law is increasingly detached from the realities of medical practice and reasonable expectations of patients. Primarily based on UK law, the work also discusses Australian, Canadian, and Singaporean law.

The book is aimed at the medical and legal fraternities as well as students and scholars of tort law. Doctors and lawyers will gain fresh insights into medical negligence; scholars will find an alternative perspective to orthodoxy with rich material to rethink theory and doctrine in negligence.

Volume 58 in the series Hart Studies in Private Law

Hart Studies in Private Law

This monograph series brings together in one place two types of book: works which examine in-depth the fundamental doctrines and principles of private law, and works which engage with the theoretical underpinnings of private law. The series thus aims to contribute to ever-evolving debates about the nature of private law such as problems of classification and taxonomy, remedies, the relationship with public law and the boundaries of private law generally.

The series includes, but is not confined to, works on contract, tort, unjust enrichment, equity, property and the conflict of laws, welcoming work which intersects with other fields of study to enable a deeper understanding of private law theory and practice.

Medical Negligence and the Duty to Advise

Beyond Autonomy

Kumaralingam Amirthalingam

•HART•
OXFORD • LONDON • NEW YORK • NEW DELHI • SYDNEY

HART PUBLISHING

Bloomsbury Publishing Plc

Kemp House, Chawley Park, Cumnor Hill, Oxford, OX2 9PH, UK

1385 Broadway, New York, NY 10018, USA

Bloomsbury Publishing Ireland Limited, 29 Earlsfort Terrace, Dublin 2, D02 AY28, Ireland

HART PUBLISHING, the Hart/Stag logo, BLOOMSBURY and the Diana logo are trademarks of Bloomsbury Publishing Plc

First published in Great Britain 2025

A catalogue record for this book is available from the British Library.

A catalogue record for this book is available from the Library of Congress.

Library of Congress Control Number: 2025945736

ISBN: HB: 978-1-50993-779-0
ePDF: 978-1-50993-781-3
ePub: 978-1-50993-780-6

Typeset by Compuscript Ltd, Shannon

For product safety related questions contact productsafety@bloomsbury.com

To find out more about our authors and books visit www.hartpublishing.co.uk. Here you will find extracts, author information, details of forthcoming events and the option to sign up for our newsletters.

In Memory of
My Father
A Amirthalingam

In Honour of
My Mother
PP Susila Devi

Dedicated to
My Wife and Two Sons
Rajshree Jetly, Krishiv Jetly Amirthalingam, Ishan Jetly Amirthalingam

PREFACE

This book is a culmination of over two decades of thinking about the nature of the tort of negligence, the role of judges and academics in developing the law, and the right balance in the doctor–patient relationship. It aims to take the current discourse beyond autonomy – which focuses on the *rights* of the patient, to agency and shared decision-making – which focus on the *relationship* between doctor and patient. Instead of a rights-based approach that is individualistic in nature, I argue for a human obligations approach that is relational in nature.

Historically, and even today, there are many doctors who cling to the idea of medical paternalism – that doctor knows best and that patients are incapable of understanding medical matters or making appropriate medical decisions. This paternalistic attitude is indefensible, and the championing of patient autonomy over the last three decades is to be lauded and welcomed. However, there are signs that the law has over-corrected. While I firmly believe that individual rights and autonomy must be respected and defended, I am less convinced that a rights-based approach provides the best path in the context of medical negligence litigation. The emphasis on rights and individualism has led to a de-emphasis of mutual obligations, caring, and interconnectedness in society.

Developments in the jurisprudence on the duty to inform and patient autonomy have created a destabilising effect on the medical profession. The aspirational aims of the law are sometimes in tension with practical limitations of healthcare services delivery and the nature of the doctor–patient relationship that is based on collaboration and trust. The emphasis on patient autonomy is also creating fissures in the coherent structure of negligence doctrine. The scope of the duty, the standard of care, causation, and the nature of damage are caught in the tussle between judicial law-making and precedent-based reasoning. This work adds to the existing literature by providing another philosophical viewpoint to analyse and rationalise the tort of negligence.

There are many friends and colleagues, too many to name, who have supported me in this work. I am grateful to all of you. I would like to acknowledge those who have read various draft chapters at different stages of development or discussed aspects of this work with me. They include Peter Cane, Gary Chan, Hillary Chua, Tina Cockburn, Tracey Evans-Chan, John Devereux, Vikki Entwistle, Andrew Gleeson, Andrew Halpin, Arif Jamal, Harold Luntz, Nicholas McBride, Colm McGrath, Jose Miola, Jonathan Montgomery, Donal Nolan, James Penner, Craig Purshouse, and Tan Zhong Xing. Thanks also to the Dean of Law, Andrew Simester, for his support and discussions on theories of liability in crime and tort. A special mention goes to Margaret Fordham, who was the Torts convenor when I joined the National University of Singapore (NUS) 25 years ago, and who has been a good friend and supporter of my work.

I had the privilege of spending one semester on sabbatical at the Centre for Biomedical Ethics at the Yong Loo Lin School of Medicine, where I had many insightful discussions with biomedical ethics experts and healthcare professionals. This work has also benefited tremendously from my interactions with the medical and legal professions in Singapore and Malaysia through the annual conferences of the Medico-Legal Society of Singapore and the Medico-Legal Society of Malaysia. A special mention goes to Dr Devanand Anantham, Dr Thirumoorthy, and Dr Lai Siang Hui, doctors with a keen interest and understanding of law, and Edmund Kronenberg, PS Ranjan, and Raja Eileen, lawyers with a keen interest and understanding of medical practice.

My student research assistants over the years, Chua Kang Le, Mazie Tan, Rachel Wam, Ryan Leong, Liew Siew Rong, Elise Khor, and Megan Tan, did excellent work and were a pleasure to work with. I am indebted to the professional staff at Hart Publishing, especially Sinead Moloney and Sasha Jawed for their professionalism, support, and flexibility, as well as Joanne Choulerton for her exemplary standards in the final editing process. Thanks also to the wonderful administrators of the research grants at NUS Law, Kris Zhao and Wendy Wee, for helping me navigate the increasing number of bureaucratic processes associated with research grants and travel.

It leaves me now to acknowledge the most important people in my life: my wife, Rajshree, for supporting me through the project and being the rock in my life, and my sons, Krishiv and Ishan, for inspiring me every day and giving joy and meaning to my life.

This research project is supported by the Ministry of Education, Singapore, under the Academic Research Fund Tier 1 (FY2017).

Kumaralingam Amirthalingam
National University of Singapore
26 May 2025

ACKNOWLEDGEMENTS

This book, which was written over a long period, drew on and reproduced parts of previously published works, listed below.

- 'Medical Duty to Advise, Patient Autonomy, and Reasonable Alternatives' (2024) 140 *Law Quarterly Review* 11
- 'Sustainable and Efficient Criminal Legal Aid: From Individual Right to Collective Interest' [2022] *Criminal Law Review* 621
- 'Upending the Medical Duty to Advise: Legislating the Standard of Care in Singapore' [2022] 22 *Medical Law International* 189
- 'Clinical Negligence and Psychiatric Injury' (2022) 138 *Law Quarterly Review* 370
- 'The *Bolam* Standard and Surgical Negligence' (2021) 37 *Journal of Professional Negligence* 137
- 'Medical Negligence and Diagnosis: Further Inroads into Bolam?' (2020) 71 *Northern Ireland Legal Quarterly* 657
- 'Judicial Law-making and the Common Law of Negligence' (2020) 27 *Tort Law Review* 155
- 'IVF Baby and Upbringing Costs – A Claim for Wrongful Parenthood' (2019) 35 *Journal of Professional Negligence* 112
- 'Reproductive Negligence: Unwanted Child or Unwanted Parenthood?' (2018) 134 *Law Quarterly Review* 15
- 'Causation and the Medical Duty to Refer' (2012) 128 *Law Quarterly Review* 208

CONTENTS

1

Introduction

There are three notable periods in the post-War development of medical negligence principles in the United Kingdom: the 1950s, the late 1980s, and the early twenty-first century. The immediate post-War period saw the establishment of the National Health Service (NHS) in 1948 and judicial decisions that were protective of the medical profession.[1] The high watermark of this period was the classic case of *Bolam v Friern Management Hospital Committee*.[2] The 1980s brought in an era of patients' rights discourse, with perhaps the most significant judgment in the UK coming in the form of a dissent in *Sidaway v Board of Governors of the Bethlem Royal Hospital and the Maudsley Hospital*,[3] in which Lord Scarman emphasised the importance of patients' rights and informed consent. From the early years of this century, the discourse has centred on patient autonomy, with the Supreme Court in *Montgomery v Lanarkshire Health Board*[4] rejecting the *Bolam* test in duty to inform cases in favour of a patient-centric approach.

This trajectory away from medical paternalism to patient autonomy was necessary and has done much to protect patients and improve healthcare outcomes. However, this trajectory, if unchecked, may undermine trust in the doctor–patient relationship and interfere with the professional autonomy of doctors. The over-correction in favour of patient autonomy was identified in a prescient article by one of the doyens of medical law, the late Margaret Brazier, who, commenting on a judgment justifying force-feeding of a patient, stated:

> I limit myself to His Lordship's suggestion that Autonomy is not the only god in the ethical, or indeed the legal, pantheon. I argue that Kay J may be right. The domination of one of many ethical principles is disturbing. Patients' rights were neglected for much of the twentieth century. Judges were too ready to endorse doctors' judgment of what was best for the patient. The past two decades have arguably over-corrected the balance.[5]

[1] See JR Maltby, CDD Hutter and KC Clayton, 'The *Woolley* and *Roe* Case' (2000) 84 *British Journal of Anaesthesia* 121. See also the comments of Lord Denning in *Roe v Ministry of Health* [1954] 2 QB 66, 86–87.

[2] *Bolam v Friern Management Hospital Committee* [1957] 1 WLR 582.

[3] *Sidaway v Board of Governors of the Bethlem Royal Hospital and the Maudsley Hospital* [1985] 1 AC 871.

[4] *Montgomery v Lanarkshire Health Board* [2015] UKSC 11; [2015] AC 1430. The groundwork for *Montgomery* was laid in *Pearce v United Bristol Healthcare NHS Trust* [1999] PIQR 53 and *Chester v Afshar* [2004] UKHL 41; [2005] 1 AC 134.

[5] M Brazier, 'Do No Harm – Do Patients Have Responsibilities Too?' (2006) 65 *Cambridge Law Journal* 397, 398.

I. The Staggering March of Autonomy[6]

Two decades on from Brazier's observation, the reign of patient autonomy over medical negligence, far from being checked, has only further entrenched itself. The aim of this book is to develop an argument based on theory and doctrine to rethink the role of autonomy in medical negligence. To be clear, this book does not aim to reverse the course on patients' rights or to reintroduce medical paternalism. Patient autonomy remains paramount when it comes to intentional interference with patients whether for clinical or research purposes. Patients must retain the right to give or withhold consent and determine what is right for them. Different considerations apply to clinical negligence.

The overemphasis on patient autonomy has blurred the line between negligence and trespass while ignoring the realities of the clinical experience and the doctor–patient relationship. Reformist academics and judges have used the tort of negligence to constrain the paternalistic attitude of the medical profession and to protect patients' rights. While this is laudable, the tort of negligence is not designed for regulation: it is backward looking and engaged only when a patient suffers injury, thus ignoring patients whose autonomy rights have been violated but who have not suffered any injury. Instead of negligence, robust enforcement of professional guidelines, ethical standards, and regulatory frameworks is a more effective means of changing medical culture and ensuring that patients' rights and interests are protected. Systemic reform and not individual liability should be the strategy.

The quaint model of a single doctor diagnosing, treating, and caring for a patient, graphically captured in the cover illustration of Harvey Teff's seminal monograph on the doctor–patient relationship,[7] may be archaic. Yet, the relationship between doctor and patient remains central to patient care and the human aspect of medicine. It is essential that the sanctity of this relationship be respected as we move toward a more egalitarian model based on shared decision-making and patient agency.

Negligence is a living tort that evolves to meet new circumstances and social expectations of the day, allowing it to remain relevant and to dominate tort law.[8] Academic opinion, socio-economic research, and policy-based advocacy are relevant and have a legitimate role to play in shaping the law. Largely through the efforts of academics, patient autonomy became the overriding concern in medical ethics, medical law, and medical regulation by the mid to late twentieth

[6] The heading pays homage to T Weir, 'The Staggering March of Negligence' in P Cane and J Stapleton (eds), *The Law of Obligations: Essays in Celebration of John Fleming* (Oxford, Oxford University Press, 1998) 97.

[7] H Teff, *Reasonable Care: Legal Perspectives on the Doctor/Patient Relationship* (Oxford, Clarendon Press, 1994).

[8] See T Weir, 'The Staggering March of Negligence' in P Cane and J Stapleton (eds), *The Law of Obligations: Essays in Celebration of John Fleming* (Oxford, Oxford University Press, 1998) 97.

century.[9] However, the voices that influence the shape and direction of the tort of negligence are not necessarily democratic or pragmatic; often the law is shaped by the elite, whose worldview may not reflect that of the general populace. Edward White offered this insightful observation in his masterful work on the history of American tort law:

> The ideas that have shaped the doctrinal content of tort law have been ideas proposed by scholars affiliated with elite educational institutions, practitioners associated with metropolitan law firms, and appellate judges that served on prominent and visible courts … Ideas that were sufficiently embedded as to have been thought beyond refutation have been abandoned; ideas that were once regarded as on the lunatic fringe have become commonplace.[10]

The movement in the Western world toward a rights-based order and the influence of academic writing on judges have shaped medical negligence law. Beyond a duty not to cause harm to the patient, doctors are now liable to patients for a failure to protect their autonomy and their right to choose.[11] Doctors may be held liable to third parties for failure to warn of health risks due to their genetic affinity with the patient.[12] The fundamental doctrines of negligence governing duty, breach, causation, and damage have been distorted to accommodate the vindication of patients' rights and protection of patient autonomy.[13] It is not the arrival of White's 'lunatic fringe', but it is revelatory of the extent to which the unorthodox has become orthodox.

Academic writings have been influential in several landmark medical negligence cases, resulting in an expansion of liability. For example, the UK Supreme Court in *Montgomery* held that the conventional test for the standard of care set out in *Bolam* should not apply to doctors' duty to inform. As will be discussed in Chapter four, this decision relied heavily on academic writing and an ideological view that championed patient autonomy as an absolute virtue. Similarly, the case of *Chester v Afshar*[14] circumvented conventional causation principles to vindicate autonomy. The Singapore Court of Appeal in *ACB v Thomson Medical Pte Ltd*[15]

[9] See HK Beecher, 'Ethics and Clinical Research' (1966) 274(24) *New England Journal of Medicine* 1354; M Pappworth, *Human Guinea Pigs: Experimentation on Man* (London, Routledge & Kegan Paul, 1967); DJ Rothman, *Strangers at the Bedside: A History of How Law and Bioethics Transformed Medical Decision Making* (New York, Basic Books, 1991); TL Beauchamp and JF Childress, *Principles of Biomedical Ethics* (New York, Oxford University Press, 1979); H Teff, *Reasonable Care: Legal Perspectives on the Doctor-Patient Relationship* (Oxford, Clarendon Press, 1994); SA McLean's *A Patient's Right to Know: Information Disclosure, the Doctor and the Law* (Aldershot, Dartmouth Publishing Co, 1989); M Brazier's *Medicine, Patients and the Law* (Harmondsworth, Penguin Books, 1987).

[10] GE White, *Tort Law in America: An Intellectual History* (New York, Oxford University Press, 2003) xi–xii.

[11] *Montgomery v Lanarkshire Health Board* [2015] UKSC 11; [2015] AC 1430; *Chester v Afshar* [2004] UKHL 41; [2005] 1 AC 134.

[12] *ABC v St George's Healthcare NHS Trust* [2020] EWHC 455.

[13] See Part II of this volume for a detailed analysis.

[14] [2024] UKHL 41; [2005] 1 AC 134.

[15] [2017] SGCA 20; [2017] 1 SLR 918.

relied heavily on academic writing to recognise a novel head of damage – loss of genetic affinity – to vindicate patient autonomy.

Research has shown that patients who are well informed and engaged in their own healthcare decisions have better healthcare outcomes.[16] It is therefore critical that patients are well-informed and involved in their own healthcare decisions. However, as patient autonomy arguments are given greater weight, doctors' professional autonomy is impacted, causing them to become reluctant to take responsibility for decisions and for proactively managing their patients.[17] Patient autonomy is vaunted for empowering patients, but this may not always be the case. Many patients are inherently vulnerable in terms of their health, their understanding of complex medical matters, and their capacity to make decisions on their own.[18]

II. The Central Argument of the Book

The central argument of this book is that the autonomy pendulum, from the rights movement in the second half of the twentieth century, has swung too far in responding to unethical or undesirable medical practices. Instead of championing patient autonomy and informed consent, this work advocates for patient agency and shared decision-making. Autonomy-based arguments in negligence reorient the doctor–patient relationship from collaborative to confrontational. Instead of relying on a rights-based paradigm, it is argued that a human obligations paradigm that recognises the interconnectedness of individuals is better suited to the tort of negligence.

The focus on patients' rights and autonomy sometimes ignores the complexities faced by doctors in making judgement calls and determining what to communicate to their patients, especially when the prognosis is bleak. Eminent physicians have taken to literature to chronical their experiences, vent their frustrations at over-regulation and under-investment in healthcare, and educate the public that the practice of medicine is shrouded in uncertainty and is as much about giving patients hope as it is about treatment.[19] Drawing on his experience, the late

[16] KE Dennis, 'Patients' Control and the Information Imperative' (1990) 39 *Nursing Research* 162.

[17] See GG Buttigeg, '*Montgomery* and its Impact on Current Medical Practice – Good or Bad?' (2019) 87 *Medico-Legal Journal* 80; I Le Gallez et al, "*Montgomery's* Legal and Practical Impact: A Systematic Review at 6 Years (2022) 28 *Journal of Evaluation in Clinical Practice* 690; KHH Kwok, EC Ip and SS Lee, 'The Conundrums of the Reasonable Patient Standard in English Medical Law' (2023) 24 *BMC Medical Ethics* Article 15.

[18] See studies cited in MA Rubin, 'The Collaborative Autonomy Model of Medical Decision-Making' (2014) 20 *Neurocrit Care* 311, 314.

[19] A Gawande, *Complications: A Surgeon's Notes on an Imperfect Science* (New York, Metropolitan Books, 2002); H Marsh, *Do No Harm: Stories of Life, Death and Brain Surgery* (London, Weidenfeld & Nicolson, 2014); P Kalanithi, *When Breath Becomes Air* (New York, Random House, 2016); S Puri, *That Good Night: Life and Medicine in the Eleventh Hour* (New York, Viking, 2019); R Clarke, *Your Life in My Hands – A Junior Doctor's Story* (London, John Blake Publishing Ltd, 2020); S Jauhar, *My Father's Brain: Life in the Shadow of Alzheimer's* (New York, Farrar, Straus and Giroux, 2023).

Henry Marsh, a renowned neurosurgeon, explains how difficult it is to give meaningful information to patients while balancing hope against reality, the patient's confidence in the doctor's ability against the risks of error, and the patient's capacity to understand information against unnecessarily frightening the patient.[20]

The relationship between doctor and patient is one that is typically ongoing and based on mutual trust – the patient trusts the doctor to respect the patient and to act in the patient's best interests, while the doctor trusts the patient to be forthcoming and to be an honest partner in the process. Patient autonomy means the patient has the right to make shared decisions with the doctor and to give or withhold consent. A failure to respect patient autonomy may expose the doctor to criminal liability, civil liability, or disciplinary sanction, but it should not be used as a backdoor to frame a collateral action in clinical negligence when a conventional claim for negligent *treatment* would fail.

III. Structure of the Book

A. Part I

Part I attempts to reimagine tort law, or at least the tort of negligence, as flowing from human obligations rather than individual rights.[21] Building on the human obligations approach, it is argued that the duty of care in negligence should be viewed from the perspective of the defendant and not the claimant. This work rejects Lord Scarman's statement that the 'doctor's duty arises from his patient's rights'.[22] Indeed, the early conception of negligence was rooted in the concept of duty and not rights. Oliver Wendell Holmes famously argued as follows:

> Torts have been thought to be infractions of rights availing against all the world. This may prove too narrow a definition, although the title includes all such rights. It contains in the first place duties of all the world to all the world; that is, duties of subjects generally to subjects generally, irrespective of any more special circumstances on either side than such as make it possible to incur a legal liability.[23]

Chapter two has two aims – to critique theoretical discourse at the meta-level and to challenge conventional wisdom that duties arise out of rights. It highlights the importance of distinguishing between descriptive, explanatory, and normative

[20] H Marsh, *Do No Harm: Stories of Life, Death and Brain Surgery* (London, Weidenfeld & Nicolson, 2014).

[21] This argument draws heavily on the works of Simone Weil, eg S Weil, *The Need for Roots: Prelude to a Declaration of Duties Toward Mankind* ((trans A Wills) New York, GP Putnam's Sons, 1952) and of O O'Neill, *Towards Justice and Virtue: A Constructive Account of Practical Reasoning* (Cambridge, Cambridge University Press, 2010).

[22] *Sidaway v Board of Governors of the Bethlem Royal Hospital and the Maudsley Hospital* [1985] 1 AC 871, 888.

[23] OW Holmes, 'The Theory of Torts' (1873) 7 *American Law Review* 652, 660.

theories in the development of the common law. Failing to distinguish between these theories risks confusion between what the law *is* and what the law *ought* to be, a distinction that is critical. Austin astutely observed in his magisterial work on jurisprudence:

> The existence of law is one thing; its merit or demerit another, whether it be or be not is one inquiry; whether it be or be not conformable to an assumed standard is another inquiry. A law which actually exists is a law though we happen to dislike it or though it vary from the text by which we regulate our approbation or disapprobation.[24]

The chapter also argues that the negligence paradigm is better served by treating duties as creating rights, instead of vice versa. This approach of starting with human obligations instead of human rights has support both in Eastern and Western philosophy;[25] it was lost in the rights-based discourse that reigned supreme from the 1970s, but it is re-emerging in contemporary discourse on the social contract.[26] The human obligations approach is superior for two reasons. It naturally defines the scope of the duty because an obligation is always directed at someone and is therefore concrete, whereas rights are against the world at large and are therefore abstract. An obligation always creates a right, but a right can exist without a corresponding obligation.[27]

Equally importantly, human obligations are relational and ensure that individuals are connected to the community. The over-emphasis on rights leads to the de-emphasis of obligations, which undermines the fabric of society based on interdependent relationships. The human obligations approach is akin to a two-way street in which both parties have mutual obligations. The rights approach, on the other hand, tends to be a one-way street where one party has demands on the other without necessarily giving anything in return. While rights discourse is important and has served us well, it has unwittingly elevated autonomy to hegemonic status in medical ethics and law, putting a strain on the doctor–patient relationship.

Chapter three explores the issues at the ground level, analysing various theoretical approaches. It is critical of the monist approach and favours the ascending pluralist approach. The tort of negligence, let alone the law of torts in general, is not well served by monist theories, which have tended to be exclusive, pitting one against the other instead of attempting to find harmony in diversity. Organisationally, all theories of tort ultimately fall within one of two meta theories, respectively based on distributive justice and corrective justice.[28] Within this duopoly, there is a range of theoretical frameworks that seek to explain or justify

[24] J Austin, *The Province of Jurisprudence Determined* (1832), WE Rumble (ed) (Cambridge, Cambridge University Press, 1995) 157.

[25] See S Weil, *The Need for Roots: Prelude to a Declaration of Duties Towards Mankind* ((trans Arthur Wills) London/ New York, Routledge, 2002).

[26] See M Shafik, *What We Owe Each Other: A New Social Contract* (Dublin, Vintage, 2002); TM Scanlon, *What We Owe To Each Other* (Cambridge MA, Belknap Press, 2000).

[27] See O O'Neil, *Towards Justice and Virtue: A Constructive Account of Practical Reasoning* (Cambridge, Cambridge University Press, 2012) 128–41.

[28] See I Englard, *Corrective and Distributive Justice: From Aristotle to Modern Times* (New York, Oxford University Press, 2009).

tort law. They include frameworks based on rights, economic analysis, welfarism, regulation, feminism, and vulnerability.

This work argues that medical negligence is best explained and justified by relational justice, vulnerability theory, and ethics of care. It cautions against rights-based theories that are absolutist, and it rejects economic analysis and regulatory theories. The doctor–patient relationship is an ongoing one that is created by mutual consent. The doctor has an affirmative duty not to cause harm to the patient and to act in the patient's best interest. It is a partnership based on trust and shared decision-making. An absolute insistence on patients' right to information and right to veto medical decisions is unrealistic and incompatible with the doctor–patient relationship.[29]

Economic analysis and regulatory theory are not suited to medical negligence. Economic analysis is based on rational choice. It ignores human emotion and intangible values. The choices involved in medical matters are complex. What is a reasonable risk to accept would differ according to individual patients, and thus economic analysis cannot provide a solution. Equally, regulatory theory is not appropriate in the field of medical negligence, as doctors are subject to professional regulation, which is determined by professionals and legislated for by Parliament. The judiciary has neither the necessary resources nor the expertise to play a regulatory role.

Chapter four then examines the concept of autonomy, which has impacted every aspect of medical negligence – duty, breach, causation, and damage. From its origins in intentional medical torts and medical research, patient autonomy entered medical negligence discourse by way of historical accident and subsequently was championed on ideological grounds in a vanguard action against medical paternalism. Its rise within medical negligence coincided with the resurgence of rights-based theories of tort law. A series of works published by leading scholars in the United Kingdom reveals the dramatic shift that occurred in the late 1980s to the early 1990s,[30] placing patient autonomy at the centre of the doctor–patient relationship.

This chapter critically examines the historical arc and various conceptions of patient autonomy. It argues that the classical, Kantian notion of autonomy is not appropriate and that a relational model is better suited to the doctor–patient relationship. The individualistic autonomy model risks transforming the tort of negligence from a duty not to cause personal injury (physical or mental) to the patient to a duty to advance the abstract rights of the patient.[31]

[29] See M Brazier, 'Do No Harm – Do Patients Have Responsibilities Too?' (2006) 65 *Cambridge Law Journal* 397.

[30] Key amongst them were I Kennedy and A Grubb's *Medical Law: Text and Materials* (Wellington, Butterworth Law, 1994); Margaret Brazier's *Medicine, Patients and the Law* (Harmondsworth, Penguin Books, 1987); Sheila McLean's *A Patient's Right to Know: Information Disclosure, the Doctor and the Law* (Aldershot, Dartmouth Publishing Co, 1989); Harvey Teff's *Reasonable Care: Legal Perspectives on the Doctor-Patient Relationship* (Oxford, Clarendon Press, 1994).

[31] For example, the right to genetic affinity recognised in *ACB v Thomson Medical Pte Ltd* [2017] SGCA 20; [2017] 1 SLR 918.

The obsession with autonomy hinders doctors from helping patients to make decisions, due to fear of being accused of violating the patient's autonomy rights by appearing to coerce or influence them. Instead of patient autonomy, the focus should be on 'respect for persons', a basic ethical principle proposed in the Belmont Report.[32] This concept protects all patients, including those with diminished capacity and those who are too vulnerable to make decisions independently. It reorients the focus from the abstract to the concrete, compelling doctors to engage with the patient and to respect the individual before them, thus preserving mutual trust.

Patients today have greater awareness of their rights, greater access to information, and greater expectations of medical success due to advances in medical science. Patients have an expectation of being fully informed and of being able to exercise control at every stage of decision-making. However, there needs to be a balance between medical beneficence and patient autonomy. Medical paternalism does not strike the right balance, as the patient's best interest is viewed from the doctor's perspective and not the patient's perspective. A different paradigm is medical maternalism,[33] which recognises both patient autonomy and patient vulnerability. A paternalist may act against the will of the patient in the belief that they are acting in the patient's best interests. A maternalist acts in the patient's best interests while respecting and supporting agency.

B. Part II

Part II of the book examines the anatomy of medical negligence in light of the theoretical analysis in Part I. While it deals with medical negligence generally, the focus is on the doctor's duty to advise the patient, and the extent to which that aspect of the doctor's duty has affected the fundamental doctrines underpinning the core elements of negligence – duty, breach, causation, and damage. The duty to advise is intimately connected to the relationship of trust that exists between doctor and patient; that trust is the critical human element of medicine that is important to defend and preserve.

Chapter five deals with the duty of care. A doctor's duty to the patient has been framed in different ways – the duty to warn, advise, inform, refer, diagnose, monitor, and follow-up. Although this framing is convenient in practice, it risks Balkanising the duty concept. Instead of fragmenting the duty, a better approach is to recognise the duty as a comprehensive one which may be breached by a failure to take care in warning, advising, diagnosing, treating, and so on. However, there

[32] National Commission for the Protection of Human Subjects of Biomedical and Behavioral Research, *Ethical Principles and Guidelines for the Protection of Human Subjects of Research* (*The Belmont Report*) (1979) B1, https://www.hhs.gov/ohrp/regulations-and-policy/belmont-report/read-the-belmont-report/index.html#xrespect.

[33] See LS Sullivan and F Niker, 'Relational Autonomy, Paternalism, and Maternalism' (2018) 21 *Ethical Theory & Moral Practice* 649.

is a risk when courts go too far in the direction of consolidating the duty, standard, and breach questions into an omnibus 'scope of duty' question. The pitfall of this approach is that it conflates the question of whether the doctor *could* have avoided harm to the claimant with the question whether the doctor is *obliged* to avoid harm to the claimant.

The chapter also draws a distinction between two strands of the duty of care that emerged in the wake of the seminal judgment in *Donoghue v Stevenson*,[34] described in this book as 'relational duty' and 'contextual duty'. The former is based on the relationship between claimant and defendant while the latter is based on the nexus between the defendant's act and the claimant's injury. The pre-*Donoghue* duty of care was a relational concept; a duty only existed in pre-existing relationships. Lord Atkin's rationalisation of the duty of care to derive a general principle should have been confined to explaining the common thread in pre-existing or intended relationships, including, for example, intended relationships such as manufacturer and consumer. Unlike relational duties, which are based on the connection (or relationship) between the parties, contextual duties are based on the connection between the *act* of the defendant and the claimant's injury.

This leads to the second qualification to Lord Atkin's general principle: any contextual duty should be restricted to acts only; it should not extend to omissions. Liability for omissions may arise only when there is a relational duty or when there is a voluntary assumption of responsibility. The doctor–patient relationship readily gives rise to affirmative duties by the doctor to the patient, but the imposition of affirmative duties on doctors to third parties is harder to justify.[35] The failure to distinguish between relational and contextual duties has contributed to doctrinal inconsistencies and encouraged recognition of affirmative duties.[36]

Chapter six explores the difference between a sociological and an ethical approach to the standard of care in critiquing the reasonable person standard. It then dives into the standard of care in medical negligence, beginning with *Bolam*, under which doctors are not negligent if their impugned practice is accepted as proper by a respectable body of medical opinion. The standard of care is thus effectively determined by peer professionals. However, the standard of care for the duty to inform and advise is no longer based on the *Bolam* peer professional test; instead, it is based on the prudent patient test. The rejection of *Bolam* can be traced to the US decision of *Canterbury v Spence*,[37] with the Australian High Court decision of *Rogers v Whitaker*[38] shaping the modern law. The United Kingdom followed suit in 2015 in the landmark decision of *Montgomery* two years before Singapore did the same in *Hii Chii Kok v Ooi Peng Jin London Lucien*.[39]

[34] *Donoghue v Stevenson* [1932] AC 562; 1932 SC (HL) 31.
[35] See for example, *ABC v St George's Healthcare NHS Trust* [2020] EWHC 455.
[36] The UK Supreme Court has recently warned against the proliferation of affirmative duties. See *Tindall v Chief Constable of Thames Valley Police* [2024] UKSC 33; [2025] AC 1046.
[37] *Canterbury v Spence* 464 F 2d 772 (1972).
[38] *Rogers v Whitaker* (1992) 175 CLR 479.
[39] *Hii Chii Kok v Ooi Peng Jin London Lucien* [2017] SGCA 38; [2017] 2 SLR 492.

Under *Montgomery*, doctors must advise patients of risks and alternative treatments that reasonably would be material to patients. This puts doctors in a bind: should they advise on a treatment option which, in their professional opinion, is not reasonable but which the patient might consider reasonable?[40] Beyond the duty to inform, the *Bolam* standard has been challenged with respect to the duty to diagnose in a narrow range of cases;[41] its application to surgeries has also come under the microscope.[42] These developments raise the question whether the standard of care should be unified under a single approach or whether a balkanisation of the standard of care is inevitable. There is a trade-off between certainty and flexibility.

Chapter seven begins with an overview of the general principles of causation and the various tests that have been developed by courts, including the but-for test, the material contribution test, and the material increase in risk test. It sets out the complexities of proving causation in medical negligence cases and considers whether the burden of proof should be reversed in some cases. Apart from evidential challenges, medical negligence litigation raises conceptual problems, including loss of chance claims,[43] causation in the duty to inform cases,[44] and causal responsibility for damage that is outside the scope of duty.[45]

At the heart of this chapter is a distinction between causation and causal responsibility. It is argued that, ultimately, the law of negligence is concerned with causal responsibility for harm caused. In most cases, causal responsibility will be established by proof of causation. However, there will be exceptional cases where causation cannot be proved on the facts, yet justice demands that the defendant be held accountable. In these cases, it is argued that causal responsibility may nonetheless be recognised by a holistic assessment of the scope of duty, the exposure to the risk of damage, and the nature of the damage. This approach is more transparent and principled, as it acknowledges that while the defendant has not caused the damage, the defendant is nonetheless responsible for exposing the claimant to the risk of suffering the very damage from which the defendant was meant to protect the claimant. Causal responsibility cannot be divorced from consideration of actionable damage, the subject of Chapter eight.

Chapter eight examines how autonomy considerations have forced courts to confront whether the tort of negligence should be restricted to protecting patients from personal injury caused by the doctor or whether it should be used to vindicate the patients' right to autonomy and freedom to choose. In short, should loss of

[40] This issue was considered by the Supreme Court in *McCulloch v Forth Valley Health Board* [2023] UKSC 26; [2024] AC 925. See K Amirthalingam, 'Medical Duty to Advise, Patient Autonomy, and Reasonable Alternatives' (2024) 140 *Law Quarterly Review* 11.

[41] *Muller v King's College Hospital NHS Foundation Trust* [2017] QB 987.

[42] *Armstrong v Royal Victoria Hospital* 2018 ONSC 2439.

[43] *Gregg v Scott* [2005] UKHL 2; [2005] 2 AC 176.

[44] *Chester v Afshar* [2024] UKHL 41; [2005] 1 AC 134; *Chappel v Hart* [1998] HCA 55; (1998) 195 CLR 232.

[45] *Khan v Meadows* [2021] UKSC 21; [2022] AC 852.

autonomy be recognised as actionable damage? While there is academic support for this, courts have so far been reluctant to recognise loss of autonomy as actionable damage in negligence. Rightly so. However, there are two exceptions where loss of autonomy should be recognised as actionable damage – reproductive negligence and genetic negligence. Here, the claimants may not have suffered personal injury, but they have suffered irreparable harm to their autonomy. Paradoxically, both these cases involve negligent acts by the doctor, not negligent failure to inform, which is where autonomy arguments have gained traction.

In the leading duty to inform cases of *Chester* and *Montgomery*, the House of Lords and the Supreme Court respectively linked the doctor's duty to inform with patient autonomy, even though the actual damage in both cases respectively was personal injury and economic loss. Autonomy discourse was used to circumvent orthodox principles of causation in *Chester* and was superfluous in *Montgomery*. The real issue in both cases was whether the patient would have taken the risk which resulted in damage had the patient been properly informed. In *Chester*, the patient apparently was willing to run the risk and therefore should have failed on the issue of causation. In *Montgomery*, the patient clearly would not have run the risk and therefore rightly succeeded.

The significance of the House of Lords' decision in *Chester v Afshar*[46] cannot be understated. The defendant surgeon negligently failed to inform the patient of a material risk of spinal surgery. The risk materialised, causing injury to the patient. However, the patient conceded that, had she been informed of the risk, she would nonetheless have proceeded with the same surgeon, albeit on a different day. Thus, on conventional principles, the failure to inform was not causally relevant to her injury as she would have been exposed to the risk anyway. The House of Lords found in favour of the patient in order to vindicate her autonomy rights. By doing so, the Court replaced medical paternalism with judicial paternalism, ignoring the patient's own decision to accept the risk.

Many academics and judges see tort law as an instrument to vindicate rights and to serve social justice. In the medical context, this is apposite to intentional invasion of patient autonomy, but less so when it comes to negligence. Linden J of the Federal Court of Canada was the torchbearer of torts, especially negligence, arguing that tort law should be a tool for empowerment of the injured, to enable them 'to confront their injurers in open court to make them answer for their harmful conduct'.[47] This confrontational framing of tort law has permeated medical negligence claims, driven by the desire to champion patient autonomy. While patient autonomy must be respected, a confrontational approach does not augur well for the doctor–patient relationship which is based on trust, dialogue, and collaboration.

[46] [2004] UKHL 41; [2005] 1 AC 134.

[47] AM Linden, 'Torts Tomorrow – Empowering the Injured' in NJ Mullany and AM Linden (eds), *Torts Tomorrow: A Tribute to John Fleming* (Sydney, LBC Information Services, 1998) 321, 322.

PART I

Reimagining the Tort of Negligence

2

Theoretical Foundations of Negligence

I. Introduction

This chapter makes a case for reimagining the theoretical foundations of negligence by championing human obligations, communitarianism, and care ethics. Current legal discourse prioritises rights over obligations, arguing that rights create corresponding duties. It is argued that the reverse should hold true, at least for the tort of negligence. A duty-based or human obligations model is superior to a rights-based approach to negligence; it aligns with the neighbour principle articulated by Lord Atkin in *Donoghue v Stevenson*,[1] which lay the foundation for the modern tort of negligence. Rights and duties are two sides of the same coin and arguing about which comes first is akin to the chicken-and-egg conundrum. However, putting duties before rights is significant from a philosophical standpoint. A human obligations paradigm is apposite to negligence because it expects defendants voluntarily to take responsibility for their risk-creating activities – the obligation creates the claim right in the claimant. It fosters a caring society that avoids the battle of rights.

Human rights have been recognised since ancient times but came to the fore in Western consciousness from the seventeenth century, before taking centre stage in the post-World War II era with the Universal Declaration of Human Rights. The modern concept of human rights has its roots in the social movements of the 1960s and 1970s.[2] In the medical context, the focus on patients' rights – embodied in patient autonomy – developed as a reaction against medical paternalism. Doctors who deliberately cause harm to a patient by operating without consent, by providing or withholding treatment by deception, by profiting through fraud, or by exploiting the vulnerabilities of patients are violating patients' rights. Patient autonomy is thus relevant to intentional harm, medical research, and professional misconduct. However, in the context of clinical negligence, where the doctor is acting in the interest of the patient but inadvertently – not deliberately – causes harm, the over-emphasis on patient autonomy risks undermining trust and collaboration between doctor and patient.[3]

[1] *Donoghue v Stevenson* [1932] AC 562; 1932 SC (HL) 31.

[2] See generally, S Moyn, *The Last Utopia: Human Rights in History* (Cambridge MA, Harvard University Press, 2010).

[3] See Chapter 4 of this volume for a discussion of autonomy and the doctor–patient relationship.

Before delving into the core arguments, the chapter sets out some general contentions about theorising, distinguishing between descriptive, explanatory, and normative theories. These categories are significant as they delineate the law as it is and the law as it ought to be – a distinction that is crucial to judicial development of the law. The tort of negligence is developed by judges in the tradition of the common law. The nature of judicial law-making is that it is precedent-based and self-correcting. Thus, decisions are binding until they are overturned or abolished by legislation. One may criticise a judgment, but as long as the judgment stands it *is* the law. Whether it *ought* to be the law is a distinct question, and judges should proceed cautiously before turning an academic 'ought' into a legal 'is'.

II. Theorising about Theories

Theories serve three functions. In the sciences, they describe phenomena (descriptive theories); they explain phenomena (explanatory theories); and they predict outcomes (predictive theories).[4] So too in law and philosophy, except that the third function is pluralist: it may be predictive, normative, or prescriptive; that is to say, theories may be used to predict how the law will develop, to justify the law as it stands, or to reform the law. To recapitulate: descriptive theories reveal *what* the law is; explanatory theories reveal *why* the law is as it is; normative theories postulate what the law *ought* to be. While these theories may overlap, the distinctions are crucial.[5]

Descriptive legal theory in the common law is closely associated with legal positivism in the tradition of Jeremy Bentham, John Austin, HLA Hart, and Hans Kelsen.[6] Legal positivism developed as a counter to natural law, insisting 'that what counts as law in any particular society is fundamentally a matter of social fact or convention'.[7] Positivists did not deny that law and morals could, and indeed often did, overlap. However, they rejected the idea that law had to be based on morality; in that sense, there was a clear conceptual separation between law and morality. Positivists drew a line between what the law *is* (legal question) and what the law *ought to be* (moral question). Rejecting the natural lawyers' claim that laws are valid only if they are moral, positivists relied on other justifications for the authority of law. Austin posited the command theory, according to which laws were commands of the Sovereign that were authoritative and had to be obeyed.[8]

[4] Editorial, 'Description, Prediction, Explanation' (2021) 5(10) *Nature Human Behaviour* 1261, https://www.nature.com/articles/s41562-021-01230-5.

[5] See generally, FJ Beltrán, JJ Moreso, DM Papayannis (eds), *Neutrality and Theory of Law* (Dordrecht, Springer, 2013).

[6] J Dickson, 'Descriptive Legal Theory' in M Sellers and S Kirste (ed), *Encyclopaedia of the Philosophy of Law and Social Philosophy* (Dordrecht, Springer, 2020) 259.

[7] JL Coleman and B Leiter, 'Legal Positivism' in D Patterson (ed), *A Companion to Philosophy of Law and Legal Theory* (Chichester, Blackwell Publishing Ltd, 2nd edn, 2010) 228.

[8] J Austin, *The Province of Jurisprudence Determined* (1832), WE Rumble (ed) (Cambridge, Cambridge University Press, 1995).

Hart, rejecting the command theory, offered instead the 'rule of recognition', arguing that law, properly enacted or judicially developed, sets common standards that citizens were obliged to obey.[9]

Crucially, positivists did not evaluate the legitimacy of the law by reference to any moral or ethical imperative. As long as the law was formally enacted or judicially recognised, it was internally self-justifying. Legal positivism was thus a natural bedfellow of descriptive theories, whose function was not to justify the law but merely to describe its essential properties. Having said that, descriptive theories have an evaluative element, as they are interpretive in nature.[10] Even Hart acknowledged that while law did not need moral justification to be authoritative, any account of legal positivism had to go beyond mere description and include explanation.[11] Explanations necessarily involve evaluation. Explanatory theories, while largely descriptive, draw on external values and perspectives, thus imbuing them with some normative elements.

Descriptive and explanatory theories make the law known and understandable. They are valuable, as they help judges and students of law make sense of cases without having to traverse every single case that has been decided. Normative theories, on the other hand, are engaged in critiquing the law and making an argument as to what the law ought to be. Treating a normative theory as descriptive erases the fundamental distinction between *is* and *ought*. Frederick Schauer explains this lucidly:

> Just as much of normative or prescriptive moral and political philosophy speaks in the voice of urging how it would be *good* for people or governments to behave, so too does at least some of normative legal philosophy speak in the voice not of what our concept of law now is, but of urging how it would be good for our concept of law to be designed or redesigned.[12]

David Hume famously argued that one cannot derive an 'ought' from an 'is' without a normative argument.[13] Equally, and in the opposite direction, one cannot rewrite history by creating an 'is' from an 'ought', an error that arises when normative theories and descriptive theories are not distinguished. The landmark UK Supreme Court decision of *Montgomery v Lanarkshire Health Board*[14] illustrates the blurring of 'is' and 'ought' in the Court's judgment on patient autonomy and the duty to inform.[15] Tort law is not static; it changes over time to meet society's evolving demands. Arguing about what tort law ought to be does not describe

[9] HLA Hart, *The Concept of Law* (Oxford, Clarendon Press, 1961).

[10] See JCP Goldberg, 'Twentieth-Century Tort Theory' (2003) 91 *Georgetown Law Journal* 513 (Conference: Symposium on the New Negligence).

[11] HLA Hart, *The Concept of Law* (Oxford, Clarendon Press, 1961) 151.

[12] F Schauer, 'The Social Construction of the Concept of Law: A Reply to Julie Dickson' (2005) 25 *Oxford Journal of Legal Studies* 493, 500.

[13] D Hume, *A Treatise on Human Nature* (1739) Book 3, Part 1, Section 1; LA Selbi-Bigge and PH Nidditch (eds), *David Hume: Treatise of Human Nature* (Oxford, Oxford University Press, 2nd edn, 2014) 469–70.

[14] *Montgomery v Lanarkshire Health Board* [2015] UKSC 11; [2015] AC 1430.

[15] See discussion in Chapter 4 of this volume.

what tort law was in the past or is at the present; it can only conjure the tort law of the future. Whether one is a positivist, naturalist, or realist, there is no avoiding the dilemma of the is/ought distinction.

Lord Atkin's opinion in *Donoghue v Stevenson*[16] illustrates how descriptive, explanatory, and normative approaches may be used to develop the law in a coherent and principled manner. Lord Atkin first describes the pattern of cases where a duty has been recognised. He then explains that these cases are all linked by some notion of wrongdoing for which the defendant ought to be held accountable. Finally, he proposes a standard for the law: drawing from moral and religious values, Lord Atkin articulated the neighbour principle. The three passages extracted below, in the order in which they appear in the judgment, demonstrate how Lord Atkin moves from the descriptive to the explanatory and finally to the normative.[17]

> The Courts are concerned with the particular relations which come before them in actual litigation, and it is sufficient to say whether the duty exists in those circumstances. The result is that the Courts have been engaged upon an elaborate classification of duties as they exist in respect of property, whether real or personal, with further divisions as to ownership, occupation or control, and distinctions based on the particular relations of the one side or the other, whether manufacturer, salesman or landlord, customer, tenant, stranger, and so on.
>
> And yet the duty which is common to all the cases where liability is established must logically be based upon some element common to the cases where it is found to exist. … At present I content myself with pointing out that in English law there must be, and is, some general conception of relations giving rise to a duty of care, of which the particular cases found in the books are but instances. The liability for negligence, whether you style it such or treat it as in other systems as a species of 'culpa,' is no doubt based upon a general public sentiment of moral wrongdoing for which the offender must pay.
>
> The rule that you are to love your neighbour becomes in law, you must not injure your neighbour; and the lawyer's question, Who is my neighbour? receives a restricted reply. You must take reasonable care to avoid acts or omissions which you can reasonably foresee would be likely to injure your neighbour. Who, then, in law is my neighbour? The answer seems to be – persons who are so closely and directly affected by my act that I ought reasonably to have them in contemplation as being so affected when I am directing my mind to the acts or omissions which are called in question.

III. Theorising about Common Law

Lord Atkin's dictum in *Donoghue v Stevenson* has its fair share of admirers and detractors. Critics view his judgment as an over-generalisation that has facilitated judicial activism in developing the tort of negligence,[18] a warning entombed in

[16] [1932] AC 562; 1932 SC (HL) 31.
[17] ibid 579–80.
[18] RFV Heuston, '*Donoghue v Stevenson* in Retrospect' (1957) 20 *Modern Law Review* 1; JC Smith and P Burns, '*Donoghue v. Stevenson*: The Not so Golden Anniversary' (1983) 46 *Modern Law Review* 147.

the dissenting opinion of Lord Buckmaster, who bemoaned the risks of judicial law-making, stating:

> The law applicable is the common law, and, though its principles are capable of application to meet new conditions not contemplated when the law was laid down, these principles cannot be changed nor can additions be made to them because any particular meritorious case seems outside their ambit.[19]

It is widely accepted that common law judges engage in law-making and that it is a legitimate function.[20] Judges employ substantive and formalist reasoning in developing the common law. There are two types of substantive reasoning: '"goal" reasons and "rightness" reasons'.[21] The former is about achieving certain desired outcomes (it is instrumentalist and forward looking) and the latter is about justifying the decision on 'socio-moral norms of rightness'[22] (it is deontological and backward looking). Formal reasoning does not rely directly on substantive reasons; it relies on existing rules, principles, or precedents. It compels a court to a particular outcome regardless of any substantive reason pointing to a different outcome. This creates a tension in the common law between principles-based reasoning and policy-based reasoning, a theme explored by Lord Goff in the 1983 Maccabean Lecture in Jurisprudence.[23] For Lord Goff, the search for principle brought out the best of both worlds: the consistency of rules and the flexibility of discretion.[24]

However, he was acutely aware of the dangers inherent in the search for principle. The first danger is the 'temptation of elegance', which ignores the natural untidiness of the common law and inadvertently excludes qualifications or exceptions to the general principle.[25] The second is the 'fallacy of the instant, complete solution', where judges believe that a principled approach to a particular problem has universal application.[26] The third is the 'danger of the unhistorical approach', which ignores the historical context of particular decisions.[27] The fourth is the 'dogmatic fallacy', which is to focus on the rule without understanding the broader principle or rationale underpinning it.[28] These dangers are equally relevant to theorising about common law.

An erroneous assumption in the search for principle and theorising about common law is that a judge is free to formulate and state a principle or rule for

[19] *Donoghue v Stevenson* [1932] AC 562, 567.
[20] See references cited below in n 36.
[21] PS Aityah and RS Summers, *Form and Substance in Anglo-American Law: A Comparative Study of Legal Reasoning, Legal Theory, and Legal Institutions* (New York, Oxford University Press, 1987) 5.
[22] ibid 6.
[23] R Goff, 'The Search for Principle' (May 1983), reproduced in W Swadling and G Jones (eds), *The Search for Principle* (Oxford. Oxford University Press, 1999) 313.
[24] ibid 324.
[25] ibid 318.
[26] ibid.
[27] ibid 319.
[28] ibid 320.

posterity. However, that is not how the common law works. In the words of Lady Hale:

> The common law is a dynamic instrument. It develops and adapts to meet new situations as they arise. Therein lies its strength. But therein also lies a danger, the danger of unbridled and unprincipled growth to match what the court perceives to be the merits of the particular case ... the words used by judges in explaining why they are deciding as they do are not be treated as if they were the words of statute, setting the rules in stone and precluding further principled development should new situations arise. These things have been said many times before by wiser judges than me, but are worth repeating in this case, where we are accepting an invitation to develop the law beyond the point which it has currently reached in this jurisdiction.[29]

Lord Goff, commenting on the declaratory theory of judicial decisions, posited a reinterpretation of the declaratory theory to reconcile it with the reality of the common law as a living system.[30] Judges decide cases according to the law as they understand it, informed by academic writing and comparative jurisprudence.[31] The judge 'may, on occasion, develop the common law in the perceived interests of justice, though as a general rule he does this "only interstitially"'.[32] Judicial law-making is the art of transforming an 'ought' into an 'is'. The common law evolves as it reflects changing values and is confronted with novel circumstances. Monist theorists who champion an eternal view of the common law, based on rights or natural law, ignore this reality.

Thus, Beever, in defence of the declaratory theory, argues that when courts alter positive law, it is only to give effect to – or to declare – a greater natural law.[33] As he puts it, 'the law that remains unaltered is not positive law but something more abstract and enduring. Fulfilling the law is a matter of making the positive law more accurately reflect this abstract and enduring law'.[34] This is a romantic notion. Judges make law – and indeed unmake law,[35] drawing on policy considerations to do so. Judicial law-making is simply the process by which judges nurture the common law, carefully moving it forward, constantly reviewing and checking, and occasionally reversing course.[36]

[29] *Woodland v Essex County Council* [2013] UKSC 66; [2014] AC 537, [28].

[30] R Goff, 'The Search for Principle' (May 1983), reproduced in W Swadling and G Jones (eds), *The Search for Principle* (Oxford, Oxford University Press, 1999) 313.

[31] ibid 378.

[32] ibid.

[33] A Beever, 'The Declaratory Theory of Law' (2013) 33 *Oxford Journal of Legal Studies* 421, 425. Beever's approach is classical Dworkin (R Dworkin, 'Hard Cases' (1975) 88 *Harvard Law Review* 1057; R Dworkin, *Law's Empire* (Cambridge MA, Belknap Press, 1986)). Support for Beever's view may be found in the majority judgments in *Donoghue v Stevenson* [1932] AC 562, 582–83 (per Lord Atkin), and 608–9 (per Lord MacMillan).

[34] A Beever, 'The Declaratory Theory of Law' (2013) 33 *Oxford Journal of Legal Studies* 421, 429.

[35] S Sugarman, 'Judges as Tort Law Un-makers: Recent California Experience with "New" Torts' (1999) 45 *DePaul Law Review* 455.

[36] British judges have commented on this over the last half century. See, for example, Lord Diplock, 'The Courts as Legislators' The Holdsworth Club Presidential Address, 26 March 1965; Lord Reid, 'The Judge as Law Maker' (1972–1973) 12 *Journal of the Society of Public Teachers of Law* 22;

In the recent decision of *Paul v Royal Wolverhampton NHS Trust*,[37] two children witnessed their father suffer a sudden heart attack and die. They sued the father's doctor for negligently treating his heart condition 14 months previously. The majority held that as the children had not witnessed the negligent event, but only the subsequent death, they could not claim for the psychiatric injury they had suffered. Lord Burrows, in a dissenting opinion, highlighted the role of judges in developing the common law to correct errors and to keep the law in line with the times. He observed:

> However, even if the better view is that treating the death as the relevant event is a development of the common law, it is in my view a justified incremental step that falls well within the traditional judicial role in correcting errors and keeping the common law up-to-date.[38]

Community expectations are a significant driver of common law developments. Prior to *Donoghue*, a duty of care was owed only when the parties were in a pre-existing relationship and were not strangers at large. Lord Atkin's judgment, based on the neighbour principle, was influenced by his understanding of what the community expected of the law, as noted in the concluding paragraph of his judgment: 'It is a proposition which I venture to say no one in Scotland or England *who was not a lawyer* would for one moment doubt' (emphasis added).[39] It was a classic, albeit not uncontroversial, instance of a common law judge turning an 'ought' into an 'is'.[40] A court has a choice in such cases. It can deflect the matter to the legislature for its action or it can go ahead and develop the law, on the assumption that the legislature could step in to reverse the court if it so chose.[41] The two opposing views are expressed respectively by Lord Hoffmann and Lord Nicholls in *Gregg v Scott*.[42]

Lord Edmund-Davies, 'Judicial Activism' (1975) 28(1) *Current Legal Problems* 1; Lord Devlin, 'Judges and Lawmakers' (1976) 39 *Modern Law Review* 1; Lord Goff, 'Judge, Jurist and Legislature' (1987) 2 *Denning Law Journal* 79; Lord Bingham, 'The Judge as Lawmaker: An English Perspective' in T Bingham, *The Business of Judging: Selected Essays and Speeches* (Oxford, Oxford University Press, 2000) chapter 2; Lord Sumption, 'The Limits of Law', 27th Sultan Azlan Shah Lecture, Kuala Lumpur, 20 November 2013; Lord Dyson, 'Are Judges Too Powerful?' Bentham Presidential Lecture, 12 March 2014; Lord Neuberger, '"Judge Not, That Ye Be Not Judged": Judging Judicial Decision-making', FA Mann Lecture 2015, 29 January 2015; Lord Neuberger, 'Implications of Tort Law Decisions' Address to Northern Ireland Personal Injury Bar's Inaugural Conference, County Down, 13 May 2017 (https://www.supremecourt.uk/docs/speech-170513.pdf).

[37] *Paul v Royal Wolverhampton NHS Trust* [2024] UKSC 1; [2025] AC 459.

[38] ibid [202].

[39] *Donoghue v Stevenson* [1932] AC 532, 599.

[40] There is always a risk of unintended consequences. See Chapter 5 of this volume, text to nn 24–57 for a critique of Lord Atkin's articulation of the duty test.

[41] This occurred following *Barker* in the United Kingdom when Parliament reversed the decision on proportionate liability. In Australia, after the High Court decided *Cattanach v Melchior* (2003) 215 CLR 1, recognising wrongful birth claims, three Australian States passed legislation to reverse *Cattanach* (Civil Law (Wrongs) Act 2002 (ACT); Civil Liability Act 2002 (NSW); and Civil Liability Act 2003 (Qld)).

[42] *Gregg v Scott* [2005] UKHL 2; [2005] 2 AC 176.

Lord Hoffmann:

> But a wholesale adoption of possible rather than probable causation as the criterion of liability *would be so radical a change in our law as to amount to a legislative act.* It would have enormous consequences for insurance companies and the National Health Service. In company with my noble and learned friends Lord Phillips of Worth Matravers and Baroness Hale of Richmond, *I think that any such change should be left to Parliament* (emphasis added).[43]

Lord Nicholls:

> More fundamentally, if a claim is well-founded in law as a matter of principle, as I believe claims of this nature are, the duty of the courts is to recognise and give effect to the claim. *If the government considers that some or all of the adverse consequences of medical negligence should be borne by patients themselves, no doubt it will consider introducing appropriate legislation in Parliament* (emphasis added).[44]

In the landmark decision of *Hii Chii Kok v Ong Peng Jin London Lucien*[45] on the duty to inform, the Chief Justice was candid in noting that the court had a responsibility to explore normative questions as to how the law ought to develop when responding to changing circumstances:

> In our judgment, it would be wrong to ignore this seismic shift in medical ethics, and in societal attitudes towards the practice of medicine, in deciding how the realities of the doctor-patient relationship are to be reflected in the applicable legal standards for doctors.[46]

Every aspect of medical negligence has been reshaped by external considerations as judges responded to social, economic, and political conditions, as well as more recently to human rights developments. The pro-doctor *Bolam* test was developed by judges in post-War Britain concerned about US-style medical litigation and the potential impact on the NHS.[47] The *Bolam* test has long been criticised for fostering a culture of judicial deference to medical experts,[48] and for being especially inappropriate when applied to the doctors' duty to inform. Judicial attitudes began to change from the late twentieth century onward as patients' rights and autonomy came to prominence, and concerns arose that doctors were not

[43] ibid [90].

[44] ibid [54].

[45] *Hii Chii Kok v Ong Peng Jin London Lucien and another* [2017] SGCA 38; [2017] 2 SLR 492.

[46] ibid [120].

[47] See JR Maltby, CDD Hutter and KC Clayton, 'The Woolley and Roe Case' (2000) 84 *British Journal of Anaesthesia* 121. See also the judicial concerns expressed in *Whitehouse v Jordan* [1981] 1 WLR 246 on the danger of the US medical crisis being replicated in the United Kingdom at the expense of the NHS.

[48] Lord Woolf, 'Are Courts Excessively Deferential to the Medical Profession?' (2001) 9 *Medical Law Review* 1, 15. An attempt to temper *Bolam* was made in *Bolitho v City and Hackney Health Authority* [1998] AC 232; [1997] UKHL 46, but with little effect. See A Maclean, 'Beyond *Bolam* and *Bolitho*' (2002) 5 *Medical Law International* 205.

disclosing appropriate information and giving proper advice to enable patients to make informed decisions.[49]

In 2015, the UK Supreme Court finally held that the *Bolam* test would no longer be applied to determine the standard of care in duty to inform cases.[50] Highlighting the paradigm shift in the doctor–patient relationship, heightened societal expectations, evolving professional standards set by the General Medical Council, patients' ready access to information, and the impact of human rights jurisprudence, including the Human Rights Act 1998, the Court declared that these legal and societal changes necessitated a change in the law. Far from the common law discovering eternal truths, judges were consciously making policy choices to steer the law in response to changing circumstances.

Judges have a responsibility to shape and nurture the common law to ensure that it remains relevant to contemporary societal needs. Occasionally, there will be radical shifts in the law which are unforeseen, but inevitable. A theory of the common law derived from cases in the nineteenth century may not fit a theory of the common law based on the twentieth century, even less so for a common law of the twenty-first century. What the law is and what the law ought to be remain two distinct issues, although they may overlap by design or by accident. Theories of common law must recognise and respect this reality.

IV. Theorising about Rights and Duties

Theoretical discourse on law and justice in the Western traditions (common law and civil law) is often framed in the language of individual rights. The rights-based approach has been influential in theorising about tort law, resulting in conventional wisdom that there can be no duty in the absence of a correlative right. Rights discourse may be necessary to explain or justify torts that are actionable per se or which result in intangible losses, but it is not necessary for the tort of negligence, which is actionable only on proof of damage. The tort of negligence, by its nature, rests on the concept of duty and not rights. Lord Atkin drew on a virtue, not a right – love thy neighbour. It is worth reflecting that contracts, torts, and equity are part of the law of *obligations* and not the law of *rights*.

The tension between obligations and rights has a long history in which each has competed for primacy. It is not a matter that lends itself to easy resolution and

[49] *Canterbury v Spence* 464 F 2d 772 (DC Cir 1972) (US); *Reibl v Hughes* (1981) 114 DLR 1 (Canada); *Rogers v Whitaker* (1992) 175 CLR 479 (Australia); *Dr Hari Krishnan v Megat Noor Ishak Megat Ibrahim* [2018] 1 MLRA 535 (Malaysia); *Montgomery v Lanarkshire Health Board* [2015] UKSC 11; [2015] AC 1430 (UK); *Hii Chii Kok v Ong Peng Jin London Lucien* [2017] SGCA 38; [2017] 2 SLR 492 (Singapore).

[50] *Montgomery v Lanarkshire Health Board* [2015] UKSC 11; [2015] AC 1430.

has been likened to the chicken-and-egg conundrum.[51] Modern social and political discourse has favoured a rights-based approach, which is appropriate in many situations. However, medical negligence is not one of them. This section argues that an approach that prioritises human obligations, communitarian values, and care ethics provides a better substratum on which to construct a theoretical framework for medical negligence.[52]

This section begins with a critique of the rights-based theory of torts, using Robert Stevens' seminal work.[53] Stevens distinguishes between the 'rights model' and the 'loss model' of tort law, the latter of which assumes that whoever causes loss should be held accountable unless there are reasons for them to be immune from liability. Stevens favours the rights model under which liability can arise only if there is an infringement of a right that the victim holds against the tortfeasor. As Stevens puts it:

> A tort is a species of wrong. A wrong is a breach of a duty owed to someone else. A breach of duty owed to someone else is an infringement of a right they have against the tortfeasor. Before a defendant can be characterized as a tortfeasor *the anterior question of whether the claimant had a right against him must be answered.* The law of torts is concerned with the secondary obligations generated by the infringement of primary rights. *The infringement of rights not the infliction of loss, is the gist of the law of torts* (emphasis added).[54]

This passage raises two problems. Stevens assesses the defendant's status as a tortfeasor by assessing the claimant's status as a rights-holder rather than by assessing the defendant's responsibility; contra Henry Aiken who argued that 'rights begin where responsibilities begin, not with the putative claimant, but with him upon whom the claim is laid'.[55] The last sentence in the quote from Stevens above is heresy to the established orthodoxy that negligence is actionable only on proof of damage.[56] If X stumbles and makes unwanted contact with Y, the latter may have an action in *trespass* if the act is intentional as their right to bodily integrity has been violated. Trespass is actionable per se because it is about protecting individual rights. However, there would be no action in *negligence* unless there is some loss or damage that is caused to Y by X. Treating infringement of rights as actionable in negligence is a step too far both philosophically and practically; it muddies

[51] E Andrew, 'Simone Weil on the Injustice of Rights-Based Doctrines' (1986) 48 *The Review of Politics* 60, 72.

[52] S Weil, *The Need for Roots: Prelude to a Declaration of Duties Toward Mankind* ((trans A Wills) New York, GP Putnam's Sons, 1952).

[53] R Stevens, *Torts and Rights* (Oxford, Oxford University Press, 2007).

[54] ibid 2 (footnotes omitted).

[55] HD Aiken, 'Rights, Human and Otherwise' (1968) 52 *The Monist* 507.

[56] See, J Stapleton, 'The Gist of Negligence – Part I' (1988) 104 *Law Quarterly Review* 213; J Stapleton, 'The Gist of Negligence – Part II' (1988) 104 *Law Quarterly Review* 389.

the waters, as seen in some of the landmark medical negligence cases involving wrongful birth,[57] loss of chance,[58] and duty to inform.[59]

Stevens recognises a distinction between a liberty and a right, arguing that individuals do not have a right to free speech but a liberty.[60] A right comes into play only when someone interferes with a liberty, and the right then creates a duty. Stevens rests his rights thesis on a series of assumptions: a tort is a wrong; a wrong is a breach of duty; a breach of duty is an infringement of a right held against the tortfeasor. From these assumptions, he concludes that a tort is an infringement of a right, without critically examining whether a duty may exist independently of a correlative right. The relationship between the three concepts – liberty, duty, and rights – is not clear. One could argue that all individuals enjoy an interest in freedom or liberty and therefore all other individuals have a duty not to interfere with that liberty. If that duty is breached, then the victim has a claim-right against the wrongdoer. In this analysis, it is the liberty that creates the duty, which in turn creates the claim-right in the victim.

Wesley Hohfeld, in the early twentieth century, set out four different conceptions of rights – rights, privileges, powers, and immunities, each coupled with a correlative concept – duties, no-rights, liability, and disability.[61] The narrow conception of rights, which correlated with duties, was viewed as a claim.[62] Stevens bases his work on this narrow conception of claim-rights.[63] However, Hohfeld also recognises the concept of liberty, which was commonly used by judges in tort cases. For example, Lord Lindley, whose judgment in *Quinn v Leatham*[64] is quoted by Hohfeld, states:

> The plaintiff had the ordinary *rights* of the British subject. He was *at liberty* to earn his living in his own way, provided he did not violate some special law prohibiting him from so doing, and provided he did not infringe the rights of other people. This *liberty* involved *the liberty* to deal with other persons who were willing to deal with him. *This*

[57] *McFarlane v Tayside Health Board* [1999] UKHL 50; [2000] 2 AC 59; *Rees v Darlington Memorial Hospital NHS Trust* [2003] UKHL 52; [2004] AC 309; *Cattanach v Melchior* [2003] HCA 38, 215 CLR 1; *ACB v Thomson Medical Pte Ltd* [2017] SGCA 20; [2017] 1 SLR 918.

[58] *Gregg v Scott* [2005] UKHL 2; [2005] 2 AC 176; *Armstrongv Quest Laboratories Pte Ltd* [2018] SGHC 66; *Wallace v Kam* [2013] HCA 19; (2013) 250 CLR 375.

[59] *Chester v Afshar* [2004] UKHL 41; [2005] 1 AC 134; *Chappel v Hart* [1998] HCA 55; (1998) 195 CLR 232.

[60] Stevens acknowledges that this is a prescriptive and not descriptive argument, referring to Article 10 of the European Convention for the Protection of Human Rights and Fundamental Freedoms, which enshrines the right to freedom of expression. R Stevens, *Torts and Rights* (Oxford, Oxford University Press, 2007) 5, fn 4.

[61] WN Hohfeld, *Fundamental Legal Concepts as Applied in Judicial Reasoning*, WW Cook (ed) (Westport CT, Greenwood Press, 1978 reprint) 10.

[62] ibid 38.

[63] R Stevens, *Torts and Rights* (Oxford, Oxford University Press, 2007) 4. See J Murphy, 'Rights, Reductionism and Tort Law' (2008) 28 *Oxford Journal of Legal Studies* 393 for a critique of Stevens' use of Hohfeldian concepts.

[64] *Quinn v Leatham* [1901] AC 495.

> *liberty is a right* recognized by law; its *correlative* is the general *duty* of every one not to prevent the free exercise of this *liberty* except so far as his own liberty of action may justify him in so doing (emphasis added by Hohfeld).[65]

Lord Lindley is crystal clear that a liberty is a right whose correlative is a duty. Hohfeld, however, treats liberty as the equivalent of privilege in his taxonomy of rights.[66] This ignores another manifestation of rights, namely interest-rights.[67] Liberty is an interest-right. It is this interest-right which gives rise to a duty on the part of others to the right-holder. If the duty is breached, then the victim has a claim-right. Thus, the claim-right chronologically is ex post the duty. In this taxonomy, interest-rights give rise to primary rights with correlative duties while claim-rights give rise to secondary rights. To put it another way, interest rights operate as shields and claim rights serve as swords. Stevens, however, rejects the notion of interest-rights, arguing as follows:

> Further, an interests-based classification causes sight to be lost of the distinction between a claim-right and a liberty. I may have an interest in being loved or happy, interests I am at liberty to pursue. I do not, however, have a general claim-right good against the rest of the world which is specific to these interests.[68]

A claim-right is not against the rest of the world, but an interest-right is. The claim-right is only good against whomever has interfered with your interest-right by breaching their duty to you. Stevens acknowledges that his rights thesis is unable to explain the tort of negligence, but instead of conceding that his theory is not universal, he dismisses the tort of negligence itself as an illegitimate construct.[69] He rejects duty-based torts, arguing that a 'duty is merely the obverse of a right'.[70] This ignores the historical fact that the tort of negligence was developed to hold accountable individuals who engage in activities that expose others, especially the vulnerable, to unreasonable risks. In an interconnected world of risks, the tort of negligence is about doing the right thing by others, not just about the rights of others. Tort law is more than just protecting rights, and negligence has its place. A trespasser may not have a right, but a duty may still be owed not to injure a trespasser.

Normatively, rights-based arguments invariably favour those who have capacity to assert their rights, sometimes to the detriment of the vulnerable in society. For example, rights-based arguments have been used by corporations, asserting their legal personhood status to claim various rights to expand their powers and privileges at the expense of individual human rights, while at the same time avoiding responsibility by hiding behind the corporate veil. Paradoxically, rights-based

[65] ibid 534.

[66] WN Hohfeld, *Fundamental Legal Concepts as Applied in Judicial Reasoning*, WW Cook (ed) (Westport CT, Greenwood Press, 1978 reprint) 42–43, 47–49.

[67] P Cane, 'Torts and Rights' (2008) 71 *Modern Law Review* 641, 643–44.

[68] R Stevens, *Torts and Rights* (Oxford, Oxford University Press, 2007) 290.

[69] ibid 295–303.

[70] ibid 291, quoting Lord Diplock LJ in *Letang v Cooper* [1951] 1 QB 232 (CA) 247.

arguments can be harnessed to advance the interests of the powerful in society at the expense of the vulnerable.[71] Ciara Torres-Spelliscy explains in vivid terms:

> The bigger picture is this: over the past decade, building on previous legal precedent from centuries before, corporations – especially large, wealthy, multinational corporations – are getting more legal rights and fewer legal responsibilities. Indeed, many corporations seem to treat the rights and responsibilities that usually attach as a package to ordinary citizens, as a buffet. While an average American citizen (the human variety) expects to abide by America's laws, pay taxes, and register for the selective service (for men), many corporations seem to have no compunction with cherry-picking the choicest rights and trying mightily to shirk as many responsibilities as possible from human rights liabilities.[72]

A. Human Obligations and Interconnectedness

Conventional Western theoretical discourse uses the language of rights instead of the language of obligations, which strips justice of virtue and renders duty a derivative concept, on the assumption that there is no duty without a correlative right. As O'Neill argues, contemporary discourse 'focuses on *recipience* rather than *action*, on *rights* rather than on *obligations*'.[73] The rights-based approach tends to obscure the possibility of duties that should exist in civil society, but which do not easily lend themselves to being framed in the vocabulary of rights. There are alternative ways of thinking about justice that respect both rights and duties, but which begin with duties rather than rights.

For example, central to Hindu philosophy and its discourse on justice is the concept of *dharma*, which at its barest means to act righteously.[74] It focuses on duties and not rights. The Baghavad Gita, an ancient text that is the cornerstone of Hindu philosophy, says, "Therefore, without being attached to the fruits of activities, one should act as a matter of duty, for by working without attachment one attains the Supreme'.[75] In Hinduism, the concept of *purusharthas* or human endeavours comprises four aspects: *dharma*, *artha*, *kama*, and *moksha*.[76] *Dharma* is about righteousness and is closely associated with human obligations

[71] The US Supreme Court recognised the right of corporations to assert First Amendment rights in their bid to fund political campaigns: *Citizens United v Federal Election Commission* 558 US 310 (2010). See C Torres-Spelliscy, 'Does "We the People" Include Corporations?' (2018) 43 *Human Rights Quarterly* 16.

[72] C Torres-Spelliscy, *Corporate Citizen?: An Argument for the Separation of Corporation and State* (Durham NC, Carolina Academic Press, 2016) 6.

[73] O O'Neill, *Towards Justice and Virtue: A Constructive Account of Practical Reasoning* (Cambridge, Cambridge University Press, 2010) 127.

[74] See M Chatterjee, 'The Concept of Dharma' in MC Doeser and JN Kraay (eds), *Facts and Values Philosophical Reflections from Western and Non-Western Perspectives* (Dordrecht, Springer, 1986) 177.

[75] *Bhagavad Gita*, Chapter 2, Verse 4.

[76] C Srivastava, 'Morality and Moral Development: Traditional Hindu Concepts' (2013) 55 *Indian Journal of Psychiatry* S283.

and duties – duty for the sake of duty.[77] *Artha* is the pursuit of human security and material needs. *Kama* is the pursuit of pleasure while *moksha* is the attainment of enlightenment and freedom from the pursuits of human endeavour. When humans pursue *artha* and *kama* at the cost of *dharma*, conflicts are inevitable.[78] Similarly, rights should not be prioritised blindly over duties or obligations.

An illuminating modern restatement of the relationship between rights and duties based on the concept of *dharma* may be found in a reply by Mahatma Gandhi to a request by HG Wells for an opinion on his draft of the Rights of Man. Gandhi replied as follows:

> Received your cable. Have carefully read your five articles. You will permit me to say that you are in the wrong track. I feel sure that I can draw up a better charter of rights than you have drawn up. But what good will it be? Who will become its guardian? If you mean propaganda or popular education, you have begun at the wrong end. I suggest the right way. Begin with a charter of Duties of Man (both M and D capitals) and I promise the rights will follow as spring follows winter. I write from experience. As a young man I began life by seeking to assert my rights and I soon discovered I had none, not even over my wife. So I began by discovering and performing my duty by my wife, my children, friends, companions, and society and I find today that I have greater rights perhaps than any living man I know. If this is too tall a claim, then I say I do not know anyone who possesses greater rights than I.[79]

Gandhi's admonition against prioritising rights over duties is not a peculiarly Eastern philosophy. There is a similar vein of thinking in the Jewish tradition, as well, of prioritising obligations over rights through its concept of *mitzvah*.[80] Robert Cover explains in an evocative article the 'myth of the Sinai' which embraces heteronomy over autonomy, signalling the necessity of 'common, mutual, reciprocal obligation'.[81] When a child reaches maturity, 'the child becomes bar or bat mitzvah, literally one who is of the obligations'.[82] The Jewish approach resonates with Aiken's argument that 'rights begin where responsibilities begin'.[83] Cover writes:

> In a jurisprudence of mitzvoth the loaded, evocative edge is at the assignment of responsibility. It is to the parent paying tuition, the householder paying his assessment, that the Law speaks eloquently and persuasively. It is for him/her that the myth resonates. This is true for all welfare functions and for ritual ones as well.[84]

[77] See WF Menski, *Hindu Law: Beyond Tradition and Modernity* (New Delhi, Oxford University Press, 2008) 94–107.

[78] ibid.

[79] R Iyer (ed), *The Moral and Political Writings of Mahatma Gandhi*, vol 3 (Oxford/ New York, Oxford University Press, 1986–1987) 492–93.

[80] See, RM Cover, 'Obligation: A Jewish Jurisprudence of the Social Order' (1987) 5 *Journal of Law and Religion* 65.

[81] ibid 68.

[82] ibid 65.

[83] See above, text to n 55.

[84] RM Cover, 'Obligation: A Jewish Jurisprudence of the Social Order' (1987) 5 *Journal of Law and Religion* 65, 69.

These philosophical traditions see obligations as empowering, in contrast to the modern Western approach in private law, which views obligations as a rope around the neck enslaving the obligation holder to the rights-holder.[85] Simone Weil, the French religious and political philosopher, writing at the end of World War II, argued passionately for a political and social order based on human obligations. Weil's obligations-based argument is grounded in her commitment to impersonal justice and to rootedness in the community.[86] The emphasis on the impersonal 'stresses what is common to all humans rather than what is unique, different, distinctive, or distinguished'.[87] Rights are personal, conditional, and alienable, whereas obligations are universal, unconditional, and inalienable. The relationship between obligations and rights is akin to that between subject (humans with obligations) and object (humans with rights).[88] Individuals only have rights when someone has obligations, or duties, to them. Thus, it has been questioned whether stateless persons have rights if no state accepts an obligation to them.[89]

As Weil puts it,

> [t]he notion of obligations comes before that of rights, which is subordinate and relative to the former. A right is not effectual by itself, but only in relation to the obligations to which it corresponds, the effective exercise of a right springing not from the individual who possesses it, but from other men who consider themselves as being under a certain obligation toward him. Recognition of an obligation makes it effectual. An obligation which goes unrecognized by anybody loses none of the full force of its existence. A right which goes unrecognized by anybody is not worth very much.[90]

Weil's human obligations theory is also premised on the idea of rootedness – that individuals belong to communities and are obliged to preserve and contribute to that community. Rights are in some ways antithetical to communitarianism. It binds the community in a negative way by demanding respect for rights in exchange for obligations. As Weil puts it, 'Rights are always asserted in a tone of contention; and when this tone is adopted, it must rely upon force in the background, or else it will be laughed at'.[91] It is combative and selfish, placing individual interests over the community. Rights are double-edged swords which can be weaponised to

[85] P Birks, *The Roman Law of Obligations* (Oxford, Oxford University Press, 2014) 3.

[86] S Weil, *The Need for Roots: Prelude to a Declaration of Duties Toward Mankind* ((trans A Wills) New York, GP Putnam's Sons, 1952) 43.

[87] E Andrew, 'Simone Weil on the Injustice of Rights-Based Doctrines' (1986) 48 *The Review of Politics* 60, 63.

[88] S Weil, *The Need for Roots: Prelude to a Declaration of Duties Toward Mankind* ((trans A Wills) New York, GP Putnam's Sons, 1952); A Etzioni, *The New Golden Rule: Community and Morality in A Democratic Society* (New York, BasicBooks, 1996) 3.

[89] H Arendt, *The Origins of Totalitarianism* (San Diego CA, Harcourt, 1976) 290–302, cited in C Hamilton, 'Simone Weil's 'Human Personality': Between the Personal and the Impersonal' (2005) 98 *The Harvard Theological Review* 187, 197.

[90] S Weil, *The Need for Roots: Prelude to a Declaration of Duties Toward Mankind* ((trans A Wills) New York, GP Putnam's Sons, 1952); A Etzioni, *The New Golden Rule: Community and Morality in A Democratic Society* (New York, BasicBooks, 1996) 3.

[91] S Miles (ed), *Simone Weil: An Anthology* (London, Penguin Books, 2005) 81.

justify violence and aggression. Witness the rights-based arguments in the United States that have been used to justify gun violence and to deny women reproductive autonomy.[92]

A distinction may be drawn from a theological perspective between *imago dei* and the *imitato dei*.[93] The theological argument is that because humans were created in God's image, they are imbued with certain inherent rights.[94] However, this ignores the *imitato dei*, wherein because humans are also created as imitators of God, they should behave in a Godly manner,[95] which means to love thy neighbour and thus embrace human obligations. Communitarianism fell out of favour, as it was seen as sacrificing individuals for the greater good, which was anathema to post-Enlightenment Western societies. The communitarian ethic with human obligations has largely been replaced by individualism and a rights-based order in the West, although varying forms of communitarianism have survived in the East and in tribal communities.

There is a new wave of communitarian thinking that seeks to balance individual rights and social responsibilities; autonomy and the common good.[96] Amitai Etzioni offers an approach to communitarianism that respects both autonomy and social order. He emphasises that communitarianism is not against individual rights, but merely against the hegemony of individual rights.[97] Thus, social order and individual autonomy need not be in tension and, indeed, can be mutually enriching. He explains this through the concept of inverted symbiosis. Take, for example, a newly formed community. As the individuals get to know each other and form social bonds, they are mindful of their mutual obligations, which strengthen social order. As social order is strengthened, individuals feel less isolated and develop 'a stronger sense of self and a more secure autonomy'.[98]

However, if the community's expectations of individuals grow beyond a certain point, social order and autonomy will begin to conflict and individualism will rise to counter the imposed social order. There is a dynamic equilibrium, or 'metastability',[99] that must be maintained in societies for social order and autonomy to co-exist in a mutually reinforcing state. This explains the rise of right-wing

[92] *Dobbs v Jackson Women's Health Organization* 597 US 215 (2022), overruling *Roe v Wade* 410 US 113 (1973) on abortion rights. On the Second Amendment gun rights, see *New York State Rifle & Pistol Association Inc v Bruen* 597 US 1 (2022); *District of Columbia v Heller* 554 US 570 (2008).

[93] N Johnson, 'When Rights Go Wrong: Simone Weil on Uprootedness and the Way Forward' *Ad Fontes*, 27 September 2023, adfontesjournal.com.

[94] GJ Wenham, *Word Biblical Commentary, Volume 1: Genesis 1–15* (Waco TX, Word Books, 1987) 30.

[95] N Johnson, 'When Rights Go Wrong: Simone Weil on Uprootedness and the Way Forward' *Ad Fontes*, 27 September 2023, adfontesjournal.com.

[96] A Etzioni, *The New Golden Rule: Community and Morality in A Democratic Society* (New York, BasicBooks, 1996); A Etzioni (ed), *The Essential Communitarian Reader* (Lanham MD, Rowman & Littlefield Publishers, Inc, 1998) xi.

[97] A Etzioni (ed), *The Essential Communitarian Reader* (Lanham MD, Rowman & Littlefield Publishers, Inc, 1998) 42.

[98] ibid 36.

[99] ibid 47.

nationalism in some countries, with the United States being the paradigm example as Americans reacted against 'Woke culture' that in their eyes threatened to destabilise the social contract.[100]

The communitarian approach resonates with feminism and relational theories of justice. The human obligations approach has also been adopted in recent scholarship on private law. Nicholas McBride, in his work on the humanity of private law, agrees that duties precede rights, observing,

> you could understand the idea of an obligation without ever having to mention the word 'right' but you could not understand the concept of a 'right that someone do x' without using the terms 'obligation' or 'duty owed to another'.[101]

Instead of rights creating duties, duties create rights.[102] McBride draws on the concept of human flourishing, asking whether the defendant's conduct would interfere with an interest of the claimant, which would affect the claimant's flourishing.

That there are obligations without correlative rights is indisputable. Onora O'Neill divides these obligations into universal obligations without rights and special obligations without rights,[103] the latter being of particular relevance to the duty of care in the tort of negligence. Universal obligations include the virtues of honesty, fairness, beneficence, and courage, amongst others.[104] These are abstract virtues, but there are parallels with the virtues in medical ethics of autonomy, non-malfeasance, beneficence, and justice.[105] The special obligations are of greater interest to understanding legal duties, and they include, for example, 'the attentiveness of a parent, the patience of someone working with handicapped adults, and the trustworthiness of an accountant'.[106]

An example of this approach in the field of medical negligence may be found in the New South Wales decision of *Woods v Lowns*.[107] Briefly, the facts were that the claimant, a young boy, suffered an epileptic fit and his sister ran to the defendant's clinic located nearby, requesting assistance. The defendant refused to come to the aid of the claimant and instead instructed the sister to have the claimant brought to him. Due to delay in treatment, the claimant suffered permanent disability. The defendant was held to owe a duty to the claimant even though there was no doctor–patient relationship, there was no prior contact between the two, and the defendant had not done anything to cause the epileptic fit. There was no basis for the boy

[100] K Alfonseca, 'What Does "Woke" Mean and Why are Some Conservatives Using It?' *ABC News*, 5 March 2025, https://abcnews.go.com/Politics/woke-conservatives/story?id=93051138.

[101] NJ McBride, *The Humanity of Private Law* (Oxford, Hart Publishing, 2019) 44.

[102] ibid 45.

[103] O O'Neill, *Towards Justice and Virtue: A Constructive Account of Practical Reasoning* (Cambridge: Cambridge University Press, 2010) 136–37.

[104] ibid 137.

[105] See generally TL Beauchamp and JF Childress, *Principles of Biomedical Ethics* (New York, Oxford University Press, 8th edn, 2019).

[106] O O'Neill, *Towards Justice and Virtue: A Constructive Account of Practical Reasoning* (Cambridge, Cambridge University Press, 2010) 137.

[107] *Woods v Lowns* (1995) 36 NSWLR 344.

to claim a right against the defendant, yet a duty was found based in part on the professional obligation of a medical practitioner.[108] Badgery-Parker J observed:

> A further matter which might be thought to bear upon the question whether a duty of care ought in some circumstances be imposed upon a doctor, the content of which is an obligation to treat someone not already a patient who is in urgent need of treatment, lies in the circumstances that a medical practitioner is, by virtue of his training, qualification and registration, permitted by the community to become and be a member of a relatively small group of persons in the community who alone are recognised as having the capacity and are accorded the privilege of affording medical treatment to those who require it.[109]

Contrary to Hohfeldian privilege, whose correlative is no-rights, Badgery-Parker's use of 'privilege' is to impose an obligation – a duty – on the privilege holder. This is the cardinal difference between a rights-based approach and a duty-based one – in the latter, it is a moral obligation to be responsible to others. It is conducive to a caring, interconnected, and interdependent society. The rights-based order has prevailed because the privileged few in society place their self-interest ahead of society, thus obstructing the possibility of a 'good society'.[110] As John Galbraith put it, 'There is democracy but in no slight measure it is the democracy of the fortunate'.[111]

Liberal philosophers from the Enlightenment and Romantic periods, rightly suspicious of authoritarian regimes, valorised freedom and autonomy. The global order has been shaped by post-Enlightenment Western values, championing individualism and human rights over communitarianism and human obligations. While this may be appropriate to restrain the power of the state and ensure individual liberty, it is not necessarily the best framework for interpersonal relations. The individualistic human rights framework is based on mistrust, power, and self-interest rather than fostering trust, community, and altruism. Challenging the orthodox view may be heresy to some who argue that the law generally should not impose affirmative duties or enforce virtues. This chapter advocates for a modest recalibration of orthodoxy to allow for a more compassionate and just society where obligations are given equal weight to rights, and in some cases should be treated as first amongst equals.

B. Ethics of Care

The ethics of care is a moral theory that takes a relational approach. It eschews an atomistic view of individuals and abstract conceptions of justice in favour of an assumption that all individuals are interdependent and interconnected.

[108] The trial judgment was upheld on appeal. *Lowns v Woods* (1996) Australian Torts Reports 81-376.
[109] (1995) 36 NSWLR 344, 358.
[110] See generally, JK Galbraith, *The Good Society: The Humane Agenda* (New York, Houghton Mifflin Company, 1996).
[111] ibid 8.

This assumption is not unlike Weil's concept of rootedness on which she based her theory of human obligations. Although the provenance of the ethics of care theory is debatable,[112] it is associated with feminist theory and was brought into mainstream discourse by Carol Gilligan, who claimed that men and women had fundamentally different approaches to moral reasoning.[113] Lawrence Kohlberg, whose work Gilligan critiqued, theorised that men had superior moral reasoning capabilities because they were more rational and applied objective criteria, including law, rights, and justice.[114]

Gilligan argued that Kohlberg's thesis was flawed because it favoured male-centric notions of moral reasoning, based on an ethic of justice. She championed an alternative approach, based on an ethic of care which she associated with women. Similarly, Sara Ruddick, writing during the same period, drew on women's experiences as mothers with their inherent maternal instinct to care in developing her theory on ethics of care.[115] Nel Noddings, another feminist theorist, also drew on maternal perspectives in her influential work, *Caring*.[116] While some of these feminists' claims have been criticised,[117] their work remains invaluable as they have created a different paradigm through which to analyse social justice.

Instead of prioritising autonomy and rights, the care lens prioritises the virtues of interconnectedness and mutual obligations. Nodding's rejection of the sanctity of principles, rights, and universal norms is especially powerful. In the introduction to *Caring*, Nodding observes how humans commit atrocities in the name of principle, to vindicate a particular right. As she puts it, 'principles function to separate us from each other. We may become dangerously self-righteous when we perceive ourselves as holding a precious principle not held by the other'.[118] A care ethic, on the other hand, does not put the self before others. It is an approach that is not just feminist but also found in communitarian societies.[119]

[112] Some argue it can be traced back to Aristotle: HJ Curzer, 'Aristotle: Founder of the Ethics of Care' (2007) 41 *The Journal of Value Inquiry* 221. See also M Mayerhoff, *On Caring* (New York, Harper & Row, 1969).

[113] C Gilligan, *In a Different Voice* (Cambridge MA, Harvard University Press, 1982). Gilligan's work has subsequently been criticised for being essentialist and based on inadequate empirical evidence. See references in Chapter 3 of this volume at n 103.

[114] L Kohlberg and C Gilligan, 'The Adolescent as a Philosopher: The Discovery of the Self in a Post-conventional World' (1971) 100 *Daedalus* 1051.

[115] S Ruddick, *Maternal Thinking: Toward a Politics of Peace* (New York, Ballentine Books, 1989).

[116] N Noddings, *Caring: A Feminine Approach to Ethics & Moral Education* (Berkeley CA, University of California Press, 1984).

[117] M Sander-Staudt, 'Care Ethics' *The Internet Encyclopedia of Philosophy* (ISSN 2161-0002, https://iep.utm.edu/care-ethics/) 18 July 2024, [3].

[118] N Noddings, *Caring: A Feminine Approach to Ethics & Moral Education* (Berkeley CA University of California Press, 1984) 5.

[119] The ethics of care is prevalent in certain Confucian, African, Asian, and traditional societies, including the Maori in New Zealand. See M Barnes, T Brannelly, L Ward and N Ward, 'Introduction: The Critical Significance of Care' in M Barnes et al (eds), *Ethics of Care. Critical Advances in International Perspective* (Bristol, Policy Press, 2015) 11.

The caring attitude is universal and embedded deeply in our childhood memories as we experienced care by our parents and others.[120] Nodding distinguishes between natural caring and ethical caring. The former concerns situations where the individual wants to care and therefore cares. The classic example is the parent who cares for the child. The latter concerns situations where the individual may not *want* to care but feels that he or she *must* care. This is when caring becomes ethical, giving rise to obligations. The obligation arises not because you desire it or because it is required to vindicate another's right; it arises as a moral imperative. You must care about others because you are connected to others in society.[121]

Ethics of care theorists have different conceptualisations of care, including practice, virtue, value, or action.[122] In this work, care ethics is used as a virtue that can balance the individualistic, rights-based paradigm of justice theories. As a moral theory, care has often been juxtaposed against justice.[123] In trying to reconcile care and justice, Virginia Held argues that care comes first, as it the foundational value without which humans cannot flourish. She uses the example of the basic unit of society, the family, which can survive injustice, but which cannot exist without care. This is not to dismiss justice, but simply to reimagine our priorities. Her argument on care and justice resonates with the general thrust of this work on the respective roles of obligations and rights, autonomy and trust. To quote:

> Within a network of caring, we can and should demand justice, but justice should not then push care to the margins, imagining justice's political embodiment as the model of morality, which is, I think, what has been done … We can decide to treat persons *as* individuals, to be the bearer of rights, for the sake of constructing just political and other institutions. But we should not forget the reality and the morality this view obscures. Persons *are* relational and interdependent. We can and should value autonomy, but it must be developed and sustained within a framework of relations of trust.[124]

Partly due to its close connection with women and feminism, care ethics has been criticised for fostering essentialism and a slave morality, consigning women to exploitative care-giving work.[125] The empirical basis for some of the claims has been challenged and some have argued that care ethics is ambiguous and theoretically indistinct. Feminist discourse has provided much of the intellectual power to the development of the ethics of care, but that does not mean that caring should be the domain of women. Historically, this was so in an unequal world where the patriarchy held power and shaped norms.

[120] ibid 5.

[121] EF Kittay, A Feminist Public Ethic of Care Meets the New Communitarian Family Policy' (2001) 111 *Ethics* 523, 535.

[122] See M Sander-Staudt, 'Care Ethics' *The Internet Encyclopedia of Philosophy* (ISSN 2161-0002, https://iep.utm.edu/care-ethics/) 18 July 2024, [2], and references therein.

[123] See V Held, 'The Meshing of Care and Justice' (1995) 2 *Hypatia* 128.

[124] ibid 132.

[125] See M Sander-Staudt, 'Care Ethics' *The Internet Encyclopedia of Philosophy* (ISSN 2161-0002, https://iep.utm.edu/care-ethics/) 18 July 2024, [3].

However, as we aspire to a more equal world, care ethics can be a valuable moral guide. Both men and women have responsibilities of care; both men and women are capable of maternalistic values and practices. These values should have a greater influence on the shape of the law and legal responsibilities. This is not to jettison rights and individual autonomy, but simply to arrive at a better equilibrium informed by a greater appreciation of the ethics of caring and duties of citizenship. Tronto has made this argument with respect to democratic politics, arguing that citizens should have responsibilities of care and not merely rights of citizenship.[126] She acknowledges that this goes beyond orthodox conceptions of the proper scope of politics and would require reconceptualisation of politics. Law and politics have developed on the 'knave mentality',[127] without considering that there can be inherent good in people and that it is not beyond law and politics to foster a caring society. As Monique Deveaux put it:

> What is often perceived as care theory's biggest liability is, from a feminist vantage point, actually its greatest strength: it is an implicitly, even explicitly, normative perspective. A care perspective relies centrally on a conception of human good and entails a deep commitment to a transformative politics.[128]

The core values of care ethics include attentiveness, responsibility, competence, responsiveness, and respect.[129] Daniel Enger focuses on three of these values: attentiveness, responsiveness, and respect. An attentive person is empathetic and is aware of others' needs. Responsiveness entails dialogue or engagement with others to understand what they need. Respect requires the carer to acknowledge the others' abilities and wishes. These values are aligned with the doctor–patient relationship and provide an ideal philosophical framework to ground the doctor's duty to inform and advise the patient.

V. Conclusion

As Stevens has ably argued, a rights-based approach does not explain the tort of negligence. However, instead of dismissing negligence as an illegitimate construct, this chapter argues that a human obligations approach offers the ideal theoretical framework. The tort of negligence, based on the neighbour principle, echoes the values of Weil's human obligations, Etzioni's communitarianism, and Gilligan's care ethics. The human obligations/ communitarianism/ care ethics approach is

[126] J Tronto, *Caring Democracy: Markets, Equality, and Justice* (New York, NYU Press, 2013) 7.

[127] The knave metaphor is borrowed from J Le Grand, 'Knights, Knaves or Pawns? Human Behaviour and Social Policy' (1997) 26 *Journal of Social Policy* 149.

[128] M Deveaux, 'Shifting Paradigms: Theorizing Care and Justice in Political Theory' (1995) 10 *Hypatia* 115, 117.

[129] J Tronto, *Moral Boundaries: A Political Argument for an Ethic of Care* (New York, Routledge, 1994) 126–36; D Enger, 'Rethinking Care Theory: The Practice of Caring and the Obligation to Care' (2005) 20 *Hypatia* 50, 54–55.

inherently relational, recognising the interconnectedness of individuals and society. A rights-based approach, while crucial for many aspects of the law including negligence, is not necessarily appropriate for medical negligence due to the unique nature of the doctor–patient relationship, the occasionally conflicting interests of key stakeholders, and the public's interest in access to healthcare.

Crucially, a rights-based approach is defensive and combative, threatening the trust that is at the core of the doctor–patient relationship. Instead of the orthodox argument that a duty exists only as a correlative of a right, it is argued that the converse is preferable – a right exists as a correlative of a duty. Regardless of which comes first, a shift toward an obligations-based philosophy is a shift in the right direction for the tort of negligence. The intrinsic value of a duty-based approach is that it imposes an affirmative duty on risk-creators to avoid causing harm to the vulnerable in society. In the medical negligence context, it imposes an obligation on doctors not just to do no harm to their patients, but also, in appropriate cases, to help patients realise their autonomy.

3

Private Law Theories and Medical Negligence

I. Introduction

Theorising on private law is a keen area of study amongst private law scholars. The literature reveals various theories postulated by academics,[1] some of which are in direct competition with each other and some of which are variations on a common theme. Some tort law scholars adopt a monist view, arguing for a singular theoretical approach while others have embraced pluralism, accepting that a combination of theories may explain different aspects of private law. This chapter favours the pluralist approach, accepting that no single theory is adequate by itself.[2] It relies on Peter Cane's organising framework, describing the anatomy of private law theory as consisting of three strands – justice theories, instrumental theories, and critical theories.[3]

Justice theories are internally-driven – they aim to justify the law based on moral criteria, including concepts of rights, wrongs, and responsibility.[4] Examples include corrective justice, distributive justice, relational justice, egalitarian justice, and rights-based concepts of justice. Instrumental theories are goal-defining – they aim to prescribe what tort law should accomplish, relying on considerations external to law. Examples include economic theory and regulatory theory. Critical theories introduce perspectives that are hidden or have been ignored by classical theories – they aim to rethink how law ought to be understood and who it should

[1] Ronen Perry argues that there are basically two major schools that have dominated tort theory – corrective justice and wealth maximisation (R Perry, 'The Role of Retributive Justice in the Common Law of Torts: A Descriptive Theory' (2006) 73 *Tennessee Law Review* 177, 179); Steven Hedley identifies three dominant approaches: corrective justice; economic theory; and formalism (S Hedley, 'The Rise and Fall of Private Law Theory' (2018) 134 *Law Quarterly Review* 214); Nicholas McBride also identifies a triumvirate – economic theory, Kantianism, and legal moralism (NJ McBride, *The Humanity of Private Law. Part 1: The Explanation* (Oxford, Oxford University Press, 2019)); John Goldberg synthesises five key approaches: Compensation-deterrence theory, enterprise liability theory, economic deterrence theory, social justice theory, and individual justice theory (JCP Goldberg, 'Symposium: Twentieth-Century Tort Theory' (2003) 91 *Georgetown Law Journal* 513).

[2] See C Purhouse, 'Flourishing Under Private Law? A Critique of McBride's Explanatory Theory' (2021) XXXIV *The Canadian Journal of Law and Jurisprudence* 239, 239–40 and references therein.

[3] P Cane, 'The Anatomy of Private Law Theory' (2005) 25 *Oxford Journal of Legal Studies* 203.

[4] ibid 205. Cane includes 'justice' as a normative concept, but that appears tautological and does not provide granular concepts of justice.

serve. Examples of these theories include vulnerability theory, feminist theory, and intersectionality theory.

The chapter reviews selected theories, arguing that the tort of negligence – at least medical negligence – is best explained by a combination of relational justice theory, feminist theory, and vulnerability theory under the broad umbrella of the human obligations approach described in Chapter two. This pluralist approach provides a solution to balance the key tension between medical beneficence and patient autonomy. The individualistic, rights-based approaches focus on patient autonomy, ignoring the realities of medical practice. While patient autonomy must be protected, doctors too should have their autonomy to act as professionals protected.[5] Medical professionals argue in favour of medical paternalism to strike the right balance between the interests of the doctor and the patient.[6] However, medical paternalism has been out of favour, and rightly so. That said, a different paradigm is possible. Drawing on human obligations, relational justice, feminism, and vulnerability, this chapter argues in favour of medical maternalism, which focuses not on the doctor and patient in isolation but on the relationship between doctor and patient.

II. Justice Theories

The literature on justice theories is dominated by the twin concepts of corrective justice and distributive justice, which have an uncanny resemblance to a similar dualism in criminal law, based on retributivism and utilitarianism.[7] This is not surprising, as both torts and crimes have shared roots in the law of wrongs. Until the twelfth century, England did not have a separate system of criminal law. As Potter observed, 'The Penal law of ancient communities is not the law of crimes; it is the law of wrongs, or to use the English technical word, of Torts'.[8] The law of wrongs consisted of four elements: outlawry; blood feud; tariffs of *wer*, *bot* and *wite*; and punishment of life and limb.[9] *Wer* was the value of compensation (*Wergeld*) paid to the victim; *bot* was the fine paid to the King; and *wite* was the tariff that demonstrated penance.

This ancient system was largely retributive, with the wrongdoer executed, outlawed, punished or forced to make compensation. Vengeance was at the

[5] ED Pellegrino, 'Patient and Physician Autonomy: Conflicting Rights and Obligations in the Physician–Patient Relationship' (1994) 10 *Contemporary Health Law Policy* 47.

[6] MS Komrad, 'A Defence of Medical Paternalism: Maximising Patients' Autonomy' (1983) 9 *Journal of Medical Ethics* 38.

[7] See GT Schwartz, 'Mixed Theories of Tort Law: Affirming both Deterrence and Corrective Justice' (1997) 75 *Texas Law Review* 1801, 1811–13.

[8] H Potter, *An Historical Introduction to English Law and its Institutions* (London, Sweet & Maxwell, 1932) 295, quoting HJ Sumner Maine, *Ancient Law* (London, John Murray, 1861) 370.

[9] F Pollock and FW Maitland, *The History of English Law Vol 2* (Ann Arbor MI, University of Michigan Press, 2nd edn, 1923) 449.

heart of any resolution of wrongs, and it could be appeased by punishment or compensation.[10] The more serious wrongs were those that affected the King's peace. A distinction gradually developed between wrongs that affected the Crown (criminal and public) and wrongs that were between individuals (tortious and private). Criminal wrongs were the subject of state sanction, while tortious wrongs were the subject of personal redress.[11] A jury system was instituted for the more serious wrongs under the reign of Henry II,[12] marking the formal separation of crime and tort. Apart from the loose public–private distinction, another distinguishing feature was that crimes focused on the defendant's blameworthiness while torts focused on the victim's loss. As noted in Bacon's Maxims:

> In capital cases in *favorem vitae*, the law will not punish in so high a degree except the malice of the will and intention do appear; but in civil trespasses and injuries that are of an inferior nature, the law doth rather consider the damage of the party wronged, than the malice of him that was the wrongdoer.[13]

This shared history is often overlooked or ignored in theorizing about torts. This is not surprising, as the goal of analytic jurisprudence in the Anglo-American tradition in the main has been 'to find universal rationalizing principles' and history is regarded as 'subversive because it exposes the rationalizing enterprise'.[14] The underlying approach in this book is sceptical of universal principles and monist theories, which often are reflective of the personal views of those espousing them. Real world problems are more nuanced and complex, requiring pluralism and contextualism. Part of the context is history.

The history of wrongs is significant as it shows that deep within tort's DNA lies the notion of vengeance – the wrongdoer must pay. Tort law doctrine arguably developed as 'a means of exacting revenge or retribution'.[15] While myriad alternative theories have been developed by academics, retribution and reciprocity remain an ingrained feature of tort law, or at least in the layperson's perception of tort law.[16] Understanding this historical truth explains why doctors are defensive about tort litigation. They perceive that their reputation is attacked and that they are being held guilty of committing a blameworthy, moral wrong instead of merely being held responsible for an avoidable adverse outcome.

[10] H Potter, *An Historical Introduction to English Law and its Institutions* (London, Sweet & Maxwell, 1932) 298.

[11] See JCP Goldberg, 'Rights and Wrongs' (1999) 97 *Michigan Law Review* 1828, 1828–29.

[12] H Potter, *An Historical Introduction to English Law and its Institutions* (London, Sweet & Maxwell, 1932) 223.

[13] F Bacon, *A Collection of some Principall Rules and Maximes of the Common Lawes of England with their Latitude and Extent* (London, 1630), cited in H Potter, *An Historical Introduction to English Law and its Institutions* (London, Sweet & Maxwell, 1932) 309.

[14] MJ Horwitz, 'The Historical Contingency of the Role of History' (1981) 90 *Yale Law Journal* 1057.

[15] MA Kotler, 'Utility, Autonomy and Motive: A Descriptive Model of the Development of Tort Doctrine' (1990) 58 *Cincinnati Law Review* 1231, 1232.

[16] See, MA Geistfeld, 'Folk Tort Law' in H Dagan and BC Zipursky (eds), *Research Handbook on Private Law Theory* (Cheltenham, Edward Elgar Publishing, 2020) 338; R Perry, 'The Role of Retributive Justice in the Common Law of Torts: A Descriptive Theory' (2006) 73 *Tennessee Law Review* 177.

This strikes at the very core of their professional identity as an honourable profession that is committed to doing no harm. Lord Denning, in characteristic evocative language, paints a vivid picture:

> Mr Marven Everett sought to liken the case against a hospital to a motor-car accident or to an accident in a factory. That is the wrong approach. In the case of an accident on the road, there ought not to be any accident if everyone used proper care; and the same applies in a factory; but in a hospital, when a person who is ill goes in for treatment, there is always some risk, no matter which care is used. Every surgical operation involves risks. It would be wrong, and, indeed, bad law, to say that simply because a misadventure or mishap occurred, the hospital and the doctors are thereby liable. It would be disastrous to the community if it were so. It would mean that a doctor examining a patient, or a surgeon operating at a table, instead of getting on with his work, would be for ever looking over his shoulder to see if someone was coming up with a dagger – for an action for negligence against a doctor is for him like unto a dagger. His professional reputation is as dear to him as his body, perhaps more so, and an action for negligence can wound his reputation as severely as a dagger can his body. You must not, therefore, find him negligent simply because something happens to go wrong; if, for instance, one of the risks inherent in an operation actually takes place or some complication ensues which lessens or takes away the benefits that were hoped for, or if in a matter of opinion he makes an error of judgement. You should only find him guilty of negligence when he falls short of the standard of a reasonably skilful medical man, in short, when he is deserving of censure – for negligence in a medical man is deserving of censure.[17]

Lord Denning's observation above rightly notes that medical negligence is distinguishable from many other forms of accidental harm where the defendant voluntarily undertakes a risky enterprise and causes injury to another person. In medical negligence cases, the claimant's health is already compromised and the doctor treating the patient often does not have the luxury of choosing to avoid the encounter; thus, some leeway is justified. However, Lord Denning unfortunately treats the falling short of expected standards as conduct that is deserving of censure, treating the negligent doctor as morally blameworthy. This imports the notion of wrongdoing, which attacks the integrity of the doctor, thus making doctors defensive when allegations of medical negligence are made against them.

The following sections respectively discuss corrective justice, distributive justice, and relational justice. It is argued that corrective justice and distributive justice are foundational to tort law, but neither is adequate on its own to explain or justify tort law. Used in combination, they provide a more convincing account that explains why an obligation arises, on whom it falls, and to whom it is owed. However, both corrective justice and distributive justice adopt an atomistic view of individuals instead of viewing them as interdependent actors in ongoing relationships. Relational justice recognises this interdependence and provides a better theoretical approach for medical negligence.

[17] *Hatcher v Black*, *The Times*, 2 July 1954.

A. Corrective Justice

As John Gardner has explained in detail, justice concerns the proper *allocation* of benefits or burdens. Distributive justice is about the right allocation of benefits and burdens according to some criterion of distribution; so, for example, medals for bravery in action should go only to those who have been brave in action. By contrast, the norm of allocation that corrective justice embodies is one in which a *misallocation* of some burden is corrected. Thus, corrective justice only operates when something has gone wrong. A tort involves one party committing a 'wrong' that results in a 'loss' to another party.

Some theorists have emphasised the nature of wrongs (corrective justice theorists) and others (distributive justice theorists) have prioritised loss allocation, based on other non-wrong-dependent criteria, to explain or justify tort law. This dualist conception of justice, based on corrective and distributive notions, has a long history going back over two millennia to Aristotle's *Nichomachean Ethics*.[18] Corrective justice is formal justice in the sense that it assumes the parties to be equal and disregards any features of their situations that are irrelevant to the particular transaction between them, for example, their wealth, intelligence, social status, and so on.[19] It is also bilateral, weighing the competing claims of the claimant and defendant with the aim of restoring the status quo within that relationship, ignoring external criteria that may affect the justice of the outcome. Ernest Weinrib, the leading voice on corrective justice put it thus:

> In Aristotle's account of corrective justice, quantitative equality pairs one party with another. Corrective justice treats the defendant's unjust gain as correlative to the plaintiff's unjust loss. The disturbance of the equality *that connects two, and only two, persons*. The injustice that corrective justice corrects is essentially bipolar (emphasis added).[20]

Weinrib recognised that Aristotle's conception of corrective justice was inadequate because Aristotle presented corrective justice as a transactional equality, without providing any criteria to evaluate that equality.[21] Weinrib fills this gap by arguing that 'the equality of corrective justice is the abstract equality of free purposive beings under the Kantian concept of right'.[22]

There are two difficulties with Weinrib's approach when applied to negligence. First, by relying on Kantian concepts of rights, Weinrib treats the loss suffered by the claimant not so much as the actual injury or harm suffered, but the violation

[18] See I Englard, *Corrective and Distributive Justice: From Aristotle to Modern Times* (New York, Oxford University Press, 2009).

[19] For a critique of this aspect of negligence and corrective justice, see J Penner, 'Don't Crash into Mick Jagger When He is Driving His Rolls Royce: Liability in Damages for Economic Loss Consequent upon a Personal Injury' in PB Miller and J Oberdiek (eds), *Civil Wrongs and Justice in Private Law* (Oxford, Oxford University Press, 2020) 253.

[20] EJ Weinrib, 'Corrective Justice' (1992) 77 *Iowa Law Review* 403, 410.

[21] EJ Weinrib, *The Idea of Private Law* (Oxford, Oxford University Press, Revised edn, 2012) 56, 57.

[22] ibid 58.

of the claimant's Kantian right.[23] This poses challenges to the law of negligence where the gist of negligence is not an infringement of an abstract right, but causation of damage that is legally recognised.[24] It will be argued in the next chapter that this Kantian rights approach is partly responsible for the rise of autonomy-based claims in medical negligence and the concomitant growth in claims based on alleged failure to obtain informed consent.[25]

The second, and more fundamental, problem is that Weinrib's corrective justice thesis only tells us that A has interfered with B's right and therefore should be accountable to B. It does not tell us why A, as a matter of principle, should be held accountable to *anyone* in the first place. Distributive justice does this work. Keating highlights this eloquently:

> Corrective justice comes into play because principles of distributive justice identify some boundary-crossings as unjust. Libertarian principles of distributive justice and permissible transfer do the real work. They determine what people are and are not entitled to do. Corrective justice is the handmaiden of distributive justice; it undoes illegitimate alteration of entitlements.[26]

This is pertinent to negligence claims where a party may be held accountable to others with whom there was no prior relationship. Take, for example, the case of *ABC v St George's Healthcare NHS Trust*.[27] The defendant's patient was the father of the claimant, his adult daughter. The patient suffered from Huntington's Disease, a known hereditary genetic condition. The claimant was thus at risk of carrying the gene and passing it on to her children. Respecting the duty of confidentiality to the patient, the defendant did not inform the claimant of her father's condition. The claimant went on to have a child who was diagnosed as carrying the gene. She sued the defendant, alleging that she was owed a duty of care. The claim was initially struck out as disclosing no cause of action, but, on appeal, it was held that whether a duty existed was a triable matter.[28] Yip J found on the facts that a duty existed, but the action failed as there was no breach of duty; she reasoned that the duty was not a freestanding duty to disclose genetic information, but only a duty to balance the claimant's interest in being informed of the genetic risk against the patient's interest and the public interest in maintaining confidentiality.[29]

[23] See A Ripstein, *Private Wrongs* (Cambridge MA, Harvard University Press, 2016) 80–122.

[24] See *Gregg v Scott* [2005] UKHL 2, [193]; [2005] 1 AC 176, 226 (per Baroness Hale). Cf, R Stevens, *Torts and Rights* (Oxford, Oxford University Press, 2007).

[25] A recent study showed a significant increase in settlements based on failure to inform following the decision in *Montgomery v Lanarkshire Health Board* [2015] UKSC 11; [2015] AC 1430. DS Wald, JP Bestwick and P Kelly, 'The Effect of the Montgomery Judgment on Settled Claims Against the National Health Service due to Failure to Inform Before Giving Consent to Treatment' (2020) 113(10) *QJM: An International Journal of Medicine* 721.

[26] GC Keating, 'Corrective Justice: Sovereign or Subordinate?' in AS Gold, et al (eds), *The Oxford Handbook of the New Private Law* (Oxford, Oxford University Press, 2020) 37, 41.

[27] *ABC v St George's Healthcare NHS Trust* [2017] EWCA Civ 336.

[28] ibid.

[29] *ABC v St George's Healthcare NHS Trust* [2020] EWHC 445 (QB).

Corrective justice does not explain or justify why the doctor should owe a duty to the claimant, given that the bilateral relationship was between the doctor and the patient, the claimant's father. The defendant had a duty of confidentiality to the patient, the deliberate breach of which would result in harm to the patient. Corrective justice demands reparation by the defendant to the patient, but it cannot shed light on why the defendant should be held accountable to the claimant. Indeed, recognising such a duty to a third party would be contrary to Weinrib's correlativity argument that 'the reason the plaintiff wins ought to be the same as the reason the defendant loses'.[30] Recognising a duty to the claimant conflicts with the doctor's duty to the patient.

Gardner provides a modified account of corrective justice by distinguishing between primary and secondary obligations.[31] Primary obligations give rise to secondary obligations, which in torts is 'a duty to repair',[32] usually satisfied by compensation, which corrects (as best as possible) the harm caused by violation of the primary obligation. Thus, corrective justice applies to the secondary obligation. However, the reason for the existence of the primary obligation may not always be explained by corrective justice. Something more may be required; it may be an alternative to corrective justice, or it may require a pluralist approach, which includes instrumental theories.[33] Corrective justice can co-exist with distributive justice or economic theory, providing a framework for interpersonal justice whose content is informed by other desiderata.[34] Corrective justice cannot function in isolation as a monist theory.

Corrective justice is also not suited to the modern tort of negligence. For example, the ancient torts of trespass, slander, and nuisance are inextricably linked to the violation of an individual's rights by the defendant. The tort of negligence, on

[30] EJ Weinrib, 'Corrective Justice in a Nutshell' (2002) 52 *University of Toronto Law Journal* 349, 351.

[31] J Gardner, *Torts and Other Wrongs* (Oxford, Oxford University Press, 2019). Other corrective theorists adopt different versions, but at their core they all insist on some type of wrong by the defendant which requires correction within a bilateral approach. It is beyond the scope of this book to explore corrective justice in detail. For more insight, the leading corrective justice theorists include GP Fletcher, *Fairness and Utility in Tort Theory*' (1972) 85 *Harvard Law Review* 537; RA Epstein, 'A Theory of Strict Liability' (1973) 2(1) *Journal of Legal Studies* 151; J Coleman, *Risks and Wrongs* (Oxford, Oxford University Press, 2002); J Coleman, 'The Structure of Tort Law' (1988) 97 *Yale Law Journal* 1233; SR Perry, 'The Moral Foundations of Tort Law' (1992) 77 *Iowa Law Review* 449; A Ripstein, *Equality, Responsibility, and the Law* (Cambridge, Cambridge University Press, 1999); A Ripstein, 'Corrective Justice' in H Dagan and BC Zipursky (eds), *Research Handbook on Private Law Theory* (Cheltenham, Edward Elgar Publishing, 2020) 255; R Stevens, *Torts and Rights* (Oxford, Oxford University Press, 2007; A Beever, *Rediscovering the Law of Negligence* (Oxford: Hart Publishing, 2007); A Beever, *A Theory of Tort Liability* (Oxford, Hart Publishing, 2016); JCP Goldberg and BC Zipursky, 'Torts as Wrongs' (2010) 88 *Texas Law Review* 917.

[32] JCP Goldberg, 'Symposium: Twentieth-Century Tort Theory' (2003) 91 *Georgetown Law Journal* 513, 570.

[33] See, GT Schwartz, 'Mixed Theories of Tort Law: Affirming both Deterrence and Corrective Justice' (1997) 75 *Texas Law Review* 1801.

[34] GC Keating, 'Corrective Justice: Sovereign or Subordinate?' in AS Gold, et al (eds), *The Oxford Handbook of the New Private Law* (Oxford, Oxford University Press, 2020); P Cane, 'The Role of Distributive Justice in Tort Law' [2001] *New Zealand Law Journal* 401.

the other hand, involves unintended harm to others as a result of activities that are not necessarily aimed at the victim. It addresses the realities of an interconnected world with risks that go beyond interpersonal moral wrongs. As Gregory Keating put it:

> A tort law of 'isolated, ungeneralised wrongs' – batteries, trespasses, slanders, and the like – is a law of bilateral wrongs. Lawsuits which seek to redress bilateral wrongs embody corrective justice in a straightforward way. When the bread and butter of tort law transforms into accidental injuries that are 'the incidents of organized activities', intuitions of corrective justice feel less compelling. Accidental harms have an impersonal quality.[35]

B. Distributive Justice

Both corrective justice and distributive justice may concern themselves with the allocation of losses suffered in the course of human interactions. Unlike corrective justice, under which the defendant's wrongdoing is the criterion for allocating the plaintiff's loss to the defendant, distributive justice spreads the loss suffered amongst others who are not necessarily wrongdoers. Indeed, the law may deny a claim under distributive justice criteria that would otherwise succeed under a corrective justice approach. A clear statement of this is found in Lord Steyn's opinion in *McFarlane v Tayside Health Board*,[36] in which a claim for wrongful birth (due to a poorly executed vasectomy) was denied:

> It is possible to view the case simply from the perspective of corrective justice. It requires somebody who has harmed another without justification to indemnify the other. On this approach the parents' claim for the cost of bringing up Catherine must succeed. But one may also approach the case from the vantage point of distributive justice. It requires a focus on the just distribution of burdens and losses among members of a society. If the matter is approached in this way, it may become relevant to ask commuters on the Underground the following question: Should the parents of an unwanted but healthy child be able to sue the doctor or hospital for compensation equivalent to the cost of bringing up the child for the years of his or her minority, i.e. until about 18 years? My Lords, I am firmly of the view that an overwhelming number of ordinary men and women would answer the question with an emphatic 'No.' And the reason for such a response would be an inarticulate premise as to what is *morally acceptable* and what is not (emphasis added).[37]

While corrective justice's norm of allocation is concerned with, and only with, redressing an imbalance between two parties, distributive justice is concerned with the fair 'distribution of the benefits and burden of economic activity among

[35] G Keating, 'Is Tort Law Private?' in J Oberdiek and P Miller (eds), *Civil Wrongs and Justice in Private Law* (Oxford, Oxford University Press, 2019).

[36] *McFarlane v Tayside Health Board* [1999] UKHL 50; [2000] 2 AC 59.

[37] ibd 82.

individuals in a society'.[38] It requires assessment of three components: the participants in the distribution; the burdens and benefits to be distributed; and the criteria for distribution.[39] As with corrective justice, Aristotle did not provide substantive criteria on which to evaluate distributive justice.[40] There are several criteria that are contenders in this context, including equity, equality, and need.[41] To these, David Miller adds Rawls' difference principle, viz to ensure the greatest distribution to the least advantaged, or in other words, to the most vulnerable.[42] The challenge for distributive justice is that there is no consensus on which value ought to be prioritised, or even on how to determine the appropriate criterion.[43] Different criteria are selected depending on the participants and things to be distributed, making distributive justice a difficult theory to apply in practice.

However, this does not make distributive justice an inferior theory. It is a substantive theory of justice that is pluralistic in nature. As Miller observes, 'beliefs about justice are pluralistic … [people] invoke several criteria of distribution and reach an overall judgment by balancing these criteria against each other'.[44] Monist theories are rarely adequate, and they are often reflections of their authors' own ideology. Take, for example, the monist theories respectively of Robert Stevens and Tsachi Keren-Paz. Stevens belongs to the corrective justice school and advocates a theory of torts that is based on rights.[45] Keren-Paz is firmly in the distributive justice school and champions egalitarianism.[46] Stevens favours a conservative, procedural approach to torts, restricting liability to claim-rights held by the victim, while Keren-Paz takes an expansive, social justice approach to extend tort protection to selected vulnerable classes.

Corrective justice and distributive justice are not mutually exclusive. As Lord Steyn observed in *McFarlane*, 'The truth is that tort law is a mosaic in which the principles of corrective justice and distributive justice are interwoven'.[47] The strength of corrective justice is its focus on the bilateral nature of the dispute, ensuring that tort law is restricted to providing interpersonal justice and not social justice. The strength of distributive justice is that it provides the substance to achieve interpersonal justice. Depending on the starting point, one could say

[38] J Lamont and C Favor, 'Distributive Justice' in N Zalta (ed), *The Stanford Encyclopedia of Philosophy* (Winter 2017 edn), https://plato.stanford.edu/archives/win2017/entries/justice-distributive/.

[39] ibid Section 1.

[40] H Dagan, *Unjust Enrichment: A Study of Private Law and Public Values* (Cambridge, Cambridge University Press, 1997) 32.

[41] M Deutsch, 'Equity, Equality and Need: What Determines Which Value Will Be Used as the Basis of Distributive Justice?' (1975) 31 *Journal of Social Issues* 137.

[42] D Miller, 'Distributive Justice: What the People Think' (1992) 102 *Ethics* 555, 559. See J Rawls, *A Theory of Justice* (Cambridge MA, Harvard University Press, 1971).

[43] Miller has shown that normative assessment of the criteria does not necessarily correlate with the empirical beliefs of people: D Miller, 'Distributive Justice: What the People Think' (1992) 102 *Ethics* 555.

[44] ibid 558.

[45] R Stevens, *Torts and Rights* (Oxford, Oxford University Press, 2007).

[46] T Keren-Paz, *Torts, Egalitarianism and Distributive Justice* (Aldershot, Ashgate Publishing, 2007).

[47] *McFarlane v Tayside Health Board* [1999] UKHL 50; [2000] 2 AC 59, 83.

that 'corrective justice provides the structure of tort law within which distributive justice operates'[48] or 'distributive justice provides the structure of tort law within which corrective justice operates'.[49] In a post-industrial risk world, the latter provides a more suitable framework for justice.

C. Relational Justice

An alternative to the duopoly of corrective and distributive justice is offered by Hanoch Dagan and Avihay Dorfman in terms of relational justice, which views private law as a means of securing 'relationships of reciprocal respect to people's self-determination and substantive equality'.[50] The fundamental difference between corrective and distributive justice on the one hand and relational justice on the other is that the former are based on the independence of individuals while the latter recognises the interdependence of individuals. 'Relational reasoning is ultimately concerned … with what we owe each other and how best to effectuate this in various settings'.[51]

Corrective justice is bilateral: it involves an arithmetical equation to determine the allocation of loss between two parties. Distributive justice is multilateral: it involves a geometric equation to allocate loss amongst several parties.[52] However, both are essentially engaged in horizontal justice. Relational justice theory bridges public and private spheres, integrating vertical and horizontal justice. The orthodox, liberal approach assigns to the state responsibility for substantive justice and obligations to enable self-determination. Thus, the state sets certain rules to ensure 'background justice',[53] through taxation and welfare schemes, amongst other things. This is vertical justice. Individuals are then free to operate within that framework with no, or minimal, obligation to ensure substantive freedom and equality as long as they respect formal equality and freedom.[54] This is horizontal justice.

Relational justice's focus on substantive freedom and equality makes it especially relevant to the medical duty to inform. 'To treat a person as substantively free is to enable her to make meaningful choices about the directions of her life, rather than merely to protect her independence from being subordinated to the choices of another'.[55] The doctor's duty to inform is not merely to respect individual

[48] P Cane, 'Distributive Justice in Tort Law' [2001] *New Zealand Law Review* 401, 413.
[49] J Gardner, *Torts and Other Wrongs* (Oxford, Oxford University Press, 2019) 102.
[50] H Dagan and A Dorfman, 'Just Relationships' (2016) 116 *Columbia Law Review* 1395, 1397.
[51] Zhong Xing Tan, 'Rethinking Relational Architecture: Interpersonal Justice Beyond Private Law' (2023) 73 *University of Toronto Law Journal* 293, 306.
[52] The arithmetic and geometric equations were first proposed by Aristotle. See KR Heidt, 'Corrective Justice from Aristotle to Second Order Liability: Who Should Pay When the Culpable Cannot?' (1990) 47 *Washington & Lee Law Review* 347, 350–53.
[53] J Rawls, *Political Liberalism* (New York, Columbia University Press, 1993) 269.
[54] R Dworkin, *Law's Empire* (Cambridge MA, Harvard University Press, 1986) 299.
[55] A Dorfman, 'Relational Justice and Torts' in H Dagan and BC Zipursky (eds), *Research Handbook on Private Law Theory* (Cheltenham, Edward Elgar Publishing, 2020) 321, 322.

autonomy and independent choice, but to respect the person and enable self-determination.[56] Relational justice fosters a collaborative relationship between doctor and patient in which the doctor has a positive duty to the patient, unlike corrective justice, which is limited to 'negative duties of non-interference' with the rights of others.[57]

Recognising that individuals are interconnected and interdependent allows us to appreciate that individuals are not always equal and that in interdependent relationships, one party may be more vulnerable than the other. This then informs the scope of duty and standard of care in negligence in ways that elude formalist conceptions of justice. For example, the duty of care owed to individuals who suffer from disabilities is different from that owed to persons without disabilities.[58] In the latter cases, both parties may be deemed equal and a negative duty of non-interference may be adequate. In the former, the parties are not equal. One is vulnerable and dependent on the other taking affirmative steps. Relational justice thus also explains and justifies affirmative duties, or duties to rescue.[59]

The standard of care is dependent not just on the abstract, objective standard of the reasonable person, but on the relationship between the defendant and the claimant. Dorfman illustrates this by pointing out the asymmetries in applying the standard of care in certain situations. For example, while defendants are generally held to a strict, objective standard, regardless of any personal disabilities, the claimant's disabilities may be considered in assessing the standard when contributory negligence is raised. Similarly, economic loss cases involving financial institutions' duty to advise illustrates how the 'vulnerability imbalance'[60] affects the standard of care. It has been judicially observed that the 'experience and sophistication'[61] of the claimant is relevant to the standard of care expected of the defendant. Thus, the defendant may be held to a higher duty when advising less sophisticated and less experienced claimants, and vice versa.

The High Court of Australia's decision in *Cook v Cook*[62] is an illustration of relational justice affecting the standard of care. The defendant in *Cook* was a learner driver who was persuaded to drive by her own daughter-in-law. Due to her inexperience, the defendant lost control of the car and had an accident, causing injury to her daughter-in-law, who sat in the passenger seat. Considering the particular circumstances and the relationship between the parties, the Court reasoned

[56] This is developed in Chapter 5 of this volume, text to nn 93–132, discussing shared decision-making and patient agency.

[57] EJ Weinrib, *Corrective Justice* (Oxford, Oxford University Press, 2012) 11.

[58] *Haley v London Electricity Board* [1964] UKHL 3; [1965] AC 778 and *Paris v Stepney Borough Council* [1950] UKHL 3; [1951] AC 367.

[59] H Dagan and A Dorfman, 'Just Relationships' (2016) 116 *Columbia Law Review* 1395, 1455.

[60] A Dorfman, 'Relational Justice and Torts' in H Dagan and BC Zipursky (eds), *Research Handbook on Private Law Theory* (Cheltenham, Edward Elgar Publishing, 2020) 321, 335.

[61] *Go Dante Yap v Bank Austria Creditanstalt AG* [2011] SGCA 39; [2011] 4 SLR 559, [46]. See also, *JP Morgan Chase Group v Springwell Navigation Corp* [2008] EWHC 1186 (Comm); *Rubenstein v HSBC Bank* [2012] EWCA Civ 1184.

[62] *Cook v Cook* (1986) 162 CLR 376.

that the defendant should be held to a lower standard than that of a reasonably qualified driver. The majority stated: 'The standard of care remains an objective one. It is, however, adjusted to fit the special relationship under which it arises'.[63]

This approach is contrary to the English approach of *Nettleship v Weston*,[64] in which the Court of Appeal, in a comparable case involving a learner driver, disregarded considerations of relational justice to hold that the standard of care remained that of a qualified driver. *Nettleship* was influenced by considerations of insurance rather than principles of tort liability and interpersonal justice. Lord Denning acknowledged this, stating, 'Morally the learner driver is not at fault; but legally she is liable to be because she is insured and the risk should fall on her'.[65] Relational justice provides a nuanced approach to determining the scope and content of duty by ensuring that interpersonal justice is adjudicated contextually and not abstractly. The majority in *Cook* expressly disavowed Lord Denning's approach, observing that considerations of social policy should be left to the legislature.[66]

III. Instrumental Theories

While justice theories may be deontological (corrective justice) or consequentialist (distributive justice), instrumental theories are always consequentialist in nature, aimed at the desired outcome of the law. Two outcomes that have been the subject of considerable academic discourse are economic efficiency and regulatory efficiency.[67]

A. Economic Theory

Economic analysis of the law has a long history,[68] flourishing in the United States in the wake of the celebrated dictum of Learned Hand J in *United States v Carroll Towing Co Inc*.[69] The Hand Formula or 'calculus of negligence' posited that, as a general rule, the assessment of negligence was based on balancing the probability of risk, the gravity of risk, and the burden of adequate precautions.[70] This formula

[63] ibid 384.

[64] *Nettleship v Weston* [1971] QB 691.

[65] ibid 700.

[66] *Cook* was subsequently overruled by the High Court of Australia in *Imbree v McNeilly* [2008] HCA 40; (2008) 236 CLR 510, which adopted the *Nettleship* position.

[67] P Cane, 'The Anatomy of Private Law Theory' (2005) 25 *Oxford Journal of Legal Studies* 203, 204.

[68] JG Backhaus (ed), *The Elgar Companion to Law and Economics* (Northampton MA, Edward Elgar Publishing, 2nd edn, 2005).

[69] *United States v Carroll Towing Co Inc* 159 F2d 169 (2d Cir 1947).

[70] A similar balancing approach is applied in the UK, Australia, and Singapore. See *Morris v West Hartlepool Steam Navigation Co* [1956] AC 552 (UK); *Wyong Shire Council v Shirt* (1980) 146 CLR 40; 29 ALR 217 (Australia); *BNJ v SMRT Trains Ltd and LTA* [2014] SGHC 286; [2014] 2 SLR 7 (Singapore).

is seen as promoting economic efficiency and lies at the root of the economic analysis school of thought.[71]

However, Learned Hand J was not propounding an economic theory of law; rather he was merely applying a common-sense balancing of risks, costs, and benefits to determine what a reasonable course of action would be. Crucially, he went on to note that if there were an accepted custom that supported an action that would not have satisfied the Hand Formula, 'custom should control'.[72] This is an implicit acknowledgment that negligence liability may be determined by factors beyond economic efficiency. Nonetheless, the economic analysis school gained a stronghold and has remained influential in tort law, especially in the United States.

Law and economics as a distinct discipline emerged in the United States in the 1960s, with the influential writings of Ronald Coase and Guido Calabresi.[73] The most prominent of the modern writers in the field is Richard Posner, a fervent advocate of economic analysis of law.[74] Posner's starting point is that 'economics is the science of rational choice in a world … in which resources are limited in relation to human wants'.[75] He proceeds on the assumption that all individuals will make rational choices to maximise their self-interest.[76] However, there will always be some options sanctioned by economic analysis that are simply unpalatable from a moral or justice perspective. Posner wryly recognises this, concluding, 'Evidently there is more to justice than economics, and this is a point the reader should keep in mind in evaluating normative statements in this book'.[77]

While economic analysis clearly fits within the instrumental theories, Posner goes further and claims that economic analysis also has explanatory power, arguing that judges understand that the common law is a 'system for maximizing the wealth of society'.[78] However, there is no empirical evidence to support this claim and it is no longer a view that is shared by the majority of law and economics scholars.[79] Posner's scholarship, while undoubtedly among the finest in the tradition, was driven by a conservative, economic ideology developed at the height of

[71] RA Posner, 'Instrumental and Noninstrumental Theories of Tort Law' (2013) 88 *Indiana Law Journal* 469.

[72] *United States v Carroll Towing Co Inc* 159 F2d 169 (2d Cir 1947) 173.

[73] RH Coase, 'The Problem of Social Cost' (1960) 3 *Journal of Law and Economics* 1. G Calabresi, 'Some Thoughts on Risk Distribution and the Law of Torts' (1961) 70 *Yale Law Journal* 499.

[74] RA Posner, *Economic Analysis of Law* (Boston MA, Little, Brown & Co, 1972); RA Posner, *Tort Law: Cases and Economic Analysis* (Boston MA, Little, Brown & Co, 1982); WM Landes and RA Posner, *The Economic Structure of Tort Law* (Harvard MA, Harvard University Press, 1987).

[75] RA Posner, *Economic Analysis of Law* (New York, Aspen Publishing, 7th edn, 2007) 3.

[76] This is often not the case, as individuals are rarely fully informed of the facts, including risks and choices available to them. See H Latin, 'Problem-Solving Behavior and Theories of Tort Liability' (1985) 73 *California Law Review* 677, 692.

[77] RA Posner, *Economic Analysis of Law* (New York, Aspen Publishing, 7th edn, 2007) 27.

[78] ibid 25; RA Posner, 'Wealth Maximization and Tort Law: A Philosophical Inquiry' in DG Owen (ed), *Philosophical Foundations of Tort Law* (Oxford, Clarendon Press, 1995) 99.

[79] S Hedley, 'The Rise and Fall of Private Law Theory' (2018) 134 *Law Quarterly Review* 214, 224.

the Cold War when individualism was at its zenith.[80] Unfortunately, Posner's zeal conflates normative and descriptive theorising, endeavouring to turn his 'ought' into an 'is'. The subsequent wave of law and economics scholars adopt a more modest approach to law and economics, accepting its limits and focusing on validating theories and arguments through empirical research.[81]

Economic analysis is purely instrumental or normative. It is not descriptive of the law as there is no empirical evidence that common law judges around the world were making decisions based on economic efficiency. Whatever the strengths and weaknesses of economic analysis of law, it has not gained a strong footing in the UK, Australia, or Singapore. Economic analysis works best when it comes to dealing with economic loss in the commercial context where the parties are equal. It fails when dealing with personal injury cases, particularly those which involve difficult moral choices. It is also ill-suited to medical negligence as economic analysis rests on the assumption of rational choice. However, patients have a plethora of personal reasons for making choices that are not always rational, or at least not 'rational' in the sense intended by economists, that is as 'self-interested wealth-maximisers'.

B. Regulatory Theory

We live in a highly regulated world in which virtually no activity can escape the touch of the regulatory state. The idea of the regulatory state represents the shift from the post-World War governance model that focused on post-War reconstruction and macroeconomic stability.[82] By the 1980s, under Reaganite and Thatcherite policies,[83] a considerable number of state-owned assets and functions were privatised. This resulted in an explosion in regulation to ensure that the private sector acted in the public interest. The state's function had metamorphosised from 'rowing to steering'.[84]

Regulation may function at three levels.[85] The first level involves a command-and-control structure, relying on rule-making, monitoring, and enforcement by regulatory authorities. The second, which has shades of responsive regulation,[86] is

[80] In the same paragraph defending the claim that the common law was about wealth maximization, Posner references the fall of communism, free-market ideology, deregulation, and the Reagan presidency. RA Posner, *Economic Analysis of Law* (New York, Aspen Publishing, 7th edn, 2007) 25.

[81] See, N Mercuro and SG Medema, *Economics and the Law: From Posner to Postmodernism and Beyond* (Princeton NJ, Princeton University Press, 2nd edn, 2006).

[82] K Yeung, 'The Regulatory State' in R Baldwin, M Cave and M Lodge, *The Oxford Handbook on Regulation* (Oxford, Oxford University Press, 2010) 64, 65.

[83] See generally S Clark, *Keynesianism, Moneterism, and the Crisis of the State* (Cheltenham, Edward Elgar Publishing, 1988); A Gamble, 'Neo-Liberalism' (2001) 25 *Capital & Class* 127.

[84] D Osborne and T Gaebler, *Reinventing Government: How the Entrepreneurial Spirit is Transforming the Public Sector* (Reading, MA, Addison-Wesley, 1992) 25.

[85] R Baldwin, C Scott and C Hood (eds), *A Reader on Regulation* (Oxford, Oxford University Press, 1998) 3–4.

[86] I Ayres and J Braithwaite, *Responsive Regulation: Transcending the Deregulation Debate* (New York, Oxford University Press, 1992).

based on a coordinated effort by various agencies that creates incentives and deterrents to guide behaviour. This includes, amongst others, government regulation, reporting and disclosure regimes, taxation, immunities, and preferential treatment as well as common law developments. The third level is the broadest, involving not just the state but the private sector and society where 'anything producing effects on behaviour is capable of being considered as regulatory'.[87] Tort laws may have a regulatory role in the second and third categories.

There are, however, significant challenges that proponents of the regulatory theory of tort laws must overcome. Courts do not possess a democratic mandate to make broad policy decisions and judges lack the expertise, evidence, and resources to evaluate the broader impact of their decisions. Tort disputes are bilateral in nature: the paramount duty of the court is to settle the dispute and deliver interpersonal justice. Further, and this is a point that is not given sufficient attention, tort law develops incrementally.[88] Each decision is merely a small, incremental step; the exceptions are the occasional landmark decisions that radically alter the law. Judgments are subject to appeal, distinctions are drawn on the facts, and with so many moving parts, including shifting social and economic trends, activism, and evolving industry guidelines, any effect of tort law in individual decisions may disappear into the background.

Structurally, tort law is part of private law, concerning horizontal disputes rather than vertical disputes involving the state.[89] However, as noted above, this divide is shrinking, and on its own is not an immovable obstacle to tort law having a regulatory function. Noting this, Cane nonetheless argues that while tort law may have a regulatory role, it would be unsafe to assume that that can be a primary or even significant role of tort law as it would conflict with two cardinal features of tort law: it is focused on protecting or vindicating the interests of the claimant over regulation or sanctioning of the defendant; and it is concerned with 'backward-looking responsibility based values' rather than 'forward-looking behaviour-modification goals',[90] which are in any event beyond the capacity of a judge to effect successfully.[91]

With respect to medical negligence specifically, there is another important dimension that must be part of the regulatory theory narrative, namely, professional regulation. The medical profession is one of the most highly regulated, with medical practitioners held to high professional and ethical standards.[92] The

[87] R Baldwin, C Scott and C Hood (eds), *A Reader on Regulation* (Oxford, Oxford University Press, 1998) 4.

[88] J Stapleton, 'Regulating Torts' in C Parker, et al (eds), *Regulating Law* (Oxford, Oxford University Press, 2004) 122, 131–32.

[89] P Cane, 'Tort Law as Regulation' (2002) 31 *Common Law World Review* 305, 309.

[90] ibid 306.

[91] J Stapleton, 'Regulating Torts' in C Parker, et al (eds), *Regulating Law* (Oxford, Oxford University Press, 2004) 122, 139.

[92] See General Medical Council, *Good Medical Practice* (2024); Singapore Medical Council, *Ethical Code and Ethical Guidelines* (2016); Medical Act 1983 (UK) Medical Registration Act 1997 (Singapore).

self-regulatory nature of the medical and legal professions makes torts less suitable, perhaps even unnecessary, as a regulatory device. Medical professionals guard their independence jealously and are faithful to their professional oaths, resulting in conflict when the law purports to impose general standards with which the profession disagrees. This is not to suggest that these professions should be immune from tort liability; it is simply to recognise that tort laws' regulatory function is greatly diminished.

Tort laws have deterrent effect, but that does not necessarily mean that they have regulatory capacity. A regulatory framework presupposes a weighing of costs, benefits, and risks of an activity, along with its social and economic impact. The law of torts functions within the silo of bilateral disputes that are highly fact-specific. Judges are confined to the evidence that is available and admissible. Further, a finding of breach of duty in negligence is a question of fact that does not set a precedent.[93] Therefore, the same conduct may be negligent under some circumstances and not so in others. This is unlike regulation, which applies uniformly in all circumstances.

IV. Critical Theories

Critical theories of law challenge orthodoxy, provide a revisionist account of history, and help make the case for reform. They are both explanatory and normative.[94] Critical theory began in Germany as a philosophical approach aimed at emancipating humans from slavery.[95] It championed democratic and egalitarian values, challenging domination by one group over another while promoting individual freedom and liberty.[96] This philosophy naturally appealed to minority and vulnerable groups that were in a perennial struggle to achieve freedom from discrimination and subjugation.

Thus, progressive scholars on race theories, feminist theories, and postcolonial theories embraced critical theory, drawing on concepts of vulnerability, group identity, and intersectionality.[97] Unlike traditional philosophical approaches that eschew social science in pursuit of abstract truth, critical theories draw on both philosophy and social science to develop theoretical approaches that are grounded and supported by empirical evidence. Thus, they can provide socially relevant and

[93] *Qualcast v Haynes* [1959] AC 743.

[94] J Bohman, 'Critical Theory' in E Zalta (ed), *The Stanford Encyclopedia of Philosophy* (Spring 2021 edn), https://plato.stanford.edu/ENTRIES/critical-theory/.

[95] ibid.

[96] M Horkheimer, *Critical Theory: Selected Essays* ((trans MJ O'Connell, et al) New York, Herder & Herder, 1992).

[97] See, for examples, references cited in NA Kohn. 'Vulnerability Theory and the Role of Government' (2014) 26 *Yale Journal of Law and Feminism* 1, fn 9.

practical solutions, unlike justice theories, which may be ideologically or politically divisive.[98]

Critical theory is fundamentally a normative theory that is critical of the Kantian concept of autonomy, liberating autonomy from the straitjacket of individualism by including societal justice and democratic values. Critical theorists acknowledge that individuals are not atomistic; they exist in interconnected relationships. Thus, freedom and autonomy must be viewed through holistic and relational lenses. This is not an anti-liberal view, just a more inclusive one. Further, critical theory, as part of social science, is inherently pluralist, rejecting universal theories. Jürgen Habermas pointedly noted: 'Whereas the natural and the cultural or hermeneutic sciences are capable of living in mutually indifferent, albeit more hostile than peaceful coexistence, the social sciences must bear the tension of divergent approaches under one roof'.[99] Pluralism fosters the co-existence of theories, which collectively provide more nuanced explanation and justification for particular areas of law.

A. Feminism and Vulnerability Theory[100]

A feminist approach to negligence, in particular the concepts of duty of care and breach of duty, provides a powerful tool to reconceptualise negligence from a negative standard of reason and caution to a positive standard of caring and concern.[101] It resonates with Weil's human obligations world view explored in Chapter two. Carol Gilligan, one of the pioneers of feminist legal theory, had demonstrated through empirical research that women's moral compass prioritised 'responsibility and contextuality' while men prioritised 'rights and abstract justice'.[102] According to Lisa Bender,

> Tort law needs to be more of a system of response and caring than it is now. Its focus should be on interdependence and collective responsibility rather than on individuality, and on safety and help for the injured rather than on 'reasonableness' and economic efficiency.[103]

[98] J Bohman, 'Critical Theory' in E Zalta (ed), *The Stanford Encyclopedia of Philosophy* (Spring 2021 edn), https://plato.stanford.edu/ENTRIES/critical-theory/.

[99] J Habermas, *The Logic of the Social Sciences* (Cambridge MA MIT Press, 1988) 3.

[100] This section draws from and reproduces parts of previously published work on a different topic: K Amirthalingam, 'Sustainable and Efficient Criminal Legal Aid: From Individual Right to Collective Interest' [2022] *Criminal Law Review* 621.

[101] L Bender, 'A Lawyer's Primer on Feminist Theory and Tort' (1988) 38 *Journal of Legal Education* 1, 25.

[102] ibid 28, citing C Gilligan, *In a Different Voice. Psychological Theory and Women's Development* (Cambridge MA, Harvard University Press, 1982) 19.

[103] ibid 4.

It is important to pause and recognise that Gilligan's work is dated and has been subject to criticism that it risks promoting essentialism and gender rigidity.[104]

This work does not rely on her empirical work and conclusions but draws inspiration from feminist theories' critical alternatives to the orthodoxy that has been dominated by male norms and privilege. Feminist theorising is fluid, evolving over time. Four waves of feminism have been identified.[105] The first wave in the late nineteenth century began in the US with the aim of emancipating women. The second wave developed in the 1960s and 1970s, challenging the traditional roles of women in the private and public spheres. The third wave, beginning in the 1990s, saw an expanding agenda beyond advocating for women's rights, embracing a wider constituency that included a range of oppressed classes.[106] It was the period of intersectionality theory,[107] a study of how different identity markers – including gender, race, and sexuality – intersected in individuals, affecting their place in society. The fourth wave finds its roots in the #MeToo Movement. Feminism today 'replaces attempts at unity with a dynamic and welcoming politics of coalition'.[108] It is pluralist and inclusive, but at its core it continues to challenge orthodoxy and to seek justice for the vulnerable.

Recognising that vulnerability is both universal and relational is key to rethinking the doctor–patient relationship and patient autonomy. The doctor–patient relationship should be one of trust, mutual respect, and partnership.[109] Vis-à-vis the patient, doctors respect the person; vis-à-vis the doctor, patients respect the professional. However, patients today have greater access to information, are more aware of their rights, and are increasingly assertive in taking control of their healthcare decisions. This can lead to friction between doctor and patient, undermining that relationship of trust. The growing emphasis on patient autonomy and

[104] See, for example, CF Epstein, *Deceptive Distinctions: Sex, Gender, and the Social Order* (New Haven CT, Yale University Press, 1988); C Tavris, *The Mismeasure of Woman: Why Women Are Not the Better Sex, the Inferior Sex, or the Opposite Sex* (New York, Touchstone, 1992); E Rackley, 'From Arachne to Charlotte: An Imaginative Revisiting of Gilligan's "In A Different Voice"' (2007) 13 *William & Mary Journal of Women & Law* 751; MS Wylie, 'The Untold Story: Carol Gilligan on Recapturing the Lost Voice of Pleasure' (2002) 26 *Psychotherapy Networker* 46; MJ Frug, 'Progressive Feminist Legal Scholarship: Can We Claim "A Different Voice"?' (1992) 15 *Harvard Women's Law Journal* 37; DM Senchuk, 'Listening to a different voice: A feminist critique of Gilligan' (1990) 10 *Studies in Philosophy and Education* 233; L Kerber et al, 'On *In a Different Voice*: An Interdisciplinary Forum' (1986) 11(2) *Signs* 304; J Auerbach et al, 'Commentary: On Gilligan's *In a Different Voice*' (1985) 11(1) *Feminist Studies* 149; D Nails, 'Social-Scientific Sexism: Gilligan's Mismeasure of Man' (1983) 50(3) *Social Research: An International Quarterly* 643; JM Broughton, 'Women's Rationality and Men's Virtues: A Critique of Gender Dualism in Gilligan's Theory of Moral Development' (1983) 50(3) *Social Research: An International Quarterly* 597.

[105] M Rampton, 'Four Waves of Feminism', *Pacific* (Fall 2008 edn), https://www.pacificu.edu/magazine/four-waves-feminism#:~:text=The%20first%20wave%20of%20feminism,with%20a%20focus%20on%20suffrage.

[106] RC Snyder, 'What Is Third-Wave Feminism? A New Directions Essay' (2008) 34 *Signs* 175.

[107] The leading proponent of intersectionality theory is K Crenshaw, 'Mapping the Margins: Intersectionality, Identity Politics, and Violence Against Women of Color' (1991) 43 *Stanford Law Review* 1241.

[108] RC Snyder, 'What Is Third-Wave Feminism? A New Directions Essay' (2008) 34 *Signs* 175, 176.

[109] See generally, O O'Neill, *Autonomy and Trust* (Cambridge, Cambridge University Press, 2002).

the move to a collaborative approach to patient care and shared decision-making further stress this relationship. It is vital to strike a balance between medical beneficence and patient autonomy, and to appreciate the nature of the doctor–patient relationship, not in its idealised form but in its non-ideal but practical form,[110] which includes acknowledging the reality that the patient is dependent on the doctor.

Vulnerability theory offers an alternative to classical liberal theories that focus on procedural equality and individual rights.[111] Vulnerability as a concept is employed in various forms,[112] providing 'a response to the primacy of the discourse of rights' in various fields of law and politics.[113] There is a growing body of literature on vulnerability theory, influenced significantly by the writings of Martha Fineman in the field of family law.[114] Vulnerability discourse has been central to much of social welfare and regulatory policies 'as a summarising concept that alerts us to the need and moral obligation to take action'.[115] Vulnerability, as an organising concept, has been used, for example, to inform policies on social housing needs; accord special protection to vulnerable victims and adults in the criminal justice system; and guide immigration and refugee decisions.[116] In the public realm, it empowers individuals (as policy-makers) and public agencies to recognise that some members of society are inherently less resilient than others and therefore deserve additional assistance in order fully to exercise their agency and to have opportunities equal to those who are more resilient. In private law, vulnerability theory facilitates individual achievement of substantive autonomy.

Laudable though liberal ideals generally are, they have in some cases entrenched systemic inequalities and prevented state intervention to help the vulnerable. These liberal ideals rely on an atomistic view of individuals, assuming that all have equal opportunities and that therefore the state should have a minimal role in ordering

[110] The distinction between ideal theory and non-ideal theory was developed by John Rawls in his work on the theory of justice. J Rawls, *A Theory of Justice: Revised Edition* (Cambridge MA, The Belknap Press, 1999) 216.

[111] Vulnerability theory does not diminish the rights of the accused person but simply puts it in the background. Fineman, who developed vulnerability theory in the context of family law, candidly admitted that her work was 'stealthily disguised human rights discourse'. MA Fineman, 'The Vulnerable Subject and the Responsive State' (2010) 60 *Emory Law Journal* 251, 255.

[112] B Mizstal, *The Challenges of Vulnerability: In Search of Strategies for a Less Vulnerable Social Life* (Basingstoke, Palgrave Macmillan, 2011).

[113] CF Stychin, 'The Vulnerable Subject of Negligence Law' (2012) 8 *International Journal of Law in Context* 337.

[114] MA Fineman, 'The Vulnerable Subject: Anchoring Equality in the Human Condition' (2008) 20 *Yale Journal of Law and Feminism* 1; MA Fineman, 'The Vulnerable Subject and the Responsive State' (2010) 60 *Emory Law Journal* 251; MA Fineman, 'Equality, Autonomy, and the Vulnerable Subject in Law and Politics' in MA Fineman and A Grear (eds), *Vulnerability: Reflections on a New Ethical Foundation for Law and Politics* (Farnham, Routledge, 2013) 1.

[115] K Brown, 'Beyond Protection: "The Vulnerable" in the Age of Austerity' in M Harrison and T Sanders (eds), *Social Policies and Social Control: New Perspectives on the 'Not-So-Big-Society* (Bristol, Bristol University Press, 2014) 39.

[116] See, K Brown, K Ecclestone and N Emmel, 'The Many Faces of Vulnerability' (2017) 17 *Social Policy and Security* 497.

society.[117] Fineman insightfully argues that the liberal philosophy driving law and politics in Western democracies is based on an idealised contractarian approach while ignoring reality:

> Individual transactions and interactions with the state and its institutions are posited to involve autonomous and independent actors in processes of negotiation, bargaining, and consent. Competence is assumed and differences in power, circumstances, or actual ability are ignored.[118]

This liberal model only recognises certain forms of vulnerability, dependent on recognised categories – infants, elderly, disabled, and so on. Fineman describes this type of dependency as 'inevitable dependency', which is accommodated within the liberal framework as the 'deserving poor'.[119] This is contrasted with 'derivative dependency',[120] which is socially imposed but viewed within the liberal contractarian framework as a matter of personal choice and therefore not deserving of sympathy. In Fineman's view every human is vulnerable in some way or to some degree. While invulnerability is not achievable, the counter to vulnerability, namely resilience, *is* achievable.[121] The more vulnerable the individual the more assistance they require to enable them to become resilient and realise their autonomy on an equal footing. The doctor–patient relationship contains elements of both inevitable and derivative dependency. While Kantian autonomy protects against medical paternalism, it fails to protect patients who may be incapable of achieving true autonomy without assistance. Vulnerability theory reconciles medical beneficence and patient autonomy within the doctor–patient relationship.

A criticism of vulnerability theory is that it may be co-opted by governments that seek to exercise greater control over citizens or to reduce access to social welfare. Karen Brown argues that vulnerability discourse has been used to expand state control of individuals, encroaching on individual liberty and privacy by increasing vetting and surveillance on the ground of protecting children 'based on assumptions about their innate vulnerability'.[122] Further, by classifying individuals

[117] See E Gordon-Bouvier, *Relational Vulnerability: Theory, Law and the Private Family* (Basingstoke, Palgrave MacMillan, 2020) 32–37. Recent global movements such as 'Black Lives Matter' and '#MeToo' have brought to the fore endemic discrimination against racial minorities and women. See generally, L Wexler, JK Robbennolt and C Murphy, '#MeToo, Time's Up, and Theories of Justice' [2019] *University of Illinois Law Review* 45; K West, K Greenland and C van Laar, 'Why some White people prefer "All Lives Matter" to "Black Lives Matter"' (2021) 60 *British Journal of Social Psychology* 1136.

[118] MA Fineman, 'The Vulnerable Subject and the Responsive State' (2010) 60 *Emory Law Journal* 251, 263.

[119] ibid 264. See also, MA Fineman, 'Evolving Images of Gender and Equality: A Feminist Journey' (2009) 43 *New England Law Review* 437, 447.

[120] This type of dependency is experienced by those who care for others, and who therefore require certain material, institutional and physical resources to be able to execute that care effectively.

[121] MA Fineman, 'The Vulnerable Subject and the Responsive State' (2010) 60 *Emory Law Journal* 251, 269.

[122] KB Brown, 'Beyond Protection: "The Vulnerable" in the Age of Austerity' in M Harrison and T Sanders (eds), *Social Policies and Social Control: New Perspectives on the 'Not-So-Big-Society'* (Bristol, Bristol University Press, 2014) 3.

or groups as vulnerable, the state is enabled to become more paternalistic, disempowering the 'vulnerable' and exerting greater control over them.[123] This can play into the hands of medical paternalism.

This 'othering' of the vulnerable may be avoided by recognising that vulnerability is a universal trait – it is an embodied human condition whereby every individual is vulnerable due to his or her innate condition or situational reality. The universal vulnerability thesis posits that all humans are vulnerable, but in different ways and to different extents, depending on personal and situational factors. Fineman emphasises that the concept of universal vulnerability extends to the situational, encompassing social, economic, political, interpersonal relationships, and relationships with the state.[124] By externalising these conditions, Fineman is able to attribute responsibility for them to the state, arguing that the state can and should distribute resources to enhance resilience where required.[125] Taking this into tort law, the same argument may be used to explain and justify affirmative duties of care.

There is a distinction between an innately vulnerable individual and a situationally vulnerable individual. Ellen Gordon-Bouvier advances the argument through her theory of relational vulnerability, recognising that external vulnerabilities can 'arise as a result of how the state and its institutions, including law, respond to our embodiment and relationality'.[126] Unlike the liberal concept of individual autonomy where individuals are seen as 'self-sufficient, rational, and disembodied', relational autonomy recognises that individuals are interdependent, inter-connected, and socially embedded. In the context of the doctor-patient relationship, patient autonomy cannot be viewed in isolation from that patient's social relationships, including the relationship with the doctor.

B. From Paternalism to Maternalism

Paternalism, especially medical paternalism, has generated a counterforce in individual autonomy as the saviour of patients' rights.[127] This tension between paternalism and autonomy is most evident in the context of intentional action,

[123] ibid 10.

[124] MA Fineman, 'Vulnerability, Resilience, and LGBT Youth' (2014) 23 *Temple Political & Civil Rights Review* 307, 318. See, C Mackenzie, 'The Importance of Relational Autonomy and Capabilities for an Ethics of Vulnerability' in C Mackenzie, W Rogers and S Dodds (eds), *Vulnerability: New Essays in Ethics and Feminist Philosophy* (New York, Oxford University Press, 2014) 33.

[125] MA Fineman, 'Equality, Autonomy, and the Vulnerable Subject in Law and Politics' in MA Fineman and A Grear (eds), *Vulnerability: Reflections on a New Ethical Foundation for Law and Politics* (Farnham, Routledge, 2013) 1; MA Fineman, 'Vulnerability and Inevitable Inequality' (2017) 4 *Oslo Law Review* 133.

[126] E Gordon-Bouvier, *Relational Vulnerability: Theory, Law and the Private Family* (Basingstoke, Palgrave Macmillan, 2020) 2.

[127] See J Katz, *The Silent World of Doctor and Patient* (Baltimore MD, Johns Hopkins University Press, Revised edn, 2002); W Gaylin and B Jennings, *The Perversion of Autonomy: Coercion and Constraints in a Liberal Society* (Washington DC, Georgetown University Press, Revised edn, 2003).

whereby the doctor consciously overrides patient autonomy in the name of the patient's 'best interest'. The classic examples include the doctor who provides a blood transfusion to a Jehovah's Witness despite being aware of the latter's non-consent to the treatment and the doctor who sterilises a woman or performs a caesarean section without her consent.[128] In both cases, the doctor is acting in the patient's best interest, albeit the best interest here is limited to the patient's physical health and not holistic wellbeing. Invariably, hard paternalism and individual autonomy result in the doctor and patient being pitted against each other, which is anathema to the doctor–patient relationship that is supposed to be based on mutual trust.

Gerald Dworkin describes paternalism as 'the interference of a state or an individual with another person, against their will, and defended or motivated by a claim that the person interfered with will be better off or protected from harm'.[129] This unfairly characterises all forms of paternalism as wrongful interferences that must be justified.[130] Recognising this, Dworkin attempts a neutral, descriptive analysis of paternalism, setting out the following conditions:

1. *Z* (or its omission) interferes with the liberty or autonomy of *Y*
2. *X* does so without the consent of *Y*
3. *X* does so only because *X* believes *Z* will improve the welfare of *Y* (where this includes preventing his welfare from diminishing), or in some way promote the interests, values, or good of *Y*.[131]

Having done so, Dworkin then demonstrates that a purely descriptive concept of paternalism is impossible as each of the conditions above is inherently normative. He then develops a taxonomical framework based on the following dichotomies to reconcile paternalism and autonomy: hard v soft paternalism; broad v narrow paternalism; weak v strong paternalism; pure v impure paternalism; and moral v welfare paternalism.[132] The soft paternalist would justify interference only 'to determine whether the person interfered with is acting voluntarily and knowledgably'.[133] If they are, and even if their actions are detrimental to their interests, the soft paternalist would refrain from interference, thus respecting individual autonomy. The hard paternalist would interfere if it were in the best interest of the person, regardless of their individual choice. The weak–strong dichotomy

[128] *Re T (Adult: refusal of medical treatment)* (1992) 142 NLJ 1125; [1992] 4 All ER 649 (CA) (Jehovah's Witness case); *Re F* [1990] 2 AC 1 (Mental patient sterilisation); *Re S (Adult: Refusal of Treatment)* [1992] Fam 123 [1992] 4 All ER 671 (Fam) (cf, *St George's Healthcare NHS Trust v S* (Guidelines) [1999] Fam 26 in which the court deferred to the patient's decision).

[129] G Dworkin, 'Paternalism' in E Zalta (ed), *The Stanford Encyclopedia of Philosophy* (Fall 2020 edn), https://plato.stanford.edu/entries/paternalism/.

[130] See C Coons and M Weber (eds), *Paternalism: Theory and Practice* (Cambridge, Cambridge University Press, 2013).

[131] G Dworkin, 'Paternalism' in E Zalta (ed), *The Stanford Encyclopedia of Philosophy* (Fall 2020 edn), https://plato.stanford.edu/entries/paternalism/.

[132] ibid.

[133] ibid.

operates similarly. In both cases, a line is drawn between procedural and substantive criteria – if the individual knowingly and voluntarily chooses to act in a way that is harmful, the weak/ soft paternalist would not interfere in order to respect individual autonomy.

While weak and soft paternalism go some way to reconciling paternalism and autonomy, they are still locked into the notion of individual autonomy and are unable to advance a positive concept of care, or caring, that is so crucial to the doctor–patient relationship. Take Dworkin's illustration of a person who wishes to jump out of a window. A weak paternalist would justify interference if, and only if, the person mistakenly believes that they will not be harmed by jumping out the window. However, the weak paternalist would not justify interference if the jumper's reason for jumping is to live spontaneously, even if it means the jumper will die instantaneously. Individuals have the right to make bad decisions; but surely, there is justification in saving people from incredibly bad choices or in proactively intervening to act in the best interest of a vulnerable person?

Instead of using paternalism, soft or otherwise, as the lens, a better model would be maternalism, a concept that draws on the feminist ethic of caring and an appreciation of vulnerability. While sharing some characteristics of soft paternalism, maternalism is distinguished by its rejection of individual autonomy in favour of relational autonomy.[134] Chapter four provides a detailed account and analysis of autonomy, which will not be repeated here. For present purposes, suffice to say that individual autonomy is based on a liberal worldview in which individuals exist independently, holding rights against each other and the world at large. As John Christman puts it, an autonomous person is 'considered an individual state, a status the person has independently of the relations or interpersonal interactions she finds herself enmeshed in'.[135] One influential strand of contemporary thinking on autonomy rejects this individualistic conception, preferring instead a relational concept. Proponents of relational autonomy posit that individuals are interdependent and interconnected, relying on interpersonal relationships and social networks. Relationships of trust and care particularly are necessary for some individuals to realise their autonomous selves.

Unlike individual autonomy, relational autonomy does not exclude external influences on autonomous agency. Thus, an 'interference' that has at heart the best interest of the affected person would not automatically be dismissed as unjustified paternalism. It would be an aspect of the complex reality of relational autonomy within which such maternalistic intervention has a proper place. A paternalist acts against the will of an individual in the belief that they are acting in the individual's best interest. A maternalist, on the other hand, acts in the individual's best interest while respecting that individual's autonomous agency. As argued in Chapter two,

[134] LS Sullivan and F Niker, 'Relational Autonomy, Paternalism, and Maternalism' (2018) 21 *Ethical Theory & Moral Practice* 649.

[135] J Christman, 'Relational Autonomy, Liberal Individualism and the Social Dynamics of Paternalism' (2014) 17 *Ethical Theory & Moral Practice* 369.

the key is respect for persons, not respect for autonomy alone. Laura Sullivan and Fay Niker describe it thus:

> If paternalism is acting in another person's best interests without due consideration of their autonomy, maternalism is acting for the benefit of another person in a way that takes that person's autonomous agency into account, despite no explicit expression of consent or assent being given by the person on whose behalf the decision is made.[136]

Two conditions must be met for maternalism to operate successfully. There must be a relationship of trust, and the intervener must know the subject of intervention sufficiently well to make an informed judgement that the intervention will support the subject's autonomy.[137] These two conditions are innate to the doctor–patient relationship, which is based on trust and professional expertise, thus making maternalism especially suited to evaluating medical interventions. Indeed, medical maternalism has been informally recognised for a long time,[138] and it is what many doctors continue to practise. However, without formal recognition as an alternative theory to paternalism, maternalistic actions remain enmeshed in the entrails of paternalism. Softer forms of paternalism cannot come to the rescue, as all forms of paternalism cannot escape the dead hand of individual autonomy.

Sullivan and Niker describe six differences between maternalism and paternalism,[139] three of which are centred on the nature of the relationship between the intervener and the subject – the significance of the relationship; the character of the relationship; and the epistemic dynamics of the relationship. Paternalistic acts are not dependent on the relationship between the parties; thus, one can act paternalistically with respect to a stranger. Maternalism presupposes 'historical and ongoing relationships'[140] where the intervener has sufficient knowledge about the subject's wants and desires. Crucially, maternalism only operates successfully within 'relationships of trust and understanding'.[141] Again, this resonates with the doctor–patient relationship, where trust and understanding are mutually reinforcing and the relationship is as important as the individual interests. Finally, the epistemic dynamics of the relationship are crucial to maternalism, as the intervention is made not on the basis of what the intervener believes is best for the subject but on the intervener's understanding of the subject's unexpressed autonomous will.[142]

Neoliberal analytical jurisprudence has sacrificed the doctor–patient relationship at the twin altars of individual autonomy and informed consent. The reality of medical practice is that doctors have to make some decisions in the best interest

[136] LS Sullivan and F Niker, 'Relational Autonomy, Paternalism, and Maternalism' (2018) 21 *Ethical Theory & Moral Practice* 649, 655.

[137] ibid.

[138] J Wilson-Barnett, 'Ethical Dilemmas in Nursing' (1986) 12 *Journal of Medical Ethics* 123, 124.

[139] LS Sullivan and F Niker, 'Relational Autonomy, Paternalism, and Maternalism' (2018) 21 *Ethical Theory & Moral Practice* 649, 655–56.

[140] ibid, 657.

[141] ibid.

[142] ibid 658–59.

of their patients as part of an ongoing relationship based on mutual trust. An illuminating example comes from the nocebo effect, the flip side of the better-known placebo effect. A placebo effect is seen in the improved clinical outcome of patients who have a positive expectation based on a misconception. For example, a patient prescribed an inert substance believing it to be a therapeutic drug may exhibit positive clinical outcomes.

The nocebo effect is the opposite, whereby the patient suffers an adverse clinical outcome due to the psychological effect of negative expectations.[143] This poses an ethical dilemma for doctors who must make decisions on what information to disclose. Should the doctor disclose the potential side effect of proposed treatment and risk the nocebo effect, thus potentially harming the patient and violating the ethical principle of non-malfeasance, or should the doctor choose non-disclosure and take the risk of falling foul of the law for failing to obtain informed consent? The authors of a study on the nocebo effect and disclosure of information concluded that it would be justifiable to withhold disclosure of negative side effects of proposed treatment in some cases to avoid the nocebo effect.[144]

V. Tying the Threads: Pluralism, Vulnerability and Maternalism

James Goudkamp and John Murphy have effectively demonstrated the failure of universal theories of tort law by empirically testing three leading theories – corrective justice theory, economic theory, and rights theory – against five aspects of tort law: duty of care; breach of duty; punitive damages; defence of illegality; and the rule in *Rylands v Fletcher*.[145] Each theory tested was able to deal with only selected parts of tort law; none was able to deal satisfactorily with all aspects of tort law. To do so effectively, a pluralist approach is required. This is so even with respect to the tort of negligence itself, which requires a pluralist approach both to the underlying theory and to the doctrines governing duty of care, standard of care, causation, and damage. The complexity and dynamism of negligence belies the assumption that it is a unitary tort.

Apart from providing a nuanced theoretical approach, a pluralist approach also provides a better account of negligence doctrine. The duty of care has been the subject of intense judicial and academic scrutiny as judges and scholars have sought to articulate a universal test for the duty of care. The United Kingdom, Australia, and Singapore each have slightly different approaches to the duty of

[143] R Hahn, 'The Nocebo Effect Phenomenon: Concept, Evidence, and Implications for Public Health' (1997) 26 *Preventive Medicine* 607.

[144] JT Fortunato, JA Wasserman and DL Menkes, 'When Respective Autonomy is Harmful: A Clinically Useful Approach to the Nocebo Effect' (2017) 17 *American Journal of Bioethics* 36.

[145] J Goudkamp and J Murphy, 'The Failure of Universal Theories of Tort Law' (2015) 21 *Legal Theory* 47.

care. In Singapore, the Court of Appeal has held that there is a single, universal approach to the duty of care.[146] Australia abandoned the search for a duty of care test, with the High Court taking a 'salient features' approach, namely examining each case in which a novel duty is claimed on its individual facts and context.[147] The United Kingdom has avowedly adopted a pluralist approach to the duty of care,[148] holding that courts could apply an assumption of responsibility approach, an incremental approach, or the three-stage approach, articulated in *Caparo Industries Plc v Dickman*,[149] consisting of inquiries into reasonable foreseeability, proximity, and policy.[150]

The standard of care is based on the reasonable person, a concept that has engendered debates as to whether it is normative or descriptive.[151] Here too, the courts have endorsed a pluralist approach, for example, by holding that the standard of care in medical negligence may be based on different tests depending on whether the allegation pertains to negligent diagnosis and treatment, or negligent failure to inform of risks or advise of alternatives.[152] Causation has several tests, including the 'but-for', 'material contribution to damage', and 'material contribution to risk' tests.[153] What constitutes actionable damage is subject to conflicting approaches. For example, wrongful birth claims have been recognised in Australia,[154] but not in the United Kingdom,[155] subject to one exception.[156] Whether loss of autonomy constitutes actionable damage is a matter hotly debated by academics and has been considered by courts.[157]

The doctor–patient relationship exists in a plethora of social and economic circumstances and cannot be governed by a unitary approach. Doctors providing healthcare services in the private sector function in an environment with resources and patient demographics that are wholly different from those experienced by

[146] *Spandeck Engineering (S) Pte Ltd v Defence Science & Technology Agency* [2007] SGCA 37; [2007] 4 SLR(R) 100.

[147] *Perre v Apand Pty Ltd* [1999] HCA 36, (1999) 198 CLR 180.

[148] *Customs and Excise Commissioners v Barclays Bank* [2007] 1 AC 181.

[149] *Caparo Industries Plc v Dickman* [1990] 2 AC 605.

[150] The Supreme Court has downplayed the three stage or tripartite inquiry in Caparo, holding that *Caparo* did not state a test but was merely as an example of incremental reasoning based on analysis of precedent. *Michael v Chief Constable of South Wales Police (Refuge and others intervening)* [2015] UKSC 2; [2015] AC 1732, [106]; *Robinson v Chief Constable of West Yorkshire Police (Rev 1)* [2018] UKSC 4; [2018] AC 736, [29].

[151] AD Miller and R Perry, 'The Reasonable Person' (2012) 87 *New York University Law Review* 323.

[152] *Montgomery v Lanarkshire Health Board* [2015] UKSC 11; [2015] AC 1430; *Rogers v Whitaker* [1992] HCA 58; (1992) 175 CLR 479; *Hii Chii Kok v Ong Peng Jin London Lucien*[2017] SGCA 38; [2017] 2 SLR 492.

[153] *Fairchild v Glenhaven Funeral Services* [2003] 1 AC 32; [2002] UKHL 22; *Chester v Afshar* [2004] UKHL 41; [2005] 1 AC 134.

[154] *Cattanach v Melchior* [2003] HCA 38; (2003) 215 CLR 1. This has been reversed by legislation: Civil Liability Act 2003 (Qld) ss 49A, 49B.

[155] *McFarlane v Tayside Health Board* [2002] 2 AC 59.

[156] *Parkinson v St James and Seacroft University Hospital NHS Trust* [2001] EWCA Civ 530, [2002] QB 266. The exception involves children born with a significant disability.

[157] C Purshouse, 'How Should Autonomy Be Defined in Medical Negligence Cases?' (2015) 10 *Clinical Ethics* 107; T Keren-Paz, 'Gender Injustice in Compensating Injury to Autonomy in English and Singaporean Negligence Law' (2019) 27 *Feminist Legal Studies* 33.

doctors in the public sector. Patients are not uniform: some have greater expectations and greater capacity to exercise autonomy; some are completely independent, while others rely on family and friends to access healthcare. The doctor may have to respond to the family members' queries, and in some cases, may have to accommodate their interests. Some patients are in long-term relationships with the doctor; in others, the doctor may see the patient only once. Often, doctors act within the constraints of insurers or healthcare institutions, affecting the independence and autonomy of their relationship with their patients.

The modern doctor–patient relationship is complex and the notion of corrective justice operating within a bilateral relationship of equals vindicating patient autonomy is unrealistic and indeed harmful. Kantian notions of patient autonomy purport to protect patients against medical paternalism, but in doing so it prevents some patients from achieving autonomy due to inevitable or derivative dependency. Drawing on Kant's innate human right to freedom, Allan Beever argues that tort law is no more or less than that: it is 'unconcerned with human needs and desires'[158] and it is unconcerned with distributive justice. Even if this is acceptable in some areas of tort law, it is anathema to medical negligence, which is at the heart of 'human needs and desires'. A pluralist approach, anchored by the concept of relational vulnerability, provides the best framework for medical negligence law.

Vulnerability has long been a significant organising principle in tort law. A doyen of tort law, Jane Stapleton, has described it as tort law's 'golden thread'.[159] The House of Lords and the High Court of Australia have long recognised the relevance of vulnerability in the tort of negligence.[160] Initially viewed in the narrower sense of innate vulnerability it has been recast as situational vulnerability, focusing on the inability of claimants to protect themselves due to their particular circumstances.[161] This incorporation of external elements in evaluating vulnerability accords with Gordon-Bouvier's theory of relational vulnerability.

In *Woolcock Street Investments Pty Ltd v CDG Pty Ltd* Kirby J explained it thus in the context of negligence:

> The vulnerability of the appellant arises from the circumstances of the case. Vulnerability is not confined to cases of poverty, disability, social disadvantage or relative economic power as the majority suggest. It extends to those who, like the plaintiffs in *Perre*, might be carrying on a profitable economic enterprise but who are exposed to an insidious risk by the acts of others about which they were unaware and against which they could not reasonably protect themselves.[162]

[158] A Beever, *A Theory of Tort Liability* (Oxford/ Portland OR, Hart Publishing, 2016) 20.

[159] J Stapleton, 'The Golden Thread at the Heart of Tort Law: Protection of the Vulnerable' in P Cane (ed), *Centenary Essays for the High Court of Australia* (Chatswood NSW, LexisNexis Butterworths, 2004) 242.

[160] *Smith v Eric S Bush* [1990] 1 AC 831; *Perre v Apand Pty Ltd* [1999] HCA 36; (1999) 198 CLR 180.

[161] See *Brookfield Multiplex Ltd v Owners Corporation Strata Plan 61288* [2014] HCA 36; (2014) 254 CLR 185, [168]–[169].

[162] *Woolcock Street Investments Pty Ltd v CDG Pty Ltd* [2004] HCA 16; (2004) 216 CLR 515, [168], citing *Perre v Apand Pty Ltd* [1999] HCA 36; (1999) 198 CLR 180.

Patients are the archetype of vulnerable persons. Their health is compromised. They are dependent on their doctors, who make decisions for and on behalf of their patients or act as 'choice architects' to enable patients to make decisions.[163] Patients invariably rely on a support network of family and friends. Relational autonomy recognises the interdependencies of doctors, patients, and third parties; it helps find the middle ground between medical beneficence and patient autonomy. The fear of disempowering patients and undermining their autonomy may be allayed by adopting maternalism as a guiding framework to evaluate medical interventions that nudge the patients to accept or make decisions that they might otherwise not be able to make on their own.

Medical maternalism is not merely a matter of semantics. It differs from soft paternalism in several ways. Most crucially, maternalism focuses on the relationship and not the parties in isolation. It serves not only to protect the autonomy of the patient but also to safeguard the doctor–patient relationship. Maternalism ensures that the doctor acts in the best interest of the patient not merely from a health-outcome perspective but from a holistic perspective which respects the patient's own unexpressed desire. It would therefore not be applicable in cases where the patient has not developed an ongoing relationship with the doctor; in such cases, a relationship of trust would not have been established, and the doctor would not have sufficient knowledge of the patient to make decisions in the patient's best interest.

Maternalism also recognises the hypocrisy of placing a duty on doctors to care for their patients while rejecting any paternalistic action. Mark Komrad put it pithily:

> Yet it is somewhat confusing for a doctor when, on the one hand, society insists on the abolition of medical paternalism, while on the other hand many individual patients still expect, hope for, and even urge (in both subtle and outright ways) the doctor to be paternalistic. Physicians have been faced with the option of indulging these expectations and receiving accolades from the patient but condemnation from society.[164]

VI. Conclusion

The theoretical literature on private law is rich, but some of the discourse is ideologically driven in pursuit of grand unifying theories that are detached from practical realities. Classical private law theorists focus on the horizontal plane of interpersonal justice, ignoring the vertical plane that incorporates public interests. This is implausible for the tort of negligence whose primary function is to

[163] AF de Araújo Lima and FI de Souza Machado, 'Physicians as Choice Architects: Paternalism and Respect for Autonomy' (2021) 29 *Revista Bioética (Impr)* 44.

[164] MS Komrad, 'A Defence of Medical Paternalism: Maximising Patients' Autonomy' (1983) 9 *Journal of Medical Ethics* 38, 40.

allocate the cost of risk, unlike contracts, whose function is to enforce agreements between parties. Policy considerations cannot be avoided. This chapter has reviewed selected theories from three categories – justice theories, instrumental theories, and critical theories. It is argued that Dagan and Dorfman's relational justice theory coupled with Gordon-Bouvier's relational vulnerability theory are apposite.

Medical negligence, above all, involves relationships – between doctor and patient; between patient and family members; and between doctor and family members. Vulnerability discourse has been at the centre of modern negligence law over the last few decades. Relational vulnerability provides an approach that reconciles the potential tension between medical beneficence and patient autonomy. While Kantian autonomy protects against medical paternalism, it ignores the interdependent, inter-connected, and socially embedded nature of individuals, thus failing to protect patients who may be incapable of achieving true autonomy without assistance. Relational vulnerability and relational justice can transform medical paternalism into medical maternalism, balancing medical beneficence and patient autonomy.

4

Patient Autonomy and the Doctor–Patient Relationship

I. Introduction

> In the third (2010) edition of their leading work on *Principles of Medical Law*, Andrew Grubb, Judith Laing and Jean McHale confidently announced that a detailed analysis of the different speeches of the House of Lords in *Sidaway v Board of Governors of the Bethlem Royal Hospital and the Maudsley Hospital* [1985] AC 871 was no longer necessary. A combination of the 2008 Guidance provided by the General Medical Council, the decision of the Court of Appeal in *Pearce v United Bristol Healthcare NHS Trust* [1999] PIQR P 53 and the decision of the House of Lords in *Chester v Afshar* [2005] 1 AC 134 meant that it could now be stated 'with a reasonable degree of confidence' that the need for informed consent was firmly part of English law (para 8.70). This case has provided us with the opportunity, not only to confirm that confident statement, but also to make it clear that the same principles apply in Scotland.
>
> *It is now well recognised that the interest which the law of negligence protects is a person's interest in their own physical and psychiatric integrity, an important feature of which is their autonomy, their freedom to decide what shall and shall not be done with their body* (the unwanted pregnancy cases are an example: see *Rees v Darlington Memorial Hospital NHS Trust* [2003] UKHL 52, [2004] 1 AC 309). Thus, as Jonathan Herring puts it in *Medical Law and Ethics* (2012), 4th ed, p 170), 'the issue is not whether enough information was given to ensure consent to the procedure, but whether there was enough information given so that the doctor was not acting negligently and giving due protection to the patient's right of autonomy' (emphasis added).[1]

These opening paragraphs of Lady Hale's judgment in *Montgomery v Lanarkshire Health Board*[2] are striking. Citing two academic sources on the medical duty to inform and patient autonomy, *Montgomery* dives headlong into the murky waters of trespass, negligence, informed consent, autonomy, and rights. These concepts are notorious for their ambiguity and imprecise use. The quote from the Grubb, Laing and McHale text appears in a paragraph directly below the heading 'battery'. The concept of informed consent discussed was in the context of trespass, yet the

[1] *Montgomery v Lanarkshire Health Board* [2015] UKSC 11; [2015] AC 1430 (per Baroness Hale of Richmond at [107]–[108]).

[2] [2015] UKSC 11; [2015] AC 1430.

authors segue into negligence, referring to *Sidaway v Bethlem Royal Hospital*,[3] *Pearce v United Bristol Healthcare NHS Trust*,[4] and *Chester v Afshar*.[5]

The conflation between trespass and negligence is seen in *Birch v University College London Hospital NHS Foundation Trust*.[6] The claimant was advised of a one per cent risk in the proposed treatment but not advised of comparative risks in alternative procedures. The court, relying on *Pearce* and *Chester*, held that the defendant had breached the duty to inform the patient of reasonable risks. Regrettably, the trial judge referred to the failure to obtain 'fully informed consent'[7] or 'properly informed consent'[8] to the procedure. What the difference is between 'fully informed' and 'properly informed' will remain forever a mystery. Regardless, the statements are patently incorrect, as the patient had in fact consented to the procedure; the negligent failure to inform, as the trial judge noted in a subsequent paragraph, merely deprived the patient of 'the opportunity to make an informed choice'.[9] Had the patient not consented to the procedure, the hospital would have been liable in trespass and there would have been no need for the judge to consider causation of damage to establish the action:[10] damage is a requirement of negligence, not trespass.

Informed consent – a tautology as one cannot give consent without being informed about what one is consenting to – is a concept that has its roots in American jurisprudence.[11] It was imported into negligence law in *Canterbury v Spence*,[12] which relied on the application of informed consent in a trespass case where it properly belongs.[13] To be clear, consent in the context of trespass is with respect to the procedure; consent in the context of negligence is with respect to the risk inherent in the procedure. Consent in trespass is transactional; it occurs at a finite point in time when the patient consents to the procedure. Consent in negligence is relational and dynamic as the doctor and patient continue their dialogue on risks and alternatives, continually adjusting to what is acceptable.

Running these two concepts of consent together, courts and commentators have equated failure to obtain informed consent with an infringement of patient autonomy, an interest that has become paramount in medical law and ethics. Yet, despite bold claims, no court in the UK, Australia, or Singapore has recognised loss of autonomy as actionable damage. The concept is used as a means to an end

[3] *Sidaway v Board of Governors of the Bethlem Royal Hospital and the Maudsley Hospital* [1985] AC 871.

[4] *Pearce v United Bristol Healthcare NHS Trust* [1999] PIQR P53.

[5] *Chester v Afshar* [2004] UKHL 41; [2005] 1 AC 134.

[6] *Birch v University College London Hospital NHS Foundation Trust* [2008] EWHC 2237.

[7] ibid [74].

[8] ibid [75].

[9] ibid [79].

[10] ibid [80]–[81].

[11] The Canadian Supreme Court wisely expressed its disdain for the use of the expression: *Reibl v Hughes* (1981) 114 DLR 1; 14 CCLT 1.

[12] *Canterbury v Spence* 464 F2d 722 (DC Cir 1972).

[13] *Schloendorff v Society of New York Hospital* 211 NY 125, 105 NE 92 (NY 1914).

to justify expanding the scope of duty,[14] to provide vindicatory damages,[15] or to circumvent difficulties in establishing causation of damage, which on conventional analysis would result in the claimant failing.[16] Autonomy is everywhere yet nowhere in medical negligence.[17]

This chapter argues that, for reasons of genealogy, philosophy, and principle, the tort of negligence and patient autonomy do not make natural bedfellows. From its origins in the Enlightenment period through its application to intentional medical torts and medical research in the wake of scandalous abuse of trust by doctors, patient autonomy entered medical negligence discourse by way of historical accident. Subsequently, it was championed on ideological grounds and embraced by patients' advocacy groups in a vanguard action against medical paternalism. The unequal doctor–patient relationship and historical medical paternalism had created an environment in which patients lacked control over medical decisions affecting them. As medical science improved so too did patients' expectations of better outcomes. Coupled with greater awareness of human rights and a consumerist-patient model, autonomy served as a potent rallying cry.

This is not to denigrate the concept of autonomy or rights discourse, which have been crucial in recalibrating the doctor–patient relationship, protecting the patient from unwanted medical interference, and allowing patients to choose how they manage their own health. Foregrounding patient autonomy was necessary to move the needle on the unhealthy culture of medical paternalism and exploitation of patients in medical research. However, over-emphasising patient autonomy risks undermining the doctor–patient relationship and the efficient delivery of healthcare in an environment of underfunded healthcare systems, bureaucratisation of healthcare services, and focus on corporate profits.[18] It weakens the bedrock of trust upon which the mutually respectful nature of the relationship rests, recasting it from a fiduciary-type relationship to a merely transactional relationship.[19]

Patient autonomy concerns traditionally were animated in cases involving experimental treatment, end-of-life decisions, and reproductive health.[20] These cases involve intentional action, deliberate choices, and moral considerations that are a world away from negligence in the context of an ongoing doctor–patient

[14] *ACB v Thomson Medical Pte Ltd* [2017] SGCA 20; [2017] 1 SLR 918.

[15] *Rees v Darlington Memorial Hospital NHS Trust* [2003] UKHL 52; [2004] AC 309.

[16] *Chester v Afshar* [2004] UKHL 41; [2005] 1 AC 134; *Chappell v Hart* [1998] HCA 55; (1998) 195 CLR 232.

[17] The term 'autonomy' appeared an astonishing 83 times in a judgment that concluded that loss of autonomy should not be recognised as actionable damage: *ACB v Thomson Medical Pte Ltd* [2017] SGCA 20; [2017] 1 SLR 918.

[18] See the British Medical Association Report, *Caring, Supportive, Collaborative: Doctors' Vision for Change in the NHS* (September 2019).

[19] While the doctor–patient relationship does not give rise to a fiduciary duty, it shares some of the characteristics of such relationships. See M Brazier, 'Patient Autonomy and Consent to Treatment: The Role of the Law' (1987) 7 *Legal Studies* 169, 191.

[20] See Chapter 8 of this volume, text to nn 141–162 for discussion of autonomy in the context of reproductive negligence.

relationship. Yet, there is an implicit assumption – witness *Montgomery*, *Chester v Afshar*,[21] and *ACB v Thomson Medical Pte Ltd*[22] – that the tort of negligence is an appropriate vehicle to vindicate infringement of autonomy claims. This chapter challenges that assumption, arguing that autonomy properly belongs to medical ethics, professionalism, and the tort of trespass.

The focus on patient autonomy has conflated the duty to inform (relevant to the tort of negligence) with consent (relevant to battery), undermining the orthodox principle that negligence is actionable only on proof of damage. The inexorable march of patient autonomy over the landscape of medical negligence has distorted conventional doctrine underpinning the duty of care, standard of care, causation, and damage. Autonomy is a vague concept that is relevant to political, social, philosophical, moral, and legal discourse. In the medical context, it is relevant to trespass, negligence, professional regulation, and medical ethics. It can mean different things depending on the context, but conceptual precision is important in the law.

II. Historical Background

Patient autonomy is a relatively new concept in medical ethics, coming to prominence in the twentieth century.[23] This pales in comparison with over two millennia going back to Hippocrates and Pythagoras when the reigning principles were beneficence and non-malfeasance.[24] Beneficence and non-malfeasance run deep in the doctors' DNA; thus, it is not surprising that doctors do not embrace patient autonomy in the way that ethicists and philosophers do.

Autonomy is now the first amongst equals in the four pillars of medical ethics – autonomy, beneficence, non-malfeasance, and justice. This quadrangular framework of medical ethics was developed in the 1970s and institutionalised by two American philosophers in their work on biomedical ethics, published in the wake of several disturbing cases of medical exploitation in the name of research.[25] The campaign for protecting patient autonomy was in part a reaction to these gross breaches of ethical and legal duties by some individuals and institutions in the medical profession. Understanding the history of the development of autonomy in medical ethics is crucial to understanding its relevance in the modern context.

The history of autonomy is intertwined with the history of informed consent. This brief overview draws on an article by Toni Saad on the history of autonomy and

[21] [2004] UKHL 41; [2005] 1 AC 134.

[22] [2017] SGCA 20; [2017] 1 SLR 918.

[23] ED Pellegrino and D Thomasma, 'The Conflict between Autonomy and Beneficence in Medical Ethics: Proposal for a Resolution' (1987) 3 *Journal of Contemporary Health Law & Policy* 23, 24.

[24] Ibid.

[25] TL Beauchamp and JF Childress, *Principles of Biomedical Ethics* (New York, Oxford University Press, 1979).

a book by Ruth Faden and Tom Beauchamp on the history of informed consent.[26] While both works examine the histories of autonomy and informed consent, Saad does so from a sceptical perspective, arguing that more than respect for autonomy there should be respect for persons. The argument is that the modern conception of autonomy, based on individualistic, libertarian values, poses a threat to the doctor–patient relationship by undermining trust. Faden and Beauchamp, on the other hand, are Whiggish in their approach, championing informed consent in arguing that patients should be empowered with all relevant information necessary to make autonomous decisions. In their view, early medical practices were dominated by principles of beneficence and non-malfeasance at the expense of autonomy. As they express it, 'To put it in the most naked form of contrast, medicine was jolted from an exclusive preoccupation with a beneficence model to awareness of an autonomous model of responsibility'.[27]

A. The Ancient to the Enlightenment Period

Broadly, the history of patient autonomy and informed consent in Western medicine may be divided into five eras – ancient, medieval, enlightenment, post-War, and human rights.[28] The dominant source for ancient Western medical ethics is Hippocrates' *Oaths*, circa fourth century BCE, one of several publications on ethics and etiquette of medical practitioners attributed to Hippocrates. The Hippocratic Oath reads as follows:

> I swear by Apollo the physician, and Asclepius, and Hygieia and Panacea and all the gods and goddesses as my witnesses, that, according to my ability and judgement, I will keep this Oath and this contract:
>
> To hold him who taught me this art equally dear to me as my parents, to be a partner in life with him, and to fulfill his needs when required; to look upon his offspring as equals to my own siblings, and to teach them this art, if they shall wish to learn it, without fee or contract; and that by the set rules, lectures, and every other mode of instruction, I will impart a knowledge of the art to my own sons, and those of my teachers, and to students bound by this contract and having sworn this Oath to the law of medicine, but to no others.

[26] T Saad, 'The History of Autonomy in Medicine from Antiquity to Principlism' (2018) 21 *Medical Healthcare and Philosophy* 125; RR Faden and TL Beauchamp, *A History and Theory of Informed Consent* (New York, Oxford University Press, 1986). See also, JF Will, 'A Brief Historical and Theoretical Perspective on Patient Autonomy and Medical Decision Making – Part I: The Beneficence Model' (2011) 139(3) *CHEST* 669; JF Will, 'A Brief Historical and Theoretical Perspective on Patient Autonomy and Medical Decision Making – Part II: The Autonomy Model' (2011) 139(6) *CHEST* 1491.

[27] RR Faden and TL Beauchamp, *A History and Theory of Informed Consent* (New York, Oxford University Press, 1986) 142.

[28] T Saad, 'The History of Autonomy in Medicine from Antiquity to Principlism' (2018) 21 *Medical Healthcare and Philosophy* 125; RR Faden and TL Beauchamp, *A History and Theory of Informed Consent* (New York, Oxford University Press, 1986). Post-War refers to World War II.

> I will use those dietary regimens which will benefit my patients according to my greatest ability and judgement, and I will do no harm or injustice to them.
>
> I will not give a lethal drug to anyone if I am asked, nor will I advise such a plan; and similarly I will not give a woman a pessary to cause an abortion.
>
> In purity and according to divine law will I carry out my life and my art.
>
> I will not use the knife, even upon those suffering from stones, but I will leave this to those who are trained in this craft.
>
> Into whatever homes I go, I will enter them for the benefit of the sick, avoiding any voluntary act of impropriety or corruption, including the seduction of women or men, whether they are free men or slaves.
>
> Whatever I see or hear in the lives of my patients, whether in connection with my professional practice or not, which ought not to be spoken of outside, I will keep secret, as considering all such things to be private.
>
> So long as I maintain this Oath faithfully and without corruption, may it be granted to me to partake of life fully and the practice of my art, gaining the respect of all men for all time. However, should I transgress this Oath and violate it, may the opposite be my fate.[29]

The second oath contains two of the central ethical tenets of medicine – beneficence and non-malfeasance. Patient autonomy is nowhere mentioned, but a common theme throughout the oaths is respect for patients. Some have argued that while the oaths do not mention autonomy, consent, or information-giving, the practice of ancient Greek physicians *did* include disclosure of information and the seeking of consent in cases where the patient was capable of understanding or was an important figure in the community.[30] As Saad wryly notes, 'It is interesting that good and respectful medical practice is observed in the absence of modern articulations of autonomy. Perhaps autonomy as we know it is not necessary for good medical practice'.[31] Nonetheless, it cannot be gainsaid that the general approach in the past was for the physician to assume authority and the patient to obey, unless the patient was someone of high social status.

This tradition strengthened in the medieval period, when physicians were permitted to deceive patients if, in their opinion, it was in the best interest of the patient. A leading figure in the thirteenth century, Henri de Mondeville, not only encouraged physicians to lie to patients to give them hope, but he also advocated threatening patients to compel them to obey their physicians.[32] Benevolent

[29] Greek Medicine – The Hippocratic Oath, trans M North, National Library of Medicine (2002), https://www.nlm.nih.gov/hmd/topics/greek-medicine/index.html#case1.

[30] See SH Miles, *The Hippocratic Oath and the Ethics of Medicine* (New York, Oxford University Press, 2004) 134; RR Faden and TL Beauchamp, *A History and Theory of Informed Consent* (New York, Oxford University Press, 1986) 62–63.

[31] T Saad, 'The History of Autonomy in Medicine from Antiquity to Principlism' (2018) 21 *Medical Healthcare and Philosophy* 125, 127.

[32] RR Faden and TL Beauchamp, *A History and Theory of Informed Consent* (New York, Oxford University Press, 1986) 63–64.

deception continues to play a limited role in modern healthcare, as doctors accept that in some cases involving especially vulnerable patients, it is necessary to deceive them to help them. Eminent medical professionals have published eloquent memoirs and biographies giving an insider's perspective on the challenges and realities that doctors face in communicating with patients.[33] While it is harder to justify deception or even withholding the truth in the modern world that places a premium on patient autonomy, it cannot be ignored that such practices were part of the delivery of medical care for centuries when beneficence was the guiding principle.

Even today, doctors struggle with truth-telling. Dr Sandeep Jauhar came to this realisation when caring for his father who suffered from dementia. As he put it:

> Truth-telling, however, can be a double-edged sword. Its demands may exist in tension with other moral imperatives, such as a son's obligation to do the best for his declining father. Personal ethics, I discovered, may come into conflict with the reality of caregiving.[34]

The modern roots of autonomy are found in the philosophical debates during the Enlightenment period, when faith-based orders, myths, and superstition were challenged by secularism, reason, and scientific method.[35] Two competing schools dominated – the moral philosophy of Immanuel Kant and the social contract theory of Jean-Jacques Rousseau. Although Kant was inspired by Rousseau, his account of autonomy was individualistic; Rousseau advocated a relational account of autonomy, recognising the interdependence of human beings. For Rousseau, the balance between individual rights and social cohesion was found in the social contract – individuals are permitted to do what is collectively agreed in a democratic society where all are equal.[36] Implicit in this approach is an agreement that individuals surrender their autonomy to the collective, which is represented by authority. This, in Kant's view, is not autonomy, but heteronomy.[37]

Kant rejects Rosseau's relational autonomy, arguing for an individualistic approach that is justified by an internal morality. According to Kant, it is not agreement but moral law that determines how individuals should act. As he put it, 'There is, therefore, only a single categorical imperative and it is this: act only according to

[33] See for example, H Marsh, *Do No Harm: Stories of Life, Death and Brain Surgery* (London, Weidenfeld & Nicolson, 2014); S Jauhar, *My Father's Brain: Life in the Shadow of Alzheimer's* (New York, Farrar, Straus and Giroux, 2023).

[34] S Jauhar, *My Father's Brain: Life in the Shadow of Alzheimer's* (New York, Farrar, Straus and Giroux, 2023) 187.

[35] D Outram, *The Enlightenment* (Cambridge, Cambridge University Press, 4th edn, 2019) 3.

[36] F Neuhouser, 'Jean-Jacques Rousseau and the Origins of Autonomy' (2011) 54 *Inquiry* 478. 487–89.

[37] The difference between autonomy and heteronomy at the fundamental level is that the former is about internal, self-governance based on personal beliefs, while the latter allows external forces to influence individual choices, including cultural and societal forces. See BEA Liddell (trans), *Kant on the Foundation of Morality: A Modern Version of the 'Grundlegung'* (Bloomington IN/ London, Indiana University Press, 1970) chapter 8, section 2, https://publish.iupress.indiana.edu/read/kant-on-the-foundation-of-morality/section/23c43e39-b4af-4761-9249-1cb8978158a2#content_54.

that maxim whereby you can at the same time will that it should become a universal law'.[38] Kant's autonomy may be equated with self-determination, based on pure reason.[39] This insistence on pure reason detaches Kantian autonomy from social context and undermines its utility as an ethical principle that can evaluate the moral value of conduct. Thus, Kant is forced to concede that because truth-telling is a universal rule, a person who is asked by a would-be murderer to disclose the location of the intended victim cannot lie and must tell the murderer where to find the victim, knowing that this could result in the death of the victim.

> Truth in utterances that cannot be avoided is the formal duty of a man to everyone, however great the disadvantage that may arise from it to him or any other; … If then we define a lie merely as an intentionally false declaration towards another man, we need not add that it must not injure another; as the jurists think proper to put in their definition (*mendacium est falsiloquium in praeiudicium alterius*). For it always injures another; if not another individual, yet mankind generally, since it vitiates the very source of justice … To be truthful (honest) in all declarations is therefore a sacred unconditional command of reason, and not to be limited by any expediency.[40]

Kant's moral autonomy evolved into personal autonomy under the liberal philosophers in the Romantic period. Autonomy was less a matter of moral imperative and more a matter of 'self-expression and development of individual practical identity';[41] it was synonymous with individualism and the right to self-determination. The leading British voices were those of David Hume and John Stuart Mill. They saw autonomy and individuality as intrinsically connected, arguing that autonomy was critical to individual liberty and the development of individual character.

Hume rejected Kant's view that reason alone determined autonomy, arguing that autonomy was shaped by passion and desire. It is desire that motivates action; therefore, an autonomous person acts according to his or her desire. Writing at a time when tyranny was a real threat to individual liberty,[42] Mill sought to place individual autonomy above societal and cultural relationships. Individuals had a right to lead authentic lives and be true to their own beliefs. While these beliefs may be shaped by the individual's social and cultural context, these relationships were always secondary to individual autonomy. These liberal conceptions of autonomy are antithetical to contemporary relational accounts of autonomy that seek to locate autonomy within an individual's web of relationships.[43]

[38] See MJ Gregor (trans and ed), I Kant, *Groundwork of the Metaphysics of Morals* (Cambridge, Cambridge University Press, 1997) xviii.

[39] ibid 3.

[40] TK Abbott (trans), *Kant's Critique of Practical Reason and Other Works on the Theory of Ethics* (London, Longmans, Green & Co, 4th edn, 1889) 362–63.

[41] J Dryden, 'Autonomy' in *The Internet Encyclopedia of Philosophy*, https://iep.utm.edu/.

[42] W Donner, 'Autonomy, Tradition, and the Enforcement of Morality' in CL Ten, *Mill's On Liberty: A Critical Guide* (Cambridge, Cambridge University Press, 2009) 138, 139.

[43] See below, section III.B. (Relational Autonomy).

Arguments based on individual autonomy did not influence medical ethics or practice during the Enlightenment or Romantic periods, when the principle of beneficence continued to reign. However, the Enlightenment did bring about a paradigm shift in information sharing. Leading figures from the eighteenth century such as Benjamin Rush, John Gregory, and Thomas Percival began to advocate sharing information with patients, not in order to secure consent or to respect autonomy, but in the belief that it was beneficial to the patient's health.[44] The shift to autonomy in bioethics took root in the post-War period in the wake of several high-profile cases of gross violations of medical ethics and a growing rights consciousness. Just as Mill embraced individualism in the fight against political oppression, so too did philosophers and ethicists valorise autonomy in the face of the tyranny of doctors.

B. The Post-War and Human Rights Period

On 9 December 1946, 23 doctors were charged with committing war crimes and crimes against humanity for their involvement in euthanasia, human experimentation, and torture.[45] The verdict included the articulation of 10 moral, ethical, and legal principles to guide medical experimentation on humans. This list, which came to be known as the Nuremberg Code, has been influential in guiding the development of ethical principles in medical research. The first principle enshrines the need for informed consent:

> The voluntary consent of the human subject is absolutely essential. This means that the person involved should have legal capacity to give consent; should be so situated as to be able to exercise free power of choice, without the intervention of any element of force, fraud, deceit, duress, overreaching, or other ulterior form of constraint or coercion; and should have sufficient knowledge and comprehension of the elements of the subject matter involved as to enable him to make an understanding and enlightened decision. This latter element requires that before the acceptance of an affirmative decision by the experimental subject there should be made known to him the nature, duration, and purpose of the experiment; the method and means by which it is to be conducted; all inconveniences and hazards reasonably to be expected; and the effects upon his health or person which may possibly come from his participation in the experiment. The duty and responsibility for ascertaining the quality of the consent rests upon each individual who initiates, directs, or engages in the experiment. It is a personal duty and responsibility which may not be delegated to another with impunity.

[44] See RR Faden and TL Beauchamp, *A History and Theory of Informed Consent* (New York, Oxford University Press, 1986) 64–70.

[45] E Shuster, 'American Doctors at the Nuremberg Medical Trial' (2018) 108 *American Journal of Public Health* 47. For information on the trial, see Harvard Law School Nuremberg Trials Project: 'NMT Case 1 – *U.S.A. v. Karl Brandt et al.*', https://nuremberg.law.harvard.edu/nmt_1_intro.

The Nuremberg Code was followed by other similar documents, including the Declaration of Geneva in 1948,[46] and the broader Declaration of Helsinki in 1964 by the World Medical Association.[47] The Helsinki Code extended the need for informed consent beyond medical research to *unproven* interventions in clinical practice. Thus, a doctor who believed that an unproven intervention would be beneficial to the patient had to seek the patient's informed consent before administering the treatment. There was no requirement yet for informed consent with respect to conventional treatment. Patient autonomy was relevant to medical research and experimental treatment, but not to conventional clinical intervention, where beneficence continued to be the guiding principle. That began to change in the 1960s and 1970s when the public learnt of widespread unethical clinical practices in the US and the UK, and the civil rights movement was at its most active.

Publications in the 1960s by Henry Beecher in the United States and Maurice Pappworth in the United Kingdom exposed widespread post-War, civilian medical research conducted without the knowledge or consent of the participants, on infants and vulnerable groups, which had resulted in numerous fatalities.[48] Perhaps the most infamous case that is emblematic of such scandalous practices is the Tuskegee Syphilis Study in which known treatment for syphilis (penicillin) was withheld from black patients to facilitate the clinical study of the spread of diseases. The study continued for 40 years from 1932, ending only after the media investigated and reported on it.[49] The Beecher article led to the establishment of the National Commission for the Protection of Human Subjects of Biomedical and Behavioral Research. The Commission published the Belmont Report in 1979, which established 'respect for persons' as a key ethical principle. However, it inadvertently enshrined patient autonomy in medicolegal ethics:

> Respect for persons incorporates at least two ethical convictions: first, that individuals should be treated as autonomous agents, and second, that persons with diminished autonomy are entitled to protection. The principle of respect for persons thus divides into two separate moral requirements: the requirement to acknowledge autonomy and the requirement to protect those with diminished autonomy.[50]

[46] WMA Declaration of Geneva (The World Medical Association, September 1948), https://www.wma.net/policies-post/wma-declaration-of-geneva/.

[47] ibid.

[48] Patients were often subject to experimental treatment without their consent up to the mid-twentieth century. See HK Beecher, 'Ethics and Clinical Research' (1966) 274(24) *New England Journal of Medicine* 1354; M Pappworth, *Human Guinea Pigs: Experimentation on Man* (London, Routledge & Kegan Paul, 1967); DJ Rothman, *Strangers at the Bedside: A History of How Law and Bioethics Transformed Medical Decision Making* (New York, Basic Books, 1991).

[49] Center for Disease Control and Prevention, 'The Untreated Syphilis Study at Tuskegee – Timeline', https://www.cdc.gov/tuskegee/about/timeline.html?CDC_AAref_Val=https://www.cdc.gov/tuskegee/timeline.htm; J Heller, 'AP was there: Black Men untreated in Tuslegee Syphilis Study', *Associated Press*, 10 May 2017, https://apnews.com/article/business-science-health-race-and-ethnicity-syphilis-e9dd07eaa4e74052878a68132cd3803a.

[50] National Commission for the Protection of Human Subjects of Biomedical and Behavioral Research, *Ethical Principles and Guidelines for the Protection of Human Subjects of Research (The Belmont Report)* (April 1979) B1.

'Respect for persons' is distinct from 'respect for autonomy' in two ways. Crucially, the former includes respecting individuals who lack (or have impaired) capacity to make autonomous decisions.[51] 'Respect for persons' places emphasis on 'respect' – it shines the spotlight on the doctors' *obligation* to respect their patients. 'Respect for autonomy' on the other hand emphasises autonomy – it shines the spotlight on the patients' *rights*.

This pivot to rights discourse in bioethics, encapsulating the libertarian view of autonomy as self-determination, was part of a broader movement in civil rights activism seeking equality for racial minorities and women. It was during the height of the broad rights movement that the landmark decision of *Canterbury v Spence*[52] was decided. Along with Paul Ramsay's publication of *The Patient as Person*[53] in 1970 and the American Health Association's publication of the Patient Bill of Rights in 1972, *Canterbury* transformed the discourse on patients' rights and informed consent. As individuals asserted their rights against the state, their relationship with the state also evolved – moving away from citizen to consumer.[54] The consumerist movement began in the immediate post-War period as a response to mass marketing of products, in order to protect consumer rights. Patient advocacy groups adopted the strategy in the 1960s and 1970s to champion autonomy and challenge medical paternalism.[55]

Canterbury involved a minor who underwent a laminectomy and ended up paralysed. There was an inherent risk of paralysis in the procedure, which was not disclosed to the claimant's mother who signed the consent forms. The US Court of Appeals for the DC Circuit imported the consent doctrine from trespass into negligence. Citing the trespass case of *Schloendorff v Society of New York Hospital*,[56] the Court stated: 'The root premise is the concept, fundamental in American jurisprudence, that "[e]very human being of adult years and sound mind has a right to determine what shall be done with his own body"'.[57] This then formed the basis for reforming the standard of care for the duty to inform in medical negligence from the 'peer professional' to the 'prudent patient' test.[58] The Court held, 'Respect for

[51] E Marshall, 'Does the Moral Philosophy of the Belmont Report Rest on a Mistake?' (1986) 8 *IRB: Ethics and Human Research* 5.

[52] 464 F2d 772, 780 (DC Cir 1972).

[53] P Ramsay, *The Patient as Person: Explorations in Medical Ethics* (New Haven CT, Yale University Press, 1970).

[54] See F Trentmann, 'The Modern Genealogy of the Consumer: Meanings, Identities and Political Synapses' in F Trentmann and J Brewer (eds), *Consuming Cultures, Global Perspectives: Historical Trajectories, Transnational Exchanges* (Oxford, Berg, 2006) 19, 43–48.

[55] N Tomes, 'Patients or Health-Care Consumers? Why the History of Contested Terms Matters' in RA Stevens, CE Rosenberg and LR Burns (eds), *History and Health Policy in the United States: Putting the Past Back In* (New Brunswick NJ, Rutgers University Press, 2006) 83.

[56] 211 NY 125, 105 NE 92, 93 (NY 1914).

[57] *Canterbury v Spence* 464 F2d 772, 780 (DC Cir 1972). The patient was aged 19 at the time of the surgery and so under the age of majority at the time.

[58] For a detailed analysis of the cases and development of the informed consent jurisprudence from *Schloendorff* to *Canterbury*, see RR Faden and TL Beauchamp, *A History and Theory of Informed Consent* (New York, Oxford University Press, 1986) 125–38.

the patient's right of self-determination on particular therapy demands a standard set by law for physicians rather than one which physicians may or may not impose upon themselves'.[59]

The American developments on patients' rights and autonomy soon crossed the Atlantic. By the 1980s, leading legal scholars in the UK were publishing important works on medical ethics, patients' rights, the duty to inform, and the standard of care, all of which placed patient autonomy at the centre of the debate, recalibrating the equilibrium in the doctor–patient relationship. Prominent among them were Margaret Brazier's *Medicine, Patients and the Law*,[60] Sheila McLean's *A Patient's Right to Know*,[61] and Harvey Teff's *Reasonable Care*.[62] Observing the trend in medico-legal discourse at the time, Teff noted, 'It is perhaps inevitable that the critical focus has centred on patients' rights'.[63] And McLean commented: 'The interest at stake – that is, the autonomy of the patient – is one which is clearly of considerable importance'.[64]

Autonomy is thus interwoven with consumerism and anti-paternalism, with the regrettable consequence of introducing mistrust and adversarialism into the doctor–patient relationship. Alex Mold documents how the repositioning of the patient as a consumer by advocacy groups changed the relationship between doctors and patients.[65] Patients reported high satisfaction rates with the services and care they received from general practitioners and hospitals in the early 1960s, but a major source of unhappiness was the lack of information provided to enable them to understand their health and to make decisions.[66] The ability to choose was increasingly valued. While individual patients were powerless to make changes, patients' organisations flourished in the 1960s and 1970s, providing a collective voice to campaign for change.[67]

Access to healthcare was seen as a right, which included the right to be informed and to make personal decisions. This extended to the rights of patients in teaching hospitals, setting up a clash between the medical profession and patients'

[59] *Canterbury v Spence* 464 F2d 772, 784 (DC Cir 1972).

[60] M Brazier's *Medicine, Patients and the Law* (Harmondsworth, Penguin Books, 1987); M Brazier, 'Patient Autonomy and Consent to Treatment: The Role of the Law' (1987) 7 *Legal Studies* 169.

[61] SA McLean's *A Patient's Right to Know: Information Disclosure, the Doctor and the Law* (Aldershot, Dartmouth Publishing Co, 1989).

[62] H Teff, *Reasonable Care: Legal Perspectives on the Doctor-Patient Relationship* (Oxford, Clarendon Press, 1994). See also the leading textbook by Ian Kennedy and Andrew Grub: I Kennedy and A Grubb, *Medical Law: Text and Materials* (Sevenoaks, Butterworths, 1989).

[63] H Teff, *Reasonable Care: Legal Perspectives on the Doctor-Patient Relationship* (Oxford, Clarendon Press, 1994) xxvii.

[64] SA McLean's *A Patient's Right to Know: Information Disclosure, the Doctor and the Law* (Aldershot, Dartmouth Publishing Co, 1989) 7.

[65] A Mold, 'Repositioning the Patient: Patient Organizations, Consumerism, and Autonomy in Britain during the 1960s and 1970s' (2013) 87 *Bulletin of the History of Medicine* 225.

[66] 60% of patients reported difficulty in getting information from hospitals. See A Cartwright, *Patients and Their Doctors: A Study of General Practice* (London, Routledge & Kegan Paul, 1967) 74.

[67] See, B Wood, *Patient Power? The Politics of Patients' Associations in Britain and America* (Buckingham, Open University Press, 2000).

groups. The Joint Consultants Committee of the British Medical Association and the Royal College of Physicians expressed concern that clinical teaching was being sacrificed at the altar of patients' rights.[68] Patient advocacy groups had moved the ground under medical practice and medical education from 'the kind of social democracy based on social rights and responsibilities … toward the individualized, consumer-oriented vision of society often associated with neoliberalism'.[69] This resonates with the arguments developed in Chapter two advocating a human obligations approach over a rights approach for medical negligence.

Autonomy-based advocacy is pertinent to debates on clinical and research ethics, professionalism, and trespass. These are areas where patient autonomy is crucial to self-determination. Clinical negligence is different. Here, there is an underlying relationship already established between doctor and patient that is based on consent and trust. Patient autonomy has a different, more nuanced role here that should not undermine the relationship of trust.

III. Concepts of Autonomy

As briefly mentioned earlier, autonomy is one of the four modern pillars of medical ethics, the other three being non-malfeasance, beneficence, and justice. This taxonomy is attributed to the groundbreaking work of Tom Beauchamp and James Childress, *Principles of Biomedical Ethics*, first published in 1979.[70] Beauchamp and Childress did not intend for autonomy to dominate medical ethics as it has done over the last few decades. Indeed, in the sixth edition of their book, the authors take pains to highlight this misinterpretation of their thesis on biomedical ethics. In the preface, they reiterate that to treat autonomy as an overriding principle is 'profoundly mistaken' and that it should not be 'an excessively individualistic, absolutistic, or overriding notion that emphasizes individual rights to the neglect or exclusion of social responsibilities'.[71]

The focus on autonomy has driven a consumerist attitude amongst patients and encouraged defensive medicine by doctors who view informed consent processes as bureaucratic.[72] Some doctors merely present various options to the patient and invite them to decide, instead of taking on the responsibility of trying to help each patient. As a reviewer of the *Montgomery* case wryly noted, 'What the judgment

[68] A Mold, 'Repositioning the Patient: Patient Organizations, Consumerism, and Autonomy in Britain during the 1960s and 1970s' (2013) 87 *Bulletin of the History of Medicine* 225, 245.

[69] ibid 247.

[70] TL Beauchamp and JF Childress, *Principles of Biomedical Ethics* (New York, Oxford University Press, 1979).

[71] TL Beauchamp and JF Childress, *Principles of Biomedical Ethics* (New York, Oxford University Press, 6th edn, 2009) viii.

[72] M Jones, 'Informed Consent and Other Fairy Stories' (1999) 7 *Medical Law Review* 103. For a more recent analysis, see I Le Gallez et al, 'Montgomery's Legal and Practical Impact: A Systematic Review at 6 Years (2022) 28 *Journal of Evaluation in Clinical Practice* 690.

fails to do is to protect those who feel overwhelmed by medical information. It denies a patient the option of saying to their doctor "do what you think is best"'.[73] The trust that is the bedrock of the doctor–patient relationship has been eroded. Onora O'Neill distills the relationship between autonomy and trust in this pithy observation:

> Trust is most readily placed in others whom we can rely on to take our interests into account, to fulfil their roles, to keep their parts in bargains. Individual autonomy is most readily expressed when we are least constrained by others and their expectations. Trust flourishes between those who are linked to one another; individual autonomy flourishes where everyone has 'space' to do their own thing. Trust belongs with relationships and (mutual) obligations; individual autonomy with rights and adversarial claims.[74]

In her critique, O'Neill conceives of autonomy in its liberal, individualistic form in the tradition of Kant and Mill, which has dominated Western political and ethical discourse. When applied to clinical interactions, autonomy is invariably reduced to a question of informed consent, with clinical practice largely guided by legal advice. Thus, respecting patient autonomy is equated with obtaining informed consent and ensuring that such consent is adequately documented to protect doctors during audits, complaints, and litigation.[75] This is a legalistic approach that does not genuinely advance patient autonomy. Patient autonomy undoubtedly is a virtue that must be protected, but it is not a monolithic concept that applies uniformly to every interaction between doctor and patient – the conception of autonomy and the context in which it is considered are key.

A. Autonomy is a Many-splendoured Thing

It is apparent that, although not used just as a synonym for qualities that are usually approved of, 'autonomy' is used in an exceedingly broad fashion. It is used sometimes as an equivalent of liberty (positive or negative in Isaiah Berlin's terminology), sometimes as equivalent to self-rule or sovereignty, sometimes as identical with freedom of the will. It is equated with dignity, integrity, individuality, independence, responsibility, and self-knowledge. It is identified with qualities of self-assertion, with critical reflection, with freedom from obligation, with absence of external causation, with knowledge of one's own interests. It is even equated by some economists with the impossibility of interpersonal comparisons. It is related

[73] G Murphy, 'Championing Autonomy – Does *Montgomery* Truly Protect Patient's Interests?' (2018) 6 *North East Law Review* 35, 52.

[74] O O'Neill, *Autonomy and Trust in Bioethics* (Cambridge, Cambridge University Press, 2002) 25.

[75] M Boulton and M Parker, 'Informed Consent in a Changing Environment' (2007) 65 *Social Science & Medicine* 2187; LH Brenner, AT Brenner and D Horowitz, 'Beyond Informed Consent: Educating the Patient' (2009) 467 *Clinical Orthopaedics & Related Research* 348; JO Olufowote, 'A Structurational Analysis of Informed Consent to Treatment: Societal Evolution, Contradiction, and Reproductions in Medical Practice' (2008) 23 *Health Communication* 292.

to actions, to beliefs, to reasons for acting, to rules, to the will of other persons, to thoughts, and to principles. Just about the only features of autonomy that are held constant from one author to another are that autonomy is a feature of persons and it is a desirable quality.[76]

Dworkin's assessment of autonomy invokes the spectre of Lewis Caroll's Humpty Dumpty:

> 'I don't know what you mean by "glory",' Alice said.
>
> Humpty Dumpty smiled contemptuously. 'Of course you don't – till I tell you. I meant "there's a nice knock-down argument for you!"'
>
> 'But "glory" doesn't mean "a nice knock-down argument",' Alice objected.
>
> 'When I use a word,' Humpty Dumpty said in rather a scornful tone, 'it means just what I choose it to mean – neither more nor less.'
>
> 'The question is,' said Alice, 'whether you *can* make words mean so many different things.'
>
> 'The question is,' said Humpty Dumpty, 'which is to be master – that's all.'[77]

Which is to be master – the doctor, the patient, the philosopher, the ethicist, or the lawyer? Having a common conception of a concept is vital for meaningful discourse, especially when that concept is the cornerstone of a legal relationship. Richard Lindley, whose work on autonomy has been influential, illustrates the point using the Israel–Palestine conflict.[78] The Camp David Accord signed in 1978 by US President Jimmy Carter, Egyptian President Anwar Sadat, and Israeli Prime Minister Menachim Begin included the promise of autonomy to the people of Palestine living in the West Bank and Gaza.[79] However, Israel's conception of autonomy differed from Egypt's conception of autonomy, and five decades on the conflict continues, claiming tens of thousands of lives with no solution for peace.[80]

It is vital to have a common understanding of autonomy in medical law and ethics, given the centrality of the concept to patients' rights and doctors' duties, and the extent to which the concept is used by various stakeholders to shape the law on medical negligence. Different conceptions of autonomy will lead to irreconcilable conflict and the risk of a suboptimal conception of autonomy prevailing at the expense of the doctor–patient relationship and justice. Lindley identifies

[76] R Dworkin, *The Theory and Practice of Autonomy* (Cambridge, Cambridge University Press, 1988) 6.

[77] L Carroll, *Alice's adventures in Wonderland and Through the Looking-glass* (Boston MA Lothrop Publishing Company, 1898) 164.

[78] R Lindley, *Autonomy* (London, Macmillan Education Ltd, 1986) 1–2.

[79] ibid; 'The Framework for Peace in the Middle East', Camp David, Maryland, 17 September 1978, https://2001-2009.state.gov/p/nea/rls/22578.htm.

[80] The latest conflict began on 7 October 2023 when Hamas attacked Israel, killing over 1,200 people and taking more than 250 hostages. Israel retaliated by waging war across Gaza, killing in excess of 50,000 people and reducing Gaza to rubble by March 2025. N Al-Mughrabi and E Farge, 'Gaza death toll: how many Palestinians has Israel's offensive killed?' *Reuters*, 24 March 2025 (https://www.reuters.com/world/middle-east/how-many-palestinians-has-israels-gaza-offensive-killed-2025-01-15/).

three conceptions of autonomy in liberal philosophy, based on the approaches respectively of Immanuel Kant, David Hume, and John Stuart Mill.[81] Kantian autonomy is based on pure reason, dictated by the universal law and uninfluenced by personal inclinations or desire. Humean autonomy is the antithesis of Kantian, permitting individuals to act as they wish so long as their preferences are not based on false suppositions or faulty reasoning.

Millean autonomy lies between the two. While Mill acknowledges that autonomy does not have to be based on pure reason and may be driven by personal desire, his approach is a thicker version of Hume's. It is not enough to pursue personal preferences based on rational beliefs; those beliefs must be subject to rational scrutiny. In Mill's account, self-determination is central to individual character. A person should not be slave to whims and fancies, but rather is required 'to reflect on the influences of her culture, to sort out those of her felt impulses which are really expressions of her unique nature, from those which are merely the product of external influences'.[82] This in an account of autonomy that is also present in Joseph Raz's influential work.[83]

Raz argues that autonomy or freedom is necessary for a valuable life. To exercise autonomy, one must have the capacity to make rational choices; the capacity to evaluate goals; the ability to act on decisions; adequate options from which to make choices; independence from others to make choices; and be the author of one's own life.[84] Importantly, Raz takes a longer view of well-being, which allows for some restriction of immediate freedom if it furthers the longer-term well-being. As Raz put it:

> Autonomy and positive freedom relate primarily to pervasive goals, projects or relationships. The autonomous person freely develops friendships and other ties with people and animals. But that he is not free to talk to Jones now does not diminish his autonomy.[85]

Lindley argues that autonomy requires individuals to evaluate their preferences rationally and act according to their highest order preference.[86] Drawing on Lindley's work, John Coggon outlines a framework based on the following three conceptions of autonomy in the medical context: ideal desire autonomy (analogous to Kantian autonomy); best desire autonomy (analogous to Millean/ Lindleyean

[81] R Lindley, *Autonomy* (London, Macmillan Education Ltd, 1986), chapters 2, 3, and 4 respectively discuss Kant, Hume, and Mill.

[82] ibid 52.

[83] *The Morality of Freedom* (Oxford, Clarendon Press, 1986).

[84] See WJ Norman, 'The Autonomy-Based Liberalism of Joseph Raz' (1989) 2 *Canadian Journal of Law & Jurisprudence* 151, 152; J Penner, 'Taking Raz Seriously: On the Value of Autonomy and its Relation to Private Law' in PB Miller and J Oberkiek (eds), *Oxford Studies in Private Law Theory Volume II* (Oxford, Oxford University Press, 2023) 79.

[85] J Raz, *The Morality of Freedom* (Oxford, Clarendon Press, 1986) 409.

[86] ibid 66.

autonomy); and current desire autonomy (analogous to Humean autonomy).[87] Coggon describes ideal desire autonomy as leading 'to an action decided upon because it reflects what a person should want, measured by reference to some purportedly universal or objective standard of values'.[88] Best desire autonomy 'leads to an action decided upon because it reflects a person's overall desire given his own values, even if this runs contrary to his immediate desire'.[89] Current desire autonomy 'leads to an action decided upon because it reflects a person's immediate inclination, ie, what he thinks he wants in a given moment without further reflection'.[90]

As foreshadowed earlier, the *conception* of autonomy and the *context* in which it is considered are key. Appreciating this, Coggon favours a pluralist approach in which all three conceptions of autonomy are relevant to medical law, depending on whether the patient is refusing unwanted intervention (trespass) or exercising choice over treatment options (negligence). Trespass involves unlawful interference due to lack of consent. Consent is real only when it is informed. How much information is required depends on the circumstances and the nature of the inquiry. For trespass, the information need only pertain to the nature of the procedure for which consent is sought. For negligence, the relevant consent is to the risk, and therefore the information provided must be pertinent to the nature of the risk.

Coggon distinguishes between cases where the patient does not have capacity and those in which the patient does. According to Coggon, the proper conception of autonomy in the former cases is ideal desire autonomy, whereas for the latter it is current desire autonomy. There appears to be a conflation of ideal desire autonomy and best interests. Capacity is a pre-requisite for autonomy; thus, where capacity is absent it is meaningless to speak of autonomy.[91] The only question is what is in the patient's best interest; this suggests that ideal desire autonomy is the equivalent of best interest, which risks the introduction of medical paternalism. Where patients have capacity, they should have the absolute right to refuse consent to unlawful interference with their bodies. This is in the context of trespass.

The situation is more nuanced when it comes to negligence and medical decision-making. Negligence does not deal in absolutes. It is about the fair allocation of risks and responsibilities based on comparative fault. It involves compromise. An absolutist conception of autonomy developed over two centuries ago as a shield against the tyranny of the ruling class is not ideally suited to a modern twentieth-century tort dealing with risk in a doctor–patient relationship that values trust and shared decision-making. Coggon expresses a preference for

[87] J Coggon, 'Varied and Principled Understandings of Autonomy in English Law: Justifiable Inconsistency of Blinkered Moralism?' (2007) 15 *Health Care Analysis* 235, 240.

[88] ibid.

[89] ibid.

[90] ibid.

[91] This is implicitly acknowledged by Dworkin: R Dworkin, *The Theory and Practice of Autonomy* (Cambridge, Cambridge University Press, 1988) 114. See also J Raz, *The Morality of Freedom* (Oxford, Clarendon Press, 1986) 372.

best desire autonomy to deal with the nuances of negligence.[92] Coggon's framework has been applied by Craig Purshouse to medical negligence.[93] However, unlike Coggon, Purshouse advocates for current desire autonomy in medical negligence cases, arguing that ideal desire autonomy and best desire autonomy are both logically flawed.

Ideal desire autonomy is rejected as it imposes external values and relies on objective standards, potentially at the expense of the subjective desires of the patient. Purshouse argues that this conception of autonomy is indistinguishable from paternalism as it purports to restrict the patient's choice to the patient's best interest. However, this criticism can be tempered by distinguishing between the *concept* of ideal desire autonomy and its *conception*. The value animating ideal desire autonomy need not be Kantianism, confined to individualistic, rational desire; it can be something else that makes the concept amenable to the aims of negligence. Negligence is about striking a balance between risk and harm, based on the concept of reasonableness. In principle, there should be no objection to introducing an objective value to the conception of autonomy. It will be argued below that such a conception may be realised within a relational framework.

Best desire autonomy has been criticised on the ground that it results in infinite regression.[94] If a second order desire is required to validate a first order desire, critics argue that there is no reason not to require a third order desire to validate the second order, and so on ad infinitum.[95] There are two ways to resolve this conundrum. Dworkin recognises the risk of infinite regression but points out that the inquiry is not directed at determining whether the desire or act is autonomous but whether the person is acting autonomously.[96] Thus, as long as the person has reflected critically on the first order desire without external manipulation or coercion, there is no need to evaluate the second order desire. This is in line with Raz's view that an individual need only have the capacity for reasoning.

Another way is to reconceptualise best desire autonomy as reflexive desire autonomy. Reflexion goes beyond reflection:

> Reflective practice is an important part of our professional development. It means we look at what went well, what didn't and this allows us to tweak and amend our approach in the future. Although this practice is necessary, it is quite passive and is done after the event.
>
> Reflexive practice, however, is much more transformational because it is often done in the moment and takes our level of understanding much deeper. Reflexive practioners

[92] J Coggon, 'Varied and Principled Understandings of Autonomy in English Law: Justifiable Inconsistency of Blinkered Moralism?' (2007) 15 *Health Care Analysis* 235, 253.

[93] C Purshouse, 'How Should Autonomy be Defined in Medical Negligence Cases?' (2015) 10 *Clinical Ethics* 107.

[94] G Dworkin, 'The Concept of Autonomy' (1981) 12/13 *GRAZER Philosophische Studien* 203, 212–13.

[95] C Purshouse, 'How Should Autonomy be Defined in Medical Negligence Cases?' (2015) 10 *Clinical Ethics* 107, 110.

[96] G Dworkin, 'The Concept of Autonomy' (1981) 12/13 *GRAZER Philosophische Studien* 203, 212.

> [sic] have a higher level of self-awareness because they are not only able to assess a situation as it is happening and tweak things as they go, but they also have the ability to look at why things are the way that they are and consider the role they are playing in the current outcome.[97]

Reflexive desire autonomy identifies the innate desire of individuals based on internal reflection and their dynamic relationship with relevant external conditions. It is not about what is in their best interest based on the paternalistic views of another person; it is about what is in their best interest based on their own reflexive process. Individual autonomy in the context of medical negligence is about medical decision-making, and a patient's choices cannot be unrestricted. One can claim unrestricted autonomy when it comes to *refusing* consent to treatment but not necessarily when it comes to *choosing* treatment. When a patient makes a choice, the doctor has the burden of implementing that choice; thus, the patient's autonomy immediately impacts on the doctor's autonomy and the doctor–patient relationship.[98] When a patient refuses treatment, the doctor's autonomy is unaffected, as the doctor no longer has a role to play.

Purshouse ignores this distinction between refusal of consent and choice of treatment, arguing that the law must be coherent and should not distinguish between trespass and negligence when it comes to autonomy. Referring to Lord Donaldson MR's observations in *Re T (Adult: Refusal of Treatment)*,[99] Purshouse draws support for current desire autonomy:

> [T]he patient's right of choice exists whether the reasons for making that choice are rational, irrational, unknown or even non-existent. That his choice is contrary to what is to be expected of the vast majority of adults is only relevant if there are other reasons for doubting his capacity to decide.[100]

Two observations need to be made at this point: one, as alluded to above, on the facts, *Re T* involved the right to *refuse* treatment, not the right to *choose* treatment; further, Lord Donaldson, immediately following the quote above, went on to state:

> But just because adults have the right to choose, it does not follow that they have in fact exercised that right. Determining whether or not they have done so is a quite different and sometimes difficult matter. And if it is clear that they have exercised their right of choice, *problems can still arise in determining what precisely they have chosen* (emphasis added).[101]

[97] 'Reflective Practice vs Reflexive Practice', *Parenta* (1 May 2019), https://www.parenta.com/2019/05/01/reflective-practice-vs-reflexive-practice/#:~:text=A%20reflective%20thinker%20will%20analyse,inwardly%20as%20well%20as%20outwardly.

[98] See for example, the concerns expressed by the Supreme Court in *McCulloch v Forth Valley Health Board* [2023] UKSC 26; [2024] AC 925.

[99] *Re T (Adult: Refusal of Treatment)* [1992] EWCA Civ 18, [3]; [1993] Fam 95, 112.

[100] C Purshouse, 'How Should Autonomy be Defined in Medical Negligence Cases?' (2015) 10 *Clinical Ethics* 107, 112.

[101] ibid.

The italicised text suggests that the patient's choice cannot always be taken at face value and may need to be further interrogated. This is closer to best desire autonomy than current desire autonomy. The appellant, a young woman who was 34 weeks pregnant, had been involved in a traffic accident and needed a blood transfusion. Her mother was a devout Jehovah's Witness who objected to blood transfusions on religious grounds. It was never established whether the appellant herself held such beliefs and, even if she did, whether she would nonetheless have consented to a blood transfusion. The appellant was in considerable pain, suffering a lung infection, and sedated with strong narcotics. Under the apparent influence of her mother, the appellant refused to consent to a blood transfusion despite not being counselled on the risks and consequences.

The doctor obtained a court order that was upheld by the Court of Appeal on the ground that there was a medical emergency justifying the doctor's actions in the patient's best interests. If the doctor had respected the appellant's current desire autonomy, the operation would not have proceeded. The case, therefore, is not illustrative of current desire autonomy but is more in line with best desire autonomy. If the appellant had not been influenced by her mother and had been fully informed, she may well have consented to the surgery. *Re T* thus does not support current desire autonomy; instead, it illustrates why best desire autonomy is better suited to cases involving medical decision-making.

While there is significant academic support for autonomy, courts have so far been reluctant to recognise loss of autonomy as actionable damage in negligence. Instead, courts have relied on autonomy arguments indirectly to provide some compensation or vindication to the claimant.[102] However, there are exceptional cases where loss of autonomy should be recognised as actionable damage – reproductive negligence and genetic negligence.[103] In these types of cases, the claimants may not have suffered personal injury, but they have suffered irreparable harm to their autonomy. Paradoxically, both these case scenarios involve negligent acts by the doctor, not negligent failure to inform, which is where autonomy arguments have been centre stage.

In the leading duty to inform cases, the House of Lords by majority in *Chester* and the Supreme Court unanimously in *Montgomery*, linked the doctor's duty to inform with patient autonomy even though the actual damage in each case was personal injury and economic loss respectively. Autonomy discourse was used to circumvent orthodox principles of causation in *Chester* and was superfluous in *Montgomery*. The real issue in both cases was whether the patient would have consented to the risk which resulted in damage had the patient been properly informed. In *Chester*, the patient, although not informed of the risk, would, on the evidence have been willing to run the risk, and therefore should have failed

[102] *Rees v Darlington Memorial Hospital NHS Trust* [2003] UKHL 52, [2004] 1 AC 309; *ACB v Thomson Medical Pte Ltd* [2017] SGCA 20; [2017] 1 SLR 918.

[103] This argument will be developed in Chapter 8 of this volume.

on causation. In *Montgomery*, the patient clearly would not have run the risk and therefore rightly succeeded.

Individual autonomy has been put in tension with beneficence, pitting a patient-centric approach against a doctor-centric approach. The need to balance autonomy and beneficence was recognised explicitly in *Hii Chii Kok v Ooi Peng Jin London Lucien*:[104]

> It is therefore incumbent on us to reconsider the advice aspect of the relationship through the lens of patient autonomy as well as the principle of beneficence and ensure that both principles are upheld. There must be a balance between both principles (as well as balance between the doctor's perspective and the patient's perspective); neither should dominate the other.

This calls for compromise. Instead of a doctor-centric or patient-centric approach, the preferred approach should be collaborative. A relational account of autonomy provides a conceptual solution to bridge the gap between beneficence and autonomy, fostering patient agency and shared decision-making.[105]

B. Relational Autonomy

Relational autonomy entered medical law and ethics discourse when courts began to consider the interests of relatives and carers who were responsible for the patient's long-term care, and ethicists introduced concepts of shared decision-making that involved family members and carers.[106] This was in recognition of the fact that the patient's decision affected not just the patient but the carers as well. The individualistic approach to autonomy ignored the carers' autonomy, focusing solely on the patient's autonomy. Over the last few decades, the scholarship on the role of the family or relatives in making decisions with or on behalf of the patient has burgeoned.[107]

However, relational autonomy is much more than just recognising the interests of family members. It is a philosophical approach that is closely linked to feminism, vulnerability, and intersectionality;[108] it rejects the rationalistic, atomistic, and abstract conception of individuals in favour of an individual who is emotional, social, and interdependent.[109] The conventional approach to autonomy in medico-legal discourse relied on a liberal philosophy that developed during the Enlightenment

[104] *Hii Chii Kok v Ooi Peng Jin London Lucien* [2017] 2 SLR 492, [120].

[105] See Chapter 5 of this volume, text to nn 93–132.

[106] R Gilbar, 'Family Involvement, Independence and Patient Autonomy in Practice' [2011] *Medical Law Review* 192, 204 and citations therein.

[107] See references at nn 111–124.

[108] J Nedelsky, 'Re-conceiving Autonomy: Sources, Thoughts and Possibilities' (1989) 1 *Yale Journal of Law and Feminism* 7; See also, C Mackenzie and N Stoljar (eds), *Relational Autonomy: Feminist Perspectives on Autonomy, Agency, and the Social Self* (New York, Oxford University Press, 2000).

[109] A Donchin, 'Understanding Autonomy Relationally: Toward a Reconfiguration of Bioethical Principles' (2001) 26 *Journal of Medicine and Philosophy* 365, 367.

period according to which autonomous decision-making was realised only when individuals made choices independently without external pressure or influence. This ignores the reality that individual identities are formed not in the abstract but in relationships with others. 'Without understanding one's identity, one cannot really be self-conscious, and true to one's own self, and thus one cannot be autonomous'.[110]

A relational approach recognises that others invariably have an influence on individuals' decision-making and that individuals consider the impact of their decisions on others. Some individuals may voluntarily delegate their autonomy to others, trusting them to make judgements on their behalf. Anita Ho illustrates this using an anecdote of a hospital ethics consultation during which the doctors considered how to treat a patient whose prognosis was poor.[111] The patient was adamant that he did not want any treatment, but his wife intervened, persuading the patient to change his mind. The doctor was suspicious of undue influence and advised the patient that he had a right to make up his own mind. This put the patient under pressure to make a decision that he was unable to make on his own, ignoring the reality of the supporting relationship between husband and wife.

A similar example comes from the Malaysian case of *Abdul Razak bin Datuk Abu Samah v Raja Badrul Hisham bin Raja Zezeman Shah*.[112] The patient was an elderly woman who had to undergo emergency surgery. She was too afraid to consent to the insertion of a Ryle's (naso-gastric) tube, which is commonly inserted to prevent the risk of aspiration. Having failed to obtain her consent, the surgery proceeded with an alternative to the Ryle's tube. Tragically, she aspirated and died. The patient's husband, who brought the action, argued that the surgical team should have consulted him and informed him of the risks so that he could have persuaded his wife to consent.

The court accepted that the patient in this case habitually depended on her husband to make decisions and indeed the husband had been actively involved in managing the patient's care. It so happened that he was away on a business trip the day before the surgery. He argued that had he been contacted, he would have refused to consent to the surgery without the insertion of the Ryle's tube and would have convinced his wife to give consent. While it is important to ensure that family members do not exert undue influence on patients, the case shows that in appropriate cases, involvement of family members may be in the best interest of the patient both in terms of the health outcomes as well as in helping the patient achieve best interest autonomy.[113]

[110] SC Lee, 'On Relational Autonomy: From Feminist Critique to Confucian Model for Clinical Practice' in SC Lee (ed), *The Family, Medical Decision-Making, and Biotechnology: Critical Reflections on Asian Moral Perspectives* (Dordrecht, Springer, 2007) 83.

[111] A Ho, 'Relational Autonomy or Undue Pressure? Family's Role in Medical Decision-making' (2008) 22 *Scandinavian Journal of Caring Sciences* 129.

[112] *Abdul Razak bin Datuk Abu Samah v Raja Badrul Hisham bin Raja Zezeman Shah* [2013] 10 MLJ 34.

[113] While the judgment arguably erred in finding that a duty was owed personally to the husband, the facts of the case demonstrate that the patient's decision would likely have been different had her husband been involved.

Accepting that others may have a legitimate interest in a patient's decision is less alien in communitarian societies in the Global South and East than in individualistic societies in the Global North and West.[114] While an over-generalisation, there is some truth in Ruiping Fan's observation that in Eastern cultures 'a family member's disease is an issue for the whole family'.[115] However, there remains the risk that patients in these cultures may be pressured by relatives and carers. This is a similar concern expressed by feminist scholars who warn that a relational account of autonomy risks subjugating the rights of women to patriarchal expectations.[116] Striking the right balance between the interests of the patient and cultural/ relational expectations is not an easy task, but it may be achieved by respecting the individual's choice to abide by societal and cultural norms or to reject them.[117]

John Hardwig adopts a pragmatic approach, arguing that both patients' and carers' autonomy must be respected equally.[118] In some cases, he accepts that the carer's autonomy may be prioritised over the patient's as the patient has a moral responsibility to those who are making a sacrifice to care for the patient.[119] Not all share this view, as ultimately it is the patients who are subject to the medical treatment and who bear the very personal and intimate consequences of the intervention on their bodies.[120] Thus, Lindemann-Nelson and Lindemann-Nelson argue that the doctor has the responsibility to mediate any dispute between patients and carers, with a mandate to protect the patients.[121]

It may be unfair to impose on doctors the responsibility to mediate between patients and carers, but it cannot be denied that the doctor, patient, and family/ carers are interconnected in a dynamic relationship. The individualistic conception of autonomy under which the doctor provides information in order for the patient independently to give 'informed consent' in an ongoing clinical relationship is detached from reality. Studies show that patients often do not fully understand the information presented and cannot remember details.[122] They invariably rely on

[114] L Blackhall et al, 'Ethnicity and Attitudes Towards Patient Autonomy' (1995) 274 *Journal of the American Medical Association* 820, cited in F Turoldo, 'Relational Autonomy and Multiculturalism' (2010) 19 *Cambridge Quarterly Healthcare Ethics* 542, 545.

[115] R Fan, 'Critical Care Ethics in Asia: Global or Local?' (1998) 6 *Journal of Medicine and Philosophy* 549, 556–57.

[116] See L Code, 'The Perversion of Autonomy and the Subjection of Women: Discourses of Social Advocacy at Century's End' in C Mackenzie and N Stoljar (eds), *Relational Autonomy: Feminist Perspectives on Autonomy, Agency, and the Social Self* (New York, Oxford University Press, 2000) 181.

[117] There is abundant literature on the concept of liberal multiculturalism, which provides a theoretical framework to strike this balance. A leading voice is that of Will Kymlicka. See, for example, W Kymlicka, *Liberalism, Community and Culture* (Oxford, Oxford University Press, 1989); W Kymlicka, 'Liberal Multiculturalism as a Political Theory of State-Minority Relations' (2018) 46 *Political Theory* 81.

[118] J Hardwig, 'What About the Family?' (1990) 22 *Hasting's Center Report* 6.

[119] See also A Ho, 'Relational Autonomy or Undue Pressure? Family's Role in Medical Decision-Making' (2008) 22 *Scandinavian Journal of Caring Sciences* 128, 133.

[120] See H Lindemann-Nelson and J Lindemann-Nelson, *The Patient in the Family* (New York, Routledge, 1995) 114–17.

[121] ibid.

[122] GN Samuel et al, 'Healthcare Professionals' and Patients' Perspectives on Consent to Clinical Genetic Testing: Moving Towards a More Relational Approach' (2017) 18 *BMC Medical Ethics* 47.

and implicitly trust doctors for guidance. The doctor–patient relationship cannot be ignored in determining patient autonomy. Just as the patient's relationship with family and carers shapes patient autonomy, so too does the patient's relationship with the doctor.

Patient autonomy (in the individualistic sense) has become inextricably entwined with informed consent. As argued earlier in this chapter, informed consent has its roots in trespass and medical research; it is not a fruitful concept in the context of the doctor's duty to inform and advise the patient of risks and alternatives that are constantly shifting. Obtaining consent has become a bureaucratic process of form filling and 'information dumping' whose primary aim is to protect the doctor from legal liability. It assumes a relationship of adversity and mistrust: the very opposite of the doctor-patient relationship, which is based on collaboration and trust.

To quote O'Neil again: 'Trust belongs with relationships and (mutual) obligations; individual autonomy with rights and adversarial claims'.[123] Relational autonomy is compatible with a relationship of trust. It behooves the doctor to respect the patient as a person and to treat the patient with 'trustworthiness, openness, and honesty'.[124] Relational autonomy emphasises mutual obligations and not individual rights. A rights-based approach to autonomy allows patients to launch a collateral medical negligence claim against doctors when an inherent, undisclosed risk materialises, and the patient suffers damage.

This is despite the reality that in most cases, patients are willing – and want – to trust their doctors as they seek treatment and care. Indeed, some would have consented to the treatment even if they were warned of the risk. Recall the case of *Chester* discussed earlier.[125] An aggressive patients' rights conception of autonomy puts doctors on the defensive, compelling them to retreat behind formalistic informed consent procedures; this does not advance patient autonomy or the doctor–patient relationship.

IV. Conclusion

The weight accorded to patient autonomy in medical negligence litigation involving allegations of failure to inform or advise has had an adverse impact on the doctor–patient relationship and has distorted conventional doctrine. Patient autonomy properly belongs to professional regulation, medical ethics, and intentional torts. It is an important value that is necessary to protect individuals from unwanted interference with their bodily integrity, but it sits uneasily in medical negligence litigation especially as an individualistic, Kantian concept.

[123] O O'Neill, *Autonomy and Trust in Bioethics* (Cambridge, Cambridge University Press, 2002) 25.

[124] GN Samuel et al, 'Healthcare Professionals' and Patients' Perspectives on Consent to Clinical Genetic Testing: Moving Towards a More Relational Approach' (2017) 18 *BMC Medical Ethics* 47, 48.

[125] For a fuller discussion, see Chapters 7 and 8 in this volume.

In so far as autonomy is relevant to the doctor–patient relationship and clinical negligence, it must be recast as a relational concept. Otherwise, autonomy risks undermining trust in the doctor–patient relationship. It is important not to lose sight of the fact that when patients make choices about treatments in exercising their 'autonomy right', they directly impinge on the autonomy of the doctor who must continue treating the patient. This is unlike the refusal of consent cases where the doctor is relieved of responsibility when the patient refuses consent.

Relational autonomy recognises the mutual interconnectedness of individuals and the limitations that such relationships impose on individual autonomy. It is aligned with virtues of care and trust, which are fundamental to the doctor-patient relationship. Patient autonomy should not be an overarching consideration in determining the content of the doctor's duty to inform or the scope of liability for any consequent injury. Doctors have a duty to explain the proposed procedure, inherent risks, and alternative options by engaging in a dialogue with patients, allowing for a reflexive shared decision-making process.

The duty to inform is not effective as a regulatory device to compel doctors to protect patient autonomy or to give patients freedom of choice. It is crucial to note that negligent failure to inform cases are litigated only when the patient suffers personal injury; in all other cases, the doctor's negligent failure to inform is unaffected by the tort of negligence. Lord Hope in Chester stated:

> The function of the law is to enable rights to be vindicated and to provide remedies when duties have been breached. Unless this is done the duty is a hollow one, stripped of all practical force and devoid of all content. It will have lost its ability to protect the patient and thus to fulfil the only purpose which brought it into existence.[126]

If the purpose of the duty is to vindicate rights and to ensure that patients are properly informed, then it fails in its mission in the vast majority of cases where patients are not provided with adequate information on risks but have the good fortune of not having the risk materialise. It is this misunderstanding of the nature of the tort of negligence and patient autonomy that has undermined both doctrinal coherence in the law and the sanctity of the doctor–patient relationship. The safeguarding of patients' autonomy and ensuring doctors provide adequate information on risks and treatment options are functions that are better left to professional regulation and ethics.

[126] *Chester v Afshar* [2004] UKHL 41; [2005] 1 AC 134, [87].

PART II

The Anatomy of Negligence

5

Reconceptualising the Duty of Care

I. Introduction

Part II of this volume draws on the theoretical arguments developed in Part I to critique the key elements of negligence. To establish liability in negligence the claimant must prove that the defendant owed the claimant a duty of care; the defendant breached that duty of care; the defendant's breach of duty caused damage to the claimant; the damage caused was recognised in law and was not too remote. These are trite propositions, but each of these elements has evolved into a complex, polysemous concept that warrants critical scrutiny. The inherent ambiguity in these concepts has resulted in internal inconsistencies and occasional deviation from principle. While flexibility in applying the law can be a virtue, it is equally important to ensure that the law remains coherent, predictable, and principled.

It will be shown that judges have used these concepts instrumentally – and sometimes arbitrarily – to shape the contours of medical negligence liability. Occasionally, the decisions ignore established precedents as judges are influenced by academic views and apply their own ideological values to remake the law. The rise and fall of negligence in the major common law jurisdictions has mirrored liberal and conservative judicial approaches. Kirby J of the High Court of Australia acknowledged this reality when he stated: 'Changing attitudes in this Court to the content of the common law of negligence have resulted in a discernible shift in the outcomes of negligence cases'.[1]

Judges embraced the rights model from the latter part of the twentieth century onward to steer medical negligence discourse away from medical paternalism; in doing so, they stretched the elements of negligence to vindicate patients' rights. The scope of the duty of care was enhanced from taking care not to cause personal injury to patients to taking care to safeguard patient autonomy and choice.[2] The standard of care with respect to the duty to inform and advise was reconceptualised and assessed not from the perspective of a reasonable doctor but that of a reasonable patient, extending in some cases to accommodating idiosyncratic

[1] *Neindorf v Junkovic* [2005] HCA 75; 80 ALJR 341, [19].

[2] These developments began in the United States and were crystallised in the landmark decision of *Canterbury v Spence* 464 F 2d 772 (DC Cir 1972).

characteristics of the particular patient.[3] Causation principles were stretched in duty to inform cases,[4] and the contours of actionable damage have been redrawn to vindicate autonomy interests.[5]

This chapter begins with a brief overview of the duty of care, followed by a historical analysis, distinguishing between two strands post-*Donoghue v Stevenson*,[6] which may be described as 'relational duty' and 'contextual duty'. The former is based on the relationship between claimant and defendant, while the latter is based on the nexus between the defendant's act and the claimant's injury. The pre-*Donoghue* duty of care was a relational concept; a duty only existed in cases of pre-existing relationships. Lord Atkin's rationalisation of the duty of care to state a general principle strictly ought to have been qualified and confined to explaining the common thread in pre-existing or intended relationships, including intended relationships such as manufacturer and consumer. However, it was treated as carte blanche to create ad hoc categories of duty based on abstract concepts of foreseeability and proximity.

Any ad hoc duty that is recognised must be contextual, viz, the relationship must be closely and directly connected to the act of the defendant. This leads to the second qualification to Lord Atkin's general principle: any contextual duty should be restricted to acts only; it should not extend to omissions. Liability for omissions may arise only when there is a relational duty or when there is a voluntary assumption of responsibility. Indeed, Edward White has noted that the early cases of negligence involved allegations of neglect – a failure to do something in the context of a relationship.[7] The failure to distinguish between relational and contextual duties has contributed to doctrinal inconsistencies and encouraged recognition of affirmative duties.

The chapter then explores two related phenomena – the fragmentation of the duty of care and the consolidation of duty and breach into a scope of duty inquiry. The fragmentation approach is evident in medical negligence, with the doctors' duty splintered into the duty to care, treat, diagnose, advise, inform, warn, refer, and follow-up, amongst others. The scope of duty approach takes a holistic assessment of duty, standard, and breach. While this has certain advantages, it risks conflating duty and breach; thus, in some cases, just because the defendant *could* have avoided injury to the claimant, liability is imposed even if a duty *should not* have arisen in the circumstances.[8]

[3] *Canterbury v Spence* 464 F 2d 772 (DC Cir 1972) (US); *Reibl v Hughes* (1981) 114 DLR 1 (Canada); *Rogers v Whitaker* (1992) 175 CLR 479 (Australia); *Foo Fio Na v Dr Soo Fook Mun* [2007] 1 MLJ 593 (Malaysia); *Montgomery v Lanarkshire Health Board* [2015] UKSC 11; [2015] AC 1430 (UK)); *Hii Chii Kok v Ooi Peng Jin London Lucien* [2017] SGCA 38; [2017] 2 SLR 492 (Singapore).

[4] *Chester v Afshar* [2004] UKHL 41; [2005] 1 AC 134; *Chappell v Hart* (1998) 295 CLR 232.

[5] *Rees v Darlington Memorial Hospital NHS Trust* [2003] UKHL 52; [2004] AC 309; *ACB v Thomson Medical Pte Ltd* [2017] SGCA 20; [2017] 1 SLR 918.

[6] *Donoghue v Stevenson* [1932] AC 562; (1932) SC (HL) 31.

[7] GE White, *Tort Law in America: An Intellectual History* (New York, Oxford University Press, 2003) 16.

[8] *ABC v St George's Healthcare NHS Trust* [2020] EWHC 455 (QB).

Finally, the chapter explores the doctor's duty to advise the patient. The conventional justification for the duty to advise is vindication of patient autonomy; this was explicit in judicial comments in *Chester v Afshar*[9] and *Montgomery v Lanarkshire Health Board*.[10] Patients are vulnerable both in terms of their knowledge deficit on medical issues and the fact that their health is compromised – patients necessarily rely on doctors to help them get better. The duty to advise addresses the knowledge deficit to facilitate a collaborative approach and shared decision-making. This chapter argues that the duty to advise should not be grounded in patient autonomy but should instead focus on patient agency, which empowers patients but also makes them responsible for their informed choices.

II. The Duty of Care

Ever since the seminal judgment of Lord Atkin in *Donoghue*, courts across the world's common law jurisdictions strove to articulate a general test for the duty of care. Despite various judicial formulations, the determination of the existence and scope of a novel duty of care comes down to three questions:

1. Could the defendant reasonably have foreseen that the claimant could be affected by the defendant's conduct?[11]
2. Would it be fair, between the parties, to hold the defendant under a legal obligation not to injure the claimant?
3. Would it be fair, in the broader public interest, to recognise such a category of duty of care?

These three questions are addressed in the three-stage framework set out in *Caparo Industries Plc v Dickman*:

> What emerges is that, in addition to the foreseeability of damage, necessary ingredients in any situation giving rise to a duty of care are that there should exist between the party owing the duty and the party to whom it is owed a relationship characterised by the law as one of 'proximity' or 'neighbourhood' and that the situation should be one in which the court considers it fair, just and reasonable that the law should impose a duty of a given scope upon the one party for the benefit of the other.[12]

[9] [2004] UKHL 41; [2005] 1 AC 134.

[10] [2015] UKSC 11; [2015] AC 1430.

[11] The inquiry is narrower for economic loss and secondary victim psychiatric injury cases, where the question is whether *loss of that nature* was foreseeable to the claimant as an individual or as a member of a limited class. *Alcock v Chief Constable of South Yorkshire* [1992] 1 AC 310; *Banca Nazionale del Lavoro SPA v Playboy Club London Limited* [2018] UKSC 43; [2018] 1 WLR 4041; *Caltex Oil (Australia) Pty Ltd v The Dredge 'Willemstad'* (1976) 136 CLR 529; 11 ALR 227; *Man Mohan Singh v Zurich Insurance (Singapore) Pte Ltd* [2008] SGCA 24; [2008] 3 SLR (R) 735.

[12] [1990] 2 AC 605 (per Lord Bridge), 617–18.

This analytical framework, based on the three-stage inquiry into foreseeability, proximity, and policy, is also applied in Canadian and Singaporean jurisprudence.[13] The United Kingdom, while not abandoning the *Caparo* approach, has endorsed a pluralist approach to the duty of care.[14] The High Court of Australia has abandoned the three-stage framework in favour of an open-textured approach identifying all the salient features in favour of and against recognising a duty.[15] A close examination of this approach suggests that the salient features may be grouped respectively into factors relevant to the proximity inquiry (affecting the two parties) and factors relevant to the policy inquiry (affecting the broader public interest).[16]

The value of having a three-stage framework of analysis is that it permits a logical sequence of inquiry beginning with foreseeability, followed by proximity, and finally policy. The foreseeability inquiry serves as a threshold requirement,[17] in the absence of which there should be no further inquiry into proximity and policy. The foreseeability inquiry anchors the proximity inquiry because it ensures the proximity inquiry is undertaken in the context of the defendant's conduct and the claimant's injury. If injury to a claimant is not even foreseeable, there is no need to determine whether the claimant is sufficiently proximate – a neighbour in the legal sense. The first two inquiries are both factual and normative while the third inquiry into policy is purely normative.

The foreseeability inquiry provides the minimum required connection between the defendant's conduct and the claimant's injury. It is a broad inquiry – anything that is not 'far-fetched or fanciful' is foreseeable,[18] yet it has a normative dimension that allows courts to find or deny foreseeability by determining what is reasonable in the circumstances.[19] The proximity inquiry is internal to the parties – it is a normative questions about interpersonal justice, whether the claimant *ought* to be treated as a legal neighbour in the Atkinian (*Donoghue v Stevenson*) sense.

[13] *Cooper v Hobart* [2001] SCR 537; *Spandeck Engineering (S) Pte Ltd v Defence Science & Technology Agency* [2007] SGCA 37; [2007] 4 SLR(R) 100.

[14] *Customs and Excise v Barclays Bank plc* [2006] UKHL 28; [2007] 1 AC 181. In *Robinson v Chief Constable of West Yorkshire Police* [2018] UKSC 4; [2018] AC 736, Lord Reed opined that *Caparo* did not set out a universal test but was merely a framework of analysis.

[15] *Perre v Apand* (1998) 198 CLR 180. Kirby J offered a stoic defence of the three-stage approach (at [259]–[260]).

[16] For example, in *Woolcock Street Investments Pty Ltd v CDG Pty Ltd* [2004] HCA 16; (2004) 216 CLR 515, [96], McHugh J listed the followed 11 salient features: reasonable foreseeability, indeterminacy of liability, autonomy of the individual, plaintiff's vulnerability to the risk, defendant's knowledge of the risk, defendant's responsibility to control third parties, outflanking the law of contract, floodgates argument, disproportionate liability, lack of a measurable standard of care, circumventing the policy of limitation legislation. The first five factors are relevant to the relationship between the two parties and thus to proximity while the next six factors are relevant to wider considerations and thus relevant to policy questions or inquiry into what is fair, just and reasonable.

[17] *Spandeck Engineering (S) Pte Ltd v Defence Science & Technology Agency* [2007] SGCA 37; [2007] 4 SLR(R) 100, [76].

[18] *Wyong Shire Council v Shirt* [1980] HCA 12; (1980) 146 CLR 40 (per Mason J), 47; *Overseas Tankship (UK) Ltd v Miller Steamship Co Pty Ltd ('The Wagon Mound') (No 2)* [1967] 1 AC 617.

[19] *Tame v New South Wales* [2002] HCA 35; (2002) 211 CLR 317.

Thus, questions of fairness and reasonableness permeate this inquiry.[20] The policy inquiry is external to the parties, looking to the potential impact on future claims of a finding on duty of care. It is about the court drawing a line in the sand.[21]

III. Relational Duty and Contextual Duty

Historically, the tort of negligence, in many respects, developed in contradistinction to the law of contract.[22] Contractual liability is based on bilateral relations, with mutually agreed intention to create legal relations. Negligence liability is unilateral; it is based on the defendant's responsibility to others for failure to take care when engaging in risk-creating activity. Contractual liability is tied to the relationship between the parties; negligence liability is tied to the conduct of the defendant that affects the claimant. Historically, negligence liability arose only when there was a pre-existing relationship between the parties and one party neglected to take care in performing its duty within that relationship.[23]

Donoghue recognised a duty in the absence of a pre-existing relationship, justifying it based on the close connection between the claimant's injury and the defendant's negligent act. This was a significant development, as *Donoghue* did not merely rationalise previous cases to find a common theme in the types of relationships that gave rise to a duty of care; it ushered in an era where a duty of care could be created from a defendant's act in the absence of any pre-existing relationship. Thus, there are two strands to the duty of care concept in *Donoghue* – relational and contextual. As White observed, 'the modern negligence principle in tort law seems to have been an intellectual response to the increased number of accidents involving persons who had no preexisting relationship with one another – "stranger" cases'.[24]

The duty of care in negligence is to take reasonable care when *engaging in an act*. That duty to take care is owed to any person who is closely and directly affected *by the act*. The duty derives from the defendant's act, unlike contractual liability which derives from the defendant's relationship (the contract) with the claimant. Prior to *Donoghue*, liability in negligence existed only within established relationships. Brett MR (later Lord Esher) observed as much in attempting to state a general principle in *Heaven v Pender*: 'If one man is near to another, or is near to the property of another, a duty lies upon him not to do that which may cause

[20] This is explicit in the Canadian approach where the Supreme Court observed that 'there must have been sufficient proximity between [the parties] such that it would be fair and just to impose a duty of care'. *Syl Apps Secure Treatment Centre v BD* 2007 SCC 38; [2007] 3 SCR 83, [34].

[21] See *White v Chief Constable of South Yorkshire* [1992] 2 AC 455 (per Lord Steyn), 500.

[22] D Ibbetson, *A Historical Introduction to the Law of Obligations* (Oxford, Oxford University Press, 2006 reprint) 170–74.

[23] GE White, *Tort Law in America: An Intellectual History* (New York, Oxford University Press, 2003) 16.

[24] ibid.

a personal injury to another, or may injure his property'.[25] Whether the true basis of liability for negligence was contractual or tortious was contested for much of the nineteenth century.[26]

The historical link between tort and contract naturally resulted in notions of assumption of responsibility infiltrating tort duty, a concept that saw a renaissance in the 1990s.[27] As Percy Winfield noted,

> [i]n the process of separating contract from tort and in the development of the tort of negligence, a confused notion about assumpsit became the germ of the duty idea. It was thought that, as assumpsit in contract always showed an 'undertaking' of liability, therefore liability in tort must show something equivalent to it.[28]

Indeed, in *Customs and Excise v Barclays Bank plc*,[29] the House of Lords considered whether voluntary assumption of responsibility could in some cases independently give rise to a duty of care.[30] More recently, Edelman J of the High Court of Australia observed that there were two distinct bases for a duty of care to arise – one based on assumption of responsibility and another based on common law principles and precedent.[31]

James Murphy, in an insightful analysis of the origin of the duty of care, stated that Brett MR's analysis in *Heaven* 'relied almost wholly upon the idea of relationship'.[32] This relational approach to the duty of care casts it as an affirmative duty, one based on human obligations, or 'humanism', as Murphy expressed it.[33] The industrial revolution in the nineteenth century saw an increase in injuries due to industrial accidents and motorised transportation, leading to more claims in negligence in the absence of a prior relationship. As James Plunkett observed, 'By the middle of the nineteenth century, then, the idea of duty was being used to explain liability in cases of both relationship and non-relationship negligence alike'.[34] However, Lord Atkin, in stating the general neighbour principle, failed to distinguish between these two strands of duty – one based on a pre-existing relationship and another created by the nature of the defendant's act, stating:

> You must take reasonable care to avoid acts or omissions which you can reasonably foresee would be likely to injure your neighbour. Who, then, in law is my neighbour?

[25] *Heaven v Pender* (1883) 11 QBD 503, 508.

[26] JC Plunkett, 'The Historical Foundation of the Duty of Care' (2015) 41 *Monash University Law Review* 716, 719–20.

[27] *Spring v Guardian Assurance plc* [1995] 2 AC 296; *Henderson v Merrett Syndicates Ltd* [1995] 2 AC 145; *White v Jones* [1995] 2 AC 207.

[28] PH Winfield, 'Duty in Tortious Negligence' (1934) 34 *Columbia Law Review* 41, 65.

[29] *Customs and Excise v Barclays Bank plc* [2006] UKHL 28; [2007] 1 AC 181.

[30] There was no consensus but at least Lord Bingham expressly noted that assumption of responsibility could provide an independent ground for a duty of care: ibid [4].

[31] *Kozarov v Victoria* [2022] HCA 12; (2022) 273 CLR 115, [100].

[32] JP Murphy, 'Evolution of the Duty of Care: Some Thoughts' (1980) 30 *DePaul Law Review* 147, 148.

[33] ibid.

[34] JC Plunkett, 'The Historical Foundation of the Duty of Care' (2015) 41 *Monash University Law Review* 716, 725.

> The answer seems to be-persons who are so closely and directly *affected by my act* that I ought reasonably to have them in contemplation as being so affected when I am directing my mind to the acts or omissions which are called in question (emphasis added).[35]

Lord Atkin states that there is a duty to take care to avoid acts or omissions that may foreseeably affect another person. He then goes on to elaborate that the legal neighbour is a person who is 'so closely and directly affected *by my act* …'. It is the defendant's act that gives rise to any duty, and the content of that duty is to take reasonable care to avoid any harmful acts or omissions related to the act giving rise to the duty. However, no distinction is made between the relational duty and the contextual duty. Strictly, the contextual duty does not arise from pure omissions.[36] The duty attaches to acts; whether reasonable care is taken is contingent on acts or omissions *related to that act*. By detaching the duty of care from the defendant's act and focusing on the relationship between the defendant and the claimant, the law of negligence opened itself to expansion of liability for omissions.

Instead of restricting defendants to a duty to *take care for their acts*, the law of negligence began to require defendants to *take care of claimants*. Liability for omissions is justified where there is a pre-existing relationship between the parties or where the defendant has voluntarily assumed responsibility to the claimant.[37] The affirmative duty is relational in these cases. However, when a duty is recognised between two strangers who are connected merely because one has been injured by the other, the contextual approach must prevail; the focus must be on the defendant's *act* and its connection with the claimant.

While individual cases may form patterns over time and lend themselves to general principles, the common law is found in individual precedents, not general principles. Drawing on Lord Atkin's statement in *Donoghue*, Lord Wilberforce in *Anns v Merton LBC* enunciated a two-stage analysis based on proximity and policy.[38] Although not intended by Lord Wilberforce, subsequent cases interpreted *Anns* proximity as equivalent to reasonable foreseeability.[39] Lord Wilberforce himself clarified his position on *Anns* in *McLoughlin v O'Brian*,[40] when he referred to Lord Atkin's statement of the neighbour principle:

> This is saying that foreseeability must be accompanied and limited by the law's judgment as to persons who ought, according to its standards of value or justice, to have been in contemplation … That foreseeability does not of itself, and automatically, lead to a duty of care is, I think, clear. I gave some examples in *Anns v Merton London Borough* [1978] AC 728, 752, *Anns* itself being one.

[35] [1932] AC 562, 580.

[36] AJE Jaffey, *The Duty of Care* (Aldershot, Dartmouth Publishing Co, 1992) 47; *Road and Traffic Authority v Dederer* [2007] HCA 42; (2007) 234 CLR 330, [51].

[37] *Tindall v Chief Constable of Thames Valley Police* [2024] UKSC 33.

[38] *Anns v Merton London Borough Council* [1978] AC 728; [1977] 2 All ER 492.

[39] See the observations of Lord Keith of Kinkel in the Privy Council decision of *Yuen Kun Yeu v Attorney-General of Hong Kong* [1988] AC 175, 191–92.

[40] *McLoughlin v O'Brian* [1983] AC 410, 420.

Anns also appeared to shift away from incrementalism, preferring a general principles approach. This naturally led to an expansive phase in the tort of negligence until the House of Lords reversed this course in *Caparo*, insisting on incrementalism.[41] It crafted a three-stage approach to the duty of care that included an assessment of reasonable foreseeability separately from proximity as well as consideration of whether imposing a duty of care would be fair, just, and reasonable in the circumstances. As Deanne J of the High Court of Australia expressed it, proximity could manifest itself as physical, circumstantial, or causal.[42] Circumstantial proximity, based on the relationship between the parties, became the cornerstone of the duty of care test in leading cases involving economic loss, psychiatric harm, and omissions.[43] As these are the categories of cases that typically receive the attention of appellate courts, duty of care has come to be seen almost exclusively through the relational lens. This, despite the absurdity of the relational approach, was laid bare by David Howarth:

> Most defendants have had no relationship at all with their claimants … The relational view of negligence claims that the reason we have a duty of care is some relationship, or relations, that we have with our potential victims. The objection to that view is that it entails either a perverse or a superfluous view of what counts as a relationship.[44]

A solution offered by Plunkett is to use interest-based duty to fill in the gap left by relational duty. This involves determining which of the interests of a potential claimant are 'worthy of protection'.[45] While superficially attractive, this approach suffers from two potential challenges. One, which Plunkett acknowledges, lies in determining which interests are worthy of protection.[46] The other is that the interest-based approach, like the rights-based approach, tackles the problem from the wrong end; it does not answer the prior question of whether the defendant should come under a legal obligation in the first place, creating a chicken-and-egg situation. The mere fact that the claimant has an interest that is worthy of protection does not justify imposing a legal duty on the defendant to safeguard that interest.

The contextual approach, on the other hand, focuses on the connection between the defendant's negligent act and the claimant's injury. Thus, in the paradigm case of the road traffic accident, a driver owes a duty to a pedestrian despite the absence of a prior relationship because there is a clear connection between the driver's *negligent act* and the claimant's injury – in Deanne J's taxonomy, there is causal proximity. As Lord Jauncey of Tullichettle observed in his dissenting opinion in

[41] K Amirthalingam, 'The 'Sunrise Crane' – Shedding New Light or Casting Old Shadows on Duty of Care' [2004] *Singapore Journal of Legal Studies* 551, 552–54.

[42] *Sutherland Shire Council v Heyman* (1985) 157 CLR 424, 497–98.

[43] The relevant factors giving rise to a relational proximity included, amongst others, assumption of responsibility, reasonable reliance, close ties, control, and vulnerability.

[44] D Howarth, 'Many Duties of Care – Or a Duty of Care? Notes from the Underground' (2006) 26 *Oxford Journal of Legal Studies* 449, 464.

[45] J Plunkett, *The Duty of Care in Negligence* (Oxford/ Portland OR, Hart Publishing, 2018) 119.

[46] ibid 120.

Page v Smith,[47] 'In the normal personal injury case arising from a factory or road accident the foreseeability of such injury arising from the negligent act seldom requires to be addressed since it is self evident from the circumstances'.

The contextual approach is based on the defendant's act, holding the defendant liable only to those who are foreseeably affected *by the act* and who are sufficiently proximate *to the act*. The contextual approach is perfectly illustrated by the secondary victim psychiatric injury cases. These are cases where the claimant suffers a psychiatric injury as a result of witnessing a horrific event befalling a loved one, caused by the negligence of the defendant. The roots of the modern approach are found in *McLoughlin v O'Brian*,[48] in which a family was involved in a catastrophic motor vehicle accident. One child died and the remaining two children along with the father suffered serious injuries. The claimant was informed of the incident and rushed to hospital to the devasting sight of her husband and children in the aftermath of the accident. She failed in her claim against the negligent lorry driver at trial on reasonable foreseeability and on appeal for policy reasons. However, she succeeded in the House of Lords.

Lord Wilberforce noted that in previous cases, liability for psychiatric injury was found only when there was physical, circumstantial, and causal proximity.[49] These 'three proximities'[50] made the claimant a legal neighbour in the Atkinian sense. It bears highlighting that the foreseeability and proximity inquiries were linked explicitly to the incident and not to the defendant. Was it foreseeable that someone like the claimant who witnessed a horrific accident resulting in tragedy to close relatives could suffer psychiatric injury? The three proximity inquiries similarly were linked to the incident and not to the relationship between the claimant and defendant. The question was whether the claimant was physically present at the incident or its immediate aftermath; whether the claimant directly witnessed the shocking incident with unaided senses; and whether the claimant had a close relationship with the victims of the accident.

The relational duty operates within existing relationships and its scope may be defined by the nature of the relationship. Thus, it could require the defendant to take affirmative action, including to advise or to warn the claimant. The contextual duty is grounded in the defendant's act, holding the defendant liable to anyone who may foreseeably be affected by the defendant's act and who may fairly be treated as the defendant's neighbour in the context of the act. Distinguishing between relational and contextual approaches to the duty of care provides a conceptual framework for judges to develop the law of negligence in a coherent, incremental manner. Failure to distinguish between these two strands of the duty of care has compelled courts

[47] *Page v Smith* [1996] 1 AC 155, 171.

[48] The leading authority commonly referred to now is *Alcock v Chief Constable of South Yorkshire Police* [1992] 1 AC 310.

[49] *McLoughlin v O'Brian* [1983] AC 410, 420, 422. The House of Lords in *Alcock v Chief Constable of South Yorkshire Police* [1992] 1 AC 310 adopted these criteria as part of the proximity inquiry.

[50] The expression was coined a decade later by Amarjeet J in *Pang Koi Fa v Lim Djoe Phing* [1993] 3 SLR 317, 326.

either to fragment the duty of care so as to restrict or extend liability, or to adopt a holistic 'scope of duty' approach that includes consideration of duty, breach, and remoteness to control the extent of the defendant's liability in negligence.[51]

Serendipitously, the UK Supreme Court recently handed down a judgment on duty of care that validates the approach developed here, distinguishing between relational and contextual duties. *Tindall v Chief Constable of Thames Valley Police*[52] involved a motor vehicle accident caused by black ice. A vehicle skidded on the ice, swerved into oncoming traffic and collided with a vehicle driven by the claimant's husband who perished in the accident. The police had been alerted to the ice just prior to the accident when another accident occurred. Having arrived at the scene with the fire brigade and ambulance, the police placed a warning sign on the road, but after assisting the accident victim and arranging for the ice to be cleared, the police left, along with the other services, leaving the ice on the road with no warning sign. The accident giving rise to the claim occurred soon after.

The issue before the Supreme Court was whether the police owed a duty of care to road users. Following a review of leading authorities on the liability in negligence of public authorities, Lord Leggatt and Lord Burrows (with whom the rest of the Court agreed) held that there was no duty in this case. Lord Legatt and Lord Burrows relied on a distinction between making matters worse and failing to confer a benefit. A duty could arise in the former case but generally not in the latter. Acknowledging the elusive distinction between the two categories, some guidance was provided:

> Another way of stating the general rule is to say that a person owes a duty to take care not to expose others to unreasonable and reasonably foreseeable risks of physical harm created by that person's own conduct. By contrast, no duty of care is in general owed to protect others from risks of physical harm which arise independently of the defendant's conduct – whether from natural causes … or third parties … there are exceptions to the general rule that there is no duty of care to protect a person from harm, for example, where the defendant has assumed a responsibility to do so or has control of a third party.[53]

Lord Legatt and Lord Burrows went on to endorse the 'interference principle' proposed by McBride and Bagshaw in their book, *Tort Law*,[54] according to which a duty of care could arise when a defendant acted in such a way to interfere with any benefit that the claimant could have received from a third party or other event, provided the defendant knew or ought reasonably to have known that their act would have that effect.[55] Apart from the interference principle, three other exceptions to the no duty rule for omissions were considered: assumption of responsibility; control over the source of the danger; and the defendant's status. The court implicitly set a high bar to satisfy these requirements. To justify a duty

[51] See for example, *Khan v Meadows* [2021] UKSC 21; [2022] AC 852.

[52] *Tindall v Chief Constable of Thames Valley Police* [2024] UKSC 33; [2025] AC 1046.

[53] ibid [44].

[54] NJ McBride and R Bagshaw, *Tort Law* (London, Pearson, 6th edn, 2018 and 7th edn, 2024).

[55] ibid [58]. The claim failed because the police did not have the requisite knowledge.

on the basis of an assumption of responsibility, the defendant must have, by words or conduct, communicated to the claimant that the defendant would take care of the claimant. To ground a duty on the basis of control, it must be shown that the defendant exercised actual control and not merely had the right to control.

The question of whether status alone may justify a duty of care was left open by the Court, although Lord Legatt and Lord Burrows noted that it should not be an adequate basis for a duty of care if none of the other principles support a duty. *Tindall* is an example of a contextual duty situation where no affirmative duty arises unless strict conditions are met. This may be contrasted with *Darnley v Croydon Health Services NHS Trust*,[56] in which the claimant who had gone to the emergency department with a head injury was negligently informed by the nurse that the waiting time would be several hours. Discouraged by that information, the claimant went home and suffered an adverse medical event, ultimately sustaining permanent brain damage. Had the claimant been informed correctly that the waiting time was only 30 minutes, he would have stayed at the emergency department and would likely have avoided harm. In this case, there was clearly a relationship between the claimant and the defendant.

By contrast, in *ABC v St George's Healthcare NHS Trust*,[57] the High Court found that the doctor owed a duty to the daughter of a patient to warn her that her father suffered from a hereditary genetic condition, which could be passed to her child were she to have children. Arguably, this case was wrongly decided. Although the claimant accompanied her father and interacted with the defendant, she herself was not in a relationship with the defendant. The defendant had not made matters worse, voluntarily assumed responsibility, or exercised control over the claimant. The only basis for a duty of care appeared to be the status of the defendant as a doctor, as someone who had the power to protect the claimant. The defendant is in a comparable position to the police in *Tindall* and should not have been held to owe a duty of care. *ABC*, like *Tindall*, involved a contextual duty.

IV. The Fragmentation of the Duty of Care and the Scope of Duty

A doctor's duty to the patient has been framed in different ways – the duty to treat, diagnose, care, warn, advise, inform, refer,[58] monitor,[59] and to follow-up.[60] Although this framing is convenient in practice, it is strictly incorrect – the law

[56] *Darnley v Croydon Health Services NHS Trust* [2018] UKSC 50; [2019] AC 831.

[57] [2020] EWHC 455 (QB).

[58] *Wright v Cambridge Medical Group* [2011] EWCA Civ 669; [2011] Med LR 496.

[59] *Surender Singh s/o Jagdish Singh v Li Man Kay* [2009] SGHC 168; [2010] 1 SLR 428. In this case, a patient died of internal hemorrhaging after surgery, allegedly due to the negligent failure of a nurse to monitor the patient.

[60] See *Ziaee v Rubino* [2023] ACTCA 7. The trial judge had found liability for failure to follow-up on a referral, but this was overturned by the Court of Appeal.

imposes a duty to take care when engaging in risk-creating activity. The crucial question is whether a duty exists – the extent and scope of the duty are posterior questions. The content of the duty is a related but separate question which depends on the circumstances: thus, a failure to warn, advise, or diagnose may demonstrate that the defendant has breached the duty of care, but this question should arise only after it is determined that a duty exists.[61] The duty in *Donoghue* was not a duty to inspect the bottles, to remove contaminants, or to warn consumers. It was a duty to take care not to harm consumers (the class of people who could foreseeably be affected by the defendant's act) in the manufacture and bottling of ginger beer; that duty could be breached by failing to inspect, or to clean, or to warn.

John Fleming long ago warned against such fragmentation:

> The general standard of conduct required by law is a necessary complement of the legal concept of 'duty'. There is not only the question 'Did the defendant owe a duty to be careful?' but also 'What precisely was required of him to discharge it?' Indeed, it is not uncommon to encounter formulations of the standard of care in terms of 'duty', as when it is asserted that a motorist is under a duty to keep a proper lookout or give a turn signal. But this method of expression is best avoided. In the first place, the duty issue is already sufficiently complex without fragmenting it further to cover an endless series of details of conduct. 'Duty' is more appropriately reserved for the problem of whether the relation between the parties (like manufacturer and consumer or occupier and trespasser) warrants the imposition upon one of an obligation of care for the benefit of the other, and it is more convenient to deal with individual conduct in terms of the legal standard of what is required to meet that obligation. Secondly, it is apt to obscure the division of functions between judge and jury. It is for the court to determine the existence of a duty relationship and to lay down in general terms the standard of care by which to measure the defendant's conduct; it is for the jury to translate the general into a particular standard suitable for the case in hand and to decide whether that standard has been attained.[62]

The fragmentation of the doctor's duty is well illustrated in the opinion of Lord Scarman in *Sidaway v Board of Governors of the Bethlem Royal Hospital*.[63] *Sidaway* was a House of Lords decision on the duty to inform, in which the House of Lords by a majority affirmed that the *Bolam* test for medical negligence applied to the duty to inform. Lord Diplock emphasised that the doctor's duty was a single, comprehensive one with a universal standard.[64] Lord Scarman dissented, holding that patients had a right to make informed decisions and that doctors should not control what information to provide. Lord Scarman was compelled to argue for a separate duty to advise because he accepted that the duty of care was a matter of

[61] In practice, these aspects may be impossible to separate, and a holistic approach may be necessary, but in theory the existence of a duty must precede an inquiry into its scope.

[62] JG Fleming, *The Law of Torts* (Sydney, LBC Information Services, 9th edn, 1998) 117–18.

[63] *Sidaway v Board of Governors of the Bethlem Royal Hospital and Maudsley Hospital* [1985] AC 871.

[64] ibid 893.

law, and that the standard of care was determined by *Bolam*. However, by creating a distinct duty to advise, Lord Scarman was able to avoid applying *Bolam*.[65]

Paradoxically, this fragmentation of the duty of care goes against the intellectual reasoning of Lord Atkin in *Donoghue*, who sought to unify isolated instances of duties. While the leading authorities differed slightly on how to express the duty of care test,[66] they all coalesced around a common concept of the tort of negligence based on general principles.[67] Thus, while the fragmented approach to the tort of negligence has been put to bed, the fragmented approach to the duty of care appears to have survived. Arguably, this is because the duty of care is a matter of law over which judges have control: fragmentation gives judges the ability to extend or restrict liability depending on the circumstances, as demonstrated by Lord Scarman in *Sidaway*.[68]

There are three ways to describe the doctor's duty of care: (i) a single, comprehensive duty with a universal test for the standard of care;[69] (ii) different sub-duties with different legal tests for the standard of care;[70] a single, comprehensive duty with a particularised approach to the standard of care.[71] Phang JA expressed a preference for the third approach in an economic loss case in the Singapore Court of Appeal:

> A duty of care in the tort of negligence … is in general imposed by law upon the tortfeasor, and as a result it is necessarily a broad duty to take such care as is reasonable in the circumstances. Hence, it is not, strictly speaking, correct to speak of a 'tortious duty to advise' without more and, in particular, without reference to any related contractual obligation … If there could be a 'tortious duty to advise', there would be no logical limit to how far a duty of care in the tort of negligence could be subdivided: the courts would be flooded with claims of specific 'tortious duties' to answer telephone calls, respond to e-mails, read the newspapers or the like … Of course, it could well be a breach of a tortious duty of care (if one was owed) for someone not to give advice in certain circumstances, but that is not the same as saying that there was a tortious duty to give advice.[72]

[65] ibid 885.

[66] *Anns v Merton London Borough Council* [1978] AC 728; *Caparo Industries Plc v Dickman* [1990] 2 AC 605; *Customs and Excise Commissioners v Barclays Bank plc* [2006] UKHL 28; [2007] AC 181.

[67] Most notably, the fragmented approach to occupiers' liability with different duties for different categories of entrants has been rejected in the major common law jurisdictions: *Herrington v British Railways Board* [1972] AC 877; *Australian Safeway Stores Pty Ltd v Zaluzna* (1987) 162 CLR 479; see *Toh Siew Kee v Ho Ah Lam Ferrocement (Pte) Ltd* [2013] SGCA 29; [2013] 3 SLR 284.

[68] Fragmenting the duty is also a strategy adopted by some academics to justify departing from conventional principles governing standard of care, causation, and actionable damage. See S Fulham-McQuillam, 'Infringement of Autonomy as Damage in Medical Negligence' (2023) 139 *Law Quarterly Review* 126, discussed in Chapter 8 of this volume, text to nn 119–132.

[69] *Sidaway v Board of Governors of the Bethlem Royal Hospital* [1985] AC 871 (per Lord Diplock), 893.

[70] ibid (per Lord Scarman) 885.

[71] *Go Dante Yap v Bank Austria Creditanstalt AG* [2011] SGCA 39; [2011] 4 SLR 559 (per Andrew Phang JA), [19] (NB: *Go Dante* was an economic loss case involving a claim by an investor against a financial institution).

[72] *Go Dante Yap v Bank Austria Creditanstalt AG* [2011] SGCA 39; [2011] 4 SLR 559, [19].

This statement is true for the relational duty but not necessarily so for the contextual duty. Where the duty is relational it can fairly be said that there is a general duty to take care not to harm the claimant as a result of the defendant's conduct. However, when the duty is contextual, it may be necessary to specify the nature of the duty. Thus, a doctor has a duty to take care not to harm a patient whether through treatment, care, diagnosis, advice, information, or warning of risk. The doctor has assumed responsibility to the patient and the patient has relied on the doctor. However, when it comes to the doctor's duty to third parties with whom there is no relationship, it is impossible to speak of a general duty to take care. The duty itself must be particularised because there is no underlying relationship to define the scope of the duty.

Yet, this is overlooked in many cases where doctors have been held to owe duties to third parties. Examples include a duty of care to third parties who are attacked by mentally ill patients negligently certified for release by psychiatrists;[73] to third parties whom the psychiatrist fails to warn of an imminent threat by a patient;[74] to intimate partners of a patient with a sexually transmissible disease;[75] and to relatives of a patient suffering from a hereditary genetic condition.[76] In each of these examples, the duty imposed on a doctor is an affirmative one – the doctor is being held liable for a pure omission despite the absence of a relationship between doctor and claimant. These are contextual duties which may be recognised only if there is a sufficiently close connection between the doctor's act and the claimant's injury.

The first two examples, involving psychiatric patients, may be distinguished from the next two. In the psychiatric cases, the doctor has some control over the patient who does not have self-control and is a known risk to others.[77] In the latter two examples, the patient has control and agency; the doctor should not be held liable for the patient's free choices. There should be no affirmative duties to a third party in the absence of a relationship unless there are exceptional circumstance, including, for example, voluntary assumption of responsibility toward such third party by the defendant.[78] The point is reaffirmed in *Barclays Bank*.[79] The relational approach permits affirmative duties as it is based on a relationship. As shown above, liability in relational duty cases is often based on omission, or as White

[73] *Palmer v Tees Health Authority* [1999] Lloyd's Rep Med 351; [2000] PNLR 87; *Selwood v Durham County Council* [2012] EWCA Civ 979; [2012] PIQR P20.

[74] *Tarasoff v Regents of the University of California* 17 Cal 3d 425 (1976).

[75] *Spillane v Wasserman* (1992) 13 CCLT (2d) 267 (Ontario HC).

[76] *ABC v St George's Healthcare NHS Trust* [2020] EWHC 455 (QB).

[77] *Home Office v Dorset Yacht Co Ltd* [1970] UKHL 2, [1970] AC 1004 is authority for the proposition that a defendant in control of individuals who are known risks may be liable to third parties for harm caused by those individuals.

[78] For a similar argument, see J Plunkett, *The Duty of Care in Negligence* (Oxford/ Portland OR, Hart Publishing, 2018) 139–44.

[79] *Customs and Excise Commissioners v Barclays Bank plc* [2006] UKHL 28; [2007] 1 AC 181 (per Lord Hoffmann) [38]–[39].

explained, on neglect.[80] An affirmative duty is compatible with the human obligations approach set out in Chapter two and is appropriate within the confines of a doctor–patient relationship.

The New South Wales case of *Woods v Lowns*,[81] in which a doctor was found to owe a duty of care to a child who suffered an epileptic seizure on a street 300m away from the doctor's clinic, is illustrative. The claimant's sister had run to the defendant's clinic seeking help. The trial judge referred to the doctor's professional duty in finding a common law duty, noting that section 27(l)(h) of the Medical Practitioners Act 1938 (NSW) was a 'very clear statement of public policy in respect of the obligation of a medical practitioner in relation to a person in need of urgent treatment'.[82] The judgment was upheld by a majority of the NSW Court of Appeal in *Lowns v Woods*,[83] albeit with a strong dissent by Mahoney JA, who reasoned, inter alia, that the defendant had no prior relationship with the claimant and had done nothing to bring himself into a relationship with the claimant; had the claimant's sister run to a different clinic, the defendant would not even have been in the picture. Mahoney JA's dissent is to be preferred.

Alternatively, instead of fragmenting the duty of care, courts sometimes amalgamate the duty, breach, and remoteness questions into an omnibus scope of duty question.[84] This also gives courts significant flexibility to extend or restrict the scope of the duty of care in any given circumstance. The danger with this approach is that it is too flexible, allowing courts to make decisions on liability based on policy considerations to 'identify the fair allocation of risk between the parties',[85] which is a question that involves evaluation of duty, breach, causation, and remoteness in one go.[86] Again, the distinction between relational duty and contextual duty is critical: the scope of the relational duty is based on the nature of the relationship and the scope of the contextual duty is based on the nature of the defendant's conduct. Any inquiry into fair allocation of risk must consider the basis of the duty.

The UK Supreme Court had occasion to examine the scope of duty question in detail in a landmark medical negligence case, *Khan v Meadows*.[87] The claimant in *Khan* was a woman who had sought medical advice on whether she carried the haemophilia gene. This knowledge was important as she planned to start a family and did not want to pass the gene to her children. The defendant negligently had the claimant tested for haemophilia without ordering genetic testing to determine

[80] See above text to n 7.

[81] *Woods v Lowns* (1995) 36 NSWLR 344.

[82] ibid 358.

[83] *Lowns v Woods* (1996) Aust Torts Rep 81-376.

[84] *Khan v Meadows* [2021] UKSC 21; [2022] AC 852; *Manchester Building Society v Grant Thornton UK LLP* [2021] UKSC 20; [2022] AC 783; *South Australia Asset Management Corp v York Montague Ltd* [1996] UKHL 10; [1997] AC 191.

[85] *Khan v Meadows* [2021] UKSC 21; [2022] AC 852, [53].

[86] This holistic approach has been championed by Lord Denning: *Roe v Ministry of Health* [1954] 2 QB 66, 85.

[87] [2021] UKSC 21; [2022] AC 852.

whether the claimant asymptomatically *carried the gene* even if she herself was not a haemophiliac. The claimant alleged that if she had known that she was carrying the haemophilia gene she would have undergone foetal testing to determine whether her child would be affected by haemophilia. She would have terminated the pregnancy if the test result had been positive.

The claimant had a child some years later who was diagnosed with haemophilia and autism. She sued the defendant, seeking damages for the additional costs of raising a child with haemophilia and autism. While the law did not permit recovery of the upkeep costs of a healthy child born due to medical negligence in sterilisation procedures or advice,[88] it allowed claims for additional costs for a disabled child.[89] Yip J in the High Court allowed the claim for both haemophilia- and autism-related costs. On appeal, the Court of Appeal disallowed the autism-related costs, allowing the haemophilia-related costs only.[90] The Supreme Court upheld the Court of Appeal's decision.

Lord Hodge and Lord Sales, with whom Lord Reed, Lady Black, and Lord Kitchin agreed, delivered the leading opinion. While there was no dispute that the defendant owed the claimant a duty of care and had been negligent, the issue was whether the defendant's liability extended to autism related losses. The judges focused on the 'scope of duty' approach applied in *Banque Bruxelles Lambert SA v Eagle Star Insurance Co Ltd; South Australia Asset Management Corp v York Montague Ltd*[91] (*SAAMCO*). *SAAMCO* involved negligent advice resulting in economic loss, but Lord Reed and Lord Sales held that the scope of duty principle had general application and was not limited to economic loss cases.

Their Lordships quoted Lord Denning's comments in *Roe v Ministry of Health*:[92]

> It seems to me that they are simply three different ways of looking at one and the same problem. Starting with the proposition that a negligent person should be liable, within reason, for the consequences of his conduct, the extent of his liability is to be found by asking the one question: is the consequence fairly to be regarded as within the risk created by the negligence? If so, the negligent person is liable for it: but otherwise not.

While *Roe* was a medical negligence case involving a negligent act causing personal injury, virtually all the cases referred to by Lord Hodge and Lord Sales involved liability for psychiatric injury, pure economic loss, and omissions. As observed by Lord Burrows,[93] these are the areas where the duty of care has real work to do in controlling the extent of liability. Thus, the scope of duty is crucial. Indeed, *Khan*

[88] *Mc Farlane v Tayside Health Board* [1999] UKHL 50; [2000] 2 AC 59. For Australia, see *Cattanach v Melchior* [2003] HCA 38; (2003) 215 CLR 1 and relevant civil liability legislation in the States and Territories. In Singapore, see *ACB v Thomson Medical Pte Ltd* [2017] SGCA 20; [2017] 1 SLR 918.

[89] *Parkinson v St James and Seacroft University Hospital NHS Trust* [2001] EWCA Civ 530; [2002] QB 266; *Groom v Selby* [2001] EWCA Civ 1522; [2002] Lloyd's Rep Med 1.

[90] *Khan v Meadows* [2017] EWHC 2990 (QB); *Khan v Meadows* [2019] EWCA Civ 152.

[91] *Banque Bruxelles Lambert SA v Eagle Star Insurance Co Ltd; South Australia Asset Management Corp v York Montague Ltd* [1996] UKHL 10; [1997] AC 191.

[92] *Roe v Ministry of Health* [1954] 2 QB 66, 85.

[93] *Khan v Meadows* [2021] UKSC 21; [2022] AC 852, [80].

itself, although arising in the context of clinical negligence, involved negligent advice causing pure economic loss. However, Lord Hodge and Lord Sales extended the scope of duty approach to all cases of clinical negligence,[94] giving courts more control over clinical negligence.

Lord Burrows adopted a more restrained approach, restricting the scope of duty rule to clinical advice and applying the *SAAMCO* rule to the narrower question of what damage the defendant ought to be liable for. Lord Legatt agreed with Lord Burrows in restricting the scope of duty approach to negligent advice. As he put it:

> In particular, these appeals are concerned solely with the liability of professional persons for giving negligent advice. Ascertaining the scope of the defendant's duty in such cases depends on identifying the matters relevant to a decision to be taken by the claimant which the defendant has undertaken responsibility for assessing and advising the claimant about. The extent of those matters may be defined by express agreement or, in the absence of such an agreement, is implied from the role of a doctor or other professional person … Whether or to what extent analogous considerations apply in other contexts, such as careless driving or the negligent performance of a surgical operation to take two examples mentioned in para 47 of the judgment of Lord Hodge and Lord Sales, is not a question which arises for decision.[95]

The judgment of Lord Hodge and Lord Sales may have far-reaching implications for the scope of the doctor's duty to advise and the precedents of *Montgomery* and *Chester*. Following *Khan*, doctors may legitimately limit the scope of their duty to advise patients by explicitly setting the boundaries.[96] As Lord Legatt stated, 'The extent of those matters may be defined by express agreement or, in the absence of such an agreement, is implied from the role of a doctor or other professional person.'[97]

V. Duty to Advise – From Autonomy to Agency

It was argued in Chapter four of this volume that patient autonomy did not properly belong to the tort of negligence. Instead of patient autonomy, courts should focus on patient agency and shared decision-making. The infiltration of patient autonomy in negligence claims was a reaction to the paternalistic model of medical practice. However, basing clinical negligence standards on patient autonomy does not provide the salve it promises. It ignores the reality that patients are vulnerable and, paradoxically, it undermines respect for patients by failing to hold them accountable for their own decisions.

[94] ibid [62].
[95] ibid [96].
[96] This would be subject to the Unfair Contract Terms Act 1977.
[97] *Khan v Meadows* [2021] UKSC 21; [2022] AC 852, [96].

The premise of the patient autonomy argument in clinical negligence cases was that it empowered patients to make decisions for themselves. However, not all patients want empowerment; what they want is respect and involvement in the decision-making process.[98] The duty to inform, instead of protecting patient autonomy, should be aimed at protecting patient agency. It should enable patients to engage in dialogue with their doctors and participate in shared decision-making. Its primary aim should be to remedy patient vulnerability through information to equalise the doctor–patient relationship; to give them the 'resilience' that they need, to use Martha Fineman's words.[99]

Empirical research on what patients want in the doctor–patient relationship showed that patients wanted doctors to listen to them and understand their perspective of their health problems; they wanted doctors to give them information about their health and treatment options; they want to be involved in the decision-making process. However, the patients had different thresholds of involvement in the decision-making process, with some preferring the doctor to make the decision on their behalf.[100] Interestingly, the findings suggested that patients who had sought a second opinion were more likely to trust the doctor to make a decision, contrary to 'the notion of the informed consumer who "shops around" and demands information and choice'.[101]

A. Shared Decision-making

Decision-making in clinical cases is complex. Before even examining the various models that exist, it is important to acknowledge that decision-making takes place in a variety of contexts. It may involve end-of-life decisions, lifesaving decisions, emergencies, consent to surgery or treatment, managing long-term, chronic conditions, and decisions about medication. The prototypical duty to advise cases, represented in the landmark decisions, tend to involve information about risks of surgery and alternative treatments.[102] These cases wrongly focus on consent and patient autonomy. Consent is relevant to trespass, both in the context of clinical care and medical research. However, it is well established in the context of defending a claim of battery that to obtain consent doctors only need to provide patients with information about the broad nature of the procedure and not details about the risks.[103]

[98] See S Vick and A Scott, 'Agency in Health Care. Examining Patients' Preferences for Attributes of the Doctor-Patient Relationship' (1998) 17 *Journal of Health Economics* 587.

[99] See Chapter 3 of this volume, text to nn 119–120.

[100] S Vick and A Scott, 'Agency in Health Care. Examining Patients' Preferences for Attributes of the Doctor-Patient Relationship' (1998) 17 *Journal of Health Economics* 587, 599.

[101] ibid.

[102] *Montgomery v Lanarkshire Health Board* [2015] UKSC 11; [2015] AC 1430; *Hii Chii Kok v Ong Peng Jin London Lucien* [2017] SGCA 38; [2017] 2 SLR 492; *Rogers v Whitaker* (1992) 175 CLR 479.

[103] *Chatterton v Gerson* [1981] 1 QB 432.

Chapter four undertook a critical analysis of patient autonomy, its history, its nature, and its role in medical law and ethics, arguing that a liberal concept of patient autonomy was incompatible with clinical negligence. McCullough and Wear reinforce the argument in a compelling article published in 1985,[104] expressly stating that 'the principle of respect for autonomy … may have been transplanted from the research into the therapeutic context without realizing that they are morally nonanalogous'.[105] Medical research aims not just to benefit the patient but more importantly to benefit future patients. The interests of the patient being experimented on and the interests of future patients may not align. Thus, it is important for the patient to have the absolute right to refuse consent and prevent interference with their body for medical research. The therapeutic context is different as, unlike the future patient whose interest may conflict with the patient, the doctor is acting solely in the best interest of the patient.

Applying an absolute approach to patient autonomy based on liberal concepts of non-interference in fact undermines the relationship of trust between doctor and patient as well as the ethical premise that doctors do no harm to the patient. Liberal conceptions of patient autonomy transform the doctor–patient relationship from one of trust to mistrust, from partnership to confrontation. The role of patient autonomy in clinical negligence is not to protect the patient from non-interference. 'Instead, respect for autonomy provides another and sometimes competing perspective on the patient's best interests, namely the patient's own perspective'.[106] Consent and the duty to inform 'should be viewed as relational, and as an on-going collaborative decision-making process between the HCP and patient. This process should be based on trustworthiness, openness and honesty'.[107]

McCullough and Wear demonstrate how a liberal conception of patient autonomy may be both under-inclusive and over-inclusive by distinguishing between acute and chronic cases.[108] Acute cases typically do not involve weighty considerations of moral values or lifestyle choices. They are often medical issues that have medical solutions which the medical professional is qualified to assess and recommend. In such cases, the doctor is obliged to provide the patient with adequate information to understand the condition, the proposed treatment and reasonable alternatives, as well as the attendant benefits and risks. Chronic cases are more complex, involving a choice of treatment (or non-treatment, ie living with the condition). It involves choice of aggressive or light treatment, adjustment of

[104] LB McCullough and S Wear, 'Respect for Autonomy and Medical Paternalism Reconsidered' (1985) 6 *Theoretical Medicine* 295.

[105] ibid 298.

[106] ibid 299.

[107] GN Samuel et al, 'Healthcare Professionals' and Patients' Perspectives on Consent to Clinical Genetic Testing: Moving Towards a More Relational Approach' (2017) 18 *British Medical Council Medical Ethics*, Article 47, p 2.

[108] LB McCullough and S Wear, 'Respect for Autonomy and Medical Paternalism Reconsidered' (1985) 6 *Theoretical Medicine* 295, 304–5.

lifestyle, and choices surrounding medication, care, and therapy. McCullough and Wear express it eloquently:

> The new ethos of respect for freedom from interference and anti-paternalism thus requires too much in acute care (all possible alternative treatment modalities must be discussed) and too little in chronic care (only alternatives must be discussed, as if they were all that mattered), with a simple-minded form or medical paternalism always at stake. Once the clinically-based distinction between acute and chronic care is re-interpreted in ethical terms, respect for autonomy and medical paternalism are freed from the distortions of the theory-driven accounts of the new ethos of medical ethics. Respect for autonomy – identifying and implementing the patient's perspective on his or her best interests – is a far richer and more nuanced ethical principle than simple freedom from interference.[109]

To use a traffic light analogy, trespass and consent involve a binary choice – red light or green light. The patient either refuses consent or provides consent. For clinical negligence, all three lights are engaged – the patient may accept some treatment (green light), reject others (red light) or proceed conditionally, constantly making judgements about the next step (amber light). The amber zone is where much of the doctor–patient relationship in ongoing clinical care resides; this is where trust and shared decision-making are crucial. There are various models of decision-making for care and treatment, including the paternalistic model, the informed decision-making model, the professional-as-agent model, and the shared decision-making model.[110]

The paternalistic model is one in which the doctor is the expert acting in the best interests of the patient, who is dependent and compliant. The doctor decides what is best for the patient and, in so far as information is given to the patient, it is given to convince the patient that the doctor's decision is best. The patient's role is passive and limited to consenting to the doctor's recommendation.[111] The informed decision-making model is in some ways the mirror image of the paternalistic model. Here, the patient drives the decision-making and has the final say. The doctor's responsibility is reduced to providing the patient with relevant information to make the decision. This model ignores the reality that many patients are vulnerable. Studies show that patients often do not remember what they have been told.[112]

The professional-as-agent model sits somewhere between the paternalistic model and the informed patient model. This model differs from the informed patient model in that it is the doctor who ultimately makes the decision.[113]

[109] ibid 307.

[110] C Charles, A Gafni and T Whelan, 'Shared Decision-making in the Medical Encounter: What Does it Mean? (Or It Takes at Least Two to Tango)' (1997) 44 *Social Science & Medicine* 681, 682.

[111] EJ Emanuel and LL Emanuel, 'Four Models of the Physician-Patient Relationship (1992) 267 *Journal of the American Medical Association* 2221, 2221.

[112] GN Samuel et al, 'Healthcare Professionals' and Patients' Perspectives on Consent to Clinical Genetic Testing: Moving Towards a More Relational Approach' (2017) 17 *British Medical Council Medical Ethics*, Article 47, p 6.

[113] RG Evans, *Strained Mercy: The Economics of Canadian Healthcare* (Toronto, Butterworths, 1984) 75.

However, it differs from the paternalistic model because the doctor here is not acting in what the doctor believes to be in the best interests of the patient. Instead, the doctor is trying to divine what the patient would have wanted to do had the patient been as well informed as the doctor on the treatment options and risks. This aligns with the maternalistic model discussed in Chapter three.[114] What is of note is that in all these models the decision is made either by the doctor or by the patient. In none of these models is there genuine shared decision-making.

Charles, Gafni, and Whelan described some key characteristics of shared decision-making,[115] which include the following. Shared decision-making must involve at least the patient and the doctor, but in some cases, it may include other doctors or healthcare professionals involved in the patient's care as well as the patient's family or carers. Both doctor and patient must take steps to participate. This does not necessarily involve full participation, and it may even include the patient devolving to the doctor the responsibility for making the decision, but it requires the patient to have been involved in the process. There must be meaningful information sharing by both doctor and patient. The patients might not use the information to contribute to the decision and may choose to outsource the decision to the doctor, but by participating and being fully informed, patients retain their agency by endorsing the decision. Finally, a treatment decision must be made with the agreement of both parties. This is the crux of shared decision-making as succinctly put by Charles, Gafni, and Whelan:

> Shared decision-making is usually depicted, either implicitly or explicitly as a type of decision-making process. But shared decision-making can also refer to an outcome, i.e. a shared or agreed upon decision … The test of a shared decision (as distinct from the decision-making process) is if both parties agree on the treatment option. This does not mean that both parties are necessarily convinced that this is the best possible treatment for this patient, but rather that both endorse it as the treatment to implement.[116]

The shared decision-making model respects the patient as a person with agency, and it ensures that both doctor and patient agree to the treatment option. This has significant repercussions for the duty to advise and potential liability in the tort of negligence. The shared decision-making model places responsibility on patients to share with their doctor relevant information that may affect their decision for personal, idiosyncratic reasons even if such information would not be material to the reasonable person. This impacts the so-called subjective limb of the *Montgomery* test, reproduced below for convenience:

> The doctor is therefore under a duty to take reasonable care to ensure that the patient is aware of any material risks involved in any recommended treatment, and of any reasonable alternative or variant treatments. The test of materiality is whether, in the circumstances of the particular case, a reasonable person in the patient's position would

[114] See Chapter 3 of this volume, text to nn 126–143.
[115] C Charles, A Gafni and T Whelan, 'Shared Decision-making in the Medical Encounter: What Does it Mean? (Or It Takes at Least Two to Tango)' (1997) 44 *Social Science & Medicine* 681, 685–88.
[116] ibid 688.

> be likely to attach significance to the risk, or the doctor is or should reasonably be aware that the particular patient would be likely to attach significance to it.[117]

The subjective limb cuts both ways. Under the subjective limb, even if the risk would not be material to a reasonable patient, a doctor must disclose a risk if it is material to the particular patient if the doctor knew or ought to have known that the patient would attach significance to it. The classic example is the professional pianist consenting to surgery for trigger finger who is not informed of a very small risk that the finger may occasionally become stiff and interfere with piano playing. This risk could be material to the pianist and under *Montgomery* should be disclosed if the doctor knew or ought to have known that it was material.

However, under the shared decision-making model the risk would have to be disclosed only if the doctor actually knew it was material to the patient; otherwise, the responsibility would be on the patient to alert the doctor to his or her particular concern. The subjective limb of *Montgomery* should be restricted to idiosyncratic *risks* known or knowable to a medical professional and should not extend to idiosyncratic *patients*. The doctor should not be under a duty to make inquiries about a patient's personal idiosyncrasies.[118]

Equally significantly, the shared decision-making model would undermine *Chester*. In this case, the claimant was not informed of a one per cent risk of an adverse outcome inherent in the proposed treatment (spinal surgery). She underwent the procedure and suffered injury. Nonetheless, she testified that even if she had been advised of the risk, she would have gone ahead with the same procedure and with the same surgeon, albeit on a different day as she would have taken more time to think about it. The House of Lords held that because she would not have had surgery on the day the risk manifested, she would not have been paralysed; thus, causation was established. This decision was ostensibly to vindicate patient autonomy. However, if the patient herself says she would go ahead and take the risk, her agency should be respected.

Under the shared decision-making model, if the patient would have consented to the risk if informed of it, she should be responsible for her decision. The doctor's duty to inform the patient of risks and options cannot exist merely to vindicate patient autonomy. The dialogic process of giving information and obtaining the patient's consent and cooperation involves reciprocity, which autonomy-driven arguments marginalise. As Draper and Sorrell argued, 'Medical Ethics is one-sided. It dwells on the ethical obligations of doctors to the exclusion of those of patients'.[119] The scope of the duty to inform should be to enable the patient to have adequate information to exercise agency in the shared decision-making process.

[117] *Montgomery v Lanarkshire Health Board* [2015] UKSC 11; [2015] AC 1430, [87].

[118] cf, the Civil Law Act 1909 (Singapore) s 37(3)(b), which imposes an affirmative duty on doctors to peruse patients' records to discover what risks could be material to the particular patient despite the patient not alerting the doctor to any particular concern.

[119] H Draper and T Sorrell, 'Patients' Responsibilities in Medical Ethics' (2002) 16 *Bioethics* 335, 335.

B. Patient Agency

Until the second half of the twentieth century, the prevailing view in healthcare was that patients were passive actors.[120] Talcott Parsons, in his influential work on social systems, drew on medical practice as a microcosm of a social system to demonstrate how individual actions could be explained by systemic theory.[121] He postulated three aspects that operated to structure systems of social action: a social system, the personality of the actors, and the cultural context in which the actors and system operate.[122] In Parsons' evaluation in the 1950s, patients were helpless and technically incompetent. The state of being sick was also viewed as detrimental to society and therefore the sick were obliged to get better. Doctors were individuals who were technically competent, had professional status, and were responsible for helping the patient.[123] This was a construction of a social system where patients were not only vulnerable but incompetent to make independent and rational decisions, relying on doctors to act in their best interest.[124]

Change came about gradually through public healthcare innovations with the realisation that patients had to take responsibility for chronic conditions and therefore needed to be empowered. This required healthcare professionals to engage with patients, educate them, and understand the patients' own perceptions of their health.[125] In the mid-1970s, a study found that patients exercised their own judgement when it came to medical prescriptions, sometime deliberately ignoring medical advice.[126] Thus began the era of patient non-compliance, or in the 1990s non-adherence,[127] and more recently resistance,[128] as a mean of exercising agency and shared decision-making.

Returning to the traffic light analogy above, with the doctor–patient relationship in the amber zone, studies have shown that patients exercise agency by selective resistance, constantly adjusting to changing circumstances and information.[129] Thus, a patient might initially refuse recommended treatment but then accede to a modified regime or accept the original recommendation after being provided with additional information by the doctor. Patients' resistance allows for more

[120] D Armstrong, 'Actors, Patients and Agency: A Recent History' (2014) 36 *Sociology of Health & Illness* 163.

[121] T Parsons, *The Social System* (Glencoe IL, Free Press, 1951).

[122] ibid 3.

[123] ibid at 295.

[124] D Armstrong, 'Actors, Patients and Agency: A Recent History' (2014) 36 *Sociology of Health & Illness* 163, 163–64.

[125] GM Hochbaum, *Public Participation in Medical Screening Programs: A Socio-Psychological Study* (Washington DC, Public Health Services Publication, 1958) 15–17.

[126] DE Hayes-Bautista, 'Modifying the Treatment: Patient Compliance, Patient Control and Medical Care' (1976) 10 *Social Science & Medicine* 233.

[127] Royal Pharmaceutical Society of Great Britain, *From Compliance to Concordance: Towards Shared Goals in Medicine Taking* (London, RPS, 1997).

[128] CJ Koenig, 'Patient Resistance as Agency in Treatment Decisions' (2011) 72 *Social Science & Medicine* 1103.

[129] M Emirbayer and A Mische, 'What is Agency?' (1998) 103 *The American Journal of Sociology* 962.

dialogue and communication between doctor and patient, enabling the patient to exercise agency.[130] It is important to understand patient resistance as an exercise of patient agency and not view the resisting patient as 'resistant problem patients'.[131] A change in healthcare culture is essential, as discussed below.

At first blush, there may not appear to be a significant difference between patient autonomy and patient agency, but there is an important distinction. Autonomy is a negative concept, empowering the patient to protect their bodily integrity by withholding consent. Agency is a positive concept that both empowers the patient and holds the patient responsible for their decisions. As Armstrong put it, 'to engage with this new world of hazard requires patients to take increasing responsibility for health-related decisions; in short, to exercise agency: that is the attribute which separates the passive patient from 1958 from the active one today'.[132] The active patient is involved in shared decision-making.

The European haemophilia consortium (EHC) Think Tank Workstream on Patient Agency identified five criteria that were relevant to patient agency: shared decision-making; patient empowerment; spectrum of engagement; cultural change; and health literacy.[133] Shared decision-making is only possible if patients have agency. It involves dialogue between doctor and patient through which, collaboratively, they arrive at a decision that is based on clinical considerations as well as the patient's preferences. It is important to recognise, especially in cases of chronic illnesses, that patients or their family members may be more knowledgeable than the doctor about their specific condition.[134] This is more so in today's information world where detailed information is easily available online.

However, and this relates to the fifth point on health literacy, just because patients have access to information does not necessarily mean that they understand that information. Doctors have a responsibility not only to advise patients of their diagnosis, treatment options, and material risks, but also to help patients digest information that they obtain from other sources. It is critical that the doctor–patient dialogue is comprehensive. Ultimately, all parties must acknowledge that decisions may not always be correct due to uncertainty of information and compromise between clinical judgement and patient preference.[135]

Patient empowerment does not mean leaving the patient to make decisions on their own, as patients are inherently vulnerable and often lack the necessary technical knowledge. To enable a patient to exercise agency, the doctor must help

[130] BA Costello and F Roberts 'Medical Recommendation as Joint Social Practice' (2001) 13 *Health Communication* 241.

[131] J Hunter, M Franken and D Balmer, 'Constructions of Patient Agency in Healthcare Settings: Textual and Patient Perspectives' (2015) 7 *Discourse, Consent & Media* 37, 42.

[132] D Armstrong, 'Actors, Patients and Agency: A Recent History' (2014) 36 *Sociology of Health & Illness* 163, 172.

[133] A Bok, D Noone and N Skouw-Rasmussen, 'Patient Agency: Key Questions and Challenges – A Report from the 1st Workshop of the EHC Think Tank Workstream on Patient Agency' (2022) 9 *Journal of Haemophilia Practice* 27.

[134] ibid 29.

[135] ibid.

the patient to understand their health condition and treatment options, including inherent risks. Unlike the autonomy model, where the doctor simply informs the patient of treatment options and related material risks before leaving the patient to decide on their own, the agency model engages doctor and patient to balance beneficence and autonomy, empowering the patient as a partner in the decision-making process.

This shared decision-making process does not preclude doctors from attempting to guide or influence patients to reach a mutually agreed decision. This is a complex aspect of shared decision-making as not all patients are equal. Some are more independent and competent, while others may wish to have all the information but still receive guidance from doctors, and yet others may wish the doctor to make decisions on their behalf. The spectrum of engagement is thus wide, 'ranging from patients who do not wish to engage or are unable to engage through to those who are very highly engaged'.[136] Importantly, genuine patient engagement may in some cases require engaging with family members or carers who can support the patient and act as intermediaries when required.

As described in Chapter two, medical practice has for much of its history been dominated by a paternalistic philosophy. The rise of autonomy over the latter half of the twentieth century was a response to that, and while the recognition of patient autonomy was crucial and welcome, it has had unintended effects on the doctor–patient relationship, pitting the virtues of beneficence against autonomy. Doctors become defensive, and instead of working with patients to reach the best outcome, some doctors simply provide patients with choices, leaving the patients with sole responsibility. This is not in the best interest of patients, and, as shown above,[137] it is not what most patients want. Shared decision-making and patient agency can help regain the middle ground as both doctors and patients share ownership of the decision and responsibility for its consequences. Doctors must accept that patients have a right to make decisions about their health and patients must accept that they cannot have autonomy without responsibility.[138]

VI. Conclusion

This chapter has argued that the evolution of the duty of care founded on Lord Atkin's dictum in *Donoghue* is flawed because it does not recognise two distinct bases for a duty – relational and contextual. A relational duty is based on a pre-existing relationship; it includes liability for omissions because parties legitimately may have expectations of affirmative action within a relationship. A contextual

[136] ibid 30.

[137] See above text to nn 98–101.

[138] 'It is not only agents who need to own outcomes. Victims do too.' P Responsibility and Fault: A Relational and Functional Approach to Responsibility' in P Cane and J Gardner (eds), *Relating to Responsibility: Essays in Honour of Tony Honoré on his 80th Birthday* (Oxford, Hart Publishing, 2011) 93.

duty, on the other hand, is created by the defendant's conduct, not the relationship between the defendant and claimant. Such a duty would rarely, if ever, justify liability for a pure omission. This distinction explains why doctors have a positive duty to inform and advise their patients but should not have a positive duty to warn third parties, unless the doctor voluntarily assumes responsibility or creates an ad hoc relationship with the third party.

The chapter then considered the doctor's duty to advise and inform the patient, arguing that this duty should not be grounded in notions of individual autonomy, but rather should be based on notions of shared decision-making and patient agency. While patient agency and patient autonomy overlap, agency connotes responsibility, which autonomy does not. Thus, under an agency approach, the patient also has responsibility in the shared decision-making process. The scope of the doctor's duty would necessarily be curtailed, as the objective would be to enable the patient to exercise agency and participate in decision-making. Once that is achieved, the patient is equally responsible for the decision. It strikes a better balance between beneficence and autonomy, and between doctors' rights and patients' rights.

6

Recalibrating the Standard of Care

I. Introduction

One aspect of medical negligence that has vexed courts and commentators more than any other is the standard of care. The orthodox test was first articulated in *Bolam v Friern Hospital Management Committee*,[1] according to which doctors could not be found negligent if their conduct was accepted as proper practice by a responsible body of medical opinion, even if there was another body of medical opinion that found the conduct negligent. This test has been criticised for allowing doctors to set their own standard.[2] The criticisms were especially stringent when the test was applied to the duty to advise and inform, the argument being that patients deserved to be given advice and information that they deemed necessary in order to make informed decisions and to protect their autonomy.

Over a period spanning half a decade, courts across the common law world repudiated *Bolam* for the duty to advise, holding that doctors must advise patients of the material risks in proposed treatment, with material risks determined not by responsible medical opinion but from the patients' perspective.[3] This splintering of the standard of care raises an important question as to whether the standard of care should vary according to the nature and scope of the duty in question. At present, the law recognises two distinct tests for the standard of care in clinical negligence, distinguishing cases involving diagnosis, care, and treatment from cases involving provision of information and advice. Can the standard of care be further fragmented by segregating diagnosis, treatment and care? The duty to advise has already been further separated into two distinct components: the duty to advise of risks in the proposed treatment and the duty to advise on alternative treatment options.[4]

With significant advancements in technology and more recently the explosive growth in artificial intelligence, there will be an expectation that doctors will use

[1] *Bolam v Friern Hospital Management Committee* [1957] 1 WLR 582.

[2] See articles listed at n 48.

[3] *Canterbury v Spence* 464 F 2d 772 (DC Cir 1972) (US); *Reibl v Hughes* (1981) 114 DLR 1 (Canada); *Rogers v Whitaker* (1992) 175 CLR 479 (Australia); *Dr Hari Krishnan v Megat Noor Ishak Megat Ibrahim* [2018] 1 MLRA 535 (Malaysia); *Montgomery v Lanarkshire Health Board* [2015] UKSC 11; [2015] AC 1430 (UK); *Hii Chii Kok v Ong Peng Jin London Lucien* [2017] SGCA 38; [2017] 2 SLR 492 (Singapore).

[4] *McCulloch v Forth Valley Health Board* [2023] UKSC 26; [2024] AC 925.

artificial intelligence and technology in diagnosis and surgery.[5] The tolerance for human error and limitations will wane. The current approach to the standard of care based on *Bolam* may be too forgiving in a world in which AI and robots that are not susceptible to human error perform diagnosis and surgery. On the other hand, the approach to the duty to advise based on *Montgomery v Lanarkshire Health Board*[6] may be too demanding if it shifts the focus of inquiry from prevention of physical harm to facilitation of informed choice and protection of personal autonomy.

The chapter begins with a critical analysis of the reasonable person as the flag-bearer of acceptable standards in negligence, highlighting some of its inherent failings both in theory and practice. The reasonable person standard is by no means value-neutral; it is shaped by philosophical preferences and policy choices of judges. The chapter then goes on to critique the law based on *Bolam* as it applies to diagnosis and surgery, before analysing the developments that led to the rejection of *Bolam* by the UK Supreme Court in *Montgomery.* The chapter agrees in principle with the *Montgomery* decision but argues that it goes too far in facilitating patient choice. This danger resulted in the Supreme Court clarifying the scope of *Montgomery* in *McCulloch v Forth Valley Health Board.*[7] These uncertainties have caused considerable angst for doctors, leading to increased stress, defensive practices, and deterioration of the doctor–patient relationship.[8] As foreshadowed in Chapter five, it is argued that the law within the clinical negligence context should be aimed not at protecting patient autonomy but patient agency and shared decision-making.

II. The Reasonable Person

The standard of care by which a defendant is judged in negligence is that of a reasonable person in the defendant's position.[9] The reasonable person or the 'man of ordinary skill and prudence',[10] is ubiquitous across the spectrum of law where judges have to determine expected standards of behaviour, whether in tort law, contract law, trust law, administrative law, or criminal law.[11] The reasonable person

[5] MA Al-Antari, 'Artificial Intelligence for Medical Diagnostics – Existing and Future AI Technology!' (2023) 13 *Diagnostics* 688; A Aamir et al, 'Exploring the Current and Prospective Role of Artificial Intelligence in Disease Diagnosis' (2024) 86(2) *Annals of Medicine & Surgery* 943; O Gumkowska-Sroka, P Kotyla and W Samborski, 'Does AI Replace Medical Doctors?' (2024) 10 *Rheumatology Forum* 59.

[6] *Montgomery v Lanarkshire Health Board* [2015] UKSC 11; [2015] AC 1430.

[7] *McCulloch v Forth Valley Health Board* [2023] UKSC 26; [2024] AC 925.

[8] See GG Buttigeg, '*Montgomery* and its Impact on Current Medical Practice – Good or Bad?' (2019) 87 *Medico-Legal Journal* 80; I Le Gallez et al, '*Montgomery's* Legal and Practical Impact: A Systematic Review at 6 Years' (2022) 28 *Journal of Evaluation in Clinical Practice* 690; KHH Kwok, EC Ip and SS Lee, 'The Conundrums of the Reasonable Patient Standard in English Medical Law' (2023) 24 *BMC Medical Ethics Article* 15.

[9] *Blyth v Birmingham Waterworks Co* (1856) 11 Ex 781, 156 ER 1047.

[10] *Vaughan v Menlove* (1837) 7 Carrington & Payne 525, 526; (1837) 173 ER 232 (CP), 232.

[11] J Gardner, 'The Many Faces of the Reasonable Person' (2015) 131 *Law Quarterly Review* 563.

test has aptly been described as 'little more than the anthropomorphic conception of justice as perceived by judges or juries'.[12] However, anthropomorphic justice dispensed by an ethnocentric judiciary is not ideal. Jury trials are less of a problem, as juries represent the communities from which they are drawn and are more likely to reflect contemporary standards in society.

Critical legal scholars have demonstrated that apparently neutral concepts such as the reasonable person may discriminate against certain groups, based on race, culture, class, or gender.[13] Historically, most judges and lawyers were male, came from the majority race or culture, and generally belonged to the upper social class.[14] Their worldview, shaped by their lived realities, frequently did not match that of other segments of society. The Judicial College of England and Wales has acknowledged this, noting: 'In many courts and tribunals there has been a wide gulf in social background and life experience between the parties and the judges making decisions'.[15] Despite progress in making judiciaries more diverse,[16] the legacy of the past remains deeply ingrained in our legal values and conceptions of justice.

Beyond the risk that judges do not always reflect ordinary community standards lies a separate risk that judges can use the standard of care to shape the law of negligence to align with their individual values and policy objectives, blurring the line between judicial and legislative function.[17] The development of medical negligence law in post-War England is a case in point. In an insightful article, three anesthesiologists analysing *Roe v Ministry of Health*,[18] demonstrated how McNair J, who was the trial judge in both *Roe* and *Bolam*, as well as Lord Denning, who was on the Court of Appeal between 1948 and 1957, steered the law in favour of doctors.[19] The authors of the article observed, 'A reluctance to find against doctors in negligence cases became a Denning characteristic'.[20] In upholding McNair J's judgment, Lord Denning concluded his opinion in *Roe* with this caution:

> But we should be doing a disservice to the community at large if we were to impose liability on hospitals and doctors for everything that happens to go wrong. Doctors

[12] S Deakin, A Johnston and B Markesinis, *Markesinis and Deakin's Tort Law* (Oxford, Clarendon Press, 6th edn, 2008) 223.

[13] DM Trubek, 'Where the Action Is: Critical Legal Studies and Empiricism' (1984) 36 *Stanford Law Review* 575. For a feminist critique of the reasonable person: M Moran, *Rethinking the Reasonable Person: An Egalitarian Reconstruction of the Objective Standard* (Oxford, Oxford University Press, 2003).

[14] See, United Kingdom Parliament, Constitution Committee – Twenty-Fifth Report, *Judicial Appointments* (7 March 2012) Chapter 3, https://publications.parliament.uk/pa/ld201012/ldselect/ldconst/272/27206.htm.

[15] Judicial College, *Equal Treatment Bench Book* (February 2021 edn), p 8.

[16] Such progress cannot be taken for granted, as seen in the backlash against the ethos of diversity, equity, and inclusion in some conservative Western states.

[17] See discussion on judicial law-making in Chapter 2 text to nn 20–50.

[18] *Roe v Ministry of Health* [1954] 2 QB 66.

[19] JR Maltby, CDD Hutter and KC Clayton, 'The Woolley and Roe Case' (2000) 84 *British Journal of Anaesthesia* 121.

[20] ibid 125.

> would be led to think more of their own safety than of the good of their patients. Initiative would be stifled and confidence shaken. A proper sense of proportion requires us to have regard to the conditions in which hospitals and doctors have to work. We must insist on due care for the patient at every point, but we must not condemn as negligence that which is only a misadventure.[21]

The influence of human rights discourse and the emphasis placed on patient autonomy have in more recent years persuaded progressive judges to depart from the *Bolam* test in cases involving the doctor's duty to inform or advise. The judges in *Montgomery* and *Hii Chii Kok v Ooi Peng Jin London Lucien*[22] expressly based their reasoning on the need to change the law to respect patient autonomy.[23] *Hii Chii Kok* and *Montgomery* also shine a spotlight on whether the reasonable person test should be assessed ethically or sociologically.[24] The ethical inquiry asks what a reasonable person *ought* to do while the sociological inquiry asks what the reasonable person *would* do. Montrose, commenting in the 1950s in the wake of the *Bolam* judgment, cautioned that 'it is important to distinguish between average practices and average standards, between what the ordinary man does and what the ordinary man thinks ought to be done'.[25]

In the period following *Donoghue v Stevenson*,[26] English law had apparently adopted the ethical standard to assess negligence.[27] This necessarily involves extra-legal considerations, raising key questions of methodology and content in incorporating such considerations. Dunn et al put it pithily:

> The challenge for the court then becomes one of determining precisely what extra-legal anchoring work ought to be achieved when this legal fiction is invoked within the legal reasoning process. For our purposes, this gives rise to two key questions that need to be settled in any thorough analysis of the *Montgomery* case: (1) what legal approach is being adopted in this formulation of the standard in the law of consent to treatment, and (2) what substantive justification, if any, could underpin and defend a criterion that is formulated in this way?[28]

[21] [1954] 2 QB 66, 86–87.

[22] *Hii Chii Kok v Ooi Peng Jin London Lucien* [2017] SGCA 38; [2017] 2 SLR 492.

[23] See especially, the comments in *Montgomery v Lanarkshire Health Board* [2015] UKSC 11; [2015] AC 1430 (per Lady Hale), [108] and in *Hii Chii Kok v Ong Peng Jin London Lucien and another* [2017] SGCA 38; [2017] 2 SLR 492 (per Menon CJ), [116]–[122].

[24] JL Montrose, 'Is Negligence and Ethical or Sociological Concept?' (1958) 21 *The Modern Law Review* 259; AD Miller and R Perry, 'The Reasonable Person' (2012) 87 *New York University Law Review* 323.

[25] JL Montrose, 'Is Negligence and Ethical or Sociological Concept?' (1958) 21 *The Modern Law Review* 259, 262.

[26] *Donoghue v Stevenson* [1932] AC 562; 1932 SC (HL) 31.

[27] WTS Stallybrass, *Salmond's Law of Torts* (London, Sweet & Maxwell, 1945) 437: 'the general practice itself may not conform to the standard of care required of a reasonably prudent man. In such a case it is not a good defence that the defendant acted in accordance with the general practice'.

[28] M Dunn, KWM Fulford, J Herring and A Handa, 'Between the Reasonable and the Particular: Deflating Autonomy in the Legal Regulation of Informed Consent to Medical Treatment' (2019) 27 *Health Care Analysis* 110, 116.

Alan Miller and Ronen Perry offer three ethical principles that may be relied on to assess reasonableness in negligence: 'welfare maximization, equal freedom, and the feminist ethic of care'.[29] Chapter three undertook an extensive review of private law theories, broadly categorised as justice theories, instrumental theories, and critical theories. It argued for a pluralist approach based on relational justice theory, vulnerability theory, and care ethics. Miller and Perry's welfare maximisation principle is based on the economic analysis of law and is utilitarian in nature. This philosophy has a strong hold on the tort of negligence in the United States,[30] tracing back to the calculus of negligence introduced by Learned Hand J in the 1940s, balancing the probability and gravity of harm against the burden of avoiding the risk.[31] However, the economic analysis approach diminishes the human element in medical negligence cases, where choices involve more than purely utilitarian considerations.

By contrast, the feminist ethic of care reconceptualises negligence, reorienting it from a negative standard of reason and caution to a positive standard of caring and concern.[32] According to Bender,

> Tort law needs to be more of a system of response and caring than it is now. Its focus should be on interdependence and collective responsibility rather than on individuality, and on safety and help for the injured rather than on 'reasonableness' and economic efficiency.[33]

The feminist approach recognises the interconnectedness of the doctor and patient, respecting the inherent moral value of medical beneficence and patient autonomy.[34]

III. Medical Negligence

There are two related questions that a court must consider in determining breach of duty. They are the standard of care by which the defendant is to be judged and the reasonableness of the defendant's response to the particular risk. The standard of care at the abstract level is a matter of law; once determined, it sets a precedent. For example, courts have held that the standard of care of a practitioner of Traditional Chinese Medicine is that of practitioners in that field, not in the field of Western medicine.[35] Courts have held that inexperience in an area of skill (eg driving) does

[29] AD Miller and R Perry, 'The Reasonable Person' (2012) 87 *New York University Law Review* 323, 327.

[30] See generally, RW Wright, 'Justice and Reasonable Care in Negligence Law' (2002) 47 *American Journal of Jurisprudence* 143 for a history and criticism of this approach.

[31] RA Posner, 'A Theory of Negligence' (1972) 1 *Journal of Legal Studies* 29, 32–33.

[32] L Bender, 'A Lawyer's Primer on Feminist Theory and Tort' (1988) 38 *Journal of Legal Education* 1, 25.

[33] ibid 4.

[34] See Chapter 3 text to nn 100–126 for discussion of some of these approaches.

[35] *Shakoor v Situ* [2001] 1 WLR 410.

not lower the standard of care;[36] thus in all such cases the inexperienced defendant is held to the standard of an experienced actor. Simlarly, the law holds children who cause harm to an objective standard based on children of a similar age.[37] A layperson who carries out certain household repairs may be held to the standard of a reasonably competent tradesperson even though the layperson does not have the requisite trade skills.[38]

Whether the defendant has fallen below the expected standard is a fact-sensitive inquiry. The question is whether the defendant acted reasonably in the face of a reasonably foreseeable risk.[39] What may be a reasonable response in one case may not be so in another case due to the vagaries of the unique circumstances of each case. In coming to its judgment on breach, a court engages in a comparative risk-benefit analysis, balancing, amongst other factors, the probability of harm, the gravity of harm, the practicability of avoiding the harm, the justifiability of taking the risk, and the social utility of the activity.[40]

What is perhaps unusual about medical negligence is that the standard of care and breach of duty inquiries often appear to be fused. Under the orthodox test set out in *Bolam*, doctors will not be found liable if they act in accordance with a standard accepted as proper by peer professionals. This gives the impression that a judicial finding of negligence is not merely against the particular defendant but against the practice itself. Thus, some doctors labour under the misguided fear that a judicial finding of what constitutes acceptable practice is binding and that doctors must comply with the judicial standard instead of relying on their own medical judgement.[41] Hence, doctors wish to preserve *Bolam* at all costs in order not to cede medical judgement to the courts.

This fear, while understandable, is arguably misplaced, as breach of duty is a question of fact. Each case is unique, and a finding of negligence in one case does not mean that there must be a finding of negligence in another similar case.[42] Just because a doctor is found negligent in one instance does not mean that another doctor will be found negligent for doing something similar, so long as the facts justify the doctor's actions. Equally, just because a doctor is not found negligent in one instance does not mean that another will be absolved in a similar situation.

[36] *Nettleship v Weston* [1971] 2 QB 691.

[37] *Mullins v Richard* [1998] 1 WLR 1304.

[38] *Wells v Cooper* [1985] 2 QB 265.

[39] *Blyth v Birmingham Waterworks Co* (1856) 11 Ex 781; 156 ER 1047; *Glasgow Corp v Muir* [1943] AC 448.

[40] *United States v Carroll Towing Co* 159 F 2d 169 (2d Cir 1947); *Morris v West Hartlepool Steam Navigation Co* [1956] AC 522; *Wyong Shire Council v Shirt* (1980) 146 CLR 40; *BNJ v SMRT Trains Ltd* [2013] SGHC 286; [2014] 2 SLR 7.

[41] See for example, this warning by Yong Pung How CJ in *Dr Khoo James v Gunapathy d/o Muniandy* [2002] SGCA 25; [2002] 1 SLR(R) 1024, [144]: 'Furthermore, the lawyer-judge in "playing doctor" at the frontiers of medical science might distort or even hamper its proper development. Excessive judicial interference raises the spectre of defensive medicine, with the attendant evils of higher medical costs and wastage of precious medical resources'.

[42] *Qualcast (Wolverhampton) Ltd v Haynes* [1959] AC 743.

A. The *Bolam* Test

The standard of care in medical negligence litigation has long been a subject of concern amongst medico-legal professionals and has also been the subject of considerable academic debate.[43] The classic test for the standard of care in medical negligence is found in the jury direction of McNair J in *Bolam*, in which he stated:

> I myself would prefer to put it this way, that he is not guilty of negligence if he has acted in accordance with a practice accepted as proper by a responsible body of medical men skilled in that particular art.[44]

Thus, whether doctors are negligent depends on whether they have adhered to accepted custom in the profession (the 'custom test'),[45] or whether they are supported by peer professional opinion (the 'peer professional' test).[46] In effect, the profession regulates itself and sets its own standards. As Lord Scarman famously declared, 'the law imposes the duty of care: but the standard of care is a matter of medical judgment'.[47]

The *Bolam* test has been criticised for encouraging medical paternalism and diminishing patient autonomy when it comes to exercising choice and to consenting to treatments.[48] It has also been criticised for inhibiting judges from carrying out their judicial function in adjudicating disputes and setting legal standards.[49] *Bolam* is seen as setting a test that is not neutral but one that is 'so firmly against the plaintiff in a medical negligence action that it is almost not worth going to

[43] See generally, M Brazier and J Miola, 'Bye-Bye *Bolam*: A Medical Revolution?' (2000) 8 *Medical Law Review* 85; R Mulheron, 'Trumping *Bolam*: A Critical Legal Analysis of *Bolitho's* "Gloss"' (2010) 69 *Cambridge Law Journal* 609; C Sappideen, '*Bolam* in Australia – More Bark than Bite?' (2010) 33 *University of New South Wales Law Journal* 386; K Amirthalingam, 'Medical Negligence and Patient Autonomy: *Bolam* Rules in Singapore and Malaysia – Revisited' (2015) 27 *Singapore Academy of Law Journal* 666.

[44] *Bolam v Friern Hospital Management Committee* [1957] 1 WLR 582, 587.

[45] The description is used and explained in A Merry and A McCall Smith, *Errors, Medicine and the Law* (Cambridge, Cambridge University Press, 2001) 166–71.

[46] R Mulheron, 'Trumping *Bolam*: A Critical Legal Analysis of *Bolitho's* "Gloss"' (2010) 69 *Cambridge Law Journal* 609; M Rizzi, 'Health Professionals' Standard of Care and Breach of Duty in Western Australia: A Requiem for the "Peer Professional" Test at a Time of Uncertainty' (2020) 26 *Torts Law Journal* 179; Workgroup to Review the Taking of Informed Consent and SMC Disciplinary Process (*Report on Recommendations*, 28 November 2019), Annex E, xv.

[47] *Sidaway v Board of Governors of the Bethlem Royal Hospital and the Maudsley Hospital* [1985] 1 AC 871, 881.

[48] M Brazier and J Miola, 'Bye-Bye *Bolam*: A Medical Revolution?' (2000) 8 *Medical Law Review* 85, 90–95. See also, D Giesen, 'Medical Malpractice and the Judicial Function in Comparative Perspective' [1993] *Medical Law International* 13; J Keown 'The Rise and Rise of "the *Bolam* test"' [1995] *Singapore Journal of Legal Studies* 342, 363; H Teff, 'The Standard of Care in Medical Negligence – Moving on from *Bolam*?' (1998) 18 *Oxford Journal of Legal Studies* 473; Lord Woolf, 'Are Courts Excessively Deferential to the Medical Profession?' (2001) 9 *Medical Law Review* 1; R Mulheron, 'Trumping *Bolam*: A Critical Legal Analysis of *Bolitho's* "Gloss"' (2010) 69 *Cambridge Law Journal* 609.

[49] Lord Woolf, 'Are Courts Excessively Deferential to the Medical Profession?' (2001) 9 *Medical Law Review* 1, 15.

court in the first place'.[50] This is unsurprising considering the history of the *Bolam* test and its underlying judicial philosophy that was pro-doctor,[51] especially in the immediate post-War era, to protect the National Health Service from liability.[52]

Applying the *Bolam* test to the fused inquiry of standard and breach results in the reasonableness of the doctor's conduct being judged sociologically or positively, rather than ethically or normatively. The question is simply whether the doctor's conduct accords with acceptable practice. This hands judgement of medical negligence to the experts because judges are not allowed to question whether acceptable practice itself is adequate.[53] The problem is exacerbated because McNair J reduced the reasonable person test to an ordinary person test:[54] a doctor will not be found negligent 'if he exercises the *ordinary* skill of an *ordinary* competent man exercising that particular art' (emphasis added).[55] The ethical standard is reduced to a sociological standard, allowing medical professionals not only to judge themselves, but to judge themselves not on the basis of how they *should* act but on how some of them *actually* act. In effect, *Bolam* endorses the lowest acceptable standard.

Responding to some of these criticisms, English judges have whittled down *Bolam* at the margins over the last three decades. Significantly, the House of Lords in *Bolitho v City & Hackney Health Authority*[56] cautioned that judges should scrutinise expert opinion and be satisfied that the opinion is logically defensible as well as reasonable, respectable and responsible before accepting it. Following this decision, Brazier and Miola published an article predicting the demise of *Bolam* in a 'velvet revolution' that would advance the interests of doctors and patients.[57] However, courts continued to give *Bolitho* a narrow reading and restricted themselves to scrutinising whether the defendant's expert opinion was logically defensible rather than focus on whether the opinion was respectable, reasonable and responsible.[58] In a detailed analysis of *Bolitho*,[59] Rachel Mulheron referred

[50] MA Fordham, 'The *Bolam* Test Lives On' [1998] *Singapore Journal of Legal Studies* 140, 148.

[51] See H Teff, *Reasonable Care: Legal Perspectives on the Doctor Patient Relationship* (Oxford, Clarendon Press, 1994) 30; JK Mason, 'Master of the Balancers; Non-Voluntary Therapy under the Mantle of Lord Donaldson' [1993] *Juridical Review* 115.

[52] J Maltby, CDD Hutter and KC Clayton, 'The Woolley and Roe Case' (2000) 84 *British Journal of Anaethesia* 121. Lord Denning made no secret of the fact that he deliberately reshaped the law in order to 'relieve the anxieties of the medical men'. Lord Denning, *The Discipline of Law* (London, Butterworths, 1979) 241.

[53] *Maynard v West Midlands Regional Health Authority* [1984] 1 WLR 634; *De Freitas v O'Brien* [1993] 4 Medical LR 281; *Whitehouse v Jordan* [1981] 1 WLR 246; *Dr Khoo James v Gunapathy d/o Muniandy* [2002] SGCA 25; [2002] 1 SLR(R) 1024.

[54] J Miola, 'The Standard of Care in Medical negligence – Still Reasonably Troublesome?' in J Richardson and E Rackley (ed), *Feminist Perspectives on Tort Law* (London, Routledge, 2012) 126, 129.

[55] *Bolam v Friern Hospital Management Committee* [1957] 1 WLR 582, 586.

[56] *Bolitho v City & Hackney Health Authority* [1997] UKHL 46; [1998] AC 232.

[57] M Brazier and J Miola, 'Bye-Bye *Bolam*: A Medical Litigation Revolution?' (2000) 8 *Medical Law Review* 85, 86.

[58] See, the analysis of post-*Bolitho* cases in A Maclean, 'Beyond *Bolam* and *Bolitho*' (2002) 5 *Medical Law International* 205.

[59] R Mulheron, 'Trumping *Bolam*: A Critical Legal Analysis of *Bolitho's* Gloss' (2010) 69 *Cambridge Law Journal* 609.

to the Singaporean interpretation of *Bolitho* in *Khoo James v Gunapathy d/o Muniandy*,[60] in which Yong Pung How CJ observed as follows:

> Interpreted liberally, *Bolitho* could unwittingly herald invasive inquiry into the merits of medical opinion. For if 'defensible' were to be given a meaning akin to 'reasonable', the *Bolam* test would only be honoured in lip service. A doctor would then be liable when his view, as represented by the defence experts, was found by the court to be unreasonable. We do not think this was the intention of the House of Lords in *Bolitho*.[61]

Thus, a defendant who is supported by an expert whose opinion is logically defensible cannot be found negligent by the court: the medical profession sets its own standards.[62] However, more recent jurisprudence suggests a bolder vision for *Bolitho*. Once apparently confined to rare and exceptional cases,[63] courts no longer impose such restrictions, treating *Bolitho* as generally applicable.[64] In 2024, an England and Wales High Court judge reiterated that 'even where the *Bolam* test is applicable, the question as to whether breach has been established is ultimately a matter for the Court, not the experts'.[65] The authoritative exposition on the contours and application of the '*Bolitho* addendum' is found in *C v North Cumbria University Hospitals NHS Trust*,[66] in which Green J set out detailed guidance on how to deal with expert evidence. Significantly, Green J disaggregated logical defensibility from the adjectival triumvirate of 'reasonable, respectable and responsible', stressing that judges had to evaluate the expert opinion holistically and test it against the evidence to determine the weight that should be accorded to it.[67]

This approach to the *Bolitho* addendum gives it more teeth, moving it slightly away from the sociological to the ethical approach. It allows judges to prevent medical experts from setting the standard if the judge does not find the expert opinion 'reasonable, respectable and responsible' or if the judge does not find the expert opinion logically defensible. *Hii Chii Kok* also breathed new life into *Bolitho*, highlighting that 'the *Bolam* test is a *proxy* or a *heuristic* for determining what a reasonable and competent doctor would do'.[68] Interpreting *Bolam* as a proxy or heuristic is profound, as it clarifies that *Bolam* is a means to an end, a distinction that was lost in the *Bolamisation* of medical negligence over several decades. The High Court of Australia, in a series of decisions in the last decade of the twentieth

[60] *Khoo James v Gunapathy d/o Muniandy* [2002] SGCA 25; [2002] 1 SLR(R) 1024.

[61] ibid, [65].

[62] A Maclean, 'Beyond *Bolam* and *Bolitho*' (2002) 5 *Medical Law International* 205, 207.

[63] R Mulheron, 'Trumping *Bolam*: A Critical Legal Analysis of *Bolitho's* Gloss' [2010] *Cambridge Law Journal* 609, 618.

[64] That *Bolitho* will no longer be treated as a rare exception was affirmed in *Lane v Worcestershire Acute Hospitals NHS Trust* [2017] EWHC 1900, [16].

[65] *Winterbotham v Shahrak* [2024] EWHC 2633 (KB), [40].

[66] *C v North Cumbria University Hospitals NHS Trust* [2014] EWHC 61 (QB).

[67] ibid [25].

[68] *Hii Chii Kok v Ong Peng Jin London Lucien* [2017] SGCA 38; [2017] 2 SLR 492, [104], [111].

century,[69] culminating in *Rosenberg v Percival*, set out an unimpeachable approach to the standard of care in medical negligence:

> As the above passage, which was quoted with approval in *Rogers v Whitaker*, makes clear, the *relevance* of professional practice and opinion was not denied; what was denied was its *conclusiveness*. In many cases, professional practice and opinion will be the primary, and in some cases it may be the only, basis upon which a court may reasonably act. But, in an action brought by a patient, the responsibility for deciding the content of the doctor's duty of care rests with the court, not with his or her professional colleagues.[70]

Rosenberg strikes the right balance between recognising that expert medical opinion is crucial to understanding what constitutes acceptable medical practice and ensuring that ultimately courts have the responsibility and power to determine whether the doctor acted negligently in the circumstances. What is objectionable about *Bolam* as understood by English courts is the assumption that judges must always defer to medical opinion unless it is illogical. This extreme position prevents a judge who fully understands both the issues and the expert medical opinion from exercising independent judgement. Unfortunately, in Australia, the elegant solution provided in *Rosenberg* was swept away by legislative reforms which were aimed at reinstating the *Bolam* test.

The legislative test adopted across the Australian States (with minor variations) is based on the standard proposed by the panel of experts appointed by the Australian Government to propose reforms to the law of negligence:[71]

> A medical practitioner is not negligent if the treatment provided was in accordance with an opinion widely held by a significant number of respected practitioners in the field, unless the court considers that the opinion was irrational.

Instead of referring to widely held medical opinion, the various statutes refer to widely accepted practice.[72] This has raised fresh questions about what constitutes a practice, when it is to be regarded as widely accepted, and when a professional practice may be disregarded as irrational.[73] The tension between the courts and the medical profession as to who determines the standard of care is most clearly seen in the Victorian case of *Boxell v Peninsula Health*.[74] The Supreme Court noted that

[69] *Rogers v Whitaker* (1992) 175 CLR 479; *Breen v Williams* (1996) 186 CLR 71; *Naxakis v Western General Hospital* (1999) 197 CLR 269.

[70] *Rosenberg v Percival* (2001) 205 CLR 434 (per Gleeson CJ), [7].

[71] Following a health insurance crisis in 2001, the Australian Government established a panel of experts chaired by Ipp J to propose reforms to tort law. One of the recommendations of the panel was to reintroduce *Bolam* in modified form: *Review of the Law of Negligence Final Report* (September 2002), Recommendation 3.

[72] See Civil Liability Act (NSW) s 5O; Wrongs Act 1958 (Vic) s 59; Civil Liability Act 2002 (WA) s 5PB.

[73] Decisions from three different states have not arrived at a uniform approach. See, *Boxell v Peninsula Health* [2019] VSC 830; *Coffey v Murrumbidgee Local Health District formerly known as Greater Murray Area Health Service* [2019] NSWSC 1265; *Child and Adolescent Health Service v Sunday John Mabior by Next Friend Mary Kelei* [2019] WASCA 151.

[74] *Boxell v Peninsula Health* [2019] VSC 830.

it was not enough for the defendant to point to an existing practice accepted by peers, but it must establish the existence of a practice *widely* accepted in Australia as competent practice. Nine experts were called in *Boxell*, four for the plaintiff and five for the defendant. Despite all five of the defendant's experts testifying that not performing a CT aortogram was acceptable, the Court did not accept that their views constituted widely accepted practice, holding that the practice defended by the defendant's experts was not 'consistent with that practised in the hospitals represented by [the plaintiff's experts]'.[75]

The Court highlighted the difference between 'a standard being commonly practised, and it being widely accepted as competent professional practice by a significant number of respected practitioners in the field'.[76] This is a departure from the *Bolam/ Bolitho* approach, as the Court rejected the defendant's experts' views not on the narrow grounds of logical indefensibility but on the Court's own assessment that the defendant's experts' practice did not comport with 'widely accepted practice'. It is still a sociological approach, but at least the standards are determined not by *any* accepted practice but *widely* accepted practice.[77] The Court went on to hold the defendant negligent, based on the facts, the evidence, and the expert opinion, finding that the defendant's failure to perform a CT aortogram to exclude a possible diagnosis of an aortic dissection constituted negligent misdiagnosis.

One aspect of *Bolam* that is often overlooked in the literature and judgments is McNair J's rider that it would be negligent of a doctor to hold to a particular 'technique if it has been proved to be contrary to what is really substantially the whole of informed medical opinion'.[78] This is especially relevant to diagnosis, as scientific advancement has led to rapid developments in diagnostic techniques, particularly with the pervasive use of technology and now artificial intelligence. Courts and the medical profession will have to confront the reality that diagnosis – unlike treatment and care – is more of a science than an art.[79] In many cases, judges will be able to rely on scientific evidence, medical literature and competing expert testimony to evaluate whether a doctor was negligent in diagnosis, as exemplified in *Boxell*.

As alluded to in Chapter five, the doctor's duty is multifaceted; it includes the duty to diagnose, treat, care, inform, advise, warn, disclose, refer, and follow-up. There is no reason why *Bolam* must apply – or apply in the same way – to every aspect.[80] *Bolam* is apposite in the realms of treatment and care which are based on

[75] ibid at [293].

[76] ibid.

[77] This avoids the problem with *Bolam* where the lowest accepted practice sets the standard.

[78] *Bolam v Friern Hospital Management Committee* [1957] 1 WLR 583, 587.

[79] See SM McKinney, et al, 'International Evaluation of an AI System for Breast Cancer Screening' (2020) 577 *Nature* 89; E Neri, et al, 'What the Radiologist Should Know about Artificial Intelligence – An ESR White Paper' (2019) 10 *Insights Imaging* 44.

[80] A leading medico-legal practitioner Simon Fox, making a similar argument, is developing a menu of standards for different aspects of the doctor's duty. See S Fox, 'The Latest on *Bolam* is Dead' 6 July 2019, www.simonfoxqc.com.

a range of factors, including the expertise of the doctor; the needs and temperament of the patient; the dynamics of the patient's medical condition; the need to balance patient autonomy and medical beneficence; the available resources; and institutional protocols. Legitimate differences of opinion and a range of options are in play.

One can sensibly speak of accepted practices in the context of treatment and care: depending on the circumstances, different professionals will favour different practices, each being reasonable. Not always so with diagnosis. While it is true that in many cases, diagnosis cannot be isolated from treatment and care as each informs and affects the other, there are some aspects of diagnosis that can be isolated and treated differently, especially those involving interpretation of pathological tests or radiological scans. Here, the issue is whether the doctor could have got the diagnosis right, and in some of these cases it would be farcical to defend as acceptable practice that which is patently wrong.

B. Diagnostic Negligence

A study in 2019 showed that diagnostic errors in three areas (vascular disease, infections and cancer) account for almost 75 per cent of cases which result in serious harm or death to the patient.[81] The study also found that the overwhelming cause of diagnostic errors is poor clinical judgement. Recognising this, medical experts have called for the development of better protocols and systems to reduce diagnostic errors, including greater reliance on computer-based tools, diagnostic performance feedback, clinical teamwork, and diagnostic education.[82] It is striking that while the medical profession has acknowledged that the leading cause of diagnostic errors resulting in harm to patients is poor clinical judgement, courts continue to apply the *Bolam* test to negligent diagnosis cases: the irony – if it needs to be spelt out – lies in the fact that the *Bolam* test defers to clinical judgement.

Having said this, there is an emerging body of cases involving cancer screening or diagnosis that raises questions about the application of *Bolam*. The starting point is *Penney and Others v East Kent Health Authority*,[83] which involved three claimants whose cervical smears taken for cancer screening were negligently reported as negative. The slides showed some abnormalities, but the experts differed as to what a reasonable cytoscreener should have seen and reported. All the experts agreed that unless the screener had absolute confidence that the smears were not cancerous, they should not report them as negative. The trial judge, Peppitt QC, held that as there were abnormalities in each smear, the screeners had failed the

[81] DE Newman-Toker, et al, 'Serious Misdiagnosis-related Harms in Malpractice Claims: The "Big Three" – Vascular Events, Infections, and Cancers' (2019) 6 *Diagnosis* 227.

[82] ibid 236; A Olson, et al, 'Competencies for Improving Diagnosis: An Interprofessional Framework for Education and Training in Health Care' (2019) 6 *Diagnosis* 335, 340.

[83] *Penney v East Kent Health Authority* [1999] EWCA Civ 3005; [2000] PNLR 323.

absolute confidence test and were negligent in reporting the smears as negative. In explaining his decision, Peppitt QC stated:

> All the experts agree that the cytoscreener was wrong. No question of *acceptable* practice was involved. The issue here to which the experts' evidence was directed was whether the cytoscreeners' conduct though wrong, was *excusable*. This seems to me to fall outside the *Bolam* Principle.[84]

On appeal, the appellants argued that Peppitt QC had failed to apply the *Bolam* test and had substituted his opinion for that of the experts. In addressing this argument, Lord Woolf MR distinguished between factual findings and diagnosis based on the factual findings, observing that the *Bolam* test 'has no application where what the judge is required to do is to make findings of fact. This is so, even where those findings of fact are the subject of conflicting expert evidence'.[85] Lord Woolf set out three questions that had to be answered, the first being the purely factual question to which *Bolam* did not apply:[86]

> What was to be seen in the slides?
>
> At the relevant time could a screener exercising reasonable care fail to see what was on the slide?
>
> Could a reasonably competent screener, aware of what a screener exercising reasonable care would observe on the slide, treat the slide as negative?

Penney was closely analysed in *Muller v King's College Hospital NHS Foundation Trust*[87] by Kerr J, who argued that Lord Woolf had included some elements of professional interpretation within 'findings of fact' to which the *Bolam* test would not apply. The relevant paragraph from *Muller* is reproduced:

> Lord Woolf was clearly treating question (i) as one of fact. Yet, by 'what was to be seen in the slides', he must have meant not merely what images the screener would physically see (a question of fact in the ordinary sense of the word), but also what *interpretation* should be placed on what was to be seen on the slides, i.e. whether, objectively, there was any indication of possible cancer. His reference to expert evidence being required to determine question (i) otherwise does not make sense. He held that the court had to decide this question without reference to the *Bolam* test.[88]

It must be emphasised that Lord Woolf affirmed that the *Bolam* test applied to diagnosis and that Kerr J accepted that he was bound by *Penney*. Nonetheless, Kerr J expressed support for the view that *Bolam* should be restricted to treatment and care, and should not be applicable to pure diagnosis, 'which was either right or wrong and, if wrong, either negligently so or not'.[89] Kerr J's dictum may

[84] ibid [36].
[85] ibid [27].
[86] ibid.
[87] *Muller v King's College Hospital NHS Foundation Trust* [2017] EWHC 128 (QB); [2017] QB 987.
[88] ibid [65].
[89] ibid [46].

be read in two ways. The more radical is to take Kerr J's words literally. *Bolam* should not apply to diagnosis and should be restricted to treatment and care, as only treatment and care require nuanced judgements where legitimate differences of opinion may exist. As Kerr J noted – diagnosis is either right or wrong. A more nuanced reading would be to recognise that there is a gradient from purely factual findings to interpretation to opinion in the realm of diagnosis. *Bolam* applies at the opinion end of the spectrum but fades away as it approaches the factual finding end. This is a grey area that will continue to pose challenges for courts and uncertainty for medico-legal practitioners.[90]

Penney has gained notoriety for its exclusion of *Bolam*/ *Bolitho* from factual findings, but in some ways, it may be more significant for its application of the 'absolute confidence' test to determine negligence in screening cases. The purpose of screening programmes is to exclude the possibility of cancer as a prevention strategy;[91] this purpose would be thwarted if the pathologist is permitted to exercise his or her professional judgement to exercise discretion in reporting screening results as negative when he or she is not absolutely certain of the result. Although *Penney* arose in the context of a general screening exercise, the absolute confidence test has been applied to pathological tests to diagnose cancer.[92] It is arguable that a distinction should be drawn between diagnosis and screening, with *Bolam* excluded only in the latter cases.[93]

Penney and *Muller* featured prominently in the Irish case of *Morrissey v Health Service Executive*.[94] Mrs Morrissey underwent two cervical screenings under the National Cervical Screening Programme run by the Government of Ireland. Both results were reported as negative. A few years later, Mrs Morrissey was diagnosed with cancer. Audits of the screening showed that her test results had been wrongly reported as negative. Mrs Morrissey and her husband sued the Health Service Executive which ran the programme and the two laboratories that carried out the screening. Applying the 'absolute confidence' test, the High Court of Ireland gave judgment in her favour. Referring to *Penney*, Cross J noted that the first question in

[90] See for example, *XXX v King's College NHS Foundation Trust* [2018] EWHC 646 (QB); *Shaw v South Tees Hospitals NHS Foundation Trust* [2019] EWHC 2280 (QB); *Lillywhite v University College London Hospitals' NHS Trust* [2005] EWCA Civ 1466. For a review and discussion of these cases, see K Amirthalingam, 'Medical Negligence and Diagnosis: Further Inroads into Bolam?' (2020) 71 *Northern Ireland Legal Quarterly* 657, 663–67.

[91] AB Miller, *Cervical Cancer Screening Programmes: Managerial Guidelines* (World Health Organisation, 1992) 1.

[92] *Manning (Executor of the Estate of Jane Louise Manning Deceased) v King's College Hospital NHS Trust* [2008] EWHC 1838. The Court held that unless the confidence level was at least 90%, a pathologist should not report it as negative; to do so would be negligent under *Bolitho* even if another pathologist would also report the result as negative (*Manning* at [189]). The decision was upheld on appeal: *Manning v Kings College Hospital NHS Trust* [2009] EWCA Civ 832; (2009) 110 BMLR 175.

[93] See for example, *Morrissey v Health Service Executive* [2020] IESC 6, para 3.4, in which the Irish Supreme Court highlighted the distinction between diagnostic tests and screening tests. See generally, N Wald and H Cuckle, 'Reporting the Assessment of Screening and Diagnostic Tests' (1989) 96 *British Journal of Obstetrics and Gynaecology* 389.

[94] *Morrissey v Health Service Executive* [2019] IEHC 268.

Lord Woolf's trilogy was purely factual and did not engage *Bolam/ Bolitho*.[95] The second and third questions were to be resolved on the absolute confidence test, not *Bolam*. Expert opinion would be relevant only to assist the Court to determine whether a reasonable screener could have had absolute confidence on the facts.

This judgment gave rise to concern that the Court had substituted the *Bolam* approach with a separate 'absolute confidence' test.[96] The Supreme Court of Ireland gave leave for a 'leapfrog' appeal to determine, amongst other things, whether the *Bolam* approach continued to apply or whether it had been displaced in cancer screening cases.[97] The Court reaffirmed the status quo – *Bolam* applies to diagnosis.[98] The judgment, while defensible and perhaps even inevitable, illuminates two problems – the abdication of the standard of care to the medical profession, and the conflation of diagnosis and screening in cancer cases.

Clarke CJ was unequivocal, stating that the Court had no role in setting the standard of care, which was to be determined by the profession itself.[99] Clarke CJ rationalised the absolute confidence test as compatible with *Bolam* on the ground that it was the test agreed to by all the experts called in *Penney* and *Morrissey*. This does not seem right. Surely, the standard is set by the law; it cannot be that in a subsequent case, if there are experts who disagree that absolute confidence is required in screening cases, the court will not apply the absolute confidence test for screening. Unlike diagnosis, where the doctor may have several options to choose from and expert evidence on accepted practice may be relevant to set the standard, screening involves a binary choice and is based on a single standard – absolute confidence. Experts have a role to assist the court to determine whether the absolute confidence test is met, but they do not set the standard in these cases. Clarke CJ recognised this dual role of experts[100] but, by conflating diagnosis and screening, was unable to accept absolute confidence as a test for screening cases.

The use of technology in diagnosis has a long history in medical practice, but the technology always had to be operated by professionals and the results had to be interpreted by professionals. Reading an X-ray requires skill, and the images are open to misinterpretation. Thus, the *Bolam* test and deference to expert opinion remain relevant. Artificial intelligence (AI) has brought about a quantum shift, with growing evidence that AI outperforms professionals in basic diagnosis and interpretation of data.[101] An article published in 2019 (ancient history by the AI timeframe) explored the impact of AI and robotics in radiology.[102]

[95] See above, text to n 86.

[96] The Irish equivalent of *Bolam* is *Dunne (an infant) v National Maternity Hospital* [1989] IR 91, but for convenience *Bolam* is used as a generic reference for the approach to medical negligence.

[97] *Morrissey v Health Service Executive* [2020] IESC 6.

[98] ibid para 6.11.

[99] ibid paras 6.14, 6.15, 6.30.

[100] ibid 6.37.

[101] M Gräf, et al, 'Comparison of Physician and Artificial Intelligence-Based Symptom Checker Diagnostic Accuracy (2022) 42 *Rheumatology International* 2167. This book will not discuss the impact of AI on medical negligence, but it is clearly an enormously significant development.

[102] S Reardon, 'Rise of Robot Radiologists' (December 2019) 576(7787) *Nature* S54.

A poignant anecdote concerned a female computer scientist, who had a mammogram in 2012, which was reported as normal by her doctors. A subsequent mammogram, MRI, and biopsy were all reported as negative. In 2014, she was diagnosed with breast cancer. She survived and spent the next four years developing an algorithm to read and interpret mammograms. When applied to her 2012 mammogram, 'the algorithm correctly predicted she was at a higher risk of developing breast cancer within five years than 98 percent of patients'.[103] Should her doctors who clearly misinterpreted the mammogram be held liable in negligence?

C. Surgical Negligence

Surgical negligence is another area where *Bolam* may not always be appropriate. The claimant in the Canadian case of *Armstrong v Royal Victoria Hospital*[104] underwent a colectomy surgery performed by the defendant. During the procedure, the defendant injured the claimant's left ureter, causing blockage and consequent damage to her left kidney, which was eventually removed. The claimant alleged that the defendant had been negligent in operating the cauterising device, a surgical instrument used to fuse tissue. An electric current is passed through the jaws of the device while it is clamped on the blood vessel to heat the blood and coagulate it, thus sealing the blood vessel. However, the heat from the device can also damage any tissue that is within two millimetres of it. To avoid this collateral damage, surgeons must ensure that the device is at least two millimetres away from any other tissue.

It was commonly accepted that the damage to the ureter in *Armstrong* was the result of thermal injury from the defendant's use of the cauterising device. Equally, it was commonly accepted that the standard of care was that of a normal, prudent surgeon. The defendant maintained that he had stayed at least five centimetres away from the ureter and that he had taken the necessary steps to avoid contact with it as well as to maintain a safe distance from it. Both parties' experts agreed that the steps taken by the defendant were those which a normal, prudent surgeon should take. The defendant's expert suggested that the injury was caused accidentally. However, the claimant's expert stressed that if the defendant had stayed at least 2 millimetres away, the thermal injury could not have happened. The fact that it *did* happen meant that the defendant must have either made contact with the ureter or was less than two millimetres away from it.

The trial judge held that the standard of care required the 'surgeon to identify, protect, and avoid direct contact with or close proximity to the ureter'.[105] Given that the injury was caused by heat from the cauterising device, it stood to reason that the defendant 'had failed to avoid direct contact or close proximity to

[103] ibid S55.
[104] *Armstrong v Royal Victoria Hospital* [2019] ONCA 963.
[105] ibid [146].

the ureter'. Ergo, the defendant was negligent. The Court of Appeal for Ontario reversed the trial judge's ruling by a 2-1 majority. The crucial question in the Court of Appeal was whether the trial judge had erred in applying the standard of care, by conflating the goal to be achieved with the steps to be taken. The majority held that the defendant was not negligent because he had taken reasonable steps to identify and protect the ureter. By taking these steps, he had discharged his duty as a prudent surgeon. The fact that he had failed to keep more than two millimetres away was not an act of negligence but a goal that was not achieved despite taking reasonable steps.

The majority rested its reasoning on the danger of conflating goals and steps. On the face of it, this argument appears credible. However, on closer analysis, it is misconstrued. The goal in *Armstrong* was to achieve a successful surgery. The steps to achieve that goal were to operate the cauterising device according to professional standards: in this case, by not coming into contact with, or being within 2 millimetres of, the surrounding tissue. There was no conflation of goals and steps by the trial judge. The majority's error was to ignore the fact that there were objectively ascertainable steps that had to be taken by the defendant, choosing instead to defer to the medical experts' opinion of what constituted accepted practice. The majority's approach would excuse doctors who simply tried their best but actually failed to do what was required of them based on their professional training and expertise. It turns *Bolam* from a professional standard test into an 'I tried my best' defence.

The dissenting judge disagreed, noting that there was no evidence to suggest that this was a case in which a prudent surgeon could, without negligence, come too close to the ureter. The judge further found that there were no unusual circumstances surrounding the surgery that were beyond the surgeon's control. It was a routine procedure which required the defendant to stay at least two millimetres away from the surrounding tissue. He failed to do so and injured the claimant, thus breaching his duty as a surgeon. The dissenting judgment in *Armstrong*, with its subsequent endorsement in that case by the Supreme Court of Canada,[106] adds to a pattern in the common law world of judges reasserting their sovereignty over the standard of care in medical negligence disputes.

It remains the case that judges may not choose between expert views when what constitutes acceptable standards is contested. However, when there is an objectively ascertainable standard – 'absolute certainty' or surgical protocols – judges are willing to rely on that standard and judge the defendant in the face of contrary opinion from the medical expert. *Armstrong* is a salutary reminder that experts should only give their opinion on general, accepted standards of medical practice and refrain from expressing judgement on the defendant's particular conduct. This may seem trite, but it is not an uncommon transgression by defendants' expert witnesses. In the Court of Appeal of England and Wales in *Smith v Southampton*

[106] *Armstrong v Ward* 2021 SCC 1; [2021] 1 SCR 3.

University Hospital NHS Trust,[107] the defendant surgeon had not closed his scissors while manipulating some tissue during surgery and inadvertently severed a nerve, causing lasting damage to the claimant patient. It was commonly accepted by the experts that the scissors should be kept closed while manipulating tissue.

However, the defendant's expert testified that the failure to do so was not necessarily negligent. On the strength of that, the trial judge held that the defendant was not negligent. Reversing the trial judge, Wall LJ noted that the judge had appeared 'to rely exclusively on the *Bolam* test', emphasising that it was 'not sufficient … simply to say that [the defendant's expert] is representative of a responsible body of medical opinion and that, as a consequence, [the defendant] was not negligent'. Judges must be cautious not to allow *Bolam* to provide cover for negligent defendants.

D. Duty to Advise and Consent to Risk

There are two ways in which consent is relevant to medical malpractice – consent to the treatment and consent to the risk. Consent to the treatment is required to give the doctor lawful authority to treat the patient, absent which the doctor would commit battery and be liable in the tort of trespass.[108] Under English law, it is well established that the patient only needs to be 'informed in broad terms of the nature of the procedure which is intended'.[109] There is no requirement to provide information that will satisfy the *Montgomery/ Hii Chii Kok* test.[110] Consent to the risk, on the other hand, is to enable the patient to decide what risks they are willing to take as well as to secure the cooperation and confidence of the patient. These are factors that are crucial to establishing trust and to 'contributing to the treatment's success'.[111] However, if the doctor negligently fails to inform the patient of a material risk, which materialises and results in damage to the patient, the doctor may be liable in negligence. Tan Keng Feng put it succinctly:

> There are two aspects to the patient's participation in medical decision-making: one pertaining to the patient's exclusive non-clinical right to self-determination, and the

[107] *Smith v Southampton University Hospital NHS Trust* [2007] EWCA Civ 387.

[108] *Chatterton v Gerson* [1981] 1 QB 432.

[109] ibid 443. See also, *Hills v Potter* [1984] 1 WLR 641.

[110] See for example, *XYZ v Warrington & Halton NHS Foundation Trust* [2016] EWHC 331 in which case the court held that consent was properly taken based on the standard information on the nature of the procedure and associated risks. See also the observation in *Shaw v Kovac* [2017] 1 WLR 4773: 'It has long been the law that where a doctor has failed to provide proper information as to risk prior to a medical procedure and that failure leads to consent being given which otherwise would have been withheld, and loss results, then that is actionable in negligence. The consent so given is not regarded as a nullity; and accordingly in the usual case the claim is not to be pleaded as one of trespass to the person (in the absence of fraud or bad faith, which has never been pleaded in the present case); see, for example, *Chatterton v Gerson* [1981] 1 QB 432, p 443 (per Bristow J)'.

[111] *Re W (A Minor) (Medical Treatment: Court's Jurisdiction)* [1993] Fam 64, 76.

other pertaining to the patient's right, shared with the doctor, to participate in clinical matters in the medical treatment process.[112]

This distinction between these two forms of consent is crucial because trespass is actionable per se, ie the patient may sue even if the patient does not suffer any damage. Failing to distinguish between gaining informed consent (trespass) and the duty to inform the patient of material risks/ information (negligence) risks inadvertently importing the *Montgomery/ Hii Chii Kok* test into trespass. The lines are already becoming blurred,[113] and the cautionary words of the Canadian Supreme Court in *Reibl v Hughes*[114] to expunge the term 'informed consent' from medical negligence discourse should be heeded.

The consent standard for trespass is rightly set at a level that is relatively easily satisfied by medical practitioners. The more demanding *Montgomery/ Hii Chii Kok* test is appropriate for negligence because here, even though the standard demands more of doctors, they will only be liable if the patient suffers some damage. Further, even when damage is suffered, the patient must still prove that it was the negligent failure to inform of risk that caused the damage. This will require patients to prove that if they had been told, they would have avoided the risk by refusing consent and foregoing treatment or opting for an alternative treatment option. This will not be an easy task for serious, non-elective procedures where the patient really does not have a choice other than the recommended treatment.[115]

Courts around the common law world, acknowledging the infelicity of applying *Bolam* to the doctor's duty to advise, have rejected the peer professional test.[116] Instead of inquiring what information or advice a responsible body of peer professionals would give, the inquiry is turned to what information or advice a reasonable patient would find material. This test may be described as the 'reasonable patient' test or 'prudent patient' test.[117] Instead of peer professionals setting the standard of disclosure, doctors must inform patients of material risks, the materiality of which is assessed from the perspective of prudent patients. Underlying this shift from the peer professional to the prudent patient test is an increasing awareness

[112] Tan Keng Feng, 'Failure of Medical Advice: Trespass or Negligence?' (1987) 7 *Legal Studies* 149, 167–68.

[113] J Herring, et al, 'Elbow Room for Best Practice? Montgomery, Patients' Values, and Balanced Decision-Making in Person-Centred Clinical Care' (2017) 25 *Medical Law Review* 582, 583.

[114] *Reibl v Hughes* (1981) 114 DLR 1.

[115] See Chapter 8 text to nn 89–107.

[116] *Canterbury v Spence* 464 F 2d 772 (DC Cir 1972) (US); *Reibl v Hughes* (1981) 114 DLR 1 (Canada); *Rogers v Whitaker* (1992) 175 CLR 479 (Australia); *Dr Hari Krishnan v Megat Noor Ishak Megat Ibrahim* [2018] 1 MLRA 535 (Malaysia); *Montgomery v Lanarkshire Health Board* [2015] UKSC 11; [2015] AC 1430 (UK); *Hii Chii Kok v Ong Peng Jin London Lucien* [2017] SGCA 38; [2017] 2 SLR 492 (Singapore).

[117] *Sidaway v Board of Governors of the Bethlem Royal Hospital* [1985] 1 AC 871, 887 (per Lord Scarman); *Hii Chii Kok v Ong Peng Jin London Lucien* [2017] SGCA 38; [2017] 2 SLR 492, [68] (per Menon CJ).

and emphasis on patient autonomy.[118] The UK Supreme Court in *Montgomery v Lanarkshire Health Board* set it out thus:

> The doctor is therefore under a duty to take reasonable care to ensure that the patient is aware of any material risks involved in any recommended treatment, and of any reasonable alternative or variant treatments. The test of materiality is whether, in the circumstances of the particular case, a reasonable person in the patient's position would be likely to attach significance to the risk, or the doctor is or should reasonably be aware that the particular patient would be likely to attach significance to it.[119]

Montgomery was adopted in Singapore in *Hii Chii Kok v Ong Peng Jin London Lucien*,[120] with some modification.[121] *Hii Chii Kok* offers a carefully reasoned framework that balances beneficence and autonomy. The Singapore Court of Appeal sets out three sequential questions.[122]

- First, was the information objectively material? This is answered based on the prudent patient test.
- Secondly, did the doctor know of the risks and alternatives, and if not, ought the doctor to have known? Here, the Court reverts to the *Bolam/ Bolitho* test to determine whether the doctor ought to have known of the risks and alternatives. A doctor who is not aware or has no reason to be aware of the risks and alternatives judged by peer professionals is not negligent.
- Thirdly, is there some reasonable justification for non-disclosure of a risk? If the first two stages are satisfied, the doctor is obliged to disclose the information unless there is reasonable justification, which includes necessity, express waiver of the right to be informed by the patient, and a limited therapeutic privilege.

The 'particular patient' limb of the material risk test has given rise to an ill-informed concern that a subjective test applies, which requires doctors to disclose all possible risks that particular patients would want to know. The provenance of this test lies in the landmark Australian High Court decision of *Rogers v Whitaker*,[123] whose approach was adopted in *Montgomery*. The claimant in *Rogers* was partially blind in one eye. Prior to the surgery, she repeatedly asked whether the surgery posed any risk to her good eye as she did not want to risk losing her eyesight completely. She was adamant that if there was any risk at all to her good eye, she

[118] See especially, the comments of Lady Hale in *Montgomery v Lanarkshire Health Board* [2015] UKSC 11; [2015] AC 1430, [108] and Menon CJ in *Hii Chii Kok v Ong Peng Jin London Lucien* [2017] SGCA 38; [2017] 2 SLR 492, [116]–[122].See also, J Miola and R Heywood, 'The Changing Face of the Pre-Operative Medical Disclosure: Placing the Patient at the Heart of the Matter' (2017) 133 *Law Quarterly Review* 296; J Gardner, 'The Many Faces of the Reasonable Person' (2015) 131 *Law Quarterly Review* 563; R Heywood, 'R.I.P. Sidaway: Patient-oriented Disclosure – A Standard Worth Waiting For?' (2015) 23 *Medical Law Review* 455.

[119] *Montgomery v Lanarkshire Health Board* [2015] UKSC 11; [2015] AC 1430, [87].

[120] [2017] SGCA 38; [2017] 2 SLR 492.

[121] For a detailed commentary on *Hii Chii Kok*, see LV Austin, '*Hii Chii Kok v (1) Ooi Peng Jin London Lucien; (2) National Cancer Centre*: Modifying Montgomery' (2019) 27 *Medical Law Review* 339.

[122] *Hii Chii Kok v Ong Peng Jin London Lucien* [2017] SGCA 38; [2017] 2 SLR 492, [131]–[153].

[123] *Rogers v Whitaker* (1992) 175 CLR 479.

would not proceed with the surgery. There was a small risk, assessed by the Court as 1 in 14,000 of sympathetic ophthalmia, which was not disclosed to the patient. The risk materialised and the claimant lost her sight in both eyes. It was in that context that the Court referred to the 'particular patient' as the particular risk in that case was relevant and material to the claimant.

It must be emphasised that in *Rogers*, the claimant made very clear her concern about the particular risk. Had the 'particular patient' limb been confined to such situations or even situations where the doctor *actually knew* about the risk from other sources, the scope of the duty to inform would be uncontroversial. The extension of the particular patient limb to situations where the doctor *ought to have known* that the risk is material to the patient is arguably unfair on the doctor. In Singapore, recent legislation codifying *Hii Chii Kok* has placed an affirmative duty on doctors to examine patient records to determine whether the patient may have idiosyncratic concerns that a reasonable person may not have.[124]

The problem with the *Montgomery/ Hii Chii Kok* test is that it has become synonymous with patient autonomy. This invariably results in an overly subjective approach that focuses on the particular patient's desire for information ex post instead of the reasonable patient's desire for information ex ante.[125] Commenting on *Montgomery's* emphasis on autonomy as the basis for the duty to inform, John Banja cautioned:

> But if a court or IRB committee someday decides that patients or research participants must be told of a nonexistent risk on the basis of an autonomy-grounded 'I would nevertheless like to know' rights plea, then we will have replaced a scientific or factual understanding of a presumptive risk with something considerably less rational. Doing so would open the floodgates of information disclosure to patients without any measure or criterion in place for deciding when to engage the shut-off valves. Unless courts and regulatory entities simply demand that all serious risks, no matter how infrequent or remote, be disclosed, it is impossible to see how an autonomy standard offers any greater reliability or objectivity than a reasonable person standard.[126]

The overreach in *Montgomery* is because the court focused on the patient's rights instead of the doctor's duty. This was the error made by Lord Scarman in his otherwise laudable dissent:

> In a medical negligence case where the issue is as to the advice and information given to the patient as to the treatment proposed, the available options, and the risk, the court is concerned primarily with a patient's right. *The doctor's duty arises from his patient's*

[124] Civil Law Act 1909 (Singapore) s 37(3)(b).

[125] Concerns about the impact of *Hii Chii Kok* led to legislative reforms in Singapore, resulting in a new s 37 introduced into the Civil Law Act 1909 (Singapore). The aim of the provision was to reintroduce the *Bolam/ Bolitho* test as a check against the *Montgomery/ Hii Chii Kok* approach to the duty to advise. However, the legislation appears to be internally inconsistent and is yet to be interpreted by the courts. For critique, see K Amirthalingam, 'Upending the Medical Duty to Advise: Legislating the Standard of Care in Singapore' (2022) 22 *Medical Law International* 189.

[126] J Banja, 'Reasonable Persons, Autonomous Persons, and Lady Hale Determining a Standard for Risk Disclosure' (2020) 50(2) *Hastings Center Report* 25, 29.

> *rights*. If one considers the scope of the doctor's duty by beginning with the right of the patient to make his own decision whether he will or will not undergo the treatment proposed, the right to be informed of significant risk and the doctor's corresponding duty are easy to understand (emphasis added).[127]

Informed consent and patient autonomy should not cast too long a shadow over the tort of negligence.[128] There is a tension between the concept of reasonableness in negligence, which is relative, and the individualistic notion of patient autonomy, which is absolute.[129] That is not to say that doctors do not owe patients a duty to provide information; it is just that the basis of that duty should not be patient autonomy but patient agency. To help the patient make an informed choice is the hallmark of collaborative autonomy and shared decision-making. This is a middle ground between medical paternalism and individualistic autonomy.[130] Unlike the obtaining of consent for treatment, which typically occurs at a finite moment, the duty to inform is continuous, as the doctor–patient relationship develops, the patient's condition and circumstances evolve, and new treatment options either present themselves or are eliminated.

Patients often do not have the confidence to make decisions on their own, preferring to be advised on what to do or even to leave it to the doctor to decide.[131] However, this is not necessarily evidence that patients do not want to exercise autonomy. In some cases, patients are consciously outsourcing the decision-making to a trusted professional but retaining the right to ask further questions while preserving the right to make an informed decision. This is described in the literature as a form of 'conscientious autonomy' or 'intellectual outsourcing'.[132] 'Autonomous choice-making requires two essential psychological elements: an internal locus of control and a sense of competent self-efficacy'.[133] Persons with an internal locus of control believe that they have control over their lives while those with an external locus of control do not, believing that others or circumstances have control over them. Self-efficacy refers to 'a sense of having the ability successfully to carry out a task and achieve a result'.[134]

[127] *Sidaway v Board of Governors of the Bethlem Royal Hospital*[1985] 1 AC 871, 888.

[128] See C Purshouse, 'Liability for Lost Autonomy in Negligence: Undermining the Coherence of Tort Law?' (2015) 22 *Torts Law Journal* 226.

[129] Individual autonomy is conflated with self-determination, agency, or liberty. See generally, G Parchomovsky and A Stein, 'Autonomy' (2021) 71 *University of Toronto Law Journal* 61; J Coggon and J Miola, 'Autonomy, Liberty, and Medical Decision-Making' (2011) 70 *Cambridge Law Journal* 523.

[130] MA Rubin, 'The Collaborative Autonomy Model of Medical Decision-Making' (2014) 20 *Neurocritical Care* 311, 312.

[131] See studies cited in MA Rubin, 'The Collaborative Autonomy Model of Medical Decision-Making' (2014) 20 *Neurocritical Care* 311, 314.

[132] VA Entwistle et al, 'Communicating about Screening' (2008) 337 *British Medical Journal* 789; R Kukla, 'Conscientious Autonomy: Displacing Decisions in Health Care' (2005) 5 *Hastings Center Report* 34. I am grateful to Dr Anantham Devanand (Head, SingHealth Duke-NUS Lung Centre; Director of the SingHealth Duke-NUS Medical Humanities Institute) for these references.

[133] BN Waller, 'The Psychological Structure of Patient Autonomy' (2002) 11 *Cambridge Quarterly of Healthcare Ethics* 257.

[134] ibid 258.

This provides a better understanding of the type of patients who are capable of exercising autonomy, the type who need assistance to achieve autonomy, and the type for whom decisions have to be made. This taxonomy may be represented by this table:

	Has self-efficacy	**Lacks self-efficacy**
Internal locus of control	Type 1	Type 2
External locus of control	Type 3	Type 4

Type 1 patients are fully capable of agency and can process complex information. Patients of type 2 have the capacity for agency but lack the ability to exercise it as they may not fully understand the condition of their health and their options. Too much information can become stressful as they want to exercise control, but they are not competent to do so. Type 3 patients are competent to make their own decisions but lack the confidence to do so. Instead of presumptively making decisions for patient types 2 and 3, doctors should help these patients by providing the necessary information, advice, and support through dialogue to enable them to exercise their agency. Type 4 patients may need the doctor to hold their hand and guide them with input from family as appropriate. The theoretical framework based on relational vulnerability explored in Chapter three supports this approach.

There is no one-size-fits-all approach to the duty to inform. The type and degree of information may vary according to the patient. This will be daunting for doctors, but at the same time, courts will also be aware of this reality and will therefore assess reasonableness according to the context and the nature of the patient. Studies show that having some degree of control through adequate information is important to the patient's health.[135] 'If the basic rule of medicine is "First, do no harm," then the harm done to patient autonomy by paternalistic medical environments and overcontrolling caregivers must be scrupulously avoided'.[136] Medical beneficence and patient autonomy can be balanced by shared decision-making and patient agency.

E. Duty to Advise and Choice of Alternative Treatments

Unlike *Montgomery*, which refers to the duty to inform of *risks* in recommended procedures and alternative options, *Hii Chii Kok* extends the material information test to the doctor's general duty to advise.

> Unlike the court in *Montgomery*, *we do not confine the scope of the information in question to material risks* concerning the recommended treatment and any reasonable

[135] KE Dennis, 'Patients' Control and the Information Imperative' (1990) 39 *Nursing Research* 162.

[136] BN Waller, 'The Psychological Structure of Patient Autonomy' (2002) 11 *Cambridge Quarterly of Healthcare Ethics* 257, 263.

> alternatives or variant treatment. In our judgment, the information which doctors ought to disclose is (a) information that would be relevant and material to a reasonable patient situated in the particular patient's position, or (b) information that a doctor knows is important to the particular patient in question (emphasis added).[137]

This potentially encroaches on aspects of the doctor's duty that should be resolved according to *Bolam*. The scope of the *Montgomery* duty was considered by the UK's Supreme Court in *McCulloch v Forth Valley Health Board*.[138] The deceased in *McCulloch* died of cardiac tamponade at home after being seen by the defendant cardiologist. The alleged negligence was the defendant's failure to advise the deceased of the option of treatment with a non-steroidal anti-inflammatory drug (NSAID). The appellants alleged that had the deceased been advised of the NSAID, he would have taken the drug and would not have died. They argued that the duty to advise of alternative options was governed by the *Montgomery* test, and should be resolved based 'on the circumstances, objectives and values of the individual patient and cannot be judged simply by the view of the doctor offering the treatment even though that view is supported by a responsible body of medical opinion'.[139] The respondents argued that *Bolam* applied. A middle ground, namely that a doctor should be under a duty to advise of alternative options that have the support of a responsible body of medical opinion even though they are *not* options that the doctor would recommend, was briefly considered and rejected by the Supreme Court.

The Lord Ordinary at first instance and the Inner House on appeal held that the *Montgomery* test only applied to disclosure of risk. Advice on treatment continued to be governed by *Hunter v Hanley*,[140] *Maynard v West Midlands Regional Health Authority*,[141] and *Bolitho*. Noting that there were different views on the prescription of the NSAID, the Lord Ordinary held that the view supporting the defendant's non-disclosure of the use of the NSAID was logically defensible. Thus, it was not negligent of the defendant not to advise the deceased of the NSAID. The Supreme Court unanimously upheld the lower courts' judgment, affirming that the duty to advise patients of alternative treatments was governed by the *Bolam* test and not the *Montgomery* test.

The Court referred to the judgment in *Duce v Worcestershire Acute Hospitals NHS Trust*,[142] which applied a two-stage test to *Montgomery*. The first stage was the identification of risks associated with an operation, which was governed by the *Bolam* test. The second stage was the materiality of the risk, which was governed by the *Montgomery* test. By analogy, the Court held that the assessment of what

[137] *Hii Chii Kok v Ong Peng Jin London Lucien* [2017] SGCA 38; [2017] 2 SLR 492 (per Menon CJ), [132].

[138] *McCulloch v Forth Valley Health Board* [2023] UKSC 26; [2024] AC 925.

[139] ibid [4].

[140] *McCulloch v Forth Valley Health Board* [2020] CSOH 40; *McCulloch v Forth Valley Health Board* [2021] CSIH 21; [2021] SCLR 361. See *Hunter v Hanley* 1955 SLT 213.

[141] *Maynard v West Midlands Regional Health Authority* [1984] 1 WLR 634.

[142] *Duce v Worcestershire Acute Hospitals NHS Trust* [2018] EWCA Civ 1307; [2018] PIQR P18.

constituted a reasonable alternative was to be determined by *Bolam*. With respect, this analogy is misplaced. *Montgomery* requires a doctor to advise patients of '*any* reasonable alternative or variant treatments' (emphasis added).[143]

Doctors cannot be expected to advise of risks of which they are not aware;[144] whether they should advise of a reasonable alternative of which they are or ought reasonably to be aware is a different question. Indeed, in *Montgomery*, Lord Kerr and Lord Reed noted that 'it is a *non sequitur* to conclude that the question whether a risk of injury, *or the availability of an alternative form of treatment*, ought to be discussed with the patient is also a matter of purely professional judgment' (emphasis added).[145] This suggests that *Montgomery* contemplated moving away from the *Bolam* test not just with respect to the duty to inform of risks, but also with respect to the duty to advise on alternative treatments. Arguably, respect for patient autonomy would demand that the patient be informed of *any* reasonable alternatives so that the patient can make an informed decision about which treatment to accept.

The Supreme Court in *McCulloch* was of the view that rejecting the *Bolam* test with respect to the duty to advise on alternative treatments could potentially force doctors to give advice contrary to their professional judgement. Their Lordships referred with approval to *AH v Greater Glasgow Health Board.*[146] Lord Boyd in *AH* used this example: a patient with a pre-existing condition is treated for another illness. There is a conventional treatment option available, but it would expose the patient to greater risk due to the patient's pre-existing condition. The doctor's clinical judgement is that the risk is too great and therefore the treatment option is not reasonable. Thus, the doctor does not advise the patient of this option. According to *AH*, as long as this decision has peer support, the doctor is not negligent in failing to advise the patient of the treatment. There are three problems with this.

First, this approach undermines the patient's right to make decisions about what risks they are willing to take, handing that power to the doctors. This is contrary to the spirit of *Montgomery*, which emphasised patients' rights and individual autonomy. Secondly, this approach conflates the duty to *advise of* an alternative treatment with a duty to *administer* that treatment. That is not correct. The duty is to advise the patient to enable the patient to make an informed decision. Surely, there is no conflict with a doctor's professional and ethical duties to advise on alternatives that they do not advocate but which are accepted by peer professionals. This leads to the third problem.

Bolam recognises that there may be several reasonable alternatives, and it establishes a negative test of negligence. If a doctor acts in accordance with a practice accepted as proper, the doctor cannot be found negligent. This does not mean that

143 *Montgomery v Lanarkshire Health Board* [2015] UKSC 11; [2015] AC 1430, [87].

144 *Duce v Worcestershire Acute Hospitals NHS Trust* [2018] EWCA Civ 1307; [2018] PIQR P18 (per Lord Hamblyn), [43].

145 *Montgomery v Lanarkshire Health Board* [2015] UKSC 11; [2015] AC 1430, [83].

146 *AH v Greater Glasgow Health Board* [2018] CSOH 57; 2018 SLT 535.

the other practices are unreasonable; indeed, they may be superior to the doctor's practice. Thus, if there is an alternative treatment that has peer support, albeit not one which the doctor supports, there is nothing improper in imposing a duty on the defendant doctor to advise the patient of those reasonable alternatives.[147] The doctor may counsel against the option, but the patient should be enabled to make an informed decision and to seek alternative treatment elsewhere.

Montgomery recognises this, noting that 'it is the doctor's responsibility to explain to her patient why she considers that one of the available treatment options is medically preferable to the others'.[148] Paradoxically, Lord Hamblen and Lord Burrows in *McCulloch* note that the doctor in *Montgomery* was under a duty to advise the claimant of the alternative of a caesarean section because even though the doctor herself did not favour that option, 'there was no responsible body of medical opinion denying that a caesarean section was a reasonable alternative'.[149] It bears noting that there was a responsible body of medical opinion supporting prescription of the NSAID. Therefore, the claimant should have been advised of that option, as is implicit in this statement by the Court:

> It is important to stress that it is not being suggested that the doctor can simply inform the patient about the treatment options that the doctor himself or herself prefers. Rather the doctor's duty of care, in line with *Montgomery*, is to inform the patient of *all* reasonable treatment options applying the professional practice test (emphasis added).[150]

McCulloch was correct in holding that *Bolam* was relevant to the duty to advise of reasonable alternatives. However, it went further than necessary, resulting in arbitrary rejection of reasonable alternatives that could be material to the patient's decision. Lord Hamblen and Lord Burrows illustrate their argument with this example.[151] There are 10 possible treatment options for a given diagnosis. All 10 have the support of a responsible body of medical opinion. The defendant doctor, exercising her clinical judgment, decides that only four of the 10 options are reasonable. The doctor's view is supported by a responsible body of medical opinion. Therefore, the doctor is entitled to exclude the other six options and advise the patient of only four options. With respect, this conclusion rests on shaky grounds.

The *Bolam* test would absolve the doctor of negligence for administering one of the four treatment options, but it does not render the other six options unreasonable. The remaining six options each have the support of a responsible body of medical opinion and the patient should be advised of these options. Let us assume the patient in the above example goes to a hospital and is randomly assigned a doctor whose professional judgement differs from the defendant doctor's judgement in the above illustration. The assigned doctor decides that the other six

[147] *McCulloch* was considered in *Butler v Ward* [2025] EWHC 877 (KB).
[148] *Montgomery v Lanarkshire Health Board* [2015] UKSC 11; [2015] AC 1430, [95].
[149] *McCulloch v Forth Valley Health Board* [2023] UKSC 26; [2024] AC 925, [62].
[150] ibid [58].
[151] ibid [57].

options are reasonable. Now the patient would have the benefit of those other options. The reasoning in *McCulloch* risks arbitrary (in)justice.[152]

Bolam protects doctors against allegations of negligence by allowing for a range of practices to be considered reasonable. Therein lies the rub. Doctors may not be held liable for adopting one practice out of a range of acceptable practices in treating the patient. When it comes to advising the patient, all reasonable options known to the doctor, or which ought to be known to the doctor, should be included in the advice to enable the patient to make an informed decision and to participate in shared decision-making. However, the Court in *McCulloch* expressly considered and rejected the argument that defendant doctors should advise patients of options that are supported by a responsible body of doctors even if the defendant doctors themselves do not subscribe to the option.[153] *McCulloch* has grappled with a thorny question that lies at the intersection of professional expertise, patient's rights, medical beneficence, and patient autonomy. The solution is pragmatic but not entirely principled. *McCulloch* may provide doctors with some deserved relief in the real world of medical practice. However, it does so at the expense of deeper engagement with the complexities of contemporary, inclusive medical practice and the evolving role of the patient in the doctor–patient relationship.

IV. Conclusion

The standard of care in medical negligence is a vexed issue that has been politicised by doctors, patients' interest groups, judges, and Government officials as the delivery of affordable and competent healthcare services affects multiple stakeholder interests which may be in tension. The conventional approach set out in *Bolam* reflected an approach to medical negligence that was protective of doctors and deferential to professional expertise. It reigned supreme during the ascendancy of medical paternalism and in the wake of the creation of the National Health Service as there was a vested interest in protecting healthcare services in the immediate post-War era. As human rights concerns and patients' activism developed in the second half of the twentieth century, *Bolam* came under attack; it was whittled down by *Bolitho* and felled by *Montgomery* with respect to the duty to advise.

The extremes represented by the doctor-centric *Bolam* test and the patient-centric *Montgomery* test attest to the political nature of medical negligence. This chapter has argued that a middle path that balances doctors' interests against patients' interests, while ensuring that judges are ultimately responsible for adjudication may be found in the approach set out by the High Court of Australia in *Rosenberg*. The chapter has also demonstrated that the approaches to the standard

[152] Indeed, the court in *Montgomery* alludes to this potential risk of arbitrariness. *Montgomery v Lanarkshire Health Board* [2015] UKSC 11; [2015] AC 1430, [84]).

[153] *McCulloch v Forth Valley Health Board* [2023] UKSC 26; [2024] AC 925, [81].

of care risk under-protecting patients in some diagnostic and surgical cases while over-exposing doctors to liability in the duty to advise cases.

The almost dogmatic emphasis of patient autonomy has been detrimental to the doctor–patient relationship, imposing unrealistic expectations on doctors and undermining trust. Patient autonomy should not be a determining factor in medical negligence; its primary function is in the areas of medical trespass and medical research. The core values underpinning the duty to advise are patient agency and shared decision-making. A doctor is under a duty to enable a patient to exercise agency and participate meaningfully in making decisions with the doctor. It must be recognised that not all patients are equally competent. The more vulnerable the patient, the more the doctor may have to do to help the patient achieve agency. In some cases, a patient may not be capable of agency and the doctor may have to take a more proactive role in consultation with the patient and family.

7

Recasting Causation

I. Introduction

In most cases, causation is a simple question of cause and effect resolved according to the laws of nature and common sense, as observed by McLachlin CJ:

> A common sense inference of 'but for' causation from proof of negligence usually flows without difficulty. Evidence connecting the breach of duty to the injury suffered may permit the judge, depending on the circumstances, to infer that the defendant's negligence probably caused the loss.[1]

Proof of causation becomes complicated when there are multiple events potentially contributing to an outcome; where scientific knowledge is incapable of identifying the cause; where an effect is contingent on the hypothetical action of a third party; or where an outcome cannot be determined except as a probability. Medical negligence is one area where causation is complicated for these reasons. Patients who suffer adverse medical outcomes sometimes face significant challenges in their quest to prove causation due to the inherent uncertainties that exist in medical negligence litigation.[2]

To begin with, patients seek medical intervention when their health is already compromised, raising questions whether any adverse outcome is due to the doctor's negligence or is inevitable. Medical negligence often involves omissions – failure to diagnose, failure to treat, failure to monitor, failure to advise. Proving causation in omissions cases raises additional challenges.[3] There is always a degree of speculation – what are the chances that the doctor could have done something to avoid the adverse outcome?

Further, in many cases, the defendant's liability is contingent on the acts or hypothetical acts of a third party. In team-based practice, causation may be contingent on the act or omission of another member of the team;[4] in cases involving duty to inform, causation may be contingent on the decision of the patient;[5] in

[1] *Clements v Clements* 2012 SCC 32; [2012] 2 SCR 181, [10].

[2] EJ Russell, 'Establishing Medical Negligence – A Herculean Task?' (1998) 3 *Scots Law Times* 17.

[3] See generally on omissions and causation, Y Abrams, 'Omissive Overdetermination: Why the Act–Omission Distinction Makes a Difference for Causal Analysis' (2022) 49 *University of Western Australia Law Review* 57.

[4] *Bolitho v City and Hackney Health Authority* [1998] 1 AC 232.

[5] *Chester v Afshar* [2004] UKHL 41; [2005] 1 AC 134.

cases involving negligent delay or failure to refer, causation may be contingent on the decision of the specialist or hospital to which the patient is referred;[6] in cases involving systemic negligence, causation may be contingent on dynamic interactions of various parties and institutional protocols.[7]

Patients' health outcomes are often uncertain for epistemological or ontological reasons.[8] The aetiology of diseases and the occurrence of iatrogenic injuries (namely, those arising as a result of medical treatment) are sometimes not fully understood by experts. Evidence of negligence or causation may not be available or accessible to the claimant, making it impossible to prove causation. Intuitively, this may be perceived as unjust, leading courts to explore alternatives to orthodox proof of causation, including recognising liability for material increase in risk, loss of chance, and loss of autonomy, or reversing the burden of proof.[9]

This chapter begins with a theoretical critique of causation and causal responsibility. It then reviews the existing doctrinal approaches to causation, including the but-for test, the necessary element of a sufficient set (NESS) test, the material contribution to damage test, and the material increase in risk test. The jurisprudence shows that courts have historically modified causation principles in favour of claimants,[10] even at the risk of undermining doctrinal coherence.[11] This underlying claimant-friendly philosophy has been amplified in medical negligence by rights discourse and patient autonomy considerations, further muddying the waters of causation.[12]

Instead of distorting the law on causation, courts – or, if necessary, the legislature – should make an explicit policy decision to reverse the burden of proof, which conventionally lies on the claimant.[13] Placing the burden of proof on the claimant is itself a policy decision. Thus, there is nothing improper in placing the burden of proof on the defendant in appropriate circumstances for policy reasons.[14] It is a cleaner way to achieve the same outcome without distorting causation principles.

[6] *Wright v Cambridge Medical Group* [2011] EWCA Civ 669; [2013] QB 312.

[7] *Noor Azlin bte Abdul Rahman v Changi General Hospital Pte Ltd* [2019] SGCA 13; [2019] 1 SLR 834.

[8] *Gregg v Scott* [2005] UKHL 2; [2005] 2 AC 176; *Armstrong v Quest Laboratories Pte Ltd* [2019] SGCA 75; [2020] 1 SLR 133, [94]–[99].

[9] See discussion below, text to nn 92–135 and Chapter 8 of this volume, text to nn 9–118.

[10] See MA Kotler, 'Utility, Autonomy and Motive: A Descriptive Model of the Development of Tort Doctrine' (1990) 58 *Cincinnati Law Review* 1231, 1235; V Black, 'The Rise and Fall of Plaintiff-Friendly Causation' (2016) 53 *Alberta Law Review* 533, 534; D Hamer, 'Chance Would be a Fine Thing: Proof of Causation and Quantum in an Unpredictable World' (1999) 23 *Melbourne University Law Review* 557, 614–28.

[11] *Fairchild v Glenhaven Funeral Services Ltd* [2002] UKHL 22; [2003] 1 AC 32.

[12] *Chester v Afshar* [2004] UKHL 41; [2005] 1 AC 134.

[13] See *Nash v Volskwagen Financial Services (UK) Ltd* [2023] EWHC 2326, reaffirming that the burden of proving causation lies on the claimant. Given the 'access to healthcare' implications and public interest that is affected, it may be appropriate for Parliament to study the issue and consider whether to legislate a reversal of the burden of proof.

[14] Under English law, the defendant bears the burden of proving any defence raised, or in some cases, in refuting an element of the cause of action. See *Armstead v Royal and Sun Alliance Insurance Company Ltd* [2024] UKSC 6; [2025] AC 406. In other jurisdictions, legislation has shifted the burden

It is apt in clinical negligence litigation where, for the reasons set out above, causation may be difficult or even impossible to prove.[15]

Alternatively, causal responsibility may be resolved by reimagining the nature of actionable damage. Instead of treating the actual injury as actionable damage, the gist of negligence may in appropriate cases be moved upstream with the physical injury or economic loss suffered used merely to quantify the loss. This was done in the Singapore Court of Appeal decision of *ACB v Thomson Medical Pte Ltd*,[16] in which the Court recognised loss of genetic affinity[17] as actionable damage and calculated damages as a percentage of the upkeep costs of the child.

II. Causal Responsibility

For analytical purposes, the tort of negligence is examined through a series of artificially distinct elements comprising duty, breach, causation, and remoteness. The first two elements together address the question of the moral responsibility of the defendant. The duty question asks whether the defendant is under a legal obligation not to harm the claimant, while the breach question asks whether the defendant has failed to live up to reasonable standards. The next two elements, causation and remoteness, address the question of causal responsibility. These questions of moral and causal responsibility are inherently normative. The nature of the defendant's moral responsibility affects the scope of the defendant's causal responsibility; in exceptional cases, a defendant may be causally responsible even if it cannot be proved that the defendant's negligence in fact caused the claimant's damage.

A. Causation and Causal Responsibility

As the causation literature uses certain terms that are not clearly defined, it is helpful to set out what these terms mean, at least as they are used in this chapter.

- *Causal responsibility* – Causal responsibility is a metaphysical, normative inquiry. In addition to factual and legal causation, it includes considerations of remoteness of damage and the scope of the duty. It is about accountability for consequences.

to the defendant in exceptional cases 'when any fact is especially within the knowledge of any person'. See Evidence Act 1893 (Singapore) s 107.

[15] As Helen Reece has persuasively argued, there is an assumption underlying orthodox rules of causal responsibility that we operate in a deterministic rather than indeterministic world where proof of causation may be impossible. H Reece, 'Losses of Chances in the Law' (1996) 59 *Modern Law Review* 188, 205.

[16] *ACB v Thomson Medical Pte Ltd* [2017] SGCA 20; [2017] 1 SLR 918, [135].

[17] Namely, where a child was conceived by IVF using, in error, genetic material from a third party rather than the patients.

- *Moral responsibility* – Moral responsibility is a metaphysical, normative inquiry based on the duty of care and breach of that duty. It is about accountability for conduct.
- *Causation* – This is an inquiry into whether the defendant's negligence has caused the claimant's damage. It has both factual and legal dimensions.
- *Factual causation* – This is a purely factual inquiry into whether the defendant's negligence is causally connected to the claimant's damage, best resolved using the 'but-for' test.
- *Legal causation* – This is a normative inquiry that has two functions. It excludes certain consequences from being attributed to the defendant's actions, and it confines the causation inquiry to the legally relevant cause (the defendant's negligence), thus excluding any other potential cause.
- *Remoteness* – This is a policy-based inquiry designed to limit the scope of the defendant's liability for damage caused, based on the foreseeability of the type of damage.
- *Scope of duty* – This is a policy-based inquiry designed to limit the scope of the defendant's duty both in terms of its content, and the persons and entities to whom the duty is owed.

At its core, causal responsibility involves inquiry into two inseparable questions: did A cause B (factual inquiry) and should A be found responsible for B (normative inquiry)? There is no bright line dividing the factual and normative inquiries. Theorists and philosophers have been locked in debate over how to define causation and how to apply it to real-world problems. A flaw in much of the discourse is the conflation of causation and causal responsibility, bogging down the discourse in the quagmire of whether causation is a factual inquiry or a normative inquiry. Epistemology and linguistics matter. The word 'causation', by its nature, implies a *factual* inquiry: thus, there is some resistance to accepting a *normative* dimension.[18] Recasting the inquiry from causation to causal responsibility seamlessly integrates the factual and the normative.

This practical division of causation into factual causation and legal causation is an approach that is well established in the common law world.[19] However, there is disagreement on whether factual causation is a purely factual inquiry or whether it includes a normative dimension. Similarly, there is debate whether legal causation is an aspect of causation or whether it is a purely policy-based restriction on causal responsibility. Stapleton's analysis reveals the ambiguous nature of legal causation,

[18] See, J Stapleton, 'Unnecessary and Insufficient Factual Causes' (2023) 16 *Journal of Tort Law* 351, 366.

[19] *Khan v Meadows* [2021] UKSC 21, [44]; [2022] AC 852, 870; *Sunny Metal & Engineering Pte Ltd v Ng Khim Ming Eric* [2007] SGCA 36; [2007] 3 SLR (R) 782.

with an apparent preference for treating legal causation purely as a policy restriction on liability rather than an aspect of causation.[20] She explains:

> The first three elements are: that the interference of which P complains is recognized as a form of 'actionable damage'; that D owed P a 'duty of care'; and that some aspect of D's conduct was a breach of that duty because it fell below the standard of care that a reasonable person would have met in the circumstances. The fourth element is the 'causation' requirement: that this breach was a 'cause' of the injury of which P complains. The terminology of the fifth element varies: in the US the requirement is generally said to be that the breach was a 'proximate cause'; while in the non-US common law world the requirement is said to be that the injury must not be 'too remote' a consequence of the breach. Functionally, this fifth element sets the normatively appropriate scope of liability for consequences of breach by D: only certain of the infinite stream of consequences of the breach will be judged to be appropriately attributed to the defendant's breach for the purposes of legal liability.[21]

This analysis suggests that causal responsibility requires proof of causation. However, while in most cases, causal responsibility hinges on establishing factual causation, it is not inconceivable that causal responsibility for an injury can be justified even in the absence of proof of factual causation. Indeed, the reforms proposed by the Ipp Committee, which shaped the legislative regime of tort liability in Australia, contain such a framework. The Civil Liability Act 2002 (NSW) provides:

> 5D. General principles
>
> 1. A determination that negligence caused particular harm comprises the following elements—
>   (a) that the negligence was a necessary condition of the occurrence of the harm (*factual causation*), and
>   (b) that it is appropriate for the scope of the negligent person's liability to extend to the harm so caused (*scope of liability*).
> 2. In determining in an exceptional case, in accordance with established principles, whether negligence that cannot be established as a necessary condition of the occurrence of harm should be accepted as establishing factual causation, the court is to consider (amongst other relevant things) whether or not and why responsibility for the harm should be imposed on the negligent party.

Sections 5D(1)(a) and 5D(1)(b) respectively set out factual and legal causation, while section 5D(2) gives courts flexibility to impose causal responsibility in the absence of a finding of causation. Unfortunately, the legislation conflates factual causation and causal responsibility in section 5D(2). To treat a negligent event that is not a necessary condition of causation as establishing factual causation is a

[20] J Stapleton, 'Cause-in-Fact and Scope of Liability for Consequences' (2003) 119 *Law Quarterly Review* 388.

[21] J Stapleton, 'Choosing What We Mean by "Causation" in the Law' (2008) 73 *Missouri Law Review* 433, 448–49.

fiction. Stapleton celebrates the UK Supreme Court decision of *Financial Conduct Authority v Arch Insurance (UK) Ltd*[22] because 'the Court confirmed the far more general legal principle that a factor may be a factual cause of an indivisible outcome even if it was neither necessary *nor sufficient* for it'.[23]

This is an argument that Stapleton has long defended.[24] However, if a factor is neither necessary nor sufficient to cause an outcome, surely it cannot be a factual cause. The examples used by Stapleton and referred to by the Court to support this argument all involve multiple, simultaneous potential causal events.[25] They involve causal responsibility for the outcome, which may be explained either on the basis of common knowledge or by aggregating the causal events.

One example involves five members of a committee voting in favour of a motion, which requires a simple majority to pass. Stapleton argues that the vote of each member is neither sufficient nor necessary for the motion to pass, but if they are part of the majority that passed the motion, each member is deemed to have caused the motion to pass. This is not factual causation, but causal responsibility, which may be explained on the basis of collective responsibility. Each committee member is fully aware that by voting in favour of the motion he or she is causally responsible if a majority is achieved. Another example involves three individuals who simultaneously lean on a car parked at the edge of a mountain. Their combined force causes the car to roll down the mountain. Each individual's force on its own is not sufficient to roll the car, but the combined force of two individuals is sufficient. By aggregating the individual forces, it is clear that the three individuals caused the car to roll down the mountain, and each is causally responsible for participating in the act.[26]

Stapleton defends her argument by reformulating the but-for test as an 'extended but-for' test, under which 'a breach is a cause of an injury only if, but for it alone, (i) the injury would not exist or (ii) an actual contribution to an element of the positive requirements for its occurrence would not exist'.[27] The first limb is the orthodox but-for test, which requires the breach to be sufficient and necessary to cause the outcome. The second, alternative, limb only requires the breach to contribute to a set of conditions which are necessary and sufficient to cause the outcome; the breach on its own need not be necessary or sufficient.

Maintaining that causation can be established even if the breach was neither necessary nor sufficient, Stapleton reintroduces the necessity and sufficiency

[22] *Financial Conduct Authority v Arch Insurance (UK) Ltd* [2021] UKSC 1; [2021] AC 649.

[23] J Stapleton, 'Unnecessary and Insufficient Factual Causes' (2023) 16 *Journal of Tort Law* 351, 352.

[24] J Stapleton, 'Reflection on Common Sense Causation in Australia' in S Degeling, J Edelman and J Goudkamp (eds), *Torts in Commercial Law* (Pyrmont, Thomson Reuters Australia, 2011) 339.

[25] J Stapleton, 'Reflection on Common Sense Causation in Australia' in S Degeling, J Edelman and J Goudkamp (eds), *Torts in Commercial Law* (Pyrmont, Thomson Reuters Australia, 2011) 339, 340–41; *Financial Conduct Authority v Arch Insurance (UK) Ltd* [2021] UKSC 1; [2021] AC 649, [184]–[185].

[26] This approach will be elaborated on below when dealing with Sarah Green's Necessary Breach Analysis. See below at text to nn 61–69.

[27] J Stapleton, 'An "Extended But-For" Test for the Causal Relation in the Law of Obligations' (2015) 35 *Oxford Journal of Legal Studies* 697, 714.

criteria in the legal causation inquiry,[28] a concept that she views as interchangeable with proximate cause and remoteness.[29] However, it is important to distinguish these concepts because of the burden of proof. The UK Supreme Court, in *Armstead v Royal and Sun Alliance Insurance Company Ltd*,[30] has held that the burden of proof with respect to legal causation (restricted in that case to intervening events that could break the chain of causation) and remoteness rests with the defendant.[31]

Together, *Financial Conduct Authority* and *Armstead* potentially place the claimant in an unduly advantageous position: the claimant does not have to prove that the defendant's act was a sufficient or necessary cause before the defendant must prove that they did not cause the claimant's damage. Perhaps a better view would be to recognise a rebuttable presumption of causation rather than place the legal burden on the defendant with respect to legal causation and remoteness, as these elements are integral to establishing the cause of action, proof of which should remain on the claimant. Having said that, it bears highlighting that the Court in *Armstead* expressly referred to the 'legal burden of proof'.[32]

It is not disputed that one may have caused damage but not be legally responsible,[33] and vice versa, be legally responsible even if it is not proven that one caused the damage.[34] This explains why, in exceptional cases, a defendant may be liable even though the claimant may not be able to prove but-for causation,[35] or even that the defendant's act was a necessary element contributing to the claimant's injury.[36] However, it is incorrect to argue that an event which is *neither necessary nor sufficient* could be a *factual* cause of an outcome.[37] All that can be said is that, depending on the nature of the defendant's moral responsibility,[38] causal responsibility may follow in cases where the defendant has only increased the risk of injury or caused the claimant to lose a chance of a better outcome.

[28] J Stapleton, 'Unnecessary and Insufficient Factual Causes' (2023) 16 *Journal of Tort Law* 351, 368–69.

[29] J Stapleton, 'Reflection on Common Sense Causation in Australia' in S Degeling, J Edelman and J Goudkamp (eds), *Torts in Commercial Law* (Pyrmont, Thomson Reuters Australia, 2011) 339, 353.

[30] *Armstead v Royal and Sun Alliance Insurance Company Ltd* [2024] UKSC 6; [2025] AC 406.

[31] Armstead's ruling on the burden of proof with respect to remoteness has been applied subsequently in a nuisance case (*Nicholas v Thomas* [2025] EWHC 752 (Ch)) and a contracts case (*AF Kopp Ltd v HSBC UK Bank PLC (Re Banking – Security for Costs)* [2024] EWHC 1004 (Ch)).

[32] ibid [60]–[64].

[33] This would include situations where the damage caused by the defendant is too remote, based on the reasonable foreseeability test established in *Overseas Tankship (UK) Ltd v Morts Dock & Engineering Company Ltd* [1961] UKPC 1; [1961] AC 388; *Overseas Tankships (UK) Limited v The Miller Steamship Co Pty Limited* [1966] UKPC 10; [1967] 1 AC 617.

[34] *The Financial Conduct Authority v Arch Insurance (UK) Ltd* [2021] UKSC 1; [2021] AC 649.

[35] *McGhee v National Coal Board* [1973] 1 WLR 1.

[36] *Fairchild v Glenhaven Funeral Services Ltd* [2002] UKHL 22; [2003] 1 AC 32.

[37] See also, S Green, *Causation in Negligence* (Oxford/ Portland OR, Hart Publishing, 2015) 20, 30.

[38] The duty to inform in clinical negligence is an example. See *Chester v Afshar* [2004] UKHL 41; [2005] 1 AC 134.

B. Theorising Causal Responsibility

If, as is argued here, causal responsibility may exist in the absence of causation, then it must also be accepted that liability for harm can exist for events outside the defendant's control. The two competing principles are the Control Principle and the Moral Luck Principle.[39] Peter Cane puts it succinctly:

> When things turn out well for a person despite their lack of control, we can say that they have good luck; and when things turn out badly for a person as a result of their lack of control, we can say that they have bad luck.[40]

The argument that moral luck is relevant to moral responsibility was first set out by Bernard Williams in his critique of Kantian rationalism and morality.[41] Williams persuasively argued against the notion that individual acts and consequences could be immune from luck. Thus, any theory of responsibility or morality cannot ignore the role that luck plays, whether positive or negative. Nagel illustrates the point with this example:

> If one negligently leaves the bath running with the baby in it, one will realize, as one bounds up the stairs toward the bathroom, that if the baby has drowned one has done something awful, whereas if it has not one has merely been careless.[42]

Nagel's illustration focuses on moral responsibility, but it can also be used to explain causal responsibility. If one negligently exposes another to an unreasonable risk, that person's liability for harm depends on whether the risk materialises. If there is no liability when the risk does not materialise, why should there not be liability when the risk does materialise? In both cases, the outcomes are based on luck: good luck in the former and bad luck in the latter. One argument developed in an earlier work,[43] is that there are some cases where negligent exposure to a risk on its own is sufficient to establish causal responsibility if that risk materialises. Support for this is found in Arthur Ripstein's concept of ownership of risk:

> The person who exposes another to a risk 'owns' the risk, and if the risk ripens into an injury, that person owns the injury. The basic idea is simple: In assigning liability, the fault system determines whose problem a certain loss is. When a risk ripens into an injury, the injury belongs to whomsoever the risk in question belongs. Reasonable

[39] See generally, K Dana, 'Moral Luck', *The Stanford Encyclopedia of Philosophy* (Spring 2025 edn), https://plato.stanford.edu/cgi-bin/encyclopedia/archinfo.cgi?entry=moral-luck.

[40] P Cane, *Responsibility in Law and Morality* (Portland OR, Hart Publishing, 2002) 67.

[41] B Williams, 'Moral Luck' in Williams, *Moral Luck: Philosophical Papers 1973–1980* (Cambridge, Cambridge University Press, 1981) 20 (chapter 2). This chapter is a slightly revised version of his original paper presenting the argument: B Williams, 'Moral Luck' (1976) *Proceedings of the Aristotelian Society* 115.

[42] T Nagel, *Mortal Questions* (New York, Cambridge University, 1979) 30–31.

[43] K Amirthalingam, 'The Changing Face of the Gist of Negligence' in J Neyers, S Pitel and E Chamberlain (eds), *Emerging Issues in Tort Law* (Oxford, Hart Publishing, 2007) 467. See, Lord Hoffmann's opinion in *Barker v Corus (UK) plc* [2006] UKHL 20; [2006] 2 AC 572, [35]–[36], acknowledging that *Fairchild* effectively treated the material increase in risk as the gist of negligence.

> risks – those risks the imposition of which is compatible with appropriate regard for the interests of others – lie where they fall. Unreasonable risks belong to those who create them; as a result, the injuries that result from unreasonable risk imposition belong to the injurers.[44]

One of the most influential contemporary thinkers on causal responsibility, Michael Moore, examines the issue in detail in his magisterial work, *Causation and Responsibility*.[45] Moore's principal interest is interrogating the relationship between causation and moral responsibility. At the outset, he makes clear the philosophical premise for his analysis of causal responsibility – retributive justice for criminal law and corrective justice for tort law.[46] Moore's analysis of causation is coloured by his underlying philosophy, which casts causation as an inquiry into the *moral blameworthiness* of the defendant for his or her actions, and not merely the *causal responsibility* of the defendant for the consequences of his or her action. Peter Cane highlights a key distinction between causal responsibility in criminal law and civil law: the former focuses on the agent's conduct while the latter is relational, considering both the agent's conduct and the impact on the victim.[47] As Cane puts it, 'Responsibility in civil law is always *to* someone as well as *for* something'.[48]

Moore equates causal responsibility with moral responsibility, and moral responsibility with legal responsibility, thus leading to the conclusion that causal responsibility is the equivalent of legal responsibility. He states:

> If causation determines both the degree of prima facie wrongfulness and the permissibility of consequentialist justification of otherwise wrongful actions in morality, then a justice-oriented tort and criminal law is justifiably focused on causation.[49]

This conclusion leans heavily into the retributive justice theory for criminal law and corrective justice theory for tort law. Moore's approach thus does not readily fit with other theoretical approaches to tort law, including distributive justice, instrumental theories, and critical theories.[50] The focus of civil liability is not solely on the moral blameworthiness of the defendant but also on the fair allocation of risks and protection of the vulnerable. Causation need not do as much heavy lifting on moral responsibility as Moore requires. It should primarily involve factual inquiry, with legal causation doing merely supplementary work. Causation and causal responsibility are two different concepts, with the former generally but not always a subset of the latter.

[44] A Ripstein, *Equality, Responsibility and the Law* (Cambridge, Cambridge University Press, 2001) 54.

[45] M Moore, *Causation and Responsibility: An Essay in Law, Morals, and Metaphysics* (New York, Oxford University Press, 2009).

[46] ibid 4.

[47] P Cane, *Responsibility in Law and Morality* (Portland OR, Hart Publishing, 2002) 50.

[48] ibid.

[49] ibid81.

[50] See Chapter 3 of this volume for discussion of these theories.

Causal responsibility is innately normative. Instead of merely inquiring whether A's conduct caused injury to B, the question is whether A *ought* to be held causally responsible for the injury suffered by B. In the negligence framework, this inquiry is carried out using the concepts of causation and remoteness.[51] Unlike the tort of negligence, criminal law does not have a concept of remoteness with which to control causal responsibility. Thus, causation in criminal law must do some of this normative work, which inevitably includes considerations of foreseeability of harm and scope of risk.[52] Moore, while recognising that causation has different functions in civil and criminal law, nonetheless has allowed notions of moral responsibility that properly belong in criminal law analysis to overshadow his analysis of causation in the context of the tort of negligence.[53]

Unlike Moore, whose analysis of causal responsibility is from the perspective of the defendant's moral blameworthiness, Lord Burrows, in the clinical negligence case of *Khan v Meadows*, rightly comes at it from the perspective of the claimant's damage. Lord Burrows set out seven questions to be considered in analysing legal liability in negligence. The first two questions deal with moral responsibility by way of duty and breach. The subsequent four questions deal with causal responsibility, disaggregating cause in fact, cause in law, remoteness, and scope of duty:

1. Was there a duty of care owed by the defendant to the claimant? (the duty of care question)
2. Was there a breach of the duty of care? (the breach, or standard of care, question)
3. Was the damage or loss factually caused by the breach? (the factual causation question)
4. Was the damage or loss too remote from the breach of duty? (the remoteness question)
5. Was the damage or loss legally caused by the breach of duty? (the legal causation, or intervening cause, question)
6. Was the damage or loss within the scope of the duty of care? (the scope of duty question)
7. Are there any defences? (the defences question).[54]

The following propositions may be drawn from the basic theoretical review of causation and causal responsibility: (i) Causation and causal responsibility are two separate concepts; (ii) Causation is primarily a question of fact; (iii) Causation must be contextual – it is whether *the defendant's breach of duty* is a cause of the claimant's damage; (iv) Causal responsibility is a normative inquiry into whether

[51] See also, P Cane, *Responsibility in Law and Morality* (Portland OR, Hart Publishing, 2002) 119.

[52] *R v Roberts* (1971) 56 Cr App R 95; *R v Maybin* [2012] SCC 24; cf *R v Royall* [1991] HCA 27, (1991) 172 CLR 378, in which the High Court of Australia acknowledged that English courts had applied the reasonable foreseeability test but was itself divided on the usefulness of reasonable foreseeability as a test for causation.

[53] Despite being a general treatise on causation and responsibility, the underlying approach is shaped by criminal law considerations. The first four chapters of the book, which develop the philosophical premise, are based on previous works of Moore analysing causation in the context of criminal liability.

[54] *Khan v Meadows* [2021] UKSC 21, [79]; [2022] AC 852, 881.

the defendant *ought to* be held responsible for the claimant's injury; (v) The extent of the defendant's causal responsibility may be influenced by the defendant's moral responsibility, which is determined by the scope of duty and nature of the breach; (vi) Causal responsibility is a metaphysical concept that includes within it consideration of the scope of duty, factual and legal causation, damage, and remoteness.

III. Legal Tests for Causation

A. But-for Test

Unlike trespass, which is actionable per se, negligence is actionable only on proof of damage. Negligent defendants are not liable unless their negligence causes legally recognised damage to the claimant. Thus, proof that the defendant's breach of duty caused the claimant damage is crucial. In most cases, proof of causation will not pose a challenge and can be resolved on the face of the facts. A negligent wielder of a sword who severs the hand of a victim with a wild swing of the sword has caused personal injury to the claimant and will be liable for foreseeable losses that flow from the injury, assuming no other act or event affected the loss. The classic 'but-for' test resolves the question and, while not perfect, it remains favoured by the courts. Academics noting the inadequacies of the but-for test have developed alternatives. These include Richard Wright's Necessary Element in a Sufficient Set (NESS) test;[55] Jane Stapleton's Extended But-For test;[56] and Sarah Green's Necessary Breach Analysis (NBA) test.[57]

(i) Variants of the 'But-for' Test

The but-for test is a negative test of causation, which excludes all possible causes except the act of the defendant, rather like Sherlock Holmes' admonition to Watson: 'When you have eliminated all which is impossible, then whatever remains, however improbable, must be the truth'.[58] However, neither the but-for test nor Holmes' edict is infallible.[59] The conventional 'but-for' test of causation struggles when it comes to situations involving multiple potential causal events operating concurrently. To illustrate: A negligently shoots B, who dies. A forensic expert may determine that the gunshot was a cause of death. However, if there was a second shooter, C, whose bullet struck B at the same time, the but-for test

[55] R Wright, 'Causation in Tort Law' (1985) 73 *California Law Review* 1735.
[56] See J Stapleton, 'Unnecessary and Insufficient Factual Causes' (2023) 16 *Journal of Tort Law* 351.
[57] S Green, *Causation in Negligence* (Oxford/ Portland OR, Hart Publishing, 2015) 10.
[58] Sir Arthur Conan Doyle, 'The Adventure of the Blanched Soldier,' in *The Adventures of Sherlock Holmes* (New York, Doubleday & Company, 1960) 1011.
[59] The Holmesian fallacy is that it is impossible to eliminate all that is impossible, namely the unknown unknowns.

fails when applied individually to each shooter, assuming that either bullet was fatal. The question, 'But for A's shot, would B have died?' will be answered in the affirmative as C's shot would have killed B. Thus, A did not cause B's death. The same result follows when the but-for test is applied to C, leading to the conclusion that neither may be proved to have caused B's death.[60]

Wright offers a solution with the NESS test. Under this, an event is a cause if it is a necessary element in a sufficient set. Wright recognises that in complex cases there may be multiple potential sets of sufficient conditions. As long as the defendant's act is a necessary element of any of these sets of sufficient conditions, it may be treated as a cause. Take the example above of the three individuals (A, B, and C) leaning against a car,[61] which requires the force of at least two individuals to roll. To determine whether A was a cause, the NESS test would ask whether the force exerted by A was a necessary element of a sufficient set. Given that two individuals constitute a sufficient set, A would be a necessary element in a set combined with either B or C.

Stapleton's solution is to focus the but-for inquiry on the defendant's breach and exclude other potential causes. Under her 'targeted but-for' approach, 'one asks whether C can, if necessary by notionally removing factors from the scene, reach a perspective where the tortious conduct does satisfy the but-for test'.[62] Stapleton would resolve the two-shooter example by removing one of the shooters and asking whether the remaining shooter's act was a but-for cause of the victim's death. This is not unlike the NESS test, and indeed Stapleton acknowledges that it is a refinement of the NESS test.[63]

Green provides further refinement with her NBA test. Green emphasises that the causal inquiry in negligence is functional and not philosophical: it is to determine whether the claimant was harmed by a tortious act and whether the defendant should be held responsible for that harm. Thus, where there are multiple tortfeasors acting simultaneously, and it is impossible to determine which defendant caused the injury, the claimant nonetheless will not fail to prove causation as long as one – or both – of the defendants was a cause. This approach of looking at the totality of the tortious conduct has parallels with the approach to contributory negligence, exemplified in *Fitzgerald v Lane*.[64]

The claimant in *Fitzgerald*, who had crossed the road against the traffic lights, was hit by a car driven by the first defendant, which propelled him into the path of a car driven by the second defendant. Both drivers, the court found, had been travelling too fast. The claimant suffered serious injuries, resulting in partial

[60] See the discussion in *Cook v Lewis* [1951] SCR 830; [1952] 1 DLR 1; *Summers v Tice* 119 P 2d (1948). Put aside advancements in ballistic science which may be able to determine which bullet caused the death.

[61] See above text to n 26.

[62] J Stapleton, 'Cause in Fact and the Scope of Liability for Consequences' (2003) 119 *Law Quarterly Review* 388, 391.

[63] ibid.

[64] *Fitzgerald v Lane* [1988] UKHL 5; [1989] 1 AC 328.

tetraplegia, but was unable to prove which defendant caused the tetraplegia. The trial judge found each defendant and the claimant equally liable and thus reduced the claimant's damages by one-third for contributory negligence. The House of Lords, agreeing with the Court of Appeal, held that the claimant's fault should be compared with the defendants' collectively rather than individually. Holding that the claimant was equally at fault, damages were reduced by 50 per cent. Lord Ackner explained the approach as follows:

> While the plaintiff's conduct has to be contrasted with that of the defendants in order to decide to what extent it is just and equitable to reduce the damages, which would be awarded to him if the defendants were solely liable, it does not involve an assessment of the extent to which the fault of each of the defendants contributed to that damage. What is being contrasted is the plaintiff's conduct on the one hand, with the totality of the tortious conduct of the defendants on the other. As previously stated, the determination of the extent of each of the defendants' responsibility for the damage is not made in the main action but in the contribution proceedings between the defendants, inter se, and this does not concern the plaintiff.[65]

Green's NBA approach, constituting a two-stage inquiry, works in a similar way:

> Stage1: Is it more likely than not that *a* defendant's breach of duty changed the normal course of events so that damage (including constituent parts of larger damage) occurred which would not otherwise have done so when it did?
>
> Stage 2, applied to each defendant individually: Was the effect of *this* defendant's breach operative when the damage occurred?[66]

It does not matter, in the shooting scenario, that the claimant (B's estate or dependents) is unable to prove which shooter's bullet caused the death as long as it can prove that *one of them* did. The NBA test is satisfied as long as the damage was caused by a breach of duty; this entitles the claimant to relief. It is then up to the two shooters to prove which one did not discharge the fatal shot. Green thus offers a principled solution to justify the policy-based outcome adopted by the court in such scenarios.[67] However, the NBA approach is applicable only when all potential causes are tortious and occur simultaneously, resulting in indivisible damage. Different considerations apply when the multiple potential causes are sequential, as the classic cases of *Baker v Willoughby*,[68] *Jobling v Associated Dairies*,[69] *Performance Cars v Abraham*,[70] and *Hotson v East Berkshire Area Health Authority*[71] illustrate.

[65] ibid 345.
[66] S Green, *Causation in Negligence* (Oxford/ Portland OR, Hart Publishing, 2015) 10.
[67] *Cook v Lewis* [1951] SCR 830; (1995) DLR (4th) 609; *Summers v Tice* 119 P 2d (1948).
[68] *Baker v Willoughby* [1970] AC 467.
[69] *Jobling v Associated Dairies Ltd* [1981] UKHL 3; [1982] AC 794.
[70] *Performance Cars Ltd v Abraham* [1962] 1 QB 33.
[71] *Hotson v East Berkshire Area Health Authority* [1988] UKHL 1; [1987] AC 750.

(ii) The Chronological Sequence Matters

In *Performance Cars*, the defendant negligently collided with a car belonging to the claimant, causing damage to a panel necessitating respraying. However, the car had previously been involved in an accident sustaining damage in the identical area, necessitating respraying. Thus, the court held that the defendant had not caused any damage because the same damage had already been sustained earlier. In *Baker*, the sequence was reversed. The defendant negligently caused the initial injury to the claimant's leg, which was subsequently amputated due to a gunshot wound during a robbery. The defendant argued that any loss attributable to him was limited to the loss of use of the leg until it was amputated. The court rightly held that the defendant had caused a permanent injury and was therefore causally responsible for the continuing loss. Had the robber been sued, the robber would have been responsible for any additional damage caused to the injured leg.

In *Baker*, while the *damage* may have been different – injured leg as opposed to amputation – the *loss* was the same: functionally, the claimant was in a similar position whether with a damaged leg or a prosthetic leg. In both these cases, a distinction must be drawn between damage (actionability in negligence) and loss (quantification of loss).[72] Both *Baker* and *Performance Cars* concerned causation of loss, not causation of damage. Damage was clearly established in both cases: the defendant in *Baker* had caused damage to the claimant's leg (and subsequent loss) while the defendant in *Performance Cars* had caused damage to the car (but no loss).

Jobling concerned causation of damage. The claimant suffered a back injury following a workplace accident, resulting in a loss of earning capacity. Three years later, the claimant was diagnosed with spondylotic myelopathy, a disease of the spine which rendered him totally unfit for work, thus destroying his earning capacity. The Lords spent much of their opinions distinguishing *Baker* on the basis that it dealt with supervening tortious events while in *Jobling*, the supervening event was non-tortious. However, this was an unnecessary distraction. Lord Keith of Kinkel came closest to identifying the critical distinction, namely that in *Jobling*, the claimant was destined ultimately to lose his ability to work due to his latent condition, regardless of the accident, whereas in *Baker*, the shooting was an uncertain event post-dating the accident. *Jobling* may be analogised with *Performance Cars*: the defendant had injured an already damaged person, although that pre-existing damage (spondylotic myelopathy) was unknown at the time of the accident. As Lord Keith put it:

> In the case of supervening illness, it is appropriate to keep in view that this is one of the ordinary vicissitudes of life, and *when one is comparing the situation resulting from the accident with the situation had there been no accident, to recognise that the illness would have overtaken the plaintiff in any event*, so that it cannot be disregarded in

[72] For the distinction between damage and loss, see D Nolan, 'Rights, Damage and Loss' (2017) 37 *Oxford Journal of Legal Studies* 255, 270–74.

arriving at proper compensation, and no more than proper compensation (emphasis added).[73]

Causation, as distinct from causal responsibility, must be assessed on the facts and circumstances as they existed at the time of the incident. Imagine an AI system that is able to obtain and assess all the relevant information, evidence, and arguments instantly and come to judgment immediately after the incident. In a *Baker*-type case, if judgment were rendered immediately after the defendant's negligence caused the claimant's leg injury, compensation would have been on the basis of a permanently damaged leg. The future robber's action does not enter the equation. In a *Jobling*-type case, AI would know that the claimant has a spinal disease which would render him unable to work in three years; therefore immediately after the workplace accident, the compensation would be assessed on the basis of a loss of three years' earnings as that was all there was to lose, and therefore that was all the loss caused by the defendant.

Ignoring the chronology of events and applying a theoretical approach leads to errors. For example, Stapleton argues that the defendant should have been found to have caused the injury in *Hotson*, but she reaches this conclusion by ignoring the chronology of events. The claimant in *Hotson* was a young boy who fell from a tree, fracturing his left femoral epiphysis (part of the hip joint). He was rushed to hospital where the doctor negligently failed to diagnose the fracture, leading to a delay in treatment, which the claimant alleged caused avascular necrosis of the epiphysis due to a loss of blood supply. The hospital conceded it was negligent but disputed causation. The hospital's expert testified that the fall was the sole cause of the avascular necrosis.[74] The claimant's expert initially agreed,[75] but subsequently retracted the testimony, suggesting that it was possible that the fall alone had not caused the avascular necrosis.[76]

The trial judge was satisfied that, on a balance of probabilities, the fall was the sole cause of the avascular necrosis. Confusion was introduced by statistical probabilities. The trial judge noted that the defendant's expert had testified that the fall was 100 per cent the cause, while the claimant's expert's revised view was that the probability of the fall being the cause was between 40 and 60 per cent. The trial judge averaged that probability to 75 per cent. It must be highlighted that these figures were used to express the judge's belief probability; that is to say, whether the judge was satisfied on the balance of probabilities.[77] 75 per cent is well over the balance of probabilities,[78] and therefore as a matter of law, the trial judge was right to find that on a balance of probabilities, the fall was the cause of the avascular

[73] *Jobling v Associated Dairies Ltd* [1981] UKHL 3; [1982] AC 794, 815.
[74] *Hotson v East Berkshire Area Health Authority* [1988] UKHL 1; [1987] AC 750, 781.
[75] ibid 780–81.
[76] ibid 781.
[77] See Chapter 8 of this volume, text to nn 38–66 on belief probabilities and statistical outcome.
[78] The civil standard of the balance of probabilities is satisfied if the judge is satisfied that a fact is more likely than not; thus, in mathematical terms more than 50% would satisfy the test.

necrosis. This may not be fair, but it is orthodoxy, as Ritchie J noted in a recent medical negligence judgment:

> So the but for test is inherently imperfect. A defendant found liable because there was a finding that on the balance of probability, at say 55%, the breach caused the damage, will pay for all of the damage. Yet if the standard of proof fails, at say only a 45% likelihood that the breach caused the damage, no damages are awarded. This is the rough and ready nature of causation in tort law.[79]

The hospital's negligence in failing to diagnose the fracture in *Hotson* would have made no difference; the conditions for avascular necrosis had been fulfilled prior to the hospital's negligence. The potential casual events did not occur simultaneously, but were sequential, which makes a difference to assessment of factual causation.[80] Yet, Stapleton argues that both the fall and the negligence caused the avascular necrosis:

> Since both the fall and the subsequent medical negligence reduced the blood supply to the hip joint they both made contributions to the mechanism by which the hip joint necrosis eventually came about, and both should be recognized as a factual cause of that injury regardless of whether the plaintiff can prove that, but for the medical negligence, the necrosis would not have occurred.[81]

In *Hotson* the trial judge made a clear finding on causation based on the evidence. Thus, the hospital's negligence could not be a cause of the avascular necrosis. On this, *Hotson* is on all fours with *Barnett v Chelsea and Kensington Hospital Management Committee*,[82] in which the defendant doctor negligently failed to attend to the claimant who had suffered arsenic poisoning. The claimant subsequently died; the court found that even if the doctor had attended in a timely manner the arsenic had already taken effect and death was inevitable. These cases remind us that causation is largely a factual inquiry and should not be conflated with causal responsibility, which is a metaphysical, normative inquiry.

It is trite that negligence liability may attach to negligent acts as well as omissions. While in principle, the law on causation remains the same, in practice the question confronting the courts is quite different, as noted by Gaudron J in *Bennett v Minister of Community Welfare*:

> [A] case based on omission or a failure to act will, in certain respects, fall for analysis in a way that differs from that appropriate for a case based on a positive act. Thus, in the case of a positive act, questions of causation are answered by reference to what, in fact, happened. In the case of an omission, they are answered by reference to what would or would not have happened had the act occurred.[83]

[79] *CNZ v Royal Bath Hospitals NHS Foundation Trust* [2023] EWHC 19 (KB), [337].

[80] Lord Toulson explicitly refers to *Hotson* on this point in *Williams v Bermuda Hospitals Board* [2016] UKPC 4; [2016] AC 888, [39].

[81] J Stapleton, 'Unnecessary and Insufficient Factual Causes' (2023) 16 *Journal of Tort Law* 351, 365–66.

[82] *Barnett v Chelsea and Kensington Hospital Management Committee* [1969] 1 QB 428.

[83] *Bennett v Minister of Community Welfare* [1992] HCA 27; (1992) 176 CLR 408, 420.

Medical negligence cases often involve liability for omissions: failure to diagnose; failure to advise; or failure to intervene. Proving causation as a result of negligent omission is much more difficult for the claimant, as the entire inquiry turns on hypothetical counterfactuals. The but-for test can be applied to acts in a relatively straightforward manner; not so to omissions.

Take, for example, the following two scenarios based on an infant who drowns in the river:

> *Scenario 1*: the defendant negligently drops an infant into the river. The causation question is whether the infant would have drowned but for the defendant dropping the infant into the river. If there were no other intervening events affecting the outcome, the but-for test answers the causation inquiry.
>
> *Scenario 2*: the defendant negligently omits to rescue a drowning infant. The causation question is whether the infant would have drowned but for the defendant omitting to rescue it. It is impossible to answer this question without considering hypotheticals. Would someone else have rescued the infant? Would the infant have drowned despite the defendant's best efforts?

B. Material Contribution to Damage

Courts rarely modify the but-for test if it results in a positive result, as the risk of unfairness to the defendant is ameliorated by an inquiry into supervening events that may overwhelm the original cause. Thus, there is less concern with false positives than false negatives.[84] However, courts sometime over-extend liability in cases of false negatives and have been criticised for having 'unduly watered down their approach to causation'.[85] Courts sympathetic to claimants have developed alternatives or modifications to the but-for test, including the 'material contribution to damage' test and the 'material increase in risk' test. These cases typically involve multiple potential causes or indivisible damage. To avoid ambiguity, it is helpful to set out definitions of the key concepts as they are used in this chapter.

- *Damage* – This refers to legally recognised damage (the 'gist of negligence'), which is necessary to ground an action in negligence
- *Loss* – This refers to the extent to which the claimant is worse off as a result of the damage, and goes to questions of quantification rather than actionability
- *Divisible* – This refers to damage or loss suffered by the claimant that may be separated into distinct components for which various defendants may be severally liable

[84] V Black, 'The Rise and Fall of Plaintiff-Friendly Causation' (2016) 53 *Alberta Law Review* 533, 534.

[85] L Klar, 'Downsizing Torts' in NJ Mullany and AM Linden (eds), *Torts Tomorrow: A Tribute to John Fleming* (Sydney, LBC Information Services, 1998) 305, 311, cited in V Black, 'The Rise and Fall of Plaintiff-Friendly Causation' (2016) 53 *Alberta Law Review* 533, 534.

- *Indivisible* – This refers to damage or loss that cannot be divided, resulting in all responsible defendants being jointly liable *in solidium*
- *Cumulative* – This refers to accretive causal mechanisms, resulting in greater damage or loss with greater exposure to the causal mechanism
- *Trigger* – This refers to causal mechanisms that operate as an on-off switch; once the damage is triggered, further exposure is irrelevant

The modern authority for the material contribution to damage approach is the judgment of the House of Lords in *Bonnington Castings Ltd v Wardlaw.*[86] The claimant had contracted a lung condition, pneumoconiosis, due to exposure to silica dust from two sources of dust – swing grinders and pneumatic hammers – at his workplace. The defendant was negligent with respect to the dust caused by the swing grinders, but not with respect to the dust emitted by the operation of the pneumatic hammers. To succeed, the claimant had to prove that his pneumoconiosis was caused by the dust from the grinders. This was impossible because the two sources of dust were indistinguishable, and the but-for test could not exclude either source as the cause. Nevertheless, the House of Lords unanimously held that the claimant had proved that the dust from the grinders materially contributed to the lung disease. Material contribution, according to Lord Reid, was any contribution that was not *de minimis.*[87] Both Lord Reid and Lord Keith of Avonholm appeared to equate this with substantial contribution.[88]

On one reading, it appears that a material contribution, if it is not negligible or if it is substantial, must necessarily be *sufficient* to cause the disease, in which case the material contribution test is compatible with the but-for test and is part of factual causation. If both events occurred simultaneously, then both can be causally responsible. If the events occurred sequentially and the injury is divisible, each event could be causally responsible for different aspects of the damage. If the injury following sequential events is indivisible, the second event is no longer causative as it would have been pre-empted by the first event.[89]

A less demanding reading would be one where the material contribution is not sufficient to cause the damage but is also not negligible. On this reading, the material contribution test is not a test for causation but a determination of causal responsibility; in other words, it is an aspect of legal causation, operating as an exception to the but-for test. On this reading, both events can be causally responsible regardless of whether the injury is divisible or indivisible, as each makes a material contribution.

The cases are not uniform on how to interpret the material contribution test and its relationship with the but-for test. *Bailey v Ministry of Defence*[90] treats

[86] *Bonnington Castings Ltd v Wardlaw* [1956] AC 613.
[87] ibid 621.
[88] ibid 622, 626.
[89] See, S Green, *Causation in Negligence* (Oxford/ Portland OR, Hart Publishing, 2015) 77–78.
[90] *Bailey v Ministry of Defence* [2008] EWCA Civ 883; [2009] 1 WLR 1052.

the material contribution test as an exception to the but-for test and *Williams v Bermuda Hospitals Board*[91] treats it as compatible with the but-for test. Lord Phillips has acknowledged the ambiguity in this concept in *Sienkiewicz v Greif (UK) Ltd*: 'I doubt whether it is ever possible to define, in quantitative terms, what for the purposes of the application of any principle of law, is *de minimis*'.[92]

C. Material Increase in Risk

The material increase in risk test provides a good illustration of the conceptual distinction between causation and causal responsibility. In these cases, there is no evidence that the defendant's negligent act caused the claimant's injury. All that can be established is that the defendant's negligent act exposed the claimant to an unreasonable risk, or that it materially increased the risk of injury to the claimant. Courts have been willing to attribute causal responsibility to the defendant in such cases. Holding the defendant to account merely for increasing the risk of injury to the claimant or exposing the claimant to an unreasonable risk may be justified on the basis of moral luck.[93]

The classic case anchoring this line of authority is *McGhee v National Coal Board*.[94] The claimant in *McGhee* suffered dermatitis following exposure to coal dust at work. The defendant was not negligent for the workplace exposure but was negligent in failing to provide washing facilities for the workers. This resulted in the workers travelling home caked in dust, thereby extending the period of exposure to the dust. The issue was whether the negligent exposure – the period during which the claimant travelled home covered in dust – caused the dermatitis. The gist of negligence in *McGhee* was really an increased risk of injury. Lord Wilberforce noted that the appellant's expert 'could not do more than say that the failure to provide showers materially increased the chance, or risk, that dermatitis might set in'.[95]

In a crucial passage, Lord Wilberforce held as follows:

> In many cases, of which the present is typical, this is impossible to prove, just because honest medical opinion cannot segregate the causes of an illness between compound causes. And if one asks which of the parties, the workman or the employers should suffer from this inherent evidential difficulty, the answer as a matter in policy or justice should be that it is the creator of the risk who, *ex hypothesi* must be taken to have foreseen the possibility of damage, who should bear its consequences.[96]

[91] *Williams v Bermuda Hospitals Board* [2016] UKPC 4; [2016] AC 888, 47.

[92] *Sienkiewicz (Administratrix of the estate of Enid Costello (deceased)) v Greif (UK) Ltd* [2011] UKSC 10; [2011] 2 AC 229, [108].

[93] See above, text to nn 38–43.

[94] *McGhee v National Coal Board* [1973] 1 WLR 1. See earlier development of this line of authority in *Bonnington Castings Ltd v Wardlaw* [1956] AC 613; and *Nicholson v Atlas Steel Foundry and Engineering Co Ltd* [1957] 1 WLR 613.

[95] *McGhee v National Coal Board* [1973] 1 WLR 1, 6.

[96] ibid.

McGhee does not apply in cases where there are independent sources of risk, in addition to the defendant's negligence. Thus, in the medical negligence case of *Wilsher v Essex Area Health Authority*,[97] the House of Lords refused to apply *McGhee*, as there were other risk factors that could have caused the claimant's injury. For over three decades, *Wilsher* served as a cryochamber for *McGhee*, not overruling it but drastically limiting its application, until the House of Lords gave *McGhee* new life in *Fairchild v Glenhaven Funeral Services Ltd*.[98] The claimants in *Fairchild*, who had been exposed to asbestos at different workplaces over their working lives, eventually contracted mesothelioma, a cancer caused by exposure to asbestos.

Mesothelioma litigation was problematic for several reasons: first, the aetiology of the disease was unclear; secondly, the incubation period for the disease ran into decades; and thirdly, in most cases the victims would have had multiple exposures to the disease-causing asbestos. The combination of these factors made it impossible for the victim to prove on the traditional 'but-for' test which exposure or exposures had contributed to the disease. At the time *Fairchild* was litigated the medical understanding of the aetiology of the disease was that it could be caused by a single exposure: it was a trigger disease and it was indivisible.[99] Once triggered by exposure, further exposure would make no difference to the progression of the cancer.

Thus, it was impossible for each claimant to prove which defendant had caused the cancer, or even whether each defendant had increased the risk. Had the claimant contracted mesothelioma after exposure at the first workplace, any further exposure at the second or third workplace would not have increased the risk. Had mesothelioma been a cumulative disease, as in *McGhee*, the claimants could have argued that each defendant had materially increased the risk of contracting cancer. Further, *McGhee* was distinguishable, as it concerned a single defendant responsible for all sources of the risk whereas in *Fairchild* there were multiple sources of the risk as the claimants had worked for different defendants. Despite these differences, the House of Lords in *Fairchild* created an exceptional rule that causation could be satisfied if the claimant could prove that a defendant had materially increased the risk of the injury occurring.

An important feature of *Fairchild* was that all the exposures to asbestos were tortious; thus, even though individual claimants could not link their cancer to a particular defendant, they could show that their cancer had a tortious cause. Green's NBA offers a principled approach to support causal responsibility on this restricted application of *Fairchild*. However, *Fairchild* has been extended beyond this in *Barker v Corus (UK) plc*,[100] in which the claimant was exposed to asbestos

[97] *Wilsher v Essex Area Health Authority* [1987] 1 QB 730.

[98] *Fairchild v Glenhaven Funeral Services Ltd* [2002] UKHL 22; [2003] 1 AC 32.

[99] This understanding subsequently changed with greater scientific understanding and in *Barker v Corus (UK) plc* [2006] UKHL 20; [2006] 2 AC 572 the court accepted that mesothelioma could be a cumulative disease, justifying proportionate liability.

[100] *Barker v Corus (UK) plc* [2006] UKHL 20; [2006] 2 AC 572.

at work and also through his own activities. Thus, it could not be said that all the exposure was tortious (as in *Fairchild*). Acknowledging that it would be fiction to hold that the actual injury in *Fairchild* was proved to have been caused by the defendant, Lord Hoffmann in the House of Lords in *Barker* held that the increased risk was itself the gist of negligence,[101] leading to the bold claim in a subsequent Court of Appeal judgment that Lord Hoffmann's interpretation of *Fairchild* constituted 'the recognition of a hitherto unrecognised tort; that of negligently increasing the risk of injury'.[102]

Lord Hoffmann went on to state that although 'the *Fairchild* exception treats the risk of contracting mesothelioma as the damage, it applies only when the disease has actually been contracted'.[103] *Barker* was patently unfair on defendants who could be held liable for a disease that could have been caused by the claimants themselves.[104] The House of Lords' solution was to apply proportionate liability, although this was promptly overturned by legislation in so far as proportionate liability applied to mesothelioma claims.[105] The third case in the mesothelioma 'material increase in risk' trilogy of cases is *Sienkiewicz v Greif (UK) Ltd*.[106]

The appellant's mother (now deceased) had been exposed to asbestos dust at the respondent's workplace and to asbestos in her home environment. Notably, the court accepted that workplace exposure amounted to an 18 per cent increase in risk.[107] The trial judge in *Sienkiewicz* applied the 'doubling of risk' approach to find against the appellant. The theory behind this doubling of risk approach was that if the defendant had more than doubled the risk, one could infer on a balance of probabilities that the defendant had caused the injury.[108] The decision was reversed on appeal, with the Court of Appeal holding that the answer was to be found in legislation. Section 3(1)(d) of the Compensation Act 2006 (UK) explicitly stated that 'material increase in risk' was a sufficient basis to prove causation in mesothelioma cases. While Smith LJ endorsed the doubling of risk approach outside the mesothelioma cases,[109] doubt was cast on this approach in the Supreme Court.[110]

[101] ibid [31]. This, as Lord Rodger of Earlsferry noted, was 'not so much reinterpreting as rewriting the key decisions in *McGhee* [1973] 1 WLR 1 and *Fairchild* [2003] 1 AC 32': *Barker v Corus (UK) plc* [2006] UKHL 20; [2006] 2 AC 572, [71].

[102] *Sienkiewicz v Greif (UK) Ltd* [2009] EWCA Civ 1159, [27]. However, the House of Lords appears to have rejected increased risk as the gist of negligence in *Rothwell v Chemical and Insulating Co Ltd and Others* [2007] UKHL 39; [2008] 1 AC 281.

[103] *Barker v Corus (UK) plc* [2006] UKHL 20; [2006] 2 AC 572, [48].

[104] This unfairness was highlighted by Lady Hale in *Sienkiewicz v Greif (UK) Ltd* [2011] UKSC 10; [2011] 2 AC 229, [168].

[105] Compensation Act 2006 (UK) s 3(2).

[106] [2011] UKSC 10; [2011] 2 AC 229.

[107] ibid [109].

[108] *XYZ and Others v Schering Health Care Ltd* [2002] EWHC 1420; (2002) 70 BMLR 88, [21]; *Novartis Grimsby Ltd v Cookson* [2007] EWCA Civ 1261, [74]; *Jones v Metal Box Ltd and Another* (Unreported, Cardiff County Court, 11 January 2007).

[109] *Sienkiewicz v Greif (UK) Ltd* [2009] EWCA Civ 1159, [23].

[110] *Sienkiewicz v Greif (UK) Ltd* [2011] UKSC 10; [2011] 2 AC 229 (per Lady Hale), [173]. The other judges also expressed reservations about using epidemiological evidence to establish causation.

Lord Hoffmann's willingness to use increased risk as a proxy for damage in exceptional cases provides the jurisprudential basis to justify the causation reasoning in *Chester v Afshar*,[111] and to recognise loss of chance in medical negligence. This approach of treating exposure to unjustifiable risk as a proxy for causal responsibility for harm when the risk materialises is not as radical as it might appear. Similar sentiments have been expressed in other contexts. For example, in *Chomentowski v Red Garter Restaurant Pty Ltd*,[112] where an employee was violently assaulted by a robber while depositing his employer's restaurant takings for the day, Mason JA in the Supreme Court of New South Wales, stated:

> The injury which the plaintiff sustained, although occasioned by deliberate human intervention, was the outcome of the very risk against which it was the duty of the defendants to safeguard the plaintiff as their employee. If, as was the case, it was the existence of that risk of injury which called for the exercise of care and the taking of precautions by the defendants, then the defendants' failure to take care may properly be regarded as the cause of the injury which occurred when the risk became an actuality.[113]

IV. Burden of Proof

The practical significance of the burden of proof lies in the fact that the party on whom the burden lies will lose when the evidence is equivocal. Ideally, judges should be able to weigh the evidence and arguments to find the truth about the facts and circumstances. The burden of proof would be of little concern in cases where the judge can make an actual finding. As Baroness Hale once noted, 'generally speaking a judge is able to make up his mind where the truth lies without needing to rely upon the burden of proof'.[114]

The burden of proof only becomes critical as a rule of last resort 'to rescue'[115] judges when they cannot determine what in fact had happened. Here, the judge turns to the burden of proof to hold that the party carrying the burden has failed, thus justifying judgment in favour of the other party. The burden of proof is little more than a handmaiden of necessity, implicit in this observation by Lord Brandon:

> No judge likes to decide cases on burden of proof if he can legitimately avoid having to do so. There are cases, however, in which, owing to the unsatisfactory state of the evidence or otherwise, deciding on a burden of proof is the only just course for him to take.[116]

[111] [2004] UKHL 41; [2005] 1 AC 134.
[112] *Chomentowski v Red Garter Restaurant Pty Ltd* (1970) 92 WN (NSW) 1070 (Sup Ct NSW).
[113] ibid 1086.
[114] *Re B (Children)* [2008] UKHL 35; [2009] AC 11, [32].
[115] ibid.
[116] *Rhesa Shipping Co SA v Edmunds, The 'Popi M'* [1985] UKHL 15; [1985] 1 WLR 948, 955.

The conventional view has always been that in a negligence action, the burden of proving the elements of negligence – duty, breach, causation, and remoteness – is on the claimant. Yet, as noted earlier,[117] the UK Supreme Court in *Armstead* appeared to reverse the burden of proof with respect to legal causation and remoteness. The claimant in *Armstead*, who had hired a car, was involved in an accident due to the negligence of a van driver. When the claimant returned the car to the hirer, it had to be repaired. The hirer then claimed from the claimant, under the terms of the hire contract, the loss incurred as a result of not having the car available for hire while it was repaired.

The claimant sued the van driver's insurer to recover her economic loss, namely her contractual debt to the hirer. She lost at trial, on appeal to the Recorder, and to the Court of Appeal, but succeeded on appeal to the Supreme Court. A critical issue in the Supreme Court was the burden of proof with respect to legal causation and remoteness. Noting that there was an 'absence of authority on the question of who has the legal burden of proof in relation to remoteness',[118] Lord Legatt and Lord Burrows held that the burden was on the defendant. They went on to affirm that the defendant also bore the burden of proving legal causation with respect to whether a subsequent intervening event broke the chain of causation.[119]

The dicta on this issue are elliptical as Lord Legatt and Lord Burrows appear to distinguish between damage and loss, stating:

> The law is also unclear as to who has the legal burden of proof in a situation where it is not in dispute that a tort has been committed (in this case, by negligently *causing physical damage* to the car, which is the damage required to complete the cause of action) and what is in issue is whether *consequential loss* is irrecoverable on the ground that it is too remote (emphasis added).[120]

Even if the remoteness point can be restricted to *loss* as opposed to *damage*, the effect of intervening events on the chain of causation as part of the legal causation inquiry has always been considered in the context of proving causation of damage, not just consequential loss. The *Wagon Mound* cases,[121] which birthed the modern remoteness rule for negligence, did not reverse the burden of proof. Referring to comments in *Blyth v Birmingham Waterworks Co*,[122] Lord Reid in *Hughes v Lord Advocate*[123] stated:

> It may be that what Lord Romer, and possibly also Lord Thankerton, had in mind was that if the cause of an accident cannot be proved then the accident may have been due

[117] Above text to nn 30–31.
[118] ibid [62].
[119] ibid [61].
[120] ibid [58].
[121] *Overseas Tankship (UK) Ltd v Morts Dock & Engineering Company Ltd ('The Wagon Mound' No 1)* [1961] UKPC 1; [1961] AC 388; *Overseas Tankship (UK) Ltd v The Miller Steamship Co Pty Limited and another ('The Wagon Mound' No 2)* [1966] UKPC 10; [1967] 1 AC 617.
[122] *Blyth v The Company of Proprietors of The Birmingham Waterworks* (1856) 11 Ex 781; 156 ER 1047.
[123] *Hughes v Lord Advocate* [1963] UKHL 1; [1963] AC 837.

> to the intrusion of some new and unforeseeable cause like the falling of a ceiling so that the damage cannot be said to have resulted from the defenders' breach of duty. If they meant no more than that, then their observations would be in line with the *well-established principle that a pursuer must prove, in the sense of making it more probable than not, that the defender's breach of duty caused the accident* (emphasis added).[124]

It is clear from the above quote that the claimant bears the burden of proof with respect to legal causation and intervening events. Lord Hoffmann in *Jolley v Sutton London Borough Council*[125] had also, prior to *Armstead*, reaffirmed that the burden of proof was on the claimant to show that the damage was not too remote. Courts in the United Kingdom have implicitly reversed the burden of proof, but only in exceptional cases where it is impossible for the claimant to prove causation and where it would be manifestly unjust to deny the claimant compensation.[126] *Armstead* turns the exception into the rule for legal causation and remoteness.

There is, of course, something to be said for the argument that as long as the claimants can prove duty of care and breach (moral responsibility) and that they have suffered damage that was within the scope of the duty, the burden should shift to the defendants to deny causal responsibility (causation and remoteness). This argument is strengthened in cases where the facts relevant to proof of causation and remoteness are uniquely within the knowledge of the defendant, as would be the case in medical negligence litigation involving diagnosis, treatment, and care. In these cases, the courts should recognise a presumption of causal responsibility, which the defendant must rebut in order to avoid liability. Gaudron J's comments in *Naxakis v Western General Hospital*[127] support this approach:

> There is, in my view, a tendency to exaggerate the difficulties associated with proof of causation, even in medical negligence cases. For the purposes of the allocation of legal responsibility, '[i]f a wrongful act or omission results in an increased risk of injury to the plaintiff and that risk eventuates, the defendant's conduct has materially contributed to the injury that the plaintiff suffers whether or not other factors also contributed to that injury occurring.' And in that situation, the trier of fact – in this case, a jury – is entitled to conclude that the act or omission caused the injury in question unless the defendant establishes that the conduct had no effect at all or that the risk would have eventuated and resulted in the damage in question in any event.[128]

The Supreme Court of Canada has also been open to reversing the burden of proof.[129] Under this approach, as long as a claimant can prove that the injury is

[124] ibid 847.

[125] *Jolley v Sutton London Borough Council* [2000] UKHL 31; [2000] 1 WLR 1082, 1091.

[126] *McGhee v National Coal Board* [1973] 1 WLR 1; *Fairchild v Glenhaven Funeral Services Ltd* [2002] UKHL 22; [2003] 1 AC 32.

[127] *Naxakis v Western General Hospital* [1999] HCA 22; (1999) 197 CLR 269.

[128] ibid [31] (footnotes omitted). It is noted that Gaudron J quoted from McHugh J's judgment in *Chappel v Hart* [1998] HCA 55; (1998) 195 CLR 232, [27].

[129] *Snell v Farell* [1990] 2 SCR 311 (per Sopinka J), 321. See also McLachlin J, 'Negligence Law – Proving the Connection' in NJ Mullany and A Linden, *Torts Tomorrow: A Tribute to John Fleming* (Sydney, LBC Information Services, 1998) 16.

within the scope of the risk to which the defendant has exposed the claimant, a prima facie case of causation will be made out. The defendant will then come under a burden to produce evidence that will displace the prima facie case. In theory, the legal burden will remain with the claimant, although in practice it might, in some cases, rest with the defendant; this was the approach of the Court of Appeal in *Wright v Cambridge Medical Group*.[130] This shifting burden approach may offer a better solution than the ongoing attempt artificially to rationalise *Fairchild* in order to turn what was in fact a policy-based exception into a general principle of causation. This is all the more so in cases where 'all the facts are peculiarly within the knowledge of the defence, … and comparatively slight evidence may be regarded as calling for an explanation'.[131]

The Singaporean decision of *Surender Singh s/o Jagdish Singh v Li Man Kay*[132] is an example of how *McGhee* and reversing the burden of proof may be applied in medical negligence litigation. The claimants were the dependants of a kidney donor who died as a result of internal haemorrhaging following an operation to remove her kidney. The claim against the surgeons was based on negligent pre-operative advice and negligent performance of the surgery, while the claim against the hospital was for negligent post-operative care. The hospital's nurse was found negligent for failing to monitor the donor on an hourly basis. It was accepted that the cause of death was internal haemorrhaging due to the slippage of the Hem-o-Lok clips used by the surgeons to secure the blood vessels. However, the Singapore High Court found that the surgeons had not been negligent. Thus, the crucial question was whether the nurse's failure to monitor had caused the patient's death.

The claimants' argument was that timely monitoring would have detected the internal bleeding, while the defendant's argument was that, if the clips had indeed slipped, the bleeding would have been too rapid for any intervention through monitoring to prevent death. Causation would fail on the authority of *Barnett*. As the evidence on the rate of bleeding was inconclusive, the trial judge applied *McGhee*, finding that the failure to monitor had increased the risk of death.[133] Thus, the defendant was causally responsible. This effectively reverses the burden, which was the point made by Lord Wilberforce in *McGhee*.[134] The judge in *Surender* also accepted the claimant's argument that by virtue of the Evidence Act 1893 section 108, the defendant bore bear the burden of proving that the deceased had been properly monitored.[135]

[130] *Wright (A child) v Cambridge Medical Group (A partnership)* [2011] EWCA Civ 669; [2013] QB 312, [75].

[131] *Parker v Paton* (1941) 41 SR (NSW) 237, 243, cited in Eggleston J, 'Probabilities and Proof' (1963) 4 *Melbourne University Law Review* 180, 186.

[132] *Surender Singh s/o Jagdish Singh v Li Man Kay* [2009] SGHC 168; [2010] 1 SLR 428.

[133] Regrettably, the Court did not consider *Wilsher v Essex Area Health Authority* [1987] 1 QB 730.

[134] See above, text to n 95.

[135] ibid [217], [220]. Section 108 provides: 'When any fact is especially within the knowledge of any person, the burden of proving that fact is upon him.'

V. Conclusion

The conventional principles of causation have been upended in exceptional cases where courts seek 'to do justice' for claimants who are unable to prove that the defendant's negligence caused their damage. Instead of creating artificial distinctions between factual and legal causation, it is better to distinguish between causation and causal responsibility. Causation remains an essentially factual inquiry, tempered with legal causation in complex cases involving multiple potential causes. Causal responsibility is a purely normative inquiry which justifies holding a defendant accountable for harm that befalls the claimant in cases where the defendant has exposed the claimant to an unjustified risk or deprived the claimant of a chance of avoiding injury.

As noted in the introduction, proving causation in medical negligence litigation is fraught with challenges as there are multiple actors, systemic failures, unknown aetiology of diseases, and complex iatrogenic injuries. Outcomes sometimes depend on the hypothetical actions or decisions of other medical professionals or even the patient. In many cases, the patient does not have access to necessary information, with most of the relevant information in the control of doctors and healthcare institutions. Applying a rigid approach to proof of causation and the burden of proof may result in injustice. This chapter has reviewed various approaches to determining causal responsibility when factual causation may be impossible to establish based on existing knowledge or the particular circumstances of the case.

Some of the judicial approaches include modified tests for causation based on material contribution to damage and material increase in risk. Some courts have reversed the burden of proof or recognised novel categories of actionable damage, including material increase in risk and loss of chance. It is impossible to resolve questions of causal responsibility without simultaneously confronting the nature of actionable damage, which is the subject of the next, and final, substantive chapter. This final chapter will return to the core concern of this book, patient autonomy, to examine how this concept has impacted the legal doctrines pertaining to causal responsibility.

8

Reimagining Damage

Damage is the gist of negligence. Thus, it is essential that claimants prove that the defendant's negligence caused them damage. It was shown in Chapter seven that this can be difficult in exceptional cases and courts have circumvented orthodox causation principles to enable claimants to succeed. An alternative approach to modifying causation rules is to reimagine what constitutes actionable damage by focusing on the intermediate harm instead of the ultimate injury. This is what Lord Hoffmann did in *Barker v Corus (UK) plc*[1] when he acknowledged that the gist of negligence in *Fairchild v Glenhaven Funeral Services Ltd*[2] was the exposure to a material risk. This chapter analyses three types of intermediate damage that have been considered by courts – material increase in risk,[3] loss of chance,[4] and loss of autonomy.[5] Loss of chance and loss of autonomy are especially relevant to medical negligence.

These interests – loss of chance and patient autonomy – may deserve protection. However, there are theoretical and practical challenges to recognising these intermediate interests as protected in negligence. Loss of chance is an illusory concept with the potential of over-extending the scope of liability. It lies at the intersection of uncertain causation, actionable damage, and quantification of loss. Patient autonomy, as demonstrated in Chapter four, is mired in controversy from its provenance to its conceptualisation. These uncertainties pose significant challenges for claimants, and courts must formulate solutions that balance policy, principle, and pragmatism.

The book comes full circle in this chapter by returning to the key theme of this work – autonomy. Courts have been reluctant to recognise loss of autonomy as actionable damage in its own right, although they have used autonomy as a proxy for damage suffered by the patient or to justify vindicatory or nominal damages.[6] Autonomy is an interest that merits protection, but

[1] *Barker v Corus (UK) plc* [2006] UKHL 20; [2006] 2 AC 572.

[2] *Fairchild v Glenhaven Funeral Services Ltd* [2002] UKHL 22; [2003] 1 AC 32.

[3] *Fairchild v Glenhaven Funeral Services Ltd* [2002] UKHL 22; [2003] 1 AC 32; *Barker v Corus (UK) plc* [2006] UKHL 20; [2006] 2 AC 572.

[4] *Gregg v Scott* [2005] UKHL 2; [2005] 2 AC 176.

[5] *Chester v Afshar* [2004] UKHL 41; [2005] 1 AC 134.

[6] ibid; *Rees v Darlington Memorial Hospital NHS Trust* [2003] UKHL 52; [2004] 1 AC 309.

courts must be careful not to distort established principles or introduce arbitrary justice. For example, the vindicatory approach to patient autonomy in the landmark case of *Chester v Afshar*[7] is problematic on two grounds. At the practical level, it wrongly equates the value of the patient's autonomy interest with the actual injury suffered. At the theoretical level, paradoxically it fails to respect patient agency by not holding patients responsible for their own choices.

However, there is one area where loss of autonomy legitimately may be treated as actionable damage, namely reproductive negligence. Reproductive health involves the most personal and intimate decisions a person makes about their bodies and their personal lives. The harm that may be suffered in the event of negligence goes beyond any physical or economic damage; it strikes at the very core of a person's identity. When a person's reproductive capabilities are damaged, when a person has an unwanted child, becomes a parent against their wishes due to the defendant's negligence,[8] or loses the ability to procreate, they suffer significant harm to their personal autonomy.

I. Material Increase in Risk and Loss of Chance

The concept of material increase in risk has been used by courts to extend the scope of causal responsibility either by circumventing orthodox requirements of proof of causation or by treating it as a new form of damage that is actionable in negligence.[9] The latter approach is controversial and appears to have been rejected by the Supreme Court in *Rothwell v Chemical and Insulating Co Ltd.*[10] Leaving aside any policy reason against recognising material increase in risk as actionable damage, there is a logical reason why it should not be so recognised. In *McGhee* and *Fairchild*, the expression used was material increase in risk, not material contribution to risk. An increase in risk presupposes the existence of that very risk factor.[11] The inquiry is necessarily directed at the ultimate damage and therefore the risk itself is not the actionable damage.

[7] [2004] UKHL 41; [2005] 1 AC 134.

[8] K Amirthalingam, 'Reproductive Negligence: Unwanted Child or Unwanted Parenthood?' (2018) 134 *Law Quarterly Review* 15.

[9] *McGhee v National Coal Board* [1973] 1 WLR 1; *Fairchild v Glenhaven Funeral Services Ltd* [2002] UKHL 22; [2003] 1 AC 32; *Barker v Corus (UK) plc* [2006] UKHL 20; [2006] 2 AC 572; *Sienkiewicz v Greif (UK) Ltd* [2011] UKSC 10; [2011] 2 AC 229.

[10] *Rothwell v Chemical and Insulating Co Ltd* [2007] UKHL 39; [2008] 1 AC 281.

[11] In *Fairchild*, one of the limitations to the material increase in risk approach was that all the risk factors had to be identical. *Fairchild v Glenhaven Funeral Services Ltd* [2002] UKHL 22; [2003] 1 AC 32, 40, 57.

A. Theorising Material Increase in Risk and Loss of Chance

A distinction may be drawn between material increase in risk and exposure to a risk.[12] Cases like *Chester v Afshar*[13] and *Chappel v Hart*,[14] which will be discussed below, involve situations where the doctor has negligently failed to inform the patient of a material risk in proposed treatment, but the patient in any event would have consented to and undergone the procedure. If the risk materialises and causes injury, the doctor may argue that the case fails on causation as the patient would have been exposed to the risk even if properly advised. Here, there is no question of *increase* in risk, but simply *exposure* to risk. In such cases, it may be argued that exposure to the risk is actionable damage,[15] as the purpose of the duty to inform is precisely to enable the patient to avoid the risk. The difficulty lies in determining what types of risks should qualify.

Kenneth Simons, in a recent article on assessing damages for lost chance of a better medical outcome, disavowed loss of chance as actionable damage, arguing instead that '*exposure to a risk* created by defendant's negligence' could be a basis for compensation (emphasis added).[16] If exposure to a risk is to be recognised as the gist of negligence, it needs to be clearly defined to avoid fanciful or speculative claims being made. One way, which is not alien to the common law, is to develop the categories that qualify incrementally.[17] These categories may be characterised by the 'nature of the risk'[18] or the 'scope of the duty'.[19]

Material increase in risk and loss of chance are sometimes viewed as two sides of the same coin,[20] both dealing with uncertain causation. Referring to *McGhee*, Lord Hobson in *Hotson v East Berkshire Area Health Authority*[21] noted: 'Material increase of the risk of contraction of dermatitis is equivalent to material decrease in the chance of escaping dermatitis'. However, material increase in risk and loss of

[12] Cf C McIvor, 'Debunking Some Judicial Myths about Epidemiology and its Relevance to UK Tort Law' (2013) 21 *Medical Law Review* 553 who refers to material *contribution* to risk when analysing *McGhee* and *Fairchild*.

[13] [2004] UKHL 41; [2005] 1 AC 134.

[14] *Chappell v Hart* [1998] HCA 55; (1998) 195 CLR 232.

[15] See also KW Simons, 'Lost Chance of a Better Medical Outcome: New Tort, New Type of Compensable Injury, or New Causation Rule?' (2024) 73 *DePaul Law Review* 547, 556.

[16] ibid 599.

[17] Dillon LJ considered such an approach to loss of chance in *Hotson v East Berkshire Area Health Authority* [1988] UKHL 1; [1987] AC 750, [217].

[18] These refer to cases where the risk is so unreasonable as to be morally unacceptable. The *McGhee/ Fairchild/ Barker/ Sienkiwicz* cases illustrate the nature of risk approach.

[19] These refer to cases where the avoidance of the particular risk is the very purpose of the duty. The scope of duty approach may be illustrated by *Gregg v* Scott [2005] UKHL 2; [2005] 2 AC 176 and *Wright (A child) v Cambridge Medical Group (A partnership)* [2011] EWCA Civ 669; [2013] QB 312, discussed below at text to nn 59–62.

[20] MA Hogg, 'Re-establishing Orthodoxy in the Realm of Causation' (2007) 11 *Edinburgh Law Review* 8, 14–15; DPT Price, 'Causation – The Lords' Lost Chance?' (1989) 38 *International and Comparative Law Quarterly* 735, 735–36.

[21] *Hotson v East Berkshire Area Health Authority* [1988] UKHL 1; [1987] AC 750, 786.

chance are conceptually distinct. Avoiding the extended exposure to dust during the travel home in *McGhee* would not have given the claimant a chance to have completely avoided the disease, which was already caused by the exposure during work.[22] Further, damages in material increase in risk cases have traditionally been assessed on the basis of the actual loss suffered by the claimant,[23] unlike damages for loss of chance, which have always been assessed as a percentage of the ultimate loss, based on 'a realistic assessment of what would have been the plaintiff's prospects of success'.[24]

These concepts of material increase in risk and loss of chance are engaged in cases where the defendant has exposed the claimant to a risk of harm and the claimant suffers that very harm, but it is impossible to prove on a balance of probabilities that the defendant's negligence caused the harm. Yet, failing to compensate the claimant risks creating pockets of immunity for defendants.[25] Material increase in risk is a heuristic device to establish a connection between the defendant's negligence and the claimant's damage in the perceived interests of justice. It belongs to the *causation* inquiry. Loss of chance, on the other hand, is itself something of value that can be recognised as a protected interest in negligence under the right conditions. It belongs to the *damage* inquiry.

The loss of chance doctrine in England may be traced to the contracts case of *Chaplin v Hicks*,[26] in which the claimant, one of the finalists in a beauty contest was deprived of the opportunity to participate in the contest due to the defendant's breach of contract. Although *Chaplin* was a contracts case where damage was not an element of the action, the loss of chance principle has been applied to negligence liability in both contract and torts.[27] It is important to distinguish between damage and loss in negligence claims,[28] as the former is an element of the action. Quantifying the loss that flows from damage has always involved speculation and probabilistic reasoning.[29]

Helen Reece draws on the distinction between deterministic and indeterministic outcomes to explain loss of chance.[30] She argues that loss of chance has no role in deterministic cases as cause and effect is already determined, with the only uncertainty being epistemic and not aleatoric. In a deterministic world, it is assumed that all cause and event relationships are capable of proof and therefore it is not unfair to impose a legal burden of proof on the claimant. Indeterministic cases, on

[22] N Jansen, 'The Idea of a Lost Chance' (1999) 19 *Oxford Journal of Legal Studies* 271, 280 was categorical: 'Therefore, *McGhee* was not a case concerning the loss of a chance'.

[23] *Barker v Corus (UK) plc* [2006] UKHL 20; [2006] 2 AC 572 was an exceptional decision that recognised proportionate liability, albeit that aspect of the judgment, in so far as it applied to mesothelioma claims, was reversed by legislation. Compensation Act 2006 (UK) s 3.

[24] *Mount v Barker Austin (A Firm)* [1998] PNLR 493, 511.

[25] KW Simons, 'Lost Chance of a Better Medical Outcome: New Tort, New Type of Compensable Injury, of New Causation Rule?' (2024) 73 *DePaul Law Review* 547, 556.

[26] *Chaplin v Hicks* [1911] KB 786.

[27] *Kitchen v RAF Association* [1958] 1 WLR 563; *Yardley v Coombes* (1963) *Sol Jo* 575.

[28] See Chapter 7 of this volume, text to nn 75–77.

[29] *Malec v JC Hutton Pty Ltd* [1990] HCA 20; (1990) 169 CLR 638.

[30] H Reece, 'Losses of Chances in the Law' (1996) 59 *Modern Law Review* 188.

the other hand, give rise to a genuine loss of chance approach to damage where outcomes may be random. It would be impossible to prove causation of damage in indeterministic cases as it is only 'the chance of the event which is caused'.[31]

A sceptical view of the loss of chance debate is that it is simply a fictional device used to circumvent uncertain causation. Nils Jansen argues that the idea of a loss of chance – whether epistemological or ontological – is an illusion.[32] Epistemological loss of chance is an illusion because there is no objective loss of chance. Cause and effect are predetermined: the loss of chance analysis is relied on only because of a lack of knowledge of cause and effect. Contrary to Reece, Jansen argues that ontological or objective loss of chance is also an illusion. According to Jansen, 'there are no such things as chances in this world: one is not able to lose a chance of surviving or gaining some money. Rather, one loses one's life or one's money'.[33] Thus, there is no such thing as a loss of chance per se.

Nonetheless, Jansen supports a loss of chance approach for tort liability, arguing that the law is concerned with social conceptions of loss. As he puts it in the context of medical negligence:

> Law is concerned with the world as it is perceived in normal language. Law, therefore, does protect chances. No one doubts that C had the duty to care for the chance of A. Her duty to treat A in time was not dependent on the condition that A in fact would survive if treated in time. And, seen from the opposite point of view, A would ask C to care for her chance. She might know that she could possibly die even if treated correctly. But nonetheless, everyone in her position would have the firm belief that he/she still had something to lose: the chance of surviving. People apparently do think that chances are important things to be legally protected.[34]

Thus, according to Jansen, if the chance of a positive outcome is an interest that deserves protection, the claimant is entitled to compensation if that interest is violated. He illustrates by drawing an analogy with a defendant who steals a claimant's money just before the claimant uses the money to place a bad bet at the casino. By stealing the claimant's money, the defendant has infringed the claimant's interest and is not entitled to argue that the claimant has suffered no loss because he or she would have lost the money in the bet. Similarly, in a loss of chance case, it would not lie in the defendant's mouth to argue that the loss would not have materialised, despite the negligent act. The chance that the risk will not materialise is not the defendant's prerogative; instead, the claimant has a right not to have the risk materialise.[35] This approach raises the perplexing question of whether a patient may recover for loss of chance of survival even if the claimant eventually survives.[36]

[31] ibid 206.

[32] N Jansen, 'The Idea of a Lost Chance' (1999) 19 *Oxford Journal of Legal Studies* 271, 280.

[33] ibid 280.

[34] ibid 281. C refers to the doctor and A refers to the patient.

[35] ibid 283.

[36] This was considered in *Gregg v Scott* [2005] UKHL 2; [2005] 2 AC 176 where the claimant in fact did survive for 10 years beyond the negligent incident. The lost chance thus did not materialise. Lord Phillips of Worth Matravers noted this (at [189]) and said that the claim failed, as the claimant had not actually lost anything.

B. Applying Loss of Chance in Practice

It is trite law that the claimant in civil claims must discharge the burden of proof on a balance of probabilities standard.[37] This standard is satisfied if the claimant can prove that his or her version of events is more likely true than the defendant's. The claimant does not have to prove beyond a reasonable doubt or to a high degree of probability. The problem arises when belief probability (an evidential matter) is conflated with outcome probability (a causation matter).[38] Belief probability goes to the burden of proof and is an all-or-nothing proposition. Thus, if the judge believes the claimant's version of events is more likely, the claimant will have succeeded in discharging the burden of proof.

The Supreme Court expressed it clearly when explaining the leading loss of chance case of *Allied Maples Group Ltd v Simmons and Simmons*. The plaintiff had been negligently advised by the defendant firm in its takeover of the Gillow group, and thereby obtained imperfect future protection against contingent liabilities of Gillow's subsidiary companies:[39]

> Allied Maples would have been better off, competently advised, if, but only if: (a) it had raised the matter with Gillow and sought improved warranties and (b) Gillow had responded by providing them. The Court of Appeal held that Allied Maples had to prove point (a) on a balance of probabilities, but that point (b) should be assessed upon the basis of loss of the chance that Gillow would have responded favourably.[40]

Allied Maples had something of value – the chance of negotiating a better outcome – that was adversely affected by the defendant's negligence. This is a key feature of the successful loss of chance cases that appears to be absent in the medical negligence cases, with the apex courts in the United Kingdom, Australia, and Canada rejecting such claims.[41] The common feature in these medical negligence cases is that the defendant doctor negligently fails to diagnose the patient in a timely manner, resulting in delays in treatment that reduce the patient's chance of achieving a good medical outcome. Where the expert evidence is that the patient had a less than even chance of a good medical outcome, the law treats the patient as having nothing to lose. Thus, the doctor's negligence is irrelevant to the ultimate adverse outcome, which in the eyes of the law would have been inevitable.

Gregg provides a good illustration of the problem. The patient, who had non-Hodgkin's lymphoma, saw the defendant general practitioner, who negligently failed to diagnose the patient and refer him to a specialist. This delayed

[37] While in theory the standard of proof is the same for all case, it has been argued that some courts have held claimants to a higher standard in medical negligence cases. See M Jones, *Medical Negligence* (London, Sweet & Maxwell, 6th edn, 2021) [3-178]–[3-180].

[38] *Armstrong v Quest Laboratories Pte Ltd* [2019] SGCA 75; [2020] 1 SLR 133, [94]–[99].

[39] *Allied Maples Group Ltd v Simmons and Simmons* [1995] 1 WLR 1602.

[40] *Perry v Raleys Solicitors* [2019] UKSC 5; [2020] AC 352, [21].

[41] *Gregg v Scott* [2005] UKHL 2; [2005] 2 AC 176; *Tabet v Gett* [2010] HCA 12; (2010) 240 CLR 537; *Laferrière v Lawson* [1991] 1 SCR 541.

his treatment by nine months. According to the expert evidence, the patient had a 42 per cent chance of survival when he saw the defendant, but that chance had been reduced to 25 per cent nine months later. The majority in the House of Lords accepted the defendant's argument that the claimant was doomed before he saw the defendant because he had a less than even chance of survival. The claimant argued that the reduced chance was of value and therefore he deserved compensation. The majority rejected the loss of chance claim on policy grounds and on the ground that a less than even chance was no chance at all.

This type of reasoning based on statistical probabilities conflates the two distinct questions in *Allied Maples*, confusing belief probability (relevant to the burden of proof) with outcome probability (relevant to damage). Statistical evidence based on epidemiological studies uses data from population studies to establish a correlation between cause and effect.[42] Thus, in *Gregg*, the statistical evidence simply means that out of 100 individuals similarly affected, 42 of them would survive, thus giving a survival rate of 42 per cent. It says nothing about the likelihood of survival of any particular individual, as it is impossible to know whether the individual patient was in the group of 42 (those who survive) or 58 (those who do not). If he were in the group of 42, he would have survived.

Clare McIvor has argued that courts have failed to use epidemiological evidence correctly; when correctly applied by experts, it can go beyond 'naked statistics' and can be personalised to the particular facts to provide a scientific method of approximating the likelihood of an adverse outcome for an individual.[43] Drawing on earlier literature,[44] McIvor argues that by carefully considering fact probabilities, belief probabilities, and sampling error probabilities, statistical evidence can help resolve causation questions.[45] Despite her trenchant criticism of the Supreme Court's use of epidemiological evidence in *Sienkiewicz v Greif (UK) Ltd*,[46] McIvor recognises that epidemiology is not a silver bullet for causal conundrums in tort law.[47]

[42] See S Gold, 'Causation in Toxic Torts: Burdens of Proof, Standards of Persuasion, and Statistical Evidence' (1986) 96 *Yale Law Journal* 376; D Harvey, 'Epidemiologic Proof of Probability: Implementing the Proportional Recovery Approach in Toxic Exposure Torts' (1984) 89 *Dickinson Law Review* 233.

[43] C McIvor, 'Debunking Some Judicial Myths about Epidemiology and its Relevance to UK Tort Law' (2013) 21 *Medical Law Review* 553.

[44] A Broadbent, 'Epidemiological Evidence in Proof of Specific Causation' (2011) 17 *Legal Theory* 237; C Miller, 'Causation in Personal Injury: Legal or Epidemiological Common Sense' (2006) 26 *Legal Studies* 544; D Barnes, 'Too Many Probabilities: Statistical Evidence of Tort Causation' (2001) 64 *Law and Contemporary Problems* 192; S Gold, 'Causation in Toxic Torts: Burdens of Proof, Standards of Persuasion, and Statistical Evidence' (1986) 96 *Yale Law Journal* 376.

[45] Fact probability refers to probabilistic evidence that the claimant's damage is likely to have flowed from the defendant's negligence; belief probability refers to the strength of the fact-finder's belief that the claimant's damage was a result of the defendant's negligence; sampling error probability refers to reliability measures of the underlying study.

[46] [2011] UKSC 10; [2011] 2 AC 229.

[47] C McIvor, 'Debunking Some Judicial Myths about Epidemiology and its Relevance to UK Tort Law' (2013) 21 *Medical Law Review* 553, 581.

C. Loss of Chance and Medical Negligence

In applying her approach to medical negligence, McIvor risks obfuscating the causation inquiry, stating:

> More straightforwardly, epidemiology may also be of assistance in medical negligence scenarios where the causal question is *whether the relevant breach of duty is actually capable of causing the harm in question*. Should the courts ever reach the point of recognising liability for lost chances of a better physical outcome, epidemiology could also be relied upon to provide scientifically robust quantification evidence (emphasis added).[48]

The causal question is not whether a breach is *capable* of causing damage but whether the breach *actually did* cause the damage. Epidemiological evidence cannot resolve the causation question in cases like *Gregg*. As McIvor rightly notes, such claimants may only succeed if the court recognises loss of chance. So, the question is whether *Gregg* should be reconsidered. One way to bring *Gregg* within the general framework of *Allied Maples* is to focus not on the patient's prognosis but on the scope of the doctor's duty. Lord Nicholls in the minority does so, arguing that the scope of the doctor's duty is to 'promote the patient's prospects of recovery by exercising due skill and care in diagnosing and treating the patient's condition'.[49]

This is similar to the reasoning of the Massachusetts Supreme Judicial Court in *Matsuyama v Birnbaum*,[50] which recognised loss of chance in medical negligence. Marshall CJ made the following observation:

> [M]edical negligence that harms the patient's chances of a more favorable outcome contravenes the expectation at the heart of the doctor-patient relationship that 'the patient will take every reasonable measure to obtain an optimal outcome for the patient'.[51]

However, these factors are germane to the scope of duty and not causation of damage. By focusing on the relationship and the expectation of patients, the court has subtly shifted the basis of liability from reliance loss to an expectation loss. While there is room for expectation losses in tort law,[52] care must be taken not to award damages for loss of chance simply because the patient's hopes and expectations of a good outcome were not met.[53] A loss of chance claim may be justified when a patient relies on the doctor and suffers a lost opportunity of obtaining

[48] ibid 583.

[49] *Gregg v Scott* [2005] UKHL 2; [2005] 2 AC 176, [25].

[50] *Matsuyama v Birnbaum* 890 NE 2d 819 (Mass 2008).

[51] ibid 835. Marshall CJ quotes KS Abraham, *Forms and Functions of Tort Law* (New York, Foundation Press, 3rd edn, 2007) 117–18.

[52] J Stapleton, 'The Normal Expectancies Measure in Tort Damages' (1997) 113 *Law Quarterly Review* 257. For a critique of Stapleton's argument, see S Smith, 'Rights, Remedies, and Normal Expectancies in Tort and Contract' (1997) 113 *Law Quarterly Review* 426.

[53] In choosing to recognise loss of chance in medical negligence by preferring the minority opinion in *Gregg*, a High Court judge in Singapore stated, 'Perhaps the description "loss of chance" has been

better prospects. This is an argument also advanced by Stephen Perry,[54] relying on autonomy as a protected interest. Instead of viewing loss of chance as actionable damage, Perry focuses on whether the claimant had detrimentally relied on the defendant.[55] A patient who suffers a loss 'of an opportunity to follow a preferable course of action'[56] suffers an interference with individual autonomy.[57]

This type of argument is apposite to cases like *Gregg*, which involved a general practitioner negligently failing to diagnose cancer and to make a timely referral. The purpose of the general practitioner's duty in such cases is to provide the patient with the opportunity of a timely referral to the appropriate specialist. The general practitioner is not expected personally to cure a patient of cancer or to prevent the occurrence or consequences of an imminent heart attack.[58] Thus, in *Gregg*, it could be argued that the doctor's negligence deprived the patient of a valuable opportunity to seek medical attention that could have helped him. Indeed, the Court of Appeal in *Wright* implicitly endorses this argument.

In *Wright v Cambridge Medical Group*,[59] the defendant general practitioner negligently delayed referring the claimant, an infant with a severe bacterial infection, to hospital.[60] The hospital doctors negligently failed to administer the correct antibiotic initially, leading to further delay in treating the claimant. Had the claimant been referred in a timely manner and been properly treated by the hospital, it was likely that she would have made a full recovery. The delay progressively increased the risk of a worse outcome and resulted in permanent damage to the claimant's hip and leg. The trial judge found against the claimant on causation.

The Court of Appeal, by a 2-1 majority, reversed the judgment. Lord Neuberger MR held that the defendant GP was precluded from arguing that the hospital's negligence, actual or hypothetical, broke the chain of causation. The doctor's negligence either would have caused the claimant to have *lost the opportunity* of proper treatment, or, if the claimant had suffered improper treatment at the hands of the hospital, to *have lost the opportunity* to sue the hospital for that improper treatment.[61] There are echoes of Jansen's argument about chances having value. Notably, Dame Janet Smith held that 'it was not within the scope of [the defendant's] duty to treat [the claimant], only to refer her as expeditiously as was practicable so as to … give her the best possible opportunity for recovery'.[62] The duty was not to cure but to give the chance of a cure.

confused with loss of "hope", perhaps they mean the same thing, but whether it is a loss of a chance or loss of hope, in this case it is still a loss'. *Armstrong v Quest Laboratories Pte Ltd* [2018] SGHC 66, [18].

54 S Perry, 'Protected Interests and Undertakings' (1992) 42 *University of Toronto Law Journal* 247.

55 ibid 250.

56 ibid 291.

57 ibid 289–90, referring to J Raz, *The Morality of Freedom* (Oxford, Clarendon Press, 1986) 144, 204.

58 *Breeze v Ahmad* [2005] EWCA Civ 223.

59 [2011] EWCA Civ 669; [2011] Med LR 496.

60 For a note on the case, setting out the arguments in more detail, see K Amirthalingam, 'Causation and the Medical Duty to Refer' (2012) 128 *Law Quarterly Review* 208.

61 [2011] EWCA Civ 669, [61].

62 ibid [129].

Hotson, *Gregg*, and *Wright* represent different points in the spectrum from deterministic to indeterministic outcomes. In *Hotson*, on the basis of belief probability, it could fairly be said that the injury was determined when the claimant fell from a tree. In *Wright* the chance depended on the hypothetical action of a third party, bringing it closer to *Allied Maples*. *Gregg* lies somewhere in the middle. Indeed, Lord Neuberger MR suggested that the Supreme Court might wish to revisit *Gregg*, and to decide whether all medical loss of chance cases should necessarily be treated in the same way.[63] Lord Hoffmann did not rule out a loss of chance claim where the chance was contingent on the actions of a third party;[64] similarly, Lord Phillips of Worth Matravers left open the possibility of such claims in appropriate circumstances.[65]

The Singapore Court of Appeal in *Armstrong v Quest Laboratories Pte Ltd*[66] has also left open the possibility of compensating for loss of chance in medical negligence. Although loss of chance was not an issue, as proof of damage on conventional principles was satisfied, the Court took the opportunity to review the law, including a detailed analysis of *Gregg*. Phang JA, giving the Court's judgment, argued that the majority in *Gregg* had fallen into error in their analysis of the claimant's prospect of survival. Because of the statistical evidence that a majority of patients in the same position as the claimant at the time he visited the defendant would not have survived despite timely treatment, the majority decided that it was more likely than not that the claimant, too, would not have survived. This is a clear example of conflating belief probability and fact probability. Phang JA recognised that statistical evidence could be 'so compelling that the court may be able to infer belief probability from fact probability',[67] but rightly cautioned that the two must not be conflated.

II. Duty to Inform

The duty to inform cases raise some tricky causation questions because liability is contingent on the hypothetical decision of the patient. Take a scenario where the surgeon negligently fails to inform the patient of a one per cent risk that the proposed spinal surgery could result in paralysis even if the surgery is performed without any negligence.[68] The patient undergoes the surgery and the risk materialises, leaving her paralysed. An action is brought, and the surgeon accepts that the

[63] ibid [84].

[64] *Gregg v Scott* [2005] UKHL 2; [2005] 2 AC 176, [83]. A point his Lordship reiterated in an extra-judicial comment when he was President of the Supreme Court. Lord Neuberger, 'Implications of Tort Law Decisions' Address to Northern Ireland Personal Injury Bar's Inaugural Conference, County Down (13 May 2017), https://jcpc.uk/uploads/speech_170513_df193a3c26.pdf.

[65] ibid [190].

[66] *Armstrong v Quest Laboratories Pte Ltd* [2019] SGCA 75; [2020] 1 SLR 133.

[67] ibid [108].

[68] These facts are loosely based on *Chester v Afshar* [2004] UKHL 41; [2005] 1 AC 134, in which there was a risk of cauda equina damage during spinal surgery. The risk materialised and adversely affected the claimant's mobility.

failure to inform was a breach of duty. There are three possible scenarios relevant to causation.

The claimant may prove that she would have refused to undergo the surgery thereby avoiding the risk. This would be a straightforward case where the claimant would succeed.[69] Alternatively, the claimant may acknowledge that even if warned of the risk, she would have gone ahead with the surgery, either because she found the risk acceptable or because she felt she had no alternative option. Here, the surgeon's negligent failure to inform is not causative of her paralysis because the negligence would not have changed the course of events.[70] This too is straightforward, and the claimant's action will fail.

Difficulties arise when the claimant argues that she would not have had the surgery as scheduled, but would have delayed it to consider her options, obtain a second opinion, or seek a different surgeon to carry out the procedure. Essentially, she would have gone ahead with the same procedure but on another occasion, with the same surgeon or with a different one. The risk remains the same. It is inherent in the procedure; it is not contingent on the skill of the surgeon; and it is random. There is no increase or decrease in risk depending on when or by whom the surgery is performed. On conventional causation analysis, the claimant would fail to prove that the negligence made a difference as she would have been exposed to the exact same risk. Yet, courts in the United Kingdom and Australia have taken the view that it would be unfair to deny the claimant recovery.

The leading UK decision is *Chester v Afshar*,[71] and it would be no exaggeration to state that this is one of the most significant, and controversial, decisions in medical negligence on causation and damage.[72] The facts are similar to the scenario described above. The House of Lords by a narrow majority of 3-2 found in favour of the claimant, with the majority leaning heavily on notions of rights, autonomy, dignity, informed consent, and informed choice. These are interests that deserve protection but, as argued in Chapter four, it is debatable whether the tort of negligence is the appropriate vehicle to protect these interests. These concepts were also used interchangeably, almost randomly, by the judges in *Chester*, conflating trespass and negligence to vindicate patient autonomy in a negligence action. Lord Walker of Gestingthorpe blurs the line between trespass and negligence with this observation:

> The surgeon's duty to advise and warn his patient is closely connected with the need for the patient's consent to submit, under anaesthesia, to invasive surgery which would (in the absence of consent) be an assault. The advice is the foundation of the consent.[73]

[69] *Birch v University College London Hospital NHS Foundation Trust* [2008] EWHC 2237 (QB); (2008) 104 BMLR 168.

[70] See for example, *Duce v Worcestershire Acute Hospitals NHS Trust* [2018] EWCA Civ 1307; [2018] PIQR P18.

[71] [2004] UKHL 41; [2005] 1 AC 134.

[72] It has provoked a litany of case note and articles both supporting and critiquing the majority judgment. See T Clark and D Nolan, 'A Critique of *Chester v Afshar*' (2014) 34 *Oxford Journal of Legal Studies* 659 and references cited at n 3 therein.

[73] *Chester v Afshar* [2004] UKHL 41; [2005] 1 AC 134, 164.

Lord Steyn falls into the same error, holding that 'as a result of the surgeon's failure to warn the patient, she cannot be said to have given informed consent to the surgery in the full legal sense'.[74] With respect, this is patently wrong, as consent in negligence is relevant to the risk and avoidance of physical injury and not about interference with bodily integrity, which is the domain of trespass. Legatt LJ in *Duce v Worcestershire Acute Hospitals NHS Trust*[75] was explicit, stating, 'The language used by Lord Steyn seems more apt to a claim in trespass to the person than to a claim founded on negligence'.[76] Lord Steyn in *Chester* quotes Ronald Dworkin's work on abortion and euthanasia, in which Dworkin argues that autonomy is about respecting 'the integrity rather than the welfare of the choosing agent'.[77] Abortion and euthanasia raise fundamentally different considerations from negligence. The duty of care in negligence is to avoid injury to the claimant: unlike trespass and end-of-life decisions, negligence is about welfare not integrity.[78]

A. Autonomy and Causation

The following discussion on causation is based on UK and Australian law where the courts have adopted a subjective approach to causation, unlike Canadian courts, which have adopted an objective approach.[79] The objective test of causation is wrong in principle as it fails to deal with the actual facts, which is the essence of the causation inquiry. The Supreme Court of Canada has preferred the objective approach for pragmatic reasons, chiefly the concern that patients will invariably claim, truthfully or not, that they would have refused consent.[80] The Australian States and Territories have retained the subjective test but introduced evidential safeguards by making inadmissible any statements by claimants as to what they would have done unless such statements are against their interest.[81] This would exclude self-serving statements.

The majority in *Chester* did not deny that their judgments were based on policy and were incompatible with fundamental principles of causation.[82] They drew

[74] ibid 146.

[75] [2018] EWCA Civ 1307; [2018] PIQR P18.

[76] ibid [88].

[77] ibid [18], quoting R Dworkin, *Life's Dominion: An Argument about Abortion, Euthanasia and Individual Freedom* (New York, Alfred A Knopf, 1993) 224.

[78] T Clark and D Nolan, 'A Critique of *Chester v Afshar*' (2014) 34 *Oxford Journal of Legal Studies* 659, 675, citing H Teff, *Reasonable Care: Legal Perspectives on the Doctor-Patient Relationship* (Oxford, Oxford University Press, 1994) xxix–xxx. See Chapter 2 of this volume on vulnerability, obligations and relational theory.

[79] *Reibl v Hughes* [1980] 2 SCR 880.

[80] See, G Robertson, 'Informed Consent Ten Years Later: The Impact of *Reibl v Hughes*' (1991) 70 *Canadian Bar Review* 423.

[81] See for example, Civil Liability Act 2002 (NSW) s 5D(3)(b).

[82] *Chester v Afshar* [2004] UKHL 41; [2005] 1 AC 134 (per Lord Steyn), [21]; (per Lord Hope of Craighead), [81]; (per Lord Walker of Gestingthorpe), [101].

inspiration from the decision of the High Court of Australia in *Chappel v Hart*.[83] In that case, the claimant was not warned of a material risk of damage to her vocal cords in the course of oesophagal surgery. As the claimant suffered from a 'relentlessly progressive'[84] condition, and surgery was the only treatment option, it was inevitable that she would have consented, if not at the time, certainly in the near future. The claimant argued that she would have gone ahead with the same injury but would have chosen a more experienced surgeon to mitigate the risk. Indeed, she subsequently underwent the same surgery for a second time to improve her condition.

The High Court of Australia, by a 3-2 majority, found in favour of the claimant. Gaudron J held that whether the claimant would have been exposed to an identical risk by consenting to surgery at a later date was irrelevant to the causation inquiry. The gist of negligence was not exposure to risk, but the actual harm sustained. Causation was satisfied because but for the surgeon's negligent failure to inform, the claimant would not have undergone surgery and suffered the damage. On the other hand, Gummow J focused on the risk, arguing that the exposure to the very risk that materialised was a strong factor supporting causal responsibility.[85] Kirby J argued that common sense and intuition led to the conclusion that causation was proven.

Both Kirby J and Gaudron J accepted the argument that a more highly-skilled surgeon could have reduced the risk. This argument was effectively rebutted by Hayne J who reiterated the purpose of the tort of negligence:

> The law of negligence is intended to compensate those who are injured as a result of departures from standards of reasonable care. It is not intended to compensate those who have received reasonable care but who may not have had the best available care. To hold that the appellant's failure to warn the respondent of the risks of the operation caused her to lose the chance of the best available care would depart from that fundamental premise of the law of negligence.[86]

McHugh J, in the minority, argued that if 'the acts or omissions of the defendant would have made no difference to the plaintiff's course of action, the defendant has not caused the harm which the plaintiff has suffered'.[87] The academic reaction to *Chappel* was largely positive[88] and, together with the majority judgments, proved

[83] *Chappel v Hart* [1998] HCA 55; (1998) 195 CLR 232.

[84] ibid [2].

[85] ibid [65]–[68]. Gummow J found support for the 'exposure to risk' theory in J Fleming, 'Probabilistic Causation in Tort Law' (1989) 68 *Canadian Bar Review* 661, 662.

[86] *Chappell v Hart* [1998] HCA 55; (1998) 195 CLR 232, [139].

[87] ibid [32].

[88] P Cane, 'A Warning about Causation' (1999) 115 *Law Quarterly Review* 21; T Honoré, 'Medical Non-disclosure, Causation and Risk: *Chappel v Hart*' (1999) 7 *Torts Law Journal* 1; M Stauch, 'Taking the Consequences for Failure to Warn of Medical Risks' (2000) 63 *Modern Law Review* 261; M Jones, '"But for" Causation in Actions for Non-disclosure of Risk' (2002) 18 *Journal of Professional Negligence* 192; A Grubb, 'Clinical Negligence: Informed Consent and Causation' (2002) 10 *Medical Law Review* 322; J Stapleton, 'Cause-in-Fact and Scope of Liability for Consequences' (2003) 119 *Law*

influential in *Chester*. The views of Tony Honoré, in particular, underscores the majority's reasoning in *Chester* when he made the following argument in a note on *Chappel*:

> Dr Chappel violated Mrs Hart's right to choose for herself, even if he did not increase the risk to her. Judges should vindicate rights that have been violated if they can do so consistently with the authority of statutes and decided cases … For Dr Chappel *did* cause the harm that Mrs Hart suffered, though not by the advice he failed to give her. He did so by operating on her and, though he operated with due care, he slit open her oesophagus with the disastrous consequences. Morally he was responsible for the outcome of what he did.[89]

Unlike *Chappel*, where only Kirby J referred to the right of the claimant,[90] *Chester* emphasised the vindication of rights to justify an exceptional approach to causation. Lord Steyn observed that one function of the duty to inform was that it 'ensures that due respect is given to the autonomy and dignity of each patient'.[91] Lord Hope of Craighead stated that the duty to inform 'has at its heart the right of the patient to make an informed choice as to whether, and if so when and by whom, to be operated on'.[92] Lord Walker of Gestingthorpe, in a single paragraph, mentioned the word 'right' three times, capping it with a nod to autonomy.[93]

Even Lord Hoffmann in the minority championed the vindication of the patient's right to choose and would have awarded modest damages by way of *solatium*.[94] Lord Bingham was the only who rejected categorically the notion that the tort of negligence should be used to compensate a patient for the loss of a right to be informed, stating:

> I do not think for my part think that the law should seek to reinforce that right by providing for the payment of potentially very large damages by a defendant whose violation of that right is not shown to have worsened the physical condition of the claimant.[95]

The academic reception of *Chester* has been mixed. Those supporting the judgment do so for different reasons. Some take the position that *Chester* can be explained on the basis of orthodox causation principles, although courts interpreting *Chester* have consistently treated it as creating an exception to the conventional principles of causation.[96] Others justify it as a legitimate exception to the causation rules

Quarterly Review 388; R Heywood, 'Informed Consent Through the Back Door?' (2005) 56 *Northern Ireland Legal Quarterly* 266.

[89] T Honoré, 'Medical Non-disclosure, Causation and Risk: *Chappel v Hart* (1999) 7 *Torts Law Journal* 1, 8.

[90] *Chappel v Hart* [1998] HCA 55; (1998) 195 CLR 232, [95], [98].

[91] *Chester v Afshar* [2004] UKHL 41; [2005] 1 AC 134, [18].

[92] ibid [86].

[93] ibid [92], citing *Sidaway v Board of Governors of the Bethlem Royal Hospital and Maudsley Hospital* [1985] AC 871.

[94] *Chester v Afshar* [2004] UKHL 41; [2005] 1 AC 134, [34].

[95] ibid [9].

[96] See *Correia v University Hospital of North Staffordshire NHS Trust* [2017] EWCA Civ 356, [24]; *Negus v Guy's and St Thomas' NHS Hospital Trust* [2021] EWHC 643 (QB), [56]; *Winterbotham v Shahrak* [2024] EWHC 2633 (KB), [86].

or by arguing that exposure to risk or loss of autonomy should be treated as the relevant damage. Those who argue that *Chester* can be reconciled with orthodox principles emphasise that the focus of inquiry should be on the injury suffered by the patient, not the risk to which the patient was exposed. All the patient has to establish is that she would not have had the surgery when she did and therefore would not have suffered the injury that she did.

According to this argument, it is irrelevant that she might choose to face the same risk on another occasion. As there was a 1–2 per cent risk, she would have a 98–99 per cent chance of not having the risk materialise on another occasion; thus, it would be overwhelmingly likely that she would not suffer the injury. *Ergo*, the but-for test is satisfied. On this argument, a patient who testifies that, if informed of the risk, she would have stopped by a church to say a prayer on the way to surgery, thereby delaying the surgery, should also succeed! Paradoxically, the surgeon could be in a better position if the risk had been much greater. In theory, if the surgeon negligently failed to advise the patient of a 50 per cent risk of paralysis, and the patient says that she would have been willing to roll the dice and have the surgery on another day, the argument is exposed as a fallacy, as now there is an even chance of the risk materialising. The patient cannot say that in all likelihood she would not have suffered the injury by having the surgery on a different day.[97]

Arguments that *Chester* is compatible with conventional causation doctrine are flawed as they ignore the legal context of the inquiry. The question is whether the claimant would have suffered the injury but for the surgeon's *negligent failure to inform*. It is impossible to answer the but-for test of causation with respect to an omission without addressing the actual event that caused the damage. It is always a hypothetical inquiry.[98] *Bolitho v City and Hackney Health Authority*[99] provides an illustration. The claimant, a two-year-old child with serious respiratory problems, was being monitored in hospital. He went into severe distress on two occasions and on each occasion the nurse called for the attending doctor. On both occasions, the doctor negligently failed to attend. Shortly after the second incident, the child suffered another respiratory event and suffered a cardiac arrest, leaving him severely disabled. The defendant admitted negligence but contested causation.

Whether the defendant's negligence caused the injury depended on what would have happened had the attending doctor or her deputy attended. The only way to avoid the cardiac arrest would have been to intubate the child to preserve his respiratory function. Causation turns not solely on the negligent failure to

[97] In practice, of course, most duty to inform cases involve a very low risk of very grave consequences, which means that as long as the claimant can prove that she would not have had the surgery on that very occasion causation will invariably be satisfied. See R Gounder, 'The Way to Chappel' (2024) 29 *Torts Law Journal* 135, 146.

[98] S Harder, 'Medical Non-Disclosure and Hypothetical Consent' (2009) 20 *King's Law Journal* 435.

[99] *Bolitho v City and Hackney Health Authority* [1997] UKHL 46; [1998] AC 232.

attend but crucially on the hypothetical actions of the doctor had she attended.[100] As the High Court of Australia observed in *Wallace v Kam*,[101] the 'determination of factual causation necessarily turns on a determination of what the patient would have chosen to do if the medical practitioner had warned of all material risks'.[102]

It cannot be determined whether the surgeon's negligent failure to inform in *Chester* caused the injury, without determining what the claimant would or would not have done. Just as it was not enough in *Bolitho* to say that causation was established because there was a breach of duty and the very injury that should have been prevented occurred, so too there cannot be a leap of causal faith between the surgeon's negligent failure to inform and the claimant's injury. Yet, this leap is made. For example, Clark and Nolan are critical of those who disagree that causation is established on orthodox principles:

> Although others have argued that the but-for test was not satisfied on the facts of *Chester*, it turns out that they are reaching the wrong conclusion because (as so often in this area of law) they are asking the wrong question … the factual causation stage is concerned with the historical connection between the breach of duty and the damage, so in a non-disclosure case the question is not whether there was a historical connection between the failure to warn and the patient *undergoing surgery*, but between the failure to warn and the patient *suffering the physical injury* … The fact that the claimant would have been exposed to the same risk even if warned was not therefore relevant at the factual causation stage, but only later, at the scope of liability stage.[103]

Curiously, courts ignore the purpose of the duty when they wish to find causal responsibility but rely on it in cases where they wish to deny causal responsibility.[104] The purpose of the duty to take care in the performance of surgery is to avoid injury to the patient. The purpose of the duty to inform patients of risks is not to avoid injury to the patient but to enable the patient to decide whether to take the risk of suffering that injury. It respects the patient's right to decide for themselves what is an acceptable risk to them. In *Wallace*, the patient underwent a surgical procedure which carried, amongst other things, the risk of neuropraxia and the risk of catastrophic paralysis. The surgeon negligently failed to warn the patient of both risks. The neuropraxia risk materialised, but the trial judge found that the patient would have consented to the surgery even if informed.

[100] The doctor said that she would not have intubated, and the court was satisfied that it would not have been negligent not to do so. Eight experts were called, five for the claimant who testified that they would have intubated and three for the defendants who testified that they would not have intubated. Applying the *Bolam* test, the judge held that the doctor was not negligent for failing to intubate as her act was accepted as proper by a responsible body of medical opinion. Only after making this determination, could it be said that the doctor's negligent failure to attend did not cause the cardiac arrest.

[101] *Wallace v Kam* [2013] HCA 19; (2013) 250 CLR 375.

[102] ibid [17].

[103] T Clark and D Nolan, 'A Critique of *Chester v Afshar*' (2014) 34 *Oxford Journal of Legal Studies* 659, 623–24. See also, J Stapleton, 'Occam's Razor Reveals an Orthodox Basis for *Chester v Afshar*' (2006) 122 *Law Quarterly Review* 426.

[104] See for example, *Wallace v Kam* [2013] HCA 19; (2013) 250 CLR 375; *Khan v Meadows* [2021] UKSC 21; [2022] AC 852.

The question then arose whether the patient would have consented to the surgery had he been informed of all material risks, including the risk of catastrophic paralysis. If he would have refused the surgery, he would not have been exposed to the risk of neuropraxia and thus would not have suffered neuropraxia. The High Court of Australia rejected this argument, holding that the surgeon was not liable for risks which the patient accepted, noting that the policy of the law in these cases was 'to protect the patient from the occurrence of physical injury *the risk of which is unacceptable* to the patient' (emphasis added).[105] Surely then, the surgeon in *Chester* should not have been liable to the claimant for a risk which was acceptable to her. *Chester* has not been applied outside of medical negligence,[106] and even within medical negligence it is applied narrowly.[107] Nonetheless, claimants now routinely include an alternative causation argument in their pleadings as a second string to the bow, relying on both conventional causation and the *Chester* exception.[108]

B. Autonomy and Damage

Unlike the majority in *Chappel*, the majority in *Chester* placed autonomy and patients' rights at the heart of their decision. Lord Steyn stated: 'Her right of autonomy and dignity can and ought to be vindicated by a narrow and modest departure from traditional causation principles'.[109] The prominence given to the protection of autonomy in *Chester* has been reinforced by the Supreme Court in *Montgomery v Lanarkshire Health Board*,[110] spurring a growing body of academic literature arguing that autonomy should be an interest protected by the tort of negligence.[111]

Arguing against patient autonomy may appear to be regressive in light of the long history of medical paternalism. Yet, it is vital to remain objective and be measured, lest the pendulum swing too far. A distinction must be drawn between infringing a patient's autonomy to make decisions in cases like *Chester* and infringing a patient's autonomy in cases like *Rees v Darlington Memorial Hospital*.[112] It is imperative to decide which concept of autonomy is to be recognised. Courts must

105 *Wallace v Kam* [2013] HCA 19; (2013) 250 CLR 375, [36].

106 *White v Paul Davidson & Taylor (A Firm)* [2004] EWCA Civ 1511; *Beary v Pall Mall Investments (a Firm)* [2005] EWCA Civ 415.

107 *Crossman v St George's Healthcare NHS Trust* [2016] EWHC 2878 (QB); *Meiklejohn v St George's Healthcare NHS Trust* [2014] EWCA Civ 120.

108 See *Winterbotham v Shahrak* [2024] EWHC 2633 (KB), [71].

109 ibid [24].

110 *Montgomery v Lanarkshire Health Board* [2015] UKSC 11; [2015] AC 1430.

111 G Turton, 'Informed Consent to Medical Treatment Post-Montgomery: Causation and Coincidence' (2018) 27 *Medical Law Review* 108; MK Smith and T Carver, 'Montgomery, Informed Consent and Causation of Harm: Lessons from Australia or a Uniquely English Approach to Patient Autonomy?' (2018) 44 *Journal of Medical Ethics* 384; S Fullham-McQuillan, 'Infringement of Autonomy as Damage in Medical Negligence' (2023) 139 *Law Quarterly Review* 126.

112 As will be developed below, the latter is a more likely candidate for recognising autonomy as actionable damage.

also grapple with the question whether loss of autonomy is actionable per se and how damages should be quantified.

Doctors clearly have a duty to inform patients of risks inherent in proposed treatment and patients have a right to be so informed. Patient autonomy and rights discourse are relevant considerations in the assessment of the duty of care and standard of care. However, autonomy is not relevant to causation of damage. In cases like *Chester*, if the patient would have gone ahead with the surgery had she been informed, the surgeon is not liable, as the negligent failure to inform would have made no difference to the outcome for the patient. If the patient would have refused to undergo the surgery, causation will be established and the surgeon found liable. In both these cases, there is no need to have recourse to autonomy-based arguments. It is only when the patient would have delayed the surgery that there is a need to consider the infringement of autonomy as a proxy for damage.

At the duty stage, it is clear enough that a failure to inform patients of a material risk deprives patients of the opportunity to make informed decisions about their bodily integrity. That is a violation of their autonomy. Lord Steyn in *Chester* proclaimed that patients 'have the right to make decisions which doctors regard as ill advised'.[113] That is true, but equally, the patient has to be responsible for a bad decision. Thus, if the claimant in *Chester*, if informed of the innate risk of cauda equina syndrome from this type of surgery, would have accepted that risk, then the patient's choice and consequences that follow must be respected.

Paradoxically, in the name of protecting patient autonomy, the court in fact denies patient agency, replacing medical paternalism with judicial paternalism. Autonomy is a passive concept – it is about the patient's freedom to make decisions about their body. Agency is an active concept – it is about the patient's actual decisions to achieve their goals. As argued in Chapters four and five, autonomy and agency are double-edged swords – the right to choose comes with responsibility for the choice. Agency necessarily connotes accountability.

Negligent failure to inform interferes with the patient's autonomy by affecting their freedom to make informed decisions. However, once they have the information, they are free to make informed decisions. A patient who chooses to accept a risk of which she is informed is exercising agency. They are then responsible for their choices. This is implicit in *Montgomery* itself where the court noted that the law as it has evolved treats patients 'as adults who are capable of understanding that medical treatment is uncertain of success and may involve risks, *accepting responsibility for the taking of risks affecting their own lives, and living with the consequences of their choices*' (emphasis added).[114]

The causation inquiry necessarily involves a hypothetical – what would the patient have done if properly advised? If the patient would have accepted the risk, they must be accountable for their decision. This is part of shared decision-making

[113] *Chester v Afshar* [2004] UKHL 41; [2005] 1 AC 134, [14].
[114] *Montgomery v Lanarkshire Health Board* [2015] UKSC 11; [2015] AC 1430, [81].

and empowerment of patients, which is the direction in which contemporary clinical practice and ethics is moving.[115] It is not unfair to deny compensation to a patient who honestly admits that he or she would have accepted the risk. Negligence is not about rewarding honesty but compensating for harm that is negligently caused; if the harm were caused by the patient's own decision, the doctor should not be held liable for failure to inform.[116] Thus, causation is established only in the first scenario where the claimant would have refused consent and avoided the surgery.[117] The second and third scenarios are indistinguishable, as in both cases the claimant was willing to accept the risk and therefore should be held accountable for his or her choice.[118]

C. Beware the Swinging Pendulum

The problem with UK jurisprudence on the duty to inform is that it has leaned too far into patients' rights and autonomy, with *Chester* and *Montgomery* being high watermarks. It was argued in Chapter two that negligence should be viewed through the lens of obligations and not rights. Gemma Turton, in an illuminating article analysing *Chester* and *Montgomery*, rightly noted as follows:

> But the purpose of negligence liability, at least on an orthodox understanding, is not to vindicate the rights of the claimant but to allocate responsibility for harm suffered. The causation requirement plays a vital role in this allocation of responsibility by requiring not only that the defendant's negligence in fact caused the damage suffered by the claimant, but also in declining to hold the doctor responsible and therefore liable for the materialisation of a risk that the claimant was willing to run.[119]

Nonetheless, *Montgomery* and *Chester* have let the proverbial cat out of the bag. Sarah Fulham-McQuillam has recently argued that these cases have 'paved the way for infringement of autonomy to be actionable damage in medical negligence, even without physical injury'.[120] This is quite a radical argument, which would extinguish the distinction between trespass and negligence and impose an unfair burden on doctors. Fulham-McQuillam acknowledges the radical nature of the argument and does not go so far as to advocate for it.[121] She merely warns that *Chester* and *Montgomery* have opened Pandora's Box.

[115] The General Medical Council has emphasised the importance of shared decision-making in its guidance: 'Decision making and consent', https://www.gmc-uk.org/professional-standards/the-professional-standards/decision-making-and-consent.

[116] See the comments on not discriminating against honest patients *Chester v Afshar* [2004] UKHL 41; [2005] 1 AC 134, [87], [101].

[117] See above, text to nn 68–71.

[118] ibid.

[119] G Turton, 'Informed Consent to Medical Treatment Post-*Montgomery*: Causation and Coincidence' (2018) 27 *Medical Law Review* 108, 130.

[120] S Fulham-McQuillam, 'Infringement of Autonomy as Damage in Medical Negligence' (2023) 139 *Law Quarterly Review* 126, 126.

[121] ibid 152.

A bold interpretation of *Montgomery* would be to fragment the doctor's duty, hiving off the duty to advise as a positive duty that stands apart from the general duty.[122] If the duty to advise is treated as *sui generis*, then, just as the standard of care could be differentiated, with *Bolam* applying to performance-based liability,[123] and *Montgomery* applying to reliance-based liability,[124] so too can the rules for causation and damage be reimagined. *Chester* has already done so for causation, and Fulham-McQuillam argues that 'the characterisation of damage could also be different based on the patient's correlative right to be warned and advised'.[125] Having said that, she acknowledges that the courts have not recognised lost autonomy as damage, noting several England and Wales Court of Appeal decisions that expressly rejected the idea of interference with autonomy as actionable damage.[126]

Montgomery held that a doctor is 'under a duty to take reasonable care to ensure that the patient is aware of any material risks involved in any recommended treatment, and of any reasonable alternative or variant treatments'.[127] The duty to advise of risks is to enable the patient to avoid the risk of injury. The duty to advise of alternatives is designed to give patients a choice. If *Montgomery* intended to protect the patient's right to choose, the test governing the disclosure of alternative options should be the same as the test governing disclosure of risks. Yet, the Supreme Court in *McCulloch v Forth Valley Health Board*[128] has held that the *Bolam* test applies to advice on alternative options. Respect for patient autonomy would demand that the patient be informed of *any* reasonable alternatives so that the patient can make an informed decision about which treatment to accept. It appears that the Supreme Court is retreating somewhat from the strong patient autonomy stance in *Montgomery*.

Proponents of the autonomy-as-damage argument must confront the ambiguous nature of autonomy. Philosophically, autonomy exists on a spectrum from a liberal, individualistic concept to a critical, relational concept. Various conceptions of autonomy have been explored in the medical negligence context, including best desire, current desire, and ideal desire.[129] Turton has argued that *Montgomery* reflected a best desire autonomy, while Craig Purshouse has argued that *Chester* reflected current desire autonomy.[130] This work has argued in Chapter four that a

[122] ibid 133.

[123] This includes the general duty to diagnose, treat, and care.

[124] This includes the duty to inform and advise. The nomenclature of performance-based and reliance-based negligence is borrowed from GT Houseman, 'Wrongful Birth as Negligence Misrepresentation' (2013) 71 *University of Toronto Faculty of Law Review* 9, 14.

[125] S Fulham-McQuillam, 'Infringement of Autonomy as Damage in Medical Negligence' (2023) 139 *Law Quarterly Review* 126, 133.

[126] *Diamond v Royal Devon and Exeter NHS Foundation Trust* [2019] EWCA Civ 585; [2019] PIQR P12; *Shaw v Kovac* [2017] EWCA Civ 1028; [2017] 1 WLR 4773; *Duce v Worcestershire Acute Hospitals NHS Trust* [2018] EWCA Civ 1307; [2018] PIQR P18.

[127] [2015] UKSC 11; [2015] AC 1430, [87].

[128] *McCulloch v Forth Valley Health Board* [2023] UKSC 26; [2024] AC 925.

[129] See Chapter 4 of this volume, text to nn 85–96.

[130] G Turton, 'Informed Consent to Medical Treatment Post-*Montgomery*: Causation and Coincidence' (2018) 27 *Medical Law Review* 108, 113; C Purshouse, 'How Should Autonomy be Defined in Medical Negligence Cases?' (2015) 10 *Clinical Ethics* 107, 111.

relational concept of autonomy based on reflexive desire is the most appropriate for medical negligence.[131] Patient autonomy in the clinical negligence context is always in a state of flux as the patient processes information, engages in dialogue with the doctor, clarifies matters, and seeks input from family or friends to reassess what is an acceptable risk.

The observations in *Powell v University Hospitals Sussex NHS Foundation Trust*[132] capture the complex realities in these duty to inform cases:

> Therefore, by the time we arrive at January 2014, Mr Chauhan had performed four surgical procedures on Mrs Powell. She had accepted his professional advice every time over that decade. She had not once gone against it. During that time, they developed [a] doctor-patient relationship and she liked him. He called her Anne. She had, as she accepted, 'built up a lot of trust' in him.
>
> She said that she would in the past talk through Mr Chauhan's advice with her husband and at least some of her children, but as she put it, 'generally' she would go with his advice. In fact, the historical record shows that at no previous point had she not followed his advice. Frankly, it is unsurprising that Mrs Powell gave the answers she did. The claimant's orthopaedic expert Mr Donnachie states that the decision about whether to choose a first stage procedure or a DAIR or DAIR plus is a very complex decision even for surgeons. This is supported by the existence of two schools of reasonable and responsible medical opinion on the question. Thus, it is completely understandable that Mrs Powell 'wouldn't know what she would have done'. Further, given that she has followed Mr Chauhan's advice uniformly and unreservedly up to January 2014 for a decade in multiple procedures, her answer of '50-50' following his advice is if anything an understatement of what would have been likely to have happened.

This chapter argues that loss of autonomy should not be viewed as actionable damage in the duty to inform cases. If it were to be recognised as actionable damage, courts would then have to determine whether a patient is entitled to sue for infringement of autonomy even when the risk does not materialise and cause injury. This is a position contemplated by Fulham-McQuillam as a potential consequence of *Chester* and *Montgomery*.[133] This would make negligence actionable per se. It would be unjust to hold a doctor liable to patients despite not causing any personal injury; such an approach would undermine trust in the doctor–patient relationship.[134]

Finally, brief mention should be made of the policy justifications in *Chester*, namely that failing to hold the defendant liable for the claimant's injury would render the duty a 'hollow one'[135] or 'drained of its content',[136] or that the modification to causation was necessary to vindicate the patient's right.[137] This is not

[131] See Chapter 4 of this volume, text to nn 97–98.

[132] *Powell v University Hospitals Sussex NHS Foundation Trust* [2023] EWHC 736 (KB), [82]–[83].

[133] S Fulham-McQuillam, 'Infringement of Autonomy as Damage in Medical Negligence' (2023) 139 *Law Quarterly Review* 126, 144–46.

[134] The autonomy and rights of the defendant are often ignored in autonomy discourse in negligence. D Nolan, 'Negligence and Autonomy' [2022] *Singapore Journal of Legal Studies* 356, 358–59.

[135] *Chester v Afshar* [2004] UKHL 41; [2005] 1 AC 134, [87] (per Lord Steyn).

[136] ibid [101] (per Lord Walker of Gestingthorpe).

[137] ibid [24] (per Lord Steyn); [33] (per Lord Hoffmann).

entirely accurate: the duty to inform is not a hollow one as causation can be established in appropriate cases.[138] Not all breaches of duty must result in compensation to the claimant. Imagine a roller-coaster operator who negligently fails to inform a rider that there is a one per cent risk of a heart attack if the rider has a heart condition. The rider suffers a heart attack on the ride and later states that had the risk been disclosed to him he would have paused to seek his wife's permission and gone ahead on the next ride, where he would have a 99 cent chance of not suffering a heart attack. Should the rider be compensated?

More importantly, by relying on these arguments, the judges in *Chester* were using the tort of negligence to perform a regulatory function rather than a compensatory one. Chapter three argued that the tort of negligence is not ideal for regulatory function. Medical professionals are tightly regulated, and patients may lodge a complaint against doctors for professional negligence or professional misconduct.[139] Given the availability of the complaints mechanism to enforce doctors' legal and ethical duties as well as to vindicate patients' right to information, it is unnecessary for the court to modify the conventional rules on causation.

III. Beyond Autonomy

A key argument in this chapter is that the autonomy-based argument that shaped the causation discourse in *Chester* is misplaced. Autonomy is relevant to the scope of duty, but it should not muddy the causation waters. Designating autonomy as the gist of negligence may circumvent the causation conundrum but no court has yet recognised loss of autonomy as damage in the duty to inform cases. The relentless focus on autonomy and desire to vindicate patients' rights risks undermining patient agency and accountability for choices. To ignore the patient's choice to accept a risk is itself a denigration of the patient's autonomy. There are, however, areas where loss of autonomy, insult to personhood,[140] or diminution of wellbeing[141] may legitimately constitute the gist of negligence.

Two emerging areas are reproductive negligence and genomic negligence. While genomics is genuinely a recent development, assisted reproduction has a long history, with the first documented case of artificial insemination occurring in the late eighteenth century.[142] However, modern technology has revolutionised assisted reproduction, bringing with it significant legal and ethical challenges. In vitro

[138] See *Birch v University College London Hospital NHS Foundation Trust* [2008] EWHC 2237 (QB); (2008) 104 BMLR 168.

[139] Each jurisdiction has a professional body regulating doctors under legislation. In the UK, it is the General Medical Council, under the Medical Act 1983. In Singapore, it is the Singapore Medical Council, under the Medical Registration Act 1997. Australian States and Territories each have their own regulatory authorities and rules.

[140] M Mortazavi, 'Torts and Personhood' (2023) 76 *Arkansas Law Review* 387.

[141] YK Zhou, 'More on What it Means to Suffer Harm' (2022) 13 *Jurisprudence* 516.

[142] W Ombelet and JV Robays, 'Artificial Insemination History: Hurdles and Milestones' (2015) 7 *Facts Views and Vision in ObGyn* 137, 138.

fertilisation (IVF) involves the extraction of the male and female gametes, with fertilisation taking place in a laboratory before the embryo is implanted.[143] The first IVF baby was born in 1978.[144] Gamete intrafallopian transfer (GIFT) involves extraction of the gametes and insertion into the fallopian tube for fertilisation to occur.[145]

Reproductive cloning technology has advanced, although it is not yet permitted as a method of reproduction.[146] Scientists have also achieved the ability to produce mature gametes from embryonic stem cells (ESC) and induced pluripotent stem cells (IPSC).[147] Unlike ESCs, ISPCs are derived from mature cell sources, including skin and blood tissue. There is now the possibility of developing sperm and ova from skin cells, allowing humans to self-replicate through in vitro gametogenesis (IVG).[148] These methods of assisted reproduction carry significant risks of negligently caused harm when the wrong gametes are used; where there is negligence in pre-implantation genetic testing, extraction and implantation of gametes; and when expectations of genetic selections are not met. There may be no injury to the child that is born but there may be unwanted or unexpected genetic traits or anomalies.

The damage in these cases is not always physical or financial, which is how the 'wrongful birth'[149] cases have conventionally been analysed.[150] Wrongful birth cases are controversial in so far as the claim includes damages for the cost of upkeep of the child. This introduces difficult moral, ethical, and policy questions which have divided courts. The House of Lords has rejected claims for upkeep cost with respect to healthy children,[151] but allowed claims where the child is born with a disability.[152] The damages are to cover the additional costs related to the disability. The High Court of Australia has allowed upkeep costs,[153] although this decision has been reversed by legislation.[154]

While rejecting upkeep costs, the apex courts in the UK and Singapore have recognised that parents in reproductive negligence cases *do* suffer some injury to

[143] C Thomas, 'Novel Assisted Reproductive Technologies and Procreative Liberty: Examining I Vitro Gametogenesis Relative to Currently Practiced Assisted Reproductive Procedures and Reproductive Cloning' (2017) 26 *Southern California Interdisciplinary Law Journal* 623, 628.

[144] L Brown and M Powell, *Louise Brown: My Life as the World's First Test-Tube Baby* (Bristol, Bristol Books CIC, 2015).

[145] ibid.

[146] Human Fertilisation and Embryology Act 2008 (UK) s 3; Human Cloning and Other Prohibited Practices Act 2004 (Singapore) s 5.

[147] G Liu, et al, 'Advances in Pluripotent Stem Cells: History, Mechanisms, Technologies, and Applications' (2020) 16 *Stem Cell Reviews and Report* 3.

[148] C Thomas, 'Novel Assisted Reproductive Technologies and Procreative Liberty: Examining I Vitro Gametogenesis Relative to Currently Practiced Assisted Reproductive Procedures and Reproductive Cloning' (2017) 26 *Southern California Interdisciplinary Law Journal* 623, 629.

[149] The expression 'wrongful birth' is used generically to refer to wrongful fertilisation, wrongful conception, wrongful pregnancy, wrongful birth, and wrongful life.

[150] See for example, C Witting, 'Physical Damage in Negligence' (2002) 61(1) *Cambridge Law Journal* 189, 196.

[151] *McFarlane v Tayside Health Board* [1999] UKHL 50; [2000] 2 AC 59; *Rees v Darlington Memorial Hospital NHS Trust* [2003] UKHL 52; [2004] 1 AC 309.

[152] *Parkinson v St James & Seacroft University Hospital NHS Trust* [2001] EWCA Civ 530; [2002] QB 266; *Groom v Selby* [2001] EWCA Civ 1522; [2002] Lloyds Med Rep 1.

[153] *Cattanach v Melchior* [2003] HCA 38; (2003) 215 CLR 1.

[154] Civil Liability Act 2003 (Qld) ss 49A, 49B.

their autonomy which deserves legal recognition. In the UK, this was done by way of a conventional award.[155] The Singapore Court of Appeal, in a decision that attracted global attention,[156] undertook a comprehensive analysis of loss of autonomy in the reproductive negligence case of *ACB v Thomson Medical Pte Ltd*.[157] The defendant fertility clinic in *ACB* negligently used the wrong sperm in an IVF procedure, resulting in the claimant giving birth to a child that was genetically hers but with no genetic connection with her husband, as the sperm came from a stranger. *ACB* was distinguishable from the orthodox wrongful birth cases, as the claimant in *ACB* actually wanted a child and was prepared for the costs of raising a child. Thus, there was no economic loss.

After a review of the wrongful birth jurisprudence, Phang JA agreed that upkeep costs should not be awarded for policy reasons but held that the claimant had suffered a loss and deserved compensation. Phang JA rejected the conventional sum approach in *Rees* and the vindicatory approach in *Chester*. Further, Phang JA held that loss of autonomy per se should not be recognised as actionable damage, arguing that it was 'too nebulous', did 'not comport with the concept of damage in the tort of negligence', and 'would undermine existing control mechanisms which keep recovery in the tort of negligence within sensible bounds'.[158]

Drawing on academic literature,[159] Phang JA recognised that genetic affinity was an interest that merited protection in reproductive negligence cases, holding:

> In our judgment, the Appellant's interest in maintaining the integrity of her reproductive plans in this very specific sense – where she has made a conscious decision to have a child with her Husband to maintain an intergenerational genetic link and to preserve 'affinity' – is one which the law should recognise and protect.[160]

[155] Lord Millet in *McFarlane v Tayside Health Board* [1999] UKHL 50; [2000] 2 AC 59 first referred to it before the majority in *Rees v Darlington Memorial Hospital NHS Trust* [2003] UKHL 52; [2004] 1 AC 309 recognised it to award the claimant a conventional sum of £15,000 for interference with her autonomy.

[156] For analyses and critique of the judgment, see D Nolan, 'Negligence and Autonomy' [2022] *Singapore Journal of Legal Studies* 356; C Purshouse, 'Autonomy, Affinity, and the Assessment of Damages: *ACB v Thomson Medical Pte Ltd* [2017] SGCA 20 and *Shaw v Kovak* [2017] EWCA Civ 1028' (2017) 26 *Medical Law Review* 675; S Todd, 'Common Law Protection for Injury to a Person's Reproductive Autonomy' (2019) 135 *Law Quarterly Review* 635; T Foxton, 'Inaccurate Conception: *ACB v Thomson Medical*' (2018) 81 *Modern Law Review* 337; J English and MJ Hafeez-Baig, '"*ACB v Thomson Medical Pte Ltd*": Recovery of Upkeep Costs, Claims for Loss of Autonomy and Loss of Genetic Affinity: Fertile Ground for Development?' (2018) 41(3) *University of Melbourne Law Review* 1360; K Amirthalingam, 'Reproductive Negligence: Unwanted Child or Unwanted Parenthood?' (2018) 134 *Law Quarterly Review* 15; VL Raposo, 'Wrongful Genetic Connection: Neither Blood of My Blood, nor Flesh of My Flesh' (2020) 23 *Medicine, Health Care and Philosophy* 309.

[157] *ACB v Thomson Medical Pte Ltd* [2017] SGCA 20; [2017] 1 SLR 918.

[158] ibid [115].

[159] Principally, D Fox, 'Reproductive Negligence' (2017) 117 *Columbia Law Review* 149; F Norton, 'Assisted Reproduction and the Frustration of Genetic Affinity: Interest, Injury, and Damages' (1999) 74 *New York University Law Review* 793; Leon R Kass, *Life, Liberty and the Defense of Dignity: The Challenge for Bioethics* (San Francisco, Encounter Books, 2002); N Priaux, 'Joy to the World! A (Healthy) Child is Born! Reconceptualizing "Harm" in Wrongful Conception' (2004) 13 *Social & Legal Studies* 5.

[160] *ACB v Thomson Medical Pte Ltd* [2017] SGCA 20; [2017] 1 SLR 918, [135].

There is growing support for the idea that negligent interference with reproductive autonomy raises unique issues and that loss of, or interference with, autonomy should be recognised as actionable damage.[161] Interference with reproductive autonomy goes well beyond wrongful birth cases – where the critical issue is whether parents of a child that they had not planned to have should be compensated for the cost of raising the child. This is certainly one aspect, but reproductive autonomy can be affected in the reverse way as well, with a person denied the opportunity to have offspring due to the negligence of the defendant;[162] or, as in the IVF mix-up cases where the parents have a child that is not genetically linked to one or both of them.[163]

The danger with recognising loss of autonomy as actionable damage in these cases is that it opens the door to further claims. Why stop at reproductive or genetic autonomy? It is beyond the scope of this work to explore these issues. They are simply raised here to acknowledge that negligent interference with certain autonomy interests should in some cases be actionable. Tsachi Keren-Paz describes three types of interference with autonomy:

> Type 1, being deprived merely of the opportunity to consent to being moved from one state of affairs to another; Type 2, being moved without consent to a subjectively inferior state of affairs; and Type 3, autonomy loss consequent upon violation of a previously protected interest.[164]

Type 3 is not about damage but loss – the actionable damage is the previously protected interest. Type 1 is the *Chester*-type situation, which it is argued here should not be treated as actionable damage. Type 2 covers situations such as interference with reproductive autonomy, which is the only type that should be recognised as actionable damage.

IV. Conclusion

This chapter has examined whether the law should extend the concept of actionable damage in medical negligence to circumvent difficulties in proving causation of the actual injury suffered. Scholars and courts have explored the feasibility of recognising intermediate interests such as material increase in risk, exposure to unreasonable risk, loss of chance, interference with autonomy, and interference with the right to make informed decisions. The debates are overwhelmingly dominated by considerations of patient autonomy and the right to informed

[161] A Christie, 'Vindicating Reproductive Autonomy in Wrongful Conception Cases' (2020) 26 *Auckland University Law Review* 178; T Keren-Paz, 'Compensating Injury to Autonomy in English Negligence Law: Inconsistent Recognition' (2018) 26 *Medical Law Review* 585.
[162] *Yearworth v North Bristol NHS Trust* [2009] EWCA Civ 37 (2009) 107 BMLR 47.
[163] *A (A Minor) v A Health and Social Services Trust* [2010] NIQB 108.
[164] T Keren-Paz, 'Compensating Injury to Autonomy in English Negligence Law: Inconsistent Recognition' (2018) 26 *Medical Law Review* 585, 586.

decision-making, which risk conflating negligence and trespass. It is vital that the boundary between the two torts is maintained, as one is actionable only on proof of damage while the other is actionable per se.

Arguments based on increased risk and loss of chance require closer scrutiny to distinguish between cases where such analysis is warranted and those where it is not. Exposure to risk may in exceptional cases ground an action, but only when the purpose of the duty is to avoid that very risk or when the risk to which the claimant is exposed is morally unacceptable. Similarly, loss of chance and statistical evidence have nuances that must be understood and applied in a logically defensible manner. Most importantly, the difference between belief probability and outcome probability must be uppermost in such cases.

Patient autonomy is an important interest that deserves legal protection. However, it has been used injudiciously in resolving causation in the duty to inform cases. *Chester* stands out as a decision in which the majority in the House of Lords was blindsided by autonomy-based arguments. Holding the defendant accountable to the claimant in such a case ignores both the scope of the defendant's duty and the agency of the patient. It flies in the face of the ethos of shared decision-making, where the patient is encouraged to play an active role in making decisions about their healthcare. It diminishes their agency when their decision to accept a risk is ignored by courts: judicial paternalism is not necessarily better than medical paternalism. From the doctor's perspective, it is patently unfair to empower patients to make choices but not hold them responsible for their choices. The interests of the patient must be balanced against the interests of the doctor.

9

Conclusion

As Margaret Brazier warned two decades ago,[1] courts have 'over-corrected the balance'[2] between medical beneficence and patient autonomy. That imbalance in favour of autonomy has been enhanced since then with decisions such as *Chester v Afshar*[3] and *Montgomery v Lanarkshire Health Board*.[4] Recently, the Supreme Court in *McCulloch v Forth Valley Health Board*[5] has signalled that autonomy-based arguments cannot be allowed to run too far. The main objective of this work has been to develop a theoretical argument to critique the role of autonomy in medical negligence and rethink the fundamental elements of duty, breach, causation, and damage.

Unlike most torts, negligence has very few restrictions with respect to the standing of the claimant or defendant, the nature of the impugned conduct, or the type of loss. The bright line is that negligence is actionable only on proof of damage that is legally recognised. Autonomy-based arguments are beginning to erode this requirement. Because liability in negligence is determined as much by policy considerations as precedents, it has become fertile ground for academic theorising and judicial law-making. Corrective justice theories and rights-based arguments have contributed to the rise of patient autonomy in medical ethics and law.

This work has championed a human obligations approach over the rights-based approach that has dominated Western legal and philosophical thinking. A human obligations approach is in tune with communitarian values, recognising the interconnectedness of individuals and society. A rights-based approach, while integral to many torts, is not necessarily appropriate to determine liability in cases involving alleged negligence in advising patients of risks in proposed treatment. It is confrontational and undermines the trust that is at the core of the doctor–patient relationship. An obligations-based approach, on the other hand, fosters collaboration, not confrontation.

Private law has been explained and critiqued by a range of theories including justice theories, instrumental theories, and critical theories. It has been argued in this work that medical negligence is best served by a combination of relational

[1] M Brazier, 'Do No Harm – Do Patients have Responsibilities Too?' (2006) 65 *Cambridge Law Journal* 397.

[2] ibid 398.

[3] *Chester v Afshar* [2004] UKHL 41; [2005] 1 AC 134.

[4] *Montgomery v Lanarkshire Health Board* [2015] UKSC 11; [2015] AC 1430.

[5] *McCulloch v Forth Valley Health Board* [2023] UKSC 26; [2024] AC 925.

justice, vulnerability theory, and care ethics. Medical negligence involves relationships – between doctor and patient; between patient and family members; and between doctor and family members, yet the law takes an individualistic approach. While individual autonomy protects against medical paternalism, it ignores the interdependent, inter-connected, and socially embedded nature of individuals. Drawing on vulnerability theory and care ethics, this work has argued in favour of medical maternalism. Medical paternalism is when the doctor decides what is in the best interest of the patient. Medical maternalism, on the other hand, is when the doctor acts in the patient's best interest while respecting and facilitating the patient's agency.[6]

In critiquing the core theme of this work – autonomy – the philosophies of Kant, Hume, and Mill have been explored. It was noted that the Kantian version of autonomy, which valorises individualism, has dominated Western discourse. Kantian autonomy is hostage to individualistic values, ignoring the mutual interconnectedness of individuals in society and the unique nature of the doctor–patient relationship, based on trust and collaboration. This work has argued for a relational account of autonomy. A relational account comports with the realities of healthcare decision-making, which often involves the input of family members and consideration of the impact of decisions on family members and caregivers.[7] Decisions are never made in isolation.

The various concepts of autonomy drawn from Kant, Hume, and Mill have been applied to medical ethics as ideal desire, current desire, and best desire autonomy. This work has argued that best desire autonomy, refined as reflexive autonomy, is best suited to the medical context. Reflexive desire autonomy identifies the innate desire of individuals, based on internal reflection and their relationship with external conditions. It is a dynamic process where the individual's priorities are subject to change with more information and external stimuli, enabling the patient to exercise authentic autonomy.

Failure to inform of the nature of, and risks inherent in, proposed treatment has its roots in the law of trespass, where issues of autonomy and consent are critical. It was adopted in the law of negligence in various Commonwealth jurisdictions as a reaction against the culture of medical paternalism and the *Bolam* test for the standard of care, which unduly favoured doctors. The emphasis on autonomy has conflated the duty to inform in negligence with obtaining consent in trespass. To reiterate: the function of the duty to inform in negligence is to provide the patient with sufficient information to decide whether or not to accept material risks in a proposed treatment. It is about consent *to the risk*, not consent *to the treatment*. Apropos the distinction between trespass and negligence, one can consent to treatment but not to undisclosed risks.

[6] See Chapter 3 of this volume, text to nn 127–144.
[7] See Chapter 4 of this volume, text to nn 106–125.

The information and advice provided to the patient in the lead up to the treatment invariably involves dialogue. Typically, a patient has discussions with the doctor, consults with friends or family, and carries out online research to become better informed of the risks and benefits of the proposed treatment before seeking final information and advice from the doctor. The patient's decision is based on an amalgam of information from various sources, with the doctor's advice carrying significant weight. The process by which a patient arrives at acceptance of risk in proposed treatment necessarily connotes acknowledgment of uncertainty. It is based on an equilibrium of trust, autonomy, and vulnerability in the doctor–patient relationship. Recall the observations in *Powell v University Hospitals Sussex NHS Foundation Trust*:[8]

> She has … 'built up a lot of trust' in him. She said that she would in the past talk through Mr Chauhan's advice with her husband and at least some of her children, but as she put it, 'generally' she would go with his advice.

Shifting the focus from patient autonomy to patient agency and shared decision-making strikes the right balance between beneficence and autonomy, and between doctors' rights and patients' rights.[9] The difference between patient agency and patient autonomy is that the former connotes responsibility, which the latter does not. Thus, under an agency approach, the patient also has responsibility in the shared decision-making process. The scope of the doctor's duty to inform and advise should be to enable the patient to exercise agency and participate in decision-making rather than to enable the patient to have freedom of choice under the autonomy model.

Studies show that not all patients have equal ability to process information and make decisions independently. Patients have different levels of health literacy, internal locus of control, and sense of competent self-efficacy,[10] The standard of care must recognise this. As *Montgomery* highlighted, there must be dialogue and genuine understanding by the patient. Yet, *Montgomery* takes an individualistic approach, requiring doctors to advise the patient of risk and of alternative options that would be material to a reasonable person *in the patient's position* or to that *particular patient*. To restate:

> The doctor is therefore under a duty to take reasonable care to ensure that the patient is aware of any material risks involved in any recommended treatment, and of any reasonable alternative or variant treatments. The test of materiality is whether, in the circumstances of the particular case, a reasonable person in the patient's position would be likely to attach significance to the risk, or the doctor is or should reasonably be aware that the particular patient would be likely to attach significance to it.[11]

[8] *Powell v University Hospitals Sussex NHS Foundation Trust* [2023] EWHC 736 (KB), [82]–[83]. See discussion in Chapter 8 of this volume, text to n 132.

[9] Much of the discourse in medical ethics and law focuses on the rights of the patient without due consideration of the rights, including professional autonomy, of doctors.

[10] See Chapter 6 of this volume, text to nn 131–135.

[11] [2015] UKSC 11; [2015] AC 1430, [87].

Who is the reasonable person in *the patient's position*? What if the patient is vulnerable, lacks internal locus of control or sense of competent self-efficacy, or is highly dependent on a family member? Should the doctor treat the patient as a reasonable person, or should the doctor treat the patient as one without an internal locus of control and be more proactive to help the patient?[12] Returning to the observation of Mark Komrad:

> Yet it is somewhat confusing for a doctor when, on the one hand, society insists on the abolition of medical paternalism, while on the other hand many individual patients still expect, hope for, and even urge (in both subtle and outright ways) the doctor to be paternalistic. Physicians have been faced with the option of indulging these expectations and receiving accolades from the patient but condemnation from society.[13]

Montgomery's second limb should be restricted to situations where the doctor has actual knowledge of a patient's special circumstances that would make the risk material to that person although not to the 'reasonable patient'. The doctor should not be under a duty proactively to inquire into potential idiosyncratic concerns, which the autonomy model may demand. In contrast to *Montgomery*, the patient agency approach would place responsibility on the patient to inform the doctor of any idiosyncratic features that make a risk material to that particular patient but not to the reasonable patient.

While UK law has not gone this far, it is possible that a court may require doctors to take proactive steps to determine subjective risk factors if it is reasonable to do so. This affirmative obligation has been legislated into effect in Singapore, where doctors must inform patients of concerns

> which the patient does not expressly communicate to the healthcare professional but which ought to be apparent to the healthcare professional from the patient's medical records that the healthcare professional has reasonable access to and *ought reasonably to review* (emphasis added).[14]

The judgment in *Chester* on causation illustrates the fallacy of autonomy-based reasoning. It was right to adopt a subjective approach to causation, unlike the Canadian approach which adopted an objective test.[15] Causation is a question of fact and therefore it is incumbent on the court to determine what the patient would have done had he or she been informed of the risk. Causation of damage would be established if the patient would have refused consent to the procedure and thus avoided the risk. In *Chester*, the patient admitted that she would have gone ahead and accepted the risk. As in all true 'negligent failure to inform' cases, the risk was random and could materialise independently of any negligence by the surgeon. Strictly, the claimant should have failed on causation. The scope of the

[12] See the examples in Chapter 4 of this volume, text to nn 110–115.

[13] MS Komrad, 'A Defence of Medical Paternalism: Maximising Patients' Autonomy' (1983) 9 *Journal of Medical Ethics* 38, 40.

[14] Civil Law Act 1909 (Singapore) s 37(3)(b).

[15] *Reibl v Hughes* (1981) 114 DLR (3d) 1; 14 CCLT 1.

duty to inform was to enable the patient to decide whether to accept the risk; it was not to take care to avoid the actual injury that occurred.

The majority in *Chester* held that the patient's autonomy rights must be vindicated. Yet, the damage that was the basis for the action in negligence against the surgeon was not loss of autonomy but the personal injury that the patient suffered; damages were assessed not based on the value of autonomy, but the value of the loss flowing from the personal injury. Autonomy, apparently, has no intrinsic value; it is parasitic on the physical injury suffered.

Imagine three patients, each not informed of an identical material risk, which if disclosed would have resulted in each patient not consenting to the procedure. In theory, each has suffered an autonomy violation – the right to make an informed decision.

- In the first patient's case, the risk does not materialise – the patient's autonomy loss is valued at zero.
- In the second patient's case, the risk materialises resulting in minor physical injury – the patient's damages are assessed at £10,000.
- In the third patient's case, the risk materialises resulting in significant physical injury – the patient's damages are assessed at £100,000.

In each case, the autonomy interest affected is the same, but the value attached to autonomy is random.

If the purpose of the duty is to vindicate rights and to ensure that patients are properly informed, then it fails in its mission in the vast majority of cases where patients are not provided with adequate information on risks but have the good fortune of not having the risk materialise or of not suffering any loss. *Chester* is fallible on another ground. Recall: the patient admitted that, after further reflection, she would have accepted the risk had she been informed of it. By disregarding the patient's own choice as to acceptable risk, the court failed to respect the patient's agency – the right to decide for herself what risks are acceptable. From the doctor's perspective, it is patently unfair to empower patients to make choices but not hold them responsible for their choices.

This work has been critical of the role of autonomy in duty to inform cases, but it does not deny that autonomy may be a protected interest in negligence in appropriate cases. The difficulty is in delimiting such cases without falling down the rabbit hole. There are at least two categories where autonomy deserves protection as actionable damage, namely reproductive negligence and genetic negligence. In these cases, the doctor's negligence may not cause any personal injury or economic loss, but it may adversely affect the patient's reproductive or genetic autonomy. Autonomy in these cases is not an abstract concept but a concrete one. As such, the arguments against recognising loss of autonomy as actionable damage are not compelling.[16]

[16] See *ACB v Thomson Medical Pte Ltd* [2017] SGCA 20; [2017] 1 SLR 918.

Patient autonomy arguments in a negligence action in the duty to inform cases force the tort of negligence into a regulatory role for which it is not designed. There is a real question whether an action in negligence for failure to advise should continue to be recognised. If it is to be used, it must be reformed to comport with the fundamental tenets of negligence and ensure that both doctors and patients are treated justly. *Chester*'s position on causation should be overruled, and the particular patient limb of the *Montgomery* test should be limited to the doctor's actual knowledge of the patient's special circumstances.

This book has argued that the emphasis on autonomy grew out of a reaction against medical paternalism as well as unethical research and clinical practices. The over-correction has distorted medical negligence doctrine, creating a tension between liability rules and the realities of medical practice. This work has sought to explain how the common law on medical negligence has developed by unpacking the underlying theoretical arguments and philosophical conceptions of autonomy that have influenced the judicial law-making process. The core arguments are that a human obligations paradigm that recognises the interconnectedness of individuals is preferrable to a rights-based approach to medical negligence, and that instead of championing individual autonomy, the focus should be on patient agency and shared decision-making.

TABLE OF CASES

UK

Ireland

Australia

Bermuda

Canada

Malaysia

Singapore

United States

TABLE OF LEGISLATION

UK

Australia

Singapore

BIBLIOGRAPHY

Books

Abbott, TK (trans), *Kant's Critique of Practical Reason and Other Works on the Theory of Ethics* (London, Longmans, Green & Co, 4th edn, 1889)

Abraham, KS, *Forms and Functions of Tort Law* (New York, Foundation Press, 3rd edn, 2007)

Aityah, PS and Summers, RS, *Form and Substance in Anglo-American Law: A Comparative Study of Legal Reasoning, Legal Theory, and Legal Institutions* (New York, Oxford University Press, 1987)

Arendt, H, *The Origins of Totalitarianism* (San Diego CA, Harcourt, 1976) 290

Austin, J, *The Province of Jurisprudence Determined* (1832), WE Rumble (ed) (Cambridge, Cambridge University Press, 1995)

Ayres, I and Braithwaite, J, *Responsive Regulation: Transcending the Deregulation Debate* (New York, Oxford University Press, 1992)

Backhaus, JG (ed), *The Elgar Companion to Law and Economics* (Northampton MA, Edward Elgar, 2nd edn, 2005)

Bacon, F, *A Collection of some Principall Rules and Maximes of the Common Lawes of England with their Latitude and Extent* (London, 1630)

Baldwin, R, Scott, C and Hood, C (eds), *A Reader on Regulation* (Oxford, Oxford University Press, 1998)

Barnes, M, et al, *Ethics of Care Critical Advances in International Perspective* (Bristol, Policy Press, 2015)

Beauchamp, TL and Childress, JF, *Principles of Biomedical Ethics* (New York, Oxford University Press, 1979)

—— *Principles of Biomedical Ethics* (New York, Oxford University Press, 8th edn, 2019)

Beever, A, *A Theory of Tort Liability* (Oxford, Hart Publishing, 2016)

—— *Rediscovering the Law of Negligence* (Oxford, Hart Publishing, 2007)

Beltrán, FJ, Moreso, JJ and Papayannis, DM (eds), *Neutrality and Theory of Law* (Dordrecht, Springer, 2013)

Birks, P, *The Roman Law of Obligations* (Oxford, Oxford University Press, 2014)

Brazier, M, *Medicine, Patients and the Law* (Harmondsworth, Penguin Books, 1987)

Brown, L and Powell, M, *Louise Brown: My Life As the World's First Test-Tube Baby* (Bristol, Bristol Books CIC, 2015)

Cane, P, *Responsibility in Law and Morality* (Portland OR, Hart Publishing, 2002)

Cartwright, A, *Patients and Their Doctors: A Study of General Practice* (London, Routledge & Kegan Paul, 1967)

Clark, S, *Keynesianism, Moneterism, and the Crisis of the State* (Cheltenham, Edward Elgar Publishing, 1988)

Clarke, R, *Your Life in My Hands – A Junior Doctor's Story* (London, John Blake Publishing Ltd, 2020)

Coleman, J, *Risks and Wrongs* (Oxford, Oxford University Press, 2002)

Coons, C and Weber, M (eds), *Paternalism: Theory and Practice* (New York, Cambridge University Press, 2013)

Dagan, H, *Unjust Enrichment: A Study of Private Law and Public Values* (Cambridge, Cambridge University Press, 1997)

Deakin, S, Johnston, A and Markesinis, B, *Markesinis and Deakin's Tort Law* (Oxford, Clarendon Press, 6th edn, 2008) 223

Dworkin, R, *Law's Empire* (Cambridge MA, Harvard University Press, 1986)

—— *Life's Dominion: An Argument about Abortion, Euthanasia, and Individual Freedom* (New York, Alfred A Knopf, 1993) 224
—— *The Theory and Practice of Autonomy* (Cambridge, Cambridge University Press, 1988)
Englard, I, *Corrective and Distributive Justice: From Aristotle to Modern Times* (New York, Oxford University Press, 2009)
Epstein, CF, *Deceptive Distinctions: Sex, Gender, and the Social Order* (New Haven CT, Yale University Press, 1988)
Etzioni, A (ed), *The Essential Communitarian Reader* (Lanham MD, Rowman & Littlefield Publishers, Inc, 1998)
Etzioni, A, *The New Golden Rule: Community and Morality in A Democratic Society* (New York, BasicBooks, 1996)
Evans, RG, *Strained Mercy: The Economics of Canadian Healthcare* (Toronto, Butterworths, 1984) 75
Faden, RR and Beauchamp, TL, *A History and Theory of Informed Consent* (New York/ Oxford, Oxford University Press, 1986)
Fleming, J, *The Law of Torts* (Sydney, LBC Information Services, 9th edn, 1998)
Galbraith, JK, *The Good Society: The Humane Agenda* (New York, Houghton Mifflin Company, 1996)
Gardner, J, *Torts and Other Wrongs* (Oxford, Oxford University Press, 2019)
Gawande, A, *Complications: A Surgeon's Notes on an Imperfect Science* (New York, Metropolitan Books, 2002)
Gaylin, W and Jennings, B, *The Perversion of Autonomy: Coercion and Constraints in a Liberal Society* (Washington DC, Georgetown University Press, 2003 (Revised edn))
Gilligan, C, *In a Different Voice* (Cambridge MA, Harvard University Press, 1982)
Gordon-Bouvier, E, *Relational Vulnerability: Theory, Law and the Private Family* (Basingstoke, Palgrave MacMillan, 2020)
Green, S, *Causation in Negligence* (Oxford/ Portland OR, Hart Publishing, 2015)
Gregor, M (ed), *Groundwork of the Metaphysics of Morals* (Cambridge, Cambridge University Press, 1997)
Habermas, J *The Logic of the Social Sciences* (Cambridge MA, MIT Press, 1988)
Hart, HLA, *The Concept of Law* (Oxford, Clarendon Press, 1961)
Hart, HLA and Honoré, T, *Causation in the Law* (New York, Oxford University Press, 2nd edn, 2002 reprint)
Hochbaum, GM, *Public Participation in Medical Screening Programs: A Socio-Psychological Study* (Washington DC, Public Health Services Publication, 1958)
Hohfeld, WN, *Fundamental Legal Concepts as Applied in Judicial Reasoning*, WW Cook (ed) (Westport CT, Greenwood Press, 1978 reprint)
Horkheimer, M, *Critical Theory: Selected Essays* ((trans O'Connell, MJ, et al) New York, Herder & Herder, 1992)
Ibbetson, D, *A Historical Introduction to the Law of Obligations* (Oxford, Oxford University Press, 2006 reprint)
Iyer, R (ed), *The Moral and Political Writings of Mahatma Gandhi* vol 3 (Oxford/ New York, Oxford University Press, 1986–87)
Jaffey, AJE, *The Duty of Care* (Aldershot, Dartmouth Publishing Co, 1992)
Jauhar, S, *My Father's Brain: Life in the Shadow of Alzheimer's* (New York, Farrar, Straus and Giroux, 2023)
Jones, M, *Medical Negligence* (London, Sweet & Maxwell, 6th edn, 2021)
Kalanithi, P, *When Breath Becomes Air* (New York, Random House, 2016)
Kass, LR, *Life, Liberty and the Defense of Dignity: The Challenge for Bioethics* (San Francisco CA, Encounter Books, 2002)
Katz, J, *The Silent World of Doctor and Patient* (Baltimore MD, Johns Hopkins University Press, 2002 (Revised edn))
Kennedy, I and Grubb, A, *Medical Law: Text and Materials* (London, Butterworths, 1989)
Keren-Paz, T, *Torts, Egalitarianism and Distributive Justice* (Farnham, Ashgate Publishing, 2007)
Kymlicka, W, *Liberalism, Community and Culture* (Oxford, Oxford University Press, 1989)

Landes, WM and Posner, RA, *The Economic Structure of Tort Law* (Cambridge MA, Harvard University Press, 1987)
Lindemann-Nelson, H and Lindemann-Nelson, J, *The Patient in the Family* (New York, Routledge, 1995)
Lindley, R, *Autonomy* (London, Macmillan Education Ltd, 1986)
Lord Denning, *The Discipline of Law* (London, Butterworths, 1979) 241
Mackenzie, C and Stoljar, N (eds), *Relational Autonomy: Feminist Perspectives on Autonomy, Agency, and the Social Self* (New York, Oxford University Press, 2000)
Marsh, H, *Do No Harm: Stories of Life, Death and Brain Surgery* (London, Weidenfeld & Nicolson, 2014)
Mayerhoff, M, *On Caring* (New York, Harper & Row, 1969)
McBride, NJ, *The Humanity of Private Law Part 1: The Explanation* (Oxford, Oxford University Press, 2019)
McLean, SA, *A Patient's Right to Know: Information Disclosure, the Doctor and the Law* (Aldershot, Dartmouth Publishing Co, 1989)
Menski, WF, *Hindu Law: Beyond Tradition and Modernity* (New Delhi, Oxford University Press, 2008)
Mercuro, N and Medema, SG, *Economics and the Law: From Posner to Postmodernism and Beyond* (Princeton NJ, Princeton University Press, 2nd edn, 2006)
Merry, A and McCall Smith, A, *Errors, Medicine and the Law* (Cambridge, Cambridge University Press, 2001)
Miles, S (ed), *Simone Weil: An Anthology* (London, Penguin Books, 2005) 81
Miles, SH, *The Hippocratic Oath and the Ethics of Medicine* (New York, Oxford University Press, 2004)
Mizstal, B, *The Challenges of Vulnerability: In Search of Strategies for a Less Vulnerable Social Life* (Basingstoke, Palgrave Macmillan, 2011)
Moore, M, *Causation and Responsibility: An Essay in Law, Morals, and Metaphysics* (New York, Oxford University Press, 2009)
Moran, M, *Rethinking the Reasonable Person: An Egalitarian Reconstruction of the Objective Standard* (Oxford, Oxford University Press, 2003)
Moyn, S, *The Last Utopia: Human Rights in History* (Cambridge MA, Harvard University Press, 2010)
Nagel, T, *Mortal Questions* (Cambridge, Cambridge University Press, 1979)
Noddings, N, *Caring: A Feminine Approach to Ethics & Moral Education* (Berkeley: University of California Press, 1984)
O'Neill, O, *Towards Justice and Virtue: A Constructive Account of Practical Reasoning* (Cambridge, Cambridge University Press, 2010)
—— *Autonomy and Trust in Bioethics* (Cambridge, Cambridge University Press, 2002)
Osborne, D and Gaebler, T, *Reinventing Government: How the Entrepreneurial Spirit is Transforming the Public Sector* (Reading MA, Addison-Wesley, 1992)
Outram, D, *The Enlightenment* (Cambridge, Cambridge University Press, 4th edn, 2019) 3
Pappworth, M, *Human Guinea Pigs: Experimentation on Man* (London, Routledge & Kegan Paul, 1967)
Parsons, T, *The Social System* (Glencoe IL, Free Press, 1951)
Plunkett, JC, *The Duty of Care in Negligence* (Oxford/ Portland OR, Hart Publishing, 2018)
Pollock, F and Maitland, FW, *The History of English Law Vol 2* (Ann Arbor MI, University of Michigan Press, 2nd edn, 1923)
Posner, RA, *Economic Analysis of Law* (Boston MA, Little, Brown Co, 1972)
—— *Tort Law: Cases and Economic Analysis* (Boston MA, Little, Brown Co, 1982)
Potter, H, *An Historical Introduction to English Law and its Institutions* (London, Sweet & Maxwell, 1932)
Puri, S, *That Good Night: Life and Medicine in the Eleventh Hour* (New York, Viking, 2019)
Ramsay, P, *The Patient as Person: Explorations in Medical Ethics* (New Haven CT, Yale University Press, 1970)
Rawls, J, *A Theory of Justice* (Cambridge MA, Harvard University Press, 1971)
—— *Political Liberalism* (New York, Columbia University Press, 1993)

Raz, J, *The Morality of Freedom* (Oxford, Clarendon Press, 1986)
Ripstein, A, *Equality, Responsibility and the Law* (Cambridge, Cambridge University Press, 2001)
—— *Private Wrongs* (Cambridge MA, Harvard University Press, 2016)
Rothman, DJ, *Strangers at the Bedside: A History of How Law and Bioethics Transformed Medical Decision Making* (New York, Basic Books, 1991)
Ruddick, S, *Maternal Thinking: Toward a Politics of Peace* (New York, Ballentine Books, 1989)
Scanlon, TM, *What We Owe To Each Other* (Cambridge MA, Belknap Press, 2000)
Shafik, M, *What We Owe Each Other: A New Social Contract* (Dublin, Vintage, 2002)
Stallybrass, WTS, *Salmond's Law of Torts* (London, Sweet & Maxwell, 1945)
Stevens, R, *Torts and Rights* (Oxford, Oxford University Press, 2007)
Tavris, C, *The Mismeasure of Woman: Why Women Are Not the Better Sex, the Inferior Sex, or the Opposite Sex* (New York, Touchstone, 1992)
Teff, H, *Reasonable Care: Legal Perspectives on the Doctor Patient Relationship* (Oxford, Clarendon Press, 1994)
Torres-Spelliscy, C, *Corporate Citizen?: An Argument for the Separation of Corporation and State* (Durham, NC, Carolina Academic Press, 2016)
Tronto, J, *Caring Democracy: Markets, Equality, and Justice* (New York, NYU Press, 2013)
—— *Moral Boundaries: A Political Argument for an Ethic of Care* (London, Routledge, 1994)
Weil, S, *The Need for Roots: Prelude to a Declaration of Duties Toward Mankind* ((trans A Wills) New York, GP Putnam's Sons, 1952)
—— *The Need for Roots: Prelude to a Declaration of Duties Towards Mankind* ((trans Arthur Wills) London/ New York, Routledge, 2002)
Weinrib, EJ, *Corrective Justice* (Oxford, Oxford University Press, 2012)
—— *The Idea of Private Law* (Oxford, Oxford University Press, Revised edn, 2012)
Wenham, GJ, *Word Biblical Commentary, Volume 1: Genesis 1–15* (Waco TX, Word Books, 1987)
White, GE, *Tort Law in America: An Intellectual History* (New York, Oxford University Press, 2003)
Williams, B, *Moral Luck: Philosophical Papers 1973–1980* (Cambridge, Cambridge University Press, 1981)
Wood, B, *Patient Power? The Politics of Patients' Associations in Britain and America* (Buckingham, Open University Press, 2000)

Book Chapters

Amirthalingam, K, 'The Changing Face of the Gist of Negligence' in Neyers, J, Pitel, S and Chamberlain, E (eds), *Emerging Issues in Tort Law* (Oxford, Hart Publishing, 2007) 467
Bohman, J, 'Critical Theory' in Zalta, E (ed), *The Stanford Encyclopedia of Philosophy* (Spring 2021 edn), https://plato.stanford.edu/ENTRIES/critical-theory/
Brown, K, 'Beyond Protection: 'The Vulnerable' in the Age of Austerity' in Harrison, M and Sanders, T (eds), *Social Policies and Social Control: New Perspectives on the 'Not-So-Big-Society'* (Bristol, Bristol University Press, 2014) 39
Cane, P, 'Responsibility and Fault: A Relational and Functional Approach to Responsibility' in Cane, P and Gardner, J (eds), *Relating to Responsibility: Essays in Honour of Tony Honoré on his 80th Birthday* (Oxford, Hart Publishing, 2011)
Chatterjee, M, 'The Concept of Dharma' in Doeser, MC and Kraay, JN (eds), *Facts and Values Philosophical Reflections from Western and Non-Western Perspectives* (Dordrecht, Springer, 1986) 177
Code, L, 'The Perversion of Autonomy and the Subjection of Women: Discourses of Social Advocacy at Century's End' in Mackenzie, C and Stoljar, N (eds), *Feminist Perspectives on Autonomy, Agency, and the Social Self* (New York, Oxford University Press, 2000) 181
Coleman, JL and Leiter, B, 'Legal Positivism' in Patterson, D (ed), *A Companion to Philosophy of Law and Legal Theory* (Oxford, Blackwell Publishing Ltd, 2nd edn, 2010) 228

Dana K, 'Moral Luck', *The Stanford Encyclopedia of Philosophy* (Spring 2025 edn), https://plato.stanford.edu/cgi-bin/encyclopedia/archinfo.cgi?entry=moral-luck

Dickson, J, 'Descriptive Legal Theory' in Sellers, M and Kirste, S (ed), *Encyclopaedia of the Philosophy of Law and Social Philosophy* (Dordrecht, Springer, 2020) 259

Donner, W, 'Autonomy, Tradition, and the Enforcement of Morality' in CL Ten, *Mill's On Liberty: A Critical Guide* (Cambridge, Cambridge University Press, 2009)

Dorfman, A 'Relational Justice and Torts' in Dagan, H and Zipursky, BC (eds), *Research Handbook on Private Law Theory* (Cheltenham, Edward Elgar Publishing, 2020)

Dryden, J, 'Autonomy' The Internet Encyclopedia of Philosophy, https://iep.utm.edu/

Dworkin, G, 'Paternalism' in Zalta, E (ed), *The Stanford Encyclopedia of Philosophy* (Fall 2020 edn), https://plato.stanford.edu/entries/paternalism/

Fineman, MA, 'Equality, Autonomy, and the Vulnerable Subject in Law and Politics' in Fineman, MA and Grear, A (eds), *Vulnerability: Reflections on a New Ethical Foundation for Law and Politics* (London, Routledge, 2013) 1

Geistfeld, MA, 'Folk Tort Law' in Dagan, H and Zipursky, BC (eds), *Research Handbook on Private Law Theory* (Cheltenham, Edward Elgar Publishing, 2020)

Goff, R, 'The Search for Principle' reproduced in Swadling, W and Jones, G (eds), *The Search for Principle* (Oxford, Oxford University Press, 1999) 313

Hoffmann, L, 'The Rise and Fall of the Economic Torts' in Degeling, S, Edelman, J and Goudkamp, J (eds), *Torts in Commercial Law* (Sydney, Law Book Co, 2011) 105

Hume, D, *A Treatise on Human Nature* (1739) Book 3, Part 1, Section 1 in Selbi-Bigge LA and Nidditch PH (eds), *David Hume: Treatise of Human Nature* (Oxford, Oxford University Press, 2nd edn, 2014)

Keating, G, 'Is Tort Law Private?' in Oberdiek, J and Miller, P (eds), *Civil Wrongs and Justice in Private Law* (Oxford: Oxford University Press, 2019)

—— 'Corrective Justice: Sovereign or Subordinate?' in Gold, AS, et al (eds), *The Oxford Handbook of the New Private Law* (Oxford: Oxford University Press, 2020)

Klar, L, 'Downsizing Torts' in Mullany, NJ and Linden, AM (eds), *Torts Tomorrow: A Tribute to John Fleming* (Sydney, LBC Information Services, 1998) 305

Lamont, J and Favor, C, 'Distributive Justice' in Zalta, N (ed), *The Stanford Encyclopedia of Philosophy* (Winter 2017 edn), https://plato.stanford.edu/archives/win2017/entries/justice-distributive/

Lee, SC, 'On Relational Autonomy: From Feminist Critique to Confucian Model for Clinical Practice' in Lee, SC (ed), *The Family, Medical Decision-Making, and Biotechnology: Critical Reflections on Asian Moral Perspectives* (Dordrecht, Springer, 2007) 83

Linden, AM, 'Torts Tomorrow – Empowering the Injured' in Mullany NJ and Linden AM (eds), *Torts Tomorrow: A Tribute to John Fleming* (Sydney, LBC Information Services, 1998) 321

Lord Bingham, 'The Judge as Lawmaker: An English Perspective' in Bingham T, *The Business of Judging: Selected Essays and Speeches* (Oxford, Oxford University Press, 2000) ch 2

Mackenzie, C, 'The Importance of Relational Autonomy and Capabilities for an Ethics of Vulnerability' in Mackenzie, C, Rogers, W and Dodds, S (eds), *Vulnerability: New Essays in Ethics and Feminist Philosophy* (New York, Oxford University Press, 2014) 33

McLachlin J, 'Negligence Law – Proving the Connection' in Mullany, NJ and Linden, A, *Torts Tomorrow: A Tribute to John Fleming* (Sydney, LBC Information Services, 1998) 16

Miola, J, 'The Standard of Care in Medical negligence – Still Reasonably Troublesome?' in Richardson, J and Rackley, E (eds), *Feminist Perspectives on Tort Law* (London, Routledge, 2012) 126

Penner, J, 'Don't Crash into Mick Jagger When He is Driving His Rolls Royce: Liability in Damages for Economic Loss Consequent upon a Personal Injury' in Miller, P and Oberdiek, J (eds), *Civil Wrongs and Justice in Private Law* (Oxford, Oxford University Press, 2020) 253

—— 'Taking Raz Seriously: On the Value of Autonomy and its Relation to Private Law' in Miller, PB and Oberkiek J (eds), *Oxford Studies in Private Law Theory Volume II* (Oxford, Oxford University Press, 2023)

Posner, RA, 'Wealth Maximization and Tort Law: A Philosophical Inquiry' in Owen, DG (ed), *Philosophical Foundations of Tort Law* (Oxford, Clarendon Press, 1995) 99

Ripstein, A, 'Corrective Justice' in Dagan, H and Zipursky, BC (eds), *Research Handbook on Private Law Theory* (Cheltenham, Edward Elgar Publishing, 2020)
Sander-Staudt, M, 'Care Ethics' *The Internet Encyclopedia of Philosophy* (ISSN 2161-0002, https://iep.utm.edu/care-ethics/
Stapleton, J, 'Reflection on Common Sense Causation in Australia' in Degeling, S, Edelman, J and Goudkamp, J (eds), *Torts in Commercial Law* (Pyrmont, Thomson Reuters Australia, 2011) 339
—— 'Regulating Torts' in Parker, C, et al (eds), *Regulating Law* (Oxford, Oxford University Press, 2004) 122
—— 'The Golden Thread at the Heart of Tort Law: Protection of the Vulnerable' in Cane, P (ed), *Centenary Essays for the High Court of Australia* (Chatswood NSW, LexisNexis Butterworths, 2004) 242
Tomes, N, 'Patients or Health-Care Consumers? Why the History of Contested Terms Matters' in Stevens, RA, Rosenberg, CE and Burns, LR (eds), *History and Health Policy in the United States: Putting the Past Back In* (New Brunswick NJ, Rutgers University Press, 2006) 83
Trentmann, F, 'The Modern Genealogy of the Consumer: Meanings, Identities and Political Synapses' in Trentmann, F and Brewer, J (eds), *Consuming Cultures, Global Perspectives: Historical Trajectories, Transnational Exchanges* (Oxford, Berg, 2006) 19
Yeung, K, 'The Regulatory State' in Baldwin, R, Cave, M and Lodge, M (eds), *The Oxford Handbook on Regulation* (Oxford, Oxford University Press, 2010) 64

Journal Articles

Aamari, A, et al, 'Exploring the Current and Prospective Role of Artificial Intelligence in Disease Diagnosis' (2024) 86 *Annals of Medicine & Surgery* 943
Abrams, Y, 'Omissive Overdetermination: Why the Act Omission Distinction Makes a Difference for Causal Analysis' (2022) 49 *University of Western Australia Law Review* 57
Aiken, HD, 'Rights, Human and Otherwise' (1968) 52 *The Monist* 507
Al-Antari, MA, 'Artificial Intelligence for Medical Diagnostics – Existing and Future AI Technology!' (2023) 13 *Diagnostics* 688
Alfonseca, K, 'What Does "Woke" Mean and Why are Some Conservatives Using It?' *ABC News*, 5 March 2025 (https://abcnews.go.com/Politics/woke-conservatives/story?id=93051138)
Amirthalingam, K, 'Causation and the Medical Duty to Refer' (2012) 128 *Law Quarterly Review* 208
—— 'Medical Duty to Advise, Patient Autonomy, and Reasonable Alternatives' (2024) 140 *Law Quarterly Review* 11
—— 'Medical Negligence and Diagnosis: Further Inroads into Bolam?' (2020) 71 *Northern Ireland Legal Quarterly* 657
—— 'Medical Negligence and Patient Autonomy: Bolam Rules in Singapore and Malaysia – Revisited' (2015) 27 *Singapore Academy of Law Journal* 666
—— 'Reproductive Negligence: Unwanted Child or Unwanted Parenthood?' (2018) 134 *Law Quarterly Review* 15
—— 'Sustainable and Efficient Criminal Legal Aid: From Individual Right to Collective Interest' [2022] *Criminal Law Review* 621
—— 'The "Sunrise Crane" – Shedding New Light or Casting Old Shadows on Duty of Care' [2004] *Singapore Journal of Legal Studies* 551
—— 'Upending the Medical Duty to Advise: Legislating the Standard of Care in Singapore' (2022) 22 *Medical Law International* 189
Andrew, E, 'Simone Weil on the Injustice of Rights-Based Doctrines' (1986) 48 *The Review of Politics* 60
Armstrong, D, 'Actors, Patients and Agency: A Recent History' (2014) 36 *Sociology of Health & Illness* 163
Auerbach, J, et al, 'Commentary: On Gilligan's "In a Different Voice"' (1985) 11 *Feminist Studies* 149

Austin, L, 'Hii Chii Kok v (1) Ooi Peng Jin London Lucien; (2) National Cancer Centre: Modifying Montgomery' (2019) 27 *Medical Law Review* 339
Banja, J, 'Reasonable Persons, Autonomous Persons, and Lady Hale Determining a Standard for Risk Disclosure' (2020) 50 *Hastings Center Report* 25
Barnes, D, 'Too Many Probabilities: Statistical Evidence of Tort Causation' (2001) 64 *Law and Contemporary Problems* 192
Beecher, HK, 'Ethics and Clinical Research' (1966) 274(24) *New England Journal of Medicine* 1354
Beever, A, 'The Declaratory Theory of Law' (2013) 33 *Oxford Journal of Legal Studies* 421
Bender, L, 'A Lawyer's Primer on Feminist Theory and Tort' (1988) 38 *Journal of Legal Education* 1
Bhagavad Gita, Chapter 2, Verse 4
Black, V, 'The Rise and Fall of Plaintiff-Friendly Causation' (2016) 53 *Alberta Law Review* 533
Blackhall, L, et al, 'Ethnicity and Attitudes Towards Patient Autonomy' (1995) 274 *Journal of the American Medical Association* 820
Bok, A, Noone, D, and Skouw-Rasmussen, N, 'Patient Agency: Key Questions and Challenges – A Report from the 1st Workshop of the EHC Think Tank Workstream on Patient Agency' (2022) 9 *Journal of Haemophilia Practice* 27
Boulton, M and Parker, M, 'Informed Consent in a Changing Environment' (2007) 65 *Social Science & Medicine* 2187
Brazier, M, 'Patient Autonomy and Consent to Treatment: The Role of the Law' (1987) 7 *Legal Studies* 169
Brazier M and Miola, J, 'Bye-Bye *Bolam*: A Medical Revolution?' (2000) 8 *Medical Law Review* 85
Brenner, LH, Brenner, AT and Horowitz, D, 'Beyond Informed Consent: Educating the Patient' (2009) 467 *Clinical Orthopaedics & Related Research* 348
Broadbent, A, 'Epidemiological Evidence in Proof of Specific Causation' (2011) 17 *Legal Theory* 237
Broughton, JM, 'Women's Rationality and Men's Virtues: A Critique of Gender Dualism in Gilligan's Theory of Moral Development' (1983) 50 *Social Research: An International Quarterly* 597
Brown, K, Ecclestone, K and Emmel, N, 'The Many Faces of Vulnerability' (2017) 17 *Social Policy and Security* 497
Buttigeg, GG, '*Montgomery* and its Impact on Current Medical Practice – Good or Bad?' (2019) 87 *Medico-Legal Journal* 80
Calabresi, G, 'Some Thoughts on Risk Distribution and the Law of Torts' (1961) 70 *Yale Law Journal* 499
Cane, P, 'A Warning about Causation' (1999) 115 *Law Quarterly Review* 21
—— 'Distributive Justice and Tort Law' [2001] *New Zealand Law Journal* 401
—— 'The Anatomy of Private Law Theory' (2005) 25 *Oxford Journal of Legal Studies* 203
—— 'Tort Law as Regulation' (2002) 31 *Common Law World Review* 305
—— 'Torts and Rights' (2008) 71 *Modern Law Review* 641
Charles, C, Gafni, A and Whelan, T, 'Shared Decision-making in the Medical Encounter: What Does it Mean? (Or It Takes at Least Two to Tango)' (1997) 44 *Social Science & Medicine* 681
Christie, A, 'Vindicating Reproductive Autonomy in Wrongful Conception Cases' (2020) 26 *Auckland University Law Review* 178
Christman, J, 'Relational Autonomy, Liberal Individualism and the Social Dynamics of Paternalism' (2014) 17 *Ethical Theory & Moral Practice* 369
Clark, T and Nolan, D, 'A Critique of *Chester v Afshar*' (2014) 34 Oxford Journal of Legal Studies 659
Coase, RH, 'The Problem of Social Cost' (1960) 3 *Journal of Law and Economics* 1
Coggon, J, 'Varied and Principled Understandings of Autonomy in English Law: Justifiable Inconsistency of Blinkered Moralism?' (2007) 15 *Health Care Analysis* 235
Coggon J and Miola, J, 'Autonomy, Liberty, and Medical Decision-Making' (2011) 70 *Cambridge Law Journal* 523
Coleman, J, 'The Structure of Tort Law' (1988) 97 *Yale Law Journal* 1233
Costello, BA and Roberts, F, 'Medical Recommendation as Joint Social Practice' (2001) 13 *Health Communication* 241

Cover, RM, 'Obligation: A Jewish Jurisprudence of the Social Order' (1987) 5 *Journal of Law and Religion* 65
Crenshaw, K, 'Mapping the Margins: Intersectionality, Identity Politics, and Violence Against Women of Color' (1991) 43 *Stanford Law Review* 1241
Curzer, HJ, 'Aristotle: Founder of the Ethics of Care' (2007) 41 *The Journal of Value Inquiry* 221
Dagan, H and Dorfman, A, 'Just Relationships' (2016) 116 *Columbia Law Review* 1395
de Araújo Lima, AF and de Souza Machado, FI, 'Physicians as Choice Architects: Paternalism and Respect for Autonomy' (2021) 29 *Revista Bioética (Impr)* 44
Dennis, KE, 'Patients' Control and the Information Imperative' (1990) 39 *Nursing Research* 162
Deutsch, M, 'Equity, Equality and Need: What Determines Which Value Will Be Used as the Basis of Distributive Justice? (1975) 31 *Journal of Social Issues* 137
Deveaux, M, 'Shifting Paradigms: Theorizing Care and Justice in Political Theory' (1995) 10 *Hypatia* 115
Donchin, A, 'Understanding Autonomy Relationally: Toward a Reconfiguration of Bioethical Principles' (2001) 26 *Journal of Medicine and Philosophy* 365
Dunn, M, et al, 'Between the Reasonable and the Particular: Deflating Autonomy in the Legal Regulation of Informed Consent to Medical Treatment' (2019) 27 *Health Care Analysis* 110
Dworkin, G, 'The Concept of Autonomy' (1981) 12/13 *GRAZER Philosophische Studien* 203
Dworkin, R, 'Hard Cases' (1975) 88 *Harvard Law Review* 1057
Editorial, 'Description, Prediction, Explanation' (2021) 5 *Nature Human Behaviour* 1261, https://www.nature.com/articles/s41562-021-01230-5
Eggleston J, 'Probabilities and Proof' (1963) 4 *Melbourne University Law Review* 180
Emanuel, EJ and Emanuel, LL, 'Four Models of the Physician-Patient Relationship' (1992) 267 *Journal of the American Medical Association* 2221
Emirbayer, M and Mische, A, 'What is Agency?' (1998) 103 *The American Journal of Sociology* 962
Enger, D, 'Rethinking Care Theory: The Practice of Caring and the Obligation to Care' (2005) 20 *Hypatia* 50
English, J and Hafeez-Baig, MJ, '*ACB v Thomson Medical Pte Ltd*: Recovery of Upkeep Costs, Claims for Loss of Autonomy and Loss of Genetic Affinity: Fertile Ground for Development?' (2018) 41 *Melbourne University Law Review* 1360
Entwistle, VA, et al, 'Communicating about Screening' (2008) 337 *British Medical Journal* 789
Epstein, RA, 'A Theory of Strict Liability' (1973) 2 *Journal of Legal Studies* 151
Fan, R, 'Critical Care Ethics in Asia: Global or Local?' (1998) 6 *Journal of Medicine and Philosophy* 549
Fineman, MA, 'Evolving Images of Gender and Equality: A Feminist Journey' (2009) 43 *New England Law Review* 437
—— 'The Vulnerable Subject and the Responsive State' (2010) 60 *Emory Law Journal* 251
—— 'The Vulnerable Subject: Anchoring Equality in the Human Condition' (2008) 20 *Yale Journal of Law and Feminism* 1
—— 'Vulnerability and Inevitable Inequality' (2017) 4 *Oslo Law Review* 133
—— 'Vulnerability, Resilience, and LGBT Youth' (2014) 23 *Temple Political & Civil Rights Review* 307
Fleming, J, 'Probabilistic Causation in Tort Law' (1989) 68 *Canadian Bar Review* 661
Fletcher, GP, 'Fairness and Utility in Tort Theory' (1972) 85 *Harvard Law Review* 537
Fordham, MA, 'The *Bolam* Test Lives On' [1998] *Singapore Journal of Legal Studies* 140
Fortunato, JT, Wasserman, JA and Menkes, DL, 'When Respective Autonomy is Harmful: A Clinically Useful Approach to the Nocebo Effect' (2017) 17 *American Journal of Bioethics* 36
Fox, D, 'Reproductive Negligence' (2017) 117 *Columbia Law Review* 149
Fox, S, 'The Latest on *Bolam* is Dead', 6 July 2019, www.simonfoxqc.com
Foxton, T, 'Inaccurate Conception: *ACB v Thomson Medical*' (2018) 81 *Modern Law Review* 337
Frug, MJ, 'Progressive Feminist Legal Scholarship: Can We Claim "A Different Voice"?' (1992) 15 *Harvard Women's Law Journal* 37
Fulham-McQuillam, S, 'Infringement of Autonomy as Damage in Medical Negligence' (2023) 139 *Law Quarterly Review* 126
Gamble, A, 'Neo-Liberalism' (2001) 25 *Capital & Class* 127
Gardner, J, 'The Many Faces of the Reasonable Person' (2015) 131 *Law Quarterly Review* 563

Giesen, D, 'Medical Malpractice and the Judicial Function in Comparative Perspective' [1993] *Medical Law International* 13

Gilbar, R, 'Family Involvement, Independence and Patient Autonomy in Practice' [2011] *Medical Law Review* 192

Gold, S, 'Causation in Toxic Torts: Burdens of Proof, Standards of Persuasion, and Statistical Evidence' (1986) 96 *Yale Law Journal* 376

Goldberg, JCP, 'Rights and Wrongs' (1999) 97 *Michigan Law Review* 1828

—— 'Twentieth-Century Tort Theory' (2003) 91 *Georgetown Law Journal* 513 (Conference: Symposium on the New Negligence)

Goldberg, JCP and Zipursky, BC, 'Torts as Wrongs' (2010) 88 *Texas Law Review* 917

Goudkamp, J and Murphy, J, 'The Failure of Universal Theories of Tort Law' (2015) 21 *Legal Theory* 47

Gounder, R, 'The Way to "Chappel": Establishing liability for breach of duty to warn in delayed consent cases' (2024) 29 *Torts Law Journal* 135

Gräf, M, et al, 'Comparison of Physician and Artificial Intelligence-Based Symptom Checker Diagnostic Accuracy' (2022) 42 *Rheumatology International* 2167

Grubb, A, 'Clinical Negligence: Informed Consent and Causation' (2002) 10 *Medical Law Review* 322

Gumkowska-Sroka, O, Kotyla, P and Samborski, W, 'Does AI Replace Medical Doctors?' (2024) 10 *Rheumatology Forum* 59

Hahn, R, 'The Nocebo Effect Phenomenon: Concept, Evidence, and Implications for Public Health' (1997) 26 *Preventive Medicine* 607

Hamer, D, 'Chance Would be a Fine Thing: Proof of Causation and Quantum in an Unpredictable World' (1999) 23 *Melbourne University Law Review* 557

Hamilton, C, 'Simone Weil's "Human Personality": Between the Personal and the Impersonal' (2005) 98 *The Harvard Theological Review* 187

Harder, S, 'Medical Non-Disclosure and Hypothetical Consent' (2009) 20 *King's Law Journal* 435

Hardwig, J, 'What About the Family?' (1990) 22 *Hastings Center Report* 6

Harvey, D, 'Epidemiologic Proof of Probability: Implementing the Proportional Recovery Approach in Toxic Exposure Torts' (1984) 89 *Dickinson Law Review* 233

Hayes-Bautista, DE, 'Modifying the Treatment: Patient Compliance, Patient Control and Medical Care' (1976) 10 *Social Science & Medicine* 233

Hedley, S, 'The Rise and Fall of Private Law Theory' (2018) 134 *Law Quarterly Review* 214

Heidt, KR, 'Corrective Justice from Aristotle to Second Order Liability: Who Should Pay When the Culpable Cannot?' (1990) 47 *Washington & Lee Law Review* 347

Held, V, 'The Meshing of Care and Justice' (1995) 2 *Hypatia* 128

Herring, J, et al, 'Elbow Room for Best Practice? Montgomery, Patients' Values, and Balanced Decision-Making in Person-Centred Clinical Care' (2017) 25 *Medical Law Review* 582

Heuston, RFV, '*Donoghue v Stevenson* in Retrospect' (1957) 20 *Modern Law Review* 1

Heywood, R, 'Informed Consent Through the Back Door?' (2005) 56 *Northern Ireland Legal Quarterly* 266

—— 'R.I.P. *Sidaway*: Patient-oriented Disclosure – A Standard Worth Waiting For?' (2015) 23 *Medical Law Review* 455

Ho, A, 'Relational Autonomy or Undue Pressure? Family's Role in Medical Decision-making' (2008) 22 *Scandinavian Journal of Caring Sciences* 129

Hogg, MA, 'Re-establishing Orthodoxy in the Realm of Causation' (2007) 11 *Edinburgh Law Review* 8

Holmes, OW, 'The Theory of Torts' (1873) 7 *American Law Review* 652

Honoré, T, 'Medical Non-disclosure, Causation and Risk. *Chappel v Hart*' (1999) 7 *Torts Law Journal* 1

Horwitz, MJ, 'The Historical Contingency of the Role of History' (1981) 90 *Yale Law Journal* 1057

Houseman, GT, 'Wrongful Birth as Negligence Misrepresentation' (2013) 71 *University of Toronto Faculty of Law Review* 9

Howarth, D, 'Many Duties of Care – Or a Duty of Care? Notes from the Underground' (2006) 26 *Oxford Journal of Legal Studies* 449

Hunter, J, Franken, M and Balmer, D, 'Construction of Patient Agency in Healthcare Settings: Textual and Patient Perspectives' (2015) 7 *Discourse, Consent & Media* 37

Jansen, N, 'The Idea of a Lost Chance' (1999) 19 *Oxford Journal of Legal Studies* 271
Johnson, N, 'When Rights Go Wrong: Simone Weil on Uprootedness and the Way Forward' *Ad Fontes*, 27 September 2023 (https://adfontesjournal.com/web-exclusives/when-rights-go-wrong-simon-weil-on-uprootedness-and-the-way-forward/)
Jones, M, '"But for" Causation in Actions for Non-disclosure of Risk' (2002) 18 *Journal of Professional Negligence* 192
—— 'Informed Consent and Other Fairy Stories' (1999) 7 *Medical Law Review* 103
Keown, J, 'The Rise and Rise of "the *Bolam* test"' [1995] *Singapore Journal of Legal Studies* 342
Kerber, L, et al, 'On 'In a Different Voice': An Interdisciplinary Forum' (1986) 11 *Signs* 304
Keren-Paz, T, 'Compensating Injury to Autonomy in English Negligence Law: Inconsistent Recognition' (2018) 26 *Medical Law Review* 585
—— 'Gender Injustice in Compensating Injury to Autonomy in English and Singaporean Negligence Law' (2019) 27 *Feminist Legal Studies* 33
Kittay, EF, 'A Feminist Public Ethic of Care Meets the New Communitarian Family Policy' (2001) 111 *Ethics* 523
Koenig, CJ, 'Patient Resistance as Agency in Treatment Decisions' (2011) 72 *Social Science & Medicine* 1103
Kohlberg, L and Gilligan, C, 'The Adolescent as a Philosopher: The Discovery of the Self in a Post-conventional World' (1971) 100 *Daedalus* 1051
Kohn, NA, 'Vulnerability Theory and the Role of Government' (2014) 26 *Yale Journal of Law and Feminism* 1
Komrad, MS, 'A Defense of Medical Paternalism: Maximising Patients' Autonomy' (1983) 9 *Journal of Medical Ethics* 38
Kotler, MA, 'Utility, Autonomy and Motive: A Descriptive Model of the Development of Tort Doctrine' (1990) 58 *Cincinnati Law Review* 1231
Kukla, R, 'Conscientious Autonomy: Displacing Decisions in Health Care' (2005) 5 *Hastings Center Report* 34
Kwok, KHH, Ip, EC and Lee, SS, 'The Conundrums of the Reasonable Patient Standard in English Medical Law' (2023) 24 *BMC Medical Ethics Article* 15
Kymlicka, W, 'Liberal Multiculturalism as a Political Theory of State-Minority Relations' (2018) 46 *Political Theory* 81
Latin, H, 'Problem-Solving Behavior and Theories of Tort Liability' (1985) 73 *California Law Review* 677
Le Gallez, I, et al, '*Montgomery's* Legal and Practical Impact: A Systematic Review at 6 Years (2022) 28 *Journal of Evaluation in Clinical Practice* 690
Le Grand, J, 'Knights, Knaves or Pawns? Human Behaviour and Social Policy' (1997) 26 *Journal of Social Policy* 149
Liu, G, et al, 'Advances in Pluripotent Stem Cells: History, Mechanisms, Technologies, and Applications' (2020) 16 *Stem Cell Reviews and Report* 3
Lord Devlin, 'Judges and Lawmakers' (1976) 39 *Modern Law Review* 1
Lord Diplock, 'The Courts as Legislators' The Holdsworth Club Presidential Address, 26 March 1965
Lord Dyson, 'Are Judges Too Powerful?' Bentham Presidential Lecture, 12 March 2014
Lord Edmund-Davies, 'Judicial Activism' [1975] *Current Legal Problems* 1
Lord Goff, 'Judge, Jurist and Legislature' (1987) 2 *Denning Law Journal* 79
Lord Neuberger, '"Judge Not, That Ye Be Not Judged": Judging Judicial Decision-making' FA Mann Lecture 2015, 29 January 2015
Lord Neuberger, 'Implications of Tort Law Decisions' Address to Northern Ireland Personal Injury Bar's Inaugural Conference, County Down, 13 May 2017 (https://www.supremecourt.uk/docs/speech-170513.pdf)
Lord Reid, 'The Judge as Law Maker' (1972–73) 12 *Journal of the Society of Public Teachers of Law* 22
Lord Sumption, 'The Limits of Law' 27th Sultan Azlan Shah Lecture, Kuala Lumpur, 20 November 2013
Lord Woolf, 'Are Courts Excessively Deferential to the Medical Profession?' (2001) 9 *Medical Law Review* 1

Lord Woolf, 'Are Courts Excessively Deferential to the Medical Profession?' (2001) 9 *Medical Law Review* 1

Maclean, A, 'Beyond *Bolam* and *Bolitho*' (2002) 5 *Medical Law International* 205

Maltby, JR, Hutter, CDD and Clayton, KC, 'The *Woolley* and *Roe* Case' (2000) 84 *British Journal of Anaesthesia* 121

Marshall, E, 'Does the Moral Philosophy of the Belmont Report Rest on a Mistake?' (1986) 8 *IRB: Ethics and Human Research* 5

Mason, J, 'Master of the Balancers; Non-Voluntary Therapy under the Mantle of Lord Donaldson' [1993] *Juridical Review* 115

McCullough, LB and Wear, S, 'Respect for Autonomy and Medical Paternalism Reconsidered' (1985) 6 *Theoretical Medicine* 295

McIvor, C, 'Debunking Some Judicial Myths about Epidemiology and its Relevance to UK Tort Law' (2013) 21 *Medical Law Review* 553

McKinney, SM, et al, 'International Evaluation of an AI System for Breast Cancer Screening' (2020) 577 *Nature* 89

Miller AD and Perry, R, 'The Reasonable Person' (2012) 87 *New York University Law Review* 323

Miller, C, 'Causation n Personal Injury: Legal or Epidemiological Common Sense' (2006) 26 *Legal Studies* 544

Miller, D, 'Distributive Justice: What the People Think' (1992) 102 *Ethics* 555

Miola, J and Heywood, R, 'The Changing Face of the Pre-Operative Medical Disclosure: Placing the Patient at the Heart of the Matter' (2017) 133 *Law Quarterly Review* 296

Mold, A, 'Repositioning the Patient: Patient Organizations, Consumerism, and Autonomy in Britain during the 1960s and 1970s' (2013) 87 *Bulletin of the History of Medicine* 225

Montrose, JL, 'Is Negligence an Ethical or Sociological Concept?' (1958) 21 *The Modern Law Review* 259

Mortazavi, M, 'Torts and Personhood' (2023) 76 *Arkansas Law Review* 387

Mulheron, R 'Trumping *Bolam*: A Critical Legal Analysis of *Bolitho*'s "Gloss"' (2010) 69 *Cambridge Law Journal* 609

Murphy, G, 'Championing Autonomy – Does *Montgomery* Truly Protect Patient's Interests?' (2018) 6 *North East Law Review* 35

Murphy, J, 'Rights, Reductionism and Tort Law' (2008) 28 *Oxford Journal of Legal Studies* 393

Murphy, JP, 'Evolution of the Duty of Care: Some Thoughts' (1980) 30 *DePaul Law Review* 147

Nails, D, 'Social-Scientific Sexism: Gilligan's Mis measure of Man' (1983) 50 *Social Research: An International Quarterly* 643

Nedelsky, J, 'Re-conceiving Autonomy: Sources, Thoughts and Possibilities' (1989) 1 *Yale Journal of Law and Feminism* 7

Neri, E, et al, 'What the Radiologist Should Know about Artificial Intelligence – An ESR White Paper' (2019) 10 *Insights Into Imaging* 44

Neuhouser, F, 'Jean-Jacques Rousseau and the Origins of Autonomy' (2011) 54 *Inquiry* 478

Newman-Toker, DE, et al, 'Serious Misdiagnosis-related Harms in Malpractice Claims: The 'Big Three' – Vascular Events, Infections, and Cancers' (2019) 6 *Diagnosis* 227

Nolan, D, 'Negligence and Autonomy' [2022] *Singapore Journal of Legal Studies* 356

—— 'Rights, Damage and Loss' (2017) 37 *Oxford Journal of Legal Studies* 255

Norman, WJ, 'The Autonomy-Based Liberalism of Joseph Raz' (1989) 2 *Canadian Journal of Law & Jurisprudence* 151

Norton, F, 'Assisted Reproduction and the Frustration of Genetic Affinity: Interest, Injury, and Damages' (1999) 74 *New York University Law Review* 793

Olson, A, et al, 'Competencies for Improving Diagnosis: An Interprofessional Framework for Education and Training in Health Care' (2019) 6 *Diagnosis* 335

Olufowote, JO, 'A Structurational Analysis of Informed Consent to Treatment: Societal Evolution, Contradiction, and Reproductions in Medical Practice' (2008) 23 *Health Communication* 292

Ombelet, W and Robays, JV, 'Artificial Insemination History: Hurdles and Milestones' (2015) 7 *Facts Views and Vision in ObGyn* 137

Parchomovsky, G and Stein, A, 'Autonomy' (2021) 71 *University of Toronto Law Journal* 61
Pellegrino, ED, 'Patient and Physician Autonomy: Conflicting Rights and Obligations in the Physician-Patient Relationship' (1994) 10 *Contemporary Health Law & Policy* 47
Pellegrino, ED and Thomasma, D, 'The Conflict between Autonomy and Beneficence in Medical Ethics: Proposal for a Resolution' (1987) 3 *Journal of Contemporary Health Law & Policy* 23
Perry, R, 'The Role of Retributive Justice in the Common Law of Torts: A Descriptive Theory' (2006) 73 *Tennessee Law Review* 177
Perry, SR, 'Protected Interests and Undertakings' (1992) 42 *University of Toronto Law Journal* 247
—— 'The Moral Foundations of Tort Law' (1992) 77 *Iowa Law Review* 449
Plunkett, JC, 'The Historical Foundation of the Duty of Care' (2015) 41 *Monash University Law Review* 716
Posner, RA, 'A Theory of Negligence' (1972) 1 *Journal of Legal Studies* 29
—— 'Instrumental and Noninstrumental Theories of Tort Law' (2013) 88 *Indiana Law Journal* 469
Priaux, N, 'Joy to the World! A (Healthy) Child is Born! Reconceptualizing "Harm" in Wrongful Conception' (2004) 13 *Social & Legal Studies* 5
Price, DPT, 'Causation – The Lords' Lost Chance?' (1989) 38 *International and Comparative Law Quarterly* 735
Purhouse, C, 'Flourishing Under Private Law? A Critique of McBride's Explanatory Theory' (2021) XXXIV *The Canadian Journal of Law and Jurisprudence* 239
—— 'Autonomy, Affinity, and the Assessment of Damages: *ACB v Thomson Medical Pte Ltd* [2017] SGCA 20 and *Shaw V Kovak* [2017] EWCA Civ 1028' (2017) 26 *Medical Law Review* 675
—— 'How Should Autonomy be Defined in Medical Negligence Cases?' (2015) 10 *Clinical Ethics* 107
—— 'Liability for Lost Autonomy in Negligence: Undermining the Coherence of Tort Law?' (2015) 22 *Torts Law Journal* 226
Rackley, E, 'From Arachne to Charlotte: An Imaginative Revisiting of Gilligan's "In A Different Voice"' (2007) 13 *William & Mary Journal of Women & Law* 751
Rampton, M, 'Four Waves of Feminism', (Fall 2008) *Pacific*, https://www.pacificu.edu/magazine/four-waves-feminism#:~:text=The%20first%20wave%20of%20feminism,with%20a%20focus%20on%20suffrage
Raposo, VL, 'Wrongful Genetic Connection: Neither Blood of My Blood, nor Flesh of My Flesh' (2020) 23 *Medicine, Health Care and Philosophy* 309
Reardon, S, 'Rise of Robot Radiologists' (December 2019) 576(7787) *Nature* S54
Reece, H, 'Losses of Chances in the Law' (1996) 59 *Modern Law Review* 188
Rizzi, M, 'Health Professionals' Standard of Care and Breach of Duty in Western Australia: A Requiem for the "Peer Professional" Test at a Time of Uncertainty' (2020) 26 *Torts Law Journal* 179
Robertson, G, 'Informed Consent Ten Years Later: The Impact of *Reibl v Hughes*' (1991) 70 *Canadian Bar Review* 423
Rubin, MA, 'The Collaborative Autonomy Model of Medical Decision-Making' (2014) 20 *Neurocritical Care* 311
Russell, EJ, 'Establishing Medical Negligence – A Herculean Task?' (1998) 3 *Scots Law Times* 17
Saad, T, 'The History of Autonomy in Medicine from Antiquity to Principlism' (2018) 21 *Medical Healthcare and Philosophy* 125
Samuel, GN, et al, 'Healthcare Professionals' and Patients' Perspectives on Consent to Clinical Genetic Testing' Moving Towards a More Relational Approach' (2017) 18 *BMC Medical Ethics* 47
Sappideen, C, '*Bolam* in Australia – More Bark than Bite?' (2010) 33 *University of New South Wales Law Journal* 386
Schauer, F, 'The Social Construction of the Concept of Law: A Reply to Julie Dickson' (2005) 25 *Oxford Journal of Legal Studies* 493
Schwartz, GT, 'Mixed Theories of Tort Law: Affirming both Deterrence and Corrective Justice' (1997) 75 *Texas Law Review* 1801
Senchuk, DM, 'Listening to a different voice: A feminist critique of Gilligan' (1990) 10 *Studies in Philosophy and Education* 233

Shuster, E, 'American Doctors at the Nuremberg Medical Trial' (2018) 108 *American Journal of Public Health* 47

Simons, KW, 'Lost Chance of a Better Medical Outcome: New Tort, New Type of Compensable Injury, of New Causation Rule?' (2024) 73 *DePaul Law Review* 547

Smith, JC and Burns, P, '*Donoghue v. Stevenson*: The Not so Golden Anniversary' (1983) 46 *Modern Law Review* 147

Smith, MK and Carver, T, '*Montgomery*, Informed Consent and Causation of Harm: Lessons from Australia or a Uniquely English Approach to Patient Autonomy?' (2018) 44 *Journal of Medical Ethics* 384

Smith, S, 'Rights, Remedies, and Normal Expectancies in Tort and Contract' (1997) 113 *Law Quarterly Review* 426

Snyder, RC, 'What Is Third-Wave Feminism? A New Directions Essay' (2008) 34 *Signs* 175

Srivastava, C, 'Morality and Moral Development: Traditional Hindu Concepts' (2013) 55 *Indian Journal of Psychiatry* S283.

Stapleton, J, 'An "Extended But-For" Test for the Causal Relation in the Law of Obligations' (2015) 35 *Oxford Journal of Legal Studies* 697

—— 'Cause-in-Fact and Scope of Liability for Consequences' (2003) 119 *Law Quarterly Review* 388

—— 'Choosing What We Mean by "Causation" in the Law' (2008) 73 *Missouri Law Review* 433

—— 'Occam's Razor Reveals an Orthodox Basis for *Chester v Afshar*' (2006) 122 *Law Quarterly Review* 426

—— 'The Gist of Negligence – Part I' (1988) 104 *Law Quarterly Review* 213

—— 'The Gist of Negligence – Part II' (1988) 104 *Law Quarterly Review* 389

—— 'The Normal Expectancies Measure in Tort Damages' (1997) 113 *Law Quarterly Review* 257

—— 'Unnecessary and Insufficient Factual Causes' (2023) 16 *Journal of Tort Law* 351

Stauch, M, 'Taking the Consequences for Failure to Warn of Medical Risks' (2000) 63 *Modern Law Review* 261

Stychin, CF, 'The Vulnerable Subject of Negligence Law' (2012) 8 *International Journal of Law in Context* 337

Sugarman, S, 'Judges as Tort Law Un-makers: Recent California Experience with "New" Torts' (1999) 45 *DePaul Law Review* 455

Sullivan, LS and Niker, F, 'Relational Autonomy, Paternalism, and Maternalism' (2018) 21 *Ethical Theory & Moral Practice* 649

Tan Keng Feng, 'Failure of Medical Advice: Trespass or Negligence?' (1987) 7 *Legal Studies* 149

Tan, ZX, 'Rethinking Relational Architecture: Interpersonal Justice Beyond Private Law' (2023) 73 *University of Toronto Law Journal* 293

Teff, H, 'The Standard of Care in Medical Negligence – Moving on from *Bolam*?' (1998) 18 *Oxford Journal of Legal Studies* 473

Thomas, C, 'Novel Assisted Reproductive Technologies and Procreative Liberty: Examining In Vitro Gametogenesis Relative to Currently Practiced Assisted Reproductive Procedures and Reproductive Cloning' (2017) 26 *Southern California Interdisciplinary Law Journal* 623

Todd, S, 'Common Law Protection for Injury to a Person's Reproductive Autonomy' (2019) 135 *Law Quarterly Review* 635

Torres-Spelliscy, C, 'Does "We the People" Include Corporations?' (2018) 43 *Human Rights Quarterly* 16

Trubek, DM, 'Where the Action Is: Critical Legal Studies and Empiricism' (1984) 36 *Stanford Law Review* 575

Turoldo, F, 'Relational Autonomy and Multiculturalism' (2010) 19 *Cambridge Quarterly of Healthcare Ethics* 542

Turton, G, 'Informed Consent to Medical Treatment Post-*Montgomery*: Causation and Coincidence' (2018) 27 *Medical Law Review* 108

Vick, S, and Scott, A, 'Agency in Health Care. Examining Patients' Preferences for Attributes of the Doctor-Patient Relationship' (1998) 17 *Journal of Health Economics* 587

Wald, DS, Bestwick, JP and Kelly, P, 'The Effect of the *Montgomery* Judgment on Settled Claims Against the National Health Service due to Failure to Inform Before Giving Consent to Treatment' (2020) 113(10) *QJM: An International Journal of Medicine* 721
Wald, N and Cuckle, H, 'Reporting the Assessment of Screening and Diagnostic Tests' (1989) 96 *British Journal of Obstetrics and Gynaecology* 389
Waller, BN, 'The Psychological Structure of Patient Autonomy' (2002) 11 *Cambridge Quarterly of Healthcare Ethics* 257
Weinrib, EJ, 'Corrective Justice in a Nutshell' (2002) 52 *University of Toronto Law Journal* 349
—— 'Corrective Justice' (1992) 77 *Iowa Law Review* 403
West, K, Greenland, K and van Laar, C, 'Why some White people prefer "All Lives Matter" to "Black Lives Matter"' (2021) 60 *British Journal of Social Psychology* 1136
Wexler, L, Robbennolt, JK and Murphy, C, '#MeToo, Time's Up, and Theories of Justice' [2019] *University of Illinois Law Review* 45
Will, JF, 'A Brief Historical and Theoretical Perspective on Patient Autonomy and Medical Decision Making – Part I: The Beneficence Model' (2011) 139(3) *CHEST* 669
—— 'A Brief Historical and Theoretical Perspective on Patient Autonomy and Medical Decision Making – Part II: The Autonomy Model' (2011) 139(6) *CHEST* 1491
Williams, B, 'Moral Luck' (1976) *Proceedings of the Aristotelian Society* 115
Wilson-Barnett, J, 'Ethical Dilemmas in Nursing' (1986) 12 *Journal of Medical Ethics* 123
Winfield, PH, 'Duty in Tortious Negligence' (1934) 34 *Columbia Law Review* 41
Witting, C, 'Physical Damage in Negligence' (2002) 61 *Cambridge Law Journal* 189
Wright, RW, 'Causation in Tort Law' (1985) 73 *California Law Review* 1735
—— 'Justice and Reasonable Care in Negligence Law' (2002) 47 *American Journal of Jurisprudence* 143
Wylie, MS, 'The Untold Story: Carol Gilligan on Recapturing the Lost Voice of Pleasure' (2002) 26 *Psychotherapy Networker* 46
Zhou, YK, 'More on What it Means to Suffer Harm' (2022) 13 *Jurisprudence* 516

Reports, Guidance and Miscellaneous Online Resources

British Medical Association Report, *Caring, Supportive, Collaborative: Doctors' Vision for Change in the NHS* (September 2019)
Department of Treasury, Australia, *Review of the Law of Negligence: Final Report* (September 2002)
General Medical Council, *Good Medical Practice* (2024)
HLS Nuremberg Trials Project: NMT Case 1 – *USA v Karl Brandt et al* (https://nuremberg.law.harvard.edu/nmt_1_intro)
Judicial College, *Equal Treatment Bench Book* (February 2021 edition)
Miller, AB, *Cervical Cancer Screening Programmes: Managerial Guidelines* (World Health Organisation, 1992) 1
National Commission for the Protection of Human Subjects of Biomedical and Behavioral Research, *Ethical Principles and Guidelines for the Protection of Human Subjects of Research (The Belmont Report)* (1979)
Royal Pharmaceutical Society of Great Britain, *From Compliance to Concordance: Towards Shared Goals in Medicine Taking* (London, RPS, 1997)
Singapore Medical Council, *Ethical Code and Ethical Guidelines* (2016)
Tuskegee Study – Timeline, https://www.cdc.gov/tuskegee/timeline.htm
United Kingdom Parliament, Constitution Committee – Twenty-Fifth Report, *Judicial Appointments* (7 March 2012) Chapter 3 (https://publications.parliament.uk/pa/ld201012/ldselect/ldconst/272/27206.htm)
WMA Declaration of Geneva – WMA – The World Medical Association (https://www.wma.net/policies-post/wma-declaration-of-geneva/)
Workgroup to Review the Taking of Informed Consent and SMC Disciplinary Process (*Report on Recommendations*, 28 November 2019)

INDEX

www.ingramcontent.com/pod-product-compliance
Ingram Content Group UK Ltd.
Pitfield, Milton Keynes, MK11 3LW, UK
UKHW020844290926
15470UKWH00004B/1545